BETWEEN QURAN AND KAFKA

BETWEEN QURAN AND KAFKA

West–Eastern Affinities

NAVID KERMANI

TRANSLATED BY TONY CRAWFORD

polity

First published in German as *Zwischen Koran und Kafka: West-östliche Erkundungen*

The translation of this work was supported by a grant from the Goethe-Institut which is funded by the German Ministry of Foreign Affairs.

Polity Press
65 Bridge Street
Cambridge CB2 1UR, UK

Polity Press
350 Main Street
Malden, MA 02148, USA

ISBN-13: 978-1-5095-0033-8
ISBN-13: 978-1-5095-0034-5 (pb)

A catalogue record for this book is available from the British Library.

Library of Congress Cataloging-in-Publication Data

Names: Kermani, Navid, 1967- author.
Title: Between Quran and Kafka : west-eastern affinities / Navid Kermani.
Other titles: Zwischen Koran und Kafka. English
Description: Malden, MA : Polity Press, 2016. | Includes bibliographical references and index. | Translated from German.
Identifiers: LCCN 2016004650 (print) | LCCN 2016008548 (ebook) | ISBN 9781509500338 (hardcover : alk. paper) | ISBN 1509500332 (hardcover : alk. paper) | ISBN 9781509500345 (pbk. : alk. paper) | ISBN 1509500340 (pbk. : alk. paper) | ISBN 9781509500369 (mobi) | ISBN 9781509500376 (epub)
Subjects: LCSH: German literature--History and criticism. | Religion and literature. | East and West.
Classification: LCC PT147 .K4713 2016 (print) | LCC PT147 (ebook) | DDC 830.9--dc23
LC record available at http://lccn.loc.gov/2016004650

Typeset in 11 on 12 JaghbUni by Servis Filmsetting Ltd, Stockport, Cheshire
Printed and bound in the UK by Clays Ltd, St. Ives PLC

For further information on Polity, visit our website: politybooks.com

CONTENTS

PREFACE

A Personal Note

After the speech I gave in the German parliament, which is appended at the end of this book, a friend of mine e-mailed me to say I had combined a poetic political correctness with the pathos of the socialist prophets in a tone, she wrote, that no one but I am capable of today – the same tone that the Jewish cosmopolitans of the nineteenth century had used in speaking of Lessing, Heine and the social idea of the prophets. 'Of course they can no longer speak today (and, if they could, they would not be allowed to do so)', my friend added, closing with the impassioned remark that I was – I will quote her again, although it will seem vain to do so in my own preface – 'the most prodigious representative' of the nineteenth-century Jewish cosmopolitans. 'That is a mighty lineage you're putting me in,' I replied to my friend, 'but to take up the idea you raise of representation of advocacy, there is probably something to it after all: what needs to be done in Germany is to fill, to the extent possible, with our limited means, experience and words, the space that became so vacant in the twentieth century.'

Since then, I have been mulling over our brief correspondence. Not that I would claim title to the inspiration, much less the superlative, that my friend had bestowed on me – she is not only a good friend but also, by her whole nature, an extraordinarily enthusiastic one, invariably exuberant in her sympathy, reliably overstated in her praise. But wasn't my answer, hastily written and promptly sent, presumptuous? I affirmed the relation in which I had placed us – but who was I thinking of besides myself? – to the Jewish thinkers and writers of the nineteenth and early twentieth centuries, in the sense that I felt not an identity, a relationship, or even an equality with them, but a legacy, with the authority and the responsibility that arise from it.

Even before receiving my friend's e-mail, I had noticed a pathos creeping into my texts at times, and even more into my public speeches, which not everyone immediately felt to be false; at times I had also noticed my audience's surprise when, without much hesitation, I connected academic or current political issues with fundamental human experiences and needs, with humanness itself, and even with the superhuman. I couldn't describe it more precisely if I wanted to; it is little more than a vague feeling that, if I were the reader and listener, I might not let another author or speaker get away so easily with what I sometimes permit myself, and what I ought to continue to permit myself, since it constitutes – for good or ill – the essence of what I have to say. That pathos is all the more remarkable since, in day-to-day life and in encounters with other people – even the people I love – I often find myself all too sober, unemotional; I seldom mention in private the primal needs and experiences that I speak of in public – too seldom, according to the occasional reproaches of the people I love. Voluntarily or not, in daily life I seem to restrain the emotionality and urgency that sometimes surprises me in my own essays and speeches. Why is that, I wondered again, and what is the source of the tone my friend was referring to, a tone that no doubt has something to do with the metaphysical orientation of my reflections?

As distasteful as I find all those interpretations that pin an author to the culture of his ancestors, for lack of a better explanation I might at one time have linked that emotionality and urgency to my Middle Eastern background. But nowadays I believe – and my friend's e-mail points in precisely this direction, which is why I only qualified her comparison rather than rejecting it outright – my tone has a different source, a thoroughly German one. I grew up with German literature and the history of German thought – that much is true – yet only sporadically with those of the present. The lineage I followed ends with the Second World War, or at the latest with the Frankfurt School, which of course was still identified in relation to the war. The tone that my friend referred to – an unusually lofty, you might say preachy, to some ears perhaps importunately existential tone in which I sometimes talk about world affairs – does it not have, rather, the sound of the nineteenth and early twentieth centuries than of some Middle Eastern ancestry? I know of no contemporary Persian or Arab author who speaks or writes that way, but of a great many German-language authors, down to Stefan Zweig, Walter Benjamin and Thomas Mann, who without a doubt wrote more elegantly, thought more profoundly, lived more vulnerably, but demonstrated the necessity of universal political ideals (whose very universality should perhaps worry us after all) by poetically translating them into concrete terms. Yes, I place Thomas Mann in this line, and

I could just as well have named Lessing or Goethe, because I am concerned here not with a specifically Jewish impetus in German literature but with a cosmopolitanism that the Jewish authors merely emphasized more often than other Germans. As a young reader I not only absorbed their ideals but evidently adopted, too, some of the pathos that my friend associated with the prophets, hence with the religious sphere.

To be sure, the religious references of my books and speeches often point to Islamic motifs and sources (but to the Bible almost as often), and the Muslim family I grew up in surely had its unconscious influence on me: my mother who veiled herself in a white chador for prayers, and only for prayers; my father who prostrated himself before God, even in the presence of my friends or at rest areas beside the motorway during long holiday drives; the perplexed looks of my friends or the other motorists. Those were experiences of foreignness, by all means, although not negative ones. None of my friends ever shunned me on account of my praying parents, and my experience of bilingualism was every bit as natural – although I learned this only many years later – as that of many other Germans up to the Second World War. In our house there was what you might indeed call a simple cosmopolitanism, one which, like that of the Jews, was rooted in religious tradition: in the quranic teaching that to each people a prophet is sent in that people's language – which is why I somehow imagined Jesus as a German, or at least associated him with Germany – and in the incessantly quoted sentence of the Prophet – who was somehow Persian to me, although actually an Arab – that the paths to God are as numerous as the breaths a man draws. While the child's concept of revelation may not have conformed to the consensus of Islamic studies, he was nonetheless greatly relieved that his friends would still be able to enter Paradise, even though their parents did not prostrate themselves before God at motorway service stations, and that at the Last Judgement it was good deeds that would count, not the exact wording of the profession of faith.

The deepest impressions on my disposition, as on any other, are those made by the images, actions and words of my early childhood. But is that why I became an Orientalist and a writer? My literary awakening was the result of the books I read, and those were, in my formative years of discovery and study, the German literature and ideas of the nineteenth and early twentieth centuries. And that German literature is not just any literature: it has specific traits, and up to the middle of the twentieth century it was steeped more than any other in transcendental matters and biblical motifs – not only God and Jesus but also death and resurrection, rapture and sacrifice; steeped in suffering both as a social and, almost to a greater extent, as a religious incrimination; and steeped in an earnestness that is itself almost holy, a seriousness that no one could deride as heartily as certain Germans themselves, since arguing with oneself has always been rather a German pursuit. Heinrich Heine for one might have skewered my books:

> A living German is already a sufficiently serious creature, but a *dead* German! A Frenchman has absolutely no idea how very serious we Germans are when dead; our faces then become much longer still, and the worms that dine off us wax melancholy if they look at us while eating.[1]

The fact that the French and the English don't bother to translate a word such as *Weltschmerz* says a great deal about their perception of the Germans, but it very probably says something about the Germans too. For my part, I loved Büchner for the metaphysical desperation that he wrote into Danton, waiting in his cell for execution, and even in matters of ethics and morals in the strict sense – that is, the issues that are proper to religion – I learned more from Adorno's *Minima Moralia* than from Muhammad.

While a remarkable number of French, English-speaking and Scandinavian authors of the nineteenth and early twentieth centuries described social conditions or related psychological states with an utterly incredible realism, the best-known German poets always directed their gaze higher – the growing vacancy of Heaven notwithstanding. The Jewish cosmopolitan Heine – to him at least I will appeal in this preface because he is the most sorely missed in the rest of the book – Heine himself expressed that gaze in his inimitable way in contrasting the materialism that had come to dominate France with German philosophy, which explains all matter as just a modification of spirit (when it admits the existence of matter at all): 'It seemed almost as if, across the Rhine, the spirit sought revenge for the insult done it on this side.'[2] Contrary to Heine's prediction, however, Germany's metaphysical grounding did not dissolve until the mid-twentieth century, when the totalitarian ideology of Nazism seemed to have discredited all overarching projects and all concepts of the collective. Broadly, German post-war literature refers demonstratively to the individual in society; it sees the human being more as a social than as an ontological entity. That was and is magnificent in many instances, and I am an admirer of it. But it was not what set me on my path.

> 'Dry with thirst, oh let my tongue cleave
> To my palate – let my right hand
> Wither off, if I forget thee
> Ever, O Jerusalem –'

Heine begins his poem 'Jehuda ben Halevy' with an allusion to the archetypal song of the Jewish people's exile, Psalm 137, verse 6. Heine's engagement with the Andalusian philosopher and poet ben Halevy is the most important signpost of his – not *return*; we cannot call it that, for Heine had not grown up religious; he seemed to be a child of the Enlightenment through and through – of his connection to the Jewish tradition, a connection by a writer formally converted to Protestantism; a connection which colours all of his late works and, at the same time, is a turn towards God the Creator of the Hebrew Bible.

> 'By the Babylonian waters
> There we sat and wept – our harps were
> Hung upon the weeping willow . . .'
> That old song – do you still know it?

The second part of the poem also begins with a quotation from Psalm 137 – the first two verses – before comparing the poet's Jewish origins with a kettle that has long been boiling inside him, a thousand years long: a black sorrow!

> That old tune – do you still know it? –
> How it starts with elegiac
> Whining, humming like a kettle
> That is seething on the hearth?
> Long has it been seething in me –
> For a thousand years. Black sorrow!
> And my wounds are licked by time
> Just as Job's dog licked his boils.
> Dog, I thank you for your spittle,
> But its coolness merely soothes me –
> Only death can really heal me,
> But, alas, I am immortal![3]

There is nothing cheerful about this – all right, we'll call it a return; it is almost two horrifying centuries, if not light years, away from the bright colours of today's migration literature. Heine bringing the Jews into his poetry is like Aeneas carrying his invalid father out of the burning city – yet with the twist that Heine himself had to fall deathly ill before his ancestors' faith appeared plausible to him. In his first public expression of his 'great transformation', a response in the *Augsburger Allgemeine Zeitung* to a report on his illness, Heine wrote:

> Very often, especially during severe convulsions of the vertebral column, a doubt comes over me whether man is indeed a two-legged god, as the late Professor Hegel assured me in Berlin twenty-five years ago. In May

> of last year I had to take to my bed, and I have never risen from it since. In the meanwhile I confess that a great revolution has taken place in me. I am no longer a godlike biped; I am no longer 'the freest German since Goethe,' as Ruge called me in better days; I am no longer the Great Pagan No. II, who was likened to the vine-crowned Bacchus, while men called my colleague No. I the Grand-ducal Jupiter of Weimar; I am no longer a comfortably stout Hellene, rejoicing in life, gayly looking down with a smile on the serious Nazarenes; I am now only a poor, dying Jew, a wasted figure of woe, a wretched being![4]

As I reflected further on my brief correspondence with my friend, the question became more and more detached from my own writings: weren't the cosmopolitans she was referring to themselves merely representatives? They, or perhaps their parents, had left the ancestral Jewish milieu, the ghetto, and had attained both a high degree of emancipation and a higher position in society, at least in their own literary and academic circles. But if we remember that, as recently as Ludwig Börne's childhood in late eighteenth-century Frankfurt, even the oldest and most respected Jews had to step off the pavement and bow deeply before an approaching Christian, regardless of his age and standing – even before Christian children and beggars – then we can form some idea of the images, sensations and words that made the deepest impression on their minds. And Heinrich Heine, who, as the nephew of a wealthy banker, had experienced only comparatively subtle forms of discrimination, was always conscious of his background. Addressing a friend in the summer of 1850, he said:

> A strange people – for thousands of years constantly beaten, constantly crying, constantly suffering, perpetually forgotten by God yet still cleaving to him, more tenaciously and loyally than any other people in the whole world! If martyrdom, patience and loyalty, endurance in calamity, if all this is ennobling, then these people are nobler than a lot of others. The history of the Middle Ages . . . shows us not a single year that is not marked for the Jews by tortures, autos-da-fé, beheadings, extortions, massacres. The Jews suffered more from the followers of Christ . . . than ever under the most brutal and primitive Poles and Hungarians, Bedouins, Iazyges and Mongols! Oh, how lovely is the religion of love! You probably know that in Rome, the Metropolis of the Faith, for two hundred years . . . the Jews were forced to run races on the last day of the Carnival, naked, in a loin-cloth, for the delectation of the mob.[5]

Heine's experiences of foreignness, which unlike mine were decidedly negative, engendered more of course than a responsibility for his people's tradition and a mandate to represent his people. That Jewish scholars advanced the Enlightenment by their very resistance to assimilation was in part an act of loyalty towards the Enlightenment itself, against the narrow Protestant version of it, against the practice of ascribing character to nations and against hypertrophic rationalism. Consequently, before the Holocaust, their pathos, if we bear in mind the word's literal sense of 'suffering, pain, disease', was rarely related only to the discrimination, the oppression, of their own people. It was the suffering, the pain, the disease of all creatures that drove them; it was their cry for redemption and justice that made them successors of the biblical prophets. None other than Heinrich Heine, in his disturbingly religious late poems, thematically and stylistically encompassing Orient and Occident – for all its injustice towards his earlier poems, there is a grain of truth in Karl Kraus's famous remark that Heine had to fall mortally ill to become a poet – none other than Heine introduced the perspective of the oppressed, the vanquished, in German literature. Yet he did not become the voice of his people in that field; rather, Heine testifies to the disasters of other, foreign peoples: the Moors and their last ruler, Boabdil of Granada, in 'King of the Moors'; the Mexican Indians who fell victim to the Spanish conquistador Cortez in 'Vitzliputzli'; and the sub-Saharan African slaves in 'The Slave Ship'. That means, to return to our own vantage point, that we do not have to have experienced comparable discrimination and oppression to become pathetic in the literal sense. In this respect, perhaps the Jewish cosmopolitans even advocated – as representatives of the Enlightenment project – the universal love of Jesus, secularized in the idea of equality. Then every poet would belong to the tribe of the Asra, 'they who perish when they love', as Heine says of the Sultan's beautiful daughter in his still more beautiful poem.[6] In any case, however, along with the Judaeo-Arabic heritage of the Enlightenment, Heine and scholars of Judaism after him felt a duty to uncover its Islamic heritage as well. And it would be a good thing if Muslim authors today, whether religious or not, would reciprocate by standing up for Europe's Jewish.

Suddenly this book's title, *Between Quran and Kafka*, took on a new meaning. Of course we had chosen it for its alliteration, which the publisher thought was catchy. But, at the same time, the Quran and Kafka really did designate two poles between which my writing oscillates: revelation and literature; religious and aesthetic experience; the history of the Islamic and the German-speaking cultures; the Orient and the Occident. But the Quran in particular, and Kafka's works in particular, were important points of reference to me for many years: unique and exemplary, neither imitable nor surpassable. Reflecting on the representative role my friend had ascribed to me, I suddenly discovered that 'Kafka' could also stand for something entirely different from what

I had had in mind and, likewise, that 'Quran' was not limited to the metonymic sense of 'Islam' or 'the Orient'. Kafka can also mean a way of participating in German literature, upholding it all the more resolutely for being ever uncertain of one's social and political affiliation. Kafka signifies something foreign, marginal, never quite belonging – something which is genuinely European and yet which transcends Europe. And the Quran – and the religion and the culture of Islam along with it – has a meaning, in my writing and my life, like that of the Torah to the Jewish thinkers and writers of the nineteenth and early twentieth centuries: it means a forthright affirmation of difference, of the facet of permanent exile, if you will, in my situation; an insistence, religious or not, on the continuing relevance of metaphysical questions in a radically secularized environment; and it also means, all my contemporaneity notwithstanding, a loyalty to my parents' and grandparents' canon and, hence, to pre-modern, non-European narratives and modes of narration.

Yes, I say affirmation, I say insistence and loyalty, and I am talking about conscious, almost demonstrative choices. Not unlike Kafka, who grew up reading Goethe and Stifter and appropriated the Jewish traditions as a student might – only gradually, relatively late, and then very avidly – I partook of German literature as my own and was an especially motivated student of it, perhaps not in spite but because of my origins. Although the culture and religion of Islam, which were taken very seriously in the home in which I grew up, in my Iranian family – but the young seem to have a reflex that repels what is important to their parents, as we learn when we become parents in our turn, if not before – I appropriated Islam only gradually, relatively late, and then very avidly, as a student. If the title were taken as indicating a temporal sequence, meaning that I started at one pole and then arrived at the other, this book would have to be called the reverse – 'Between Kafka and Quran' – for, when I think about it, it was via Kafka that I arrived at the Quran. It was originally an aesthetic interest, formed by my literary and essentially German reading, that drew me to Islam, and onward from there to all aspects of religion. But then the title would not have ended on the long, open vowel, and that was more important to me than a biographical logic which no one would have noticed anyway.

The friend who sent me the e-mail is named Almut Shulamit Bruckstein Çoruh, and she is herself the model of a Jewish cosmopolitan. In her new book *House of Taswir* she records a gesture that is paradigmatic of the spokesman's role. In old Herbert Stein's bookstore in Jerusalem, Almut found the Quran translation by the rabbinical scholar Lazarus Goldschmidt in its first edition of 1916. It begins with the words:

> AL-QURAN
> that is
> THE READING
> The revelation of
> Muhammad ibn Abdullah
> the Prophet of God
> put into writing by
> Abdulkaaba Abdullah Abu-Bakr
> translated by
> Lazarus Goldschmidt
> in the year 1334 of the Flight, or 1916
> of the Incarnation.

'The Flight' is of course Muhammad's emigration from Mecca, the beginning of the Islamic calendar. 'The Incarnation' denotes the Christian calendar, not simply by its pragmatic abbreviation 'AD', but by explicit reference to the substance of Christian dogma. What a beautiful, surprising gesture on the part of a great rabbi to use the two neighbouring calendars – simultaneously and with equal rank, while omitting that of his own tradition – and to take their theology seriously![7]

Almut wrote to me that she, too, would elaborate on the idea in her e-mail, which had been just as hastily written as my answer. In the meantime, readers will judge for themselves whether there is anything to the notion of the writer as a representative, which would be an honour but much more a responsibility. Whatever the judgement may be, that role in Germany is appallingly vacant.

— 1 —

DON'T FOLLOW THE POETS!

The Quran and Poetry

Muhammad lived from 570 to 632. When he was about forty, his visions and, more importantly, his auditory revelations began, and they would continue until his death, a period of some twenty-two years. He recited the revelations to his compatriots, addressing his neighbours in Mecca directly, but at the same time speaking to all Arabs. He delivered to them 'an Arabic recitation', *qur'ānan ᶜarabīyan*; the word 'quran' means nothing other than 'recitation' or 'that which is to be recited', and in the early surahs it is often used without the definite article – it had not yet become a proper noun. Over and over again, the Quran distinguishes between an 'Arabic' and a possible 'foreign-langugage' (*aᶜjami*) revelation, one not addressed to the Arabs in particular; indeed, in the history of religion there is no other text that so often and so emphatically points out and reflects on the obvious fact that it is composed in a particular language. Thus in surah 41, verse 44:

> And if we had made it
> a non-Arabic *qur'ān* (*qur'ānan aᶜjamīyan*),
> They would have said,
> 'Why are its verses not clear?
> What does it mean: a
> Non-Arabic *qur'ān*
> And an Arab speaker!'

Thus Muhammad appeared as the 'Arab' speaker of a message that God sent to all peoples.

> We have sent no Messenger
> Save with the tongue of his people, that he might make all clear to them.[1]

To hold such a concept of revelation, the Arabs must have felt themselves to be a community, in contrast to other communities and peoples, the non-Arabs. Although today that may go without saying, it was by no means self-evident in the seventh century in view of the political situation, the geographical conditions, and the tribal structure of society on the Arabian peninsula. The Arabs of the *Jahiliyyah*, the pre-Islamic period, were not united by any alliance or common political platform. On the contrary: clans raided one another; blood feuds tore the country apart. The most important form of organization by far, dominating the individual's world view and personal attachments, was the tribe. Yet the countless clans, socially and culturally highly diverse, regularly at war with one another, considered themselves a single people: the Arabic language was, in spite of all conflicts, the unifying element on the Arabian peninsula in the early seventh century. Although each tribe spoke its own dialect, which was difficult for members of other tribes to understand, the formal language of Arabic poetry, the *ᶜarabīya*, reigned over all the tribal dialects. Poetry was the foundation of a shared identity; it bore the roots of a unified memory that defied disintegration.

The situation might be compared with that of Germany in the late eighteenth century, when literature helped the small and tiny states to develop a common, specifically 'German' identity. And yet the Arabs' situation was different. In the early seventh century they were desert dwellers, living at oases, interconnected only by the merchants' caravans and the regular wars between the tribes, which were an economic activity in their own right (the word 'razzia', descended from Arabic and still current in German, recalls those plundering raids). There were few other contacts between the individual tribes and practically no means of communication. Only the rudiments of writing were generally known; almost everyone was illiterate; and the various dialects were so different at that time that communication between one native tongue and another was difficult at best. And yet, in a territory as big as a third of all Europe, from Yemen in the south to Syria in the north, from the fringes of modern-day Iraq to the borders of Egypt, ancient Arabic poetry, with its ceremonial language, its sophisticated techniques and its very strict norms and standards, was a constant. 'How this was achieved we do not know and most probably shall never learn', the Israeli Orientalist Shlomo D. Goitein wrote of this astounding circumstance.[2]

Ancient Arabic poetry is a highly complex edifice. Its vocabulary, its grammatical peculiarities and its detailed norms were passed down from generation to generation, and only the greatest of the time mastered all its subtleties. No one dared call himself a poet until he had studied under one for years or decades. Muhammad grew up in a world in which the poetic word was revered almost religiously, and he had not learned the difficult craft of poetry before he began reciting verses to his contemporaries. Initially, the Quran was not a text written down from beginning to end but consisted of separate recitable units, which only later coalesced into a whole text. The earliest surahs were dominated by dramatic scenarios of disaster and damnation, calls for spiritual and ethical repentance, and appeals for equality and responsibility among people. Their wording was insistent and forceful, and they fascinated the listeners of the time by their pulsating rhythms, their poignant onomatopoeia, their fantastic array of images. And yet Muhammad's preaching was different from poetry, and also from the rhymed prose of the soothsayers, the second form of inspired, structured oratory at that time. It strangely violated the norms of ancient Arabic poetry: its narratives went a different way; it suspended metre; the themes, the metaphors, the whole ideological thrust of the early Quran, unlike the conservative, affirmative poetry of that time – all of it was new to Muhammad's contemporaries and amounted to a revolutionary change in the world they lived in. At the same time, the application of the verses almost always conformed to the rules of ancient Arabic poetry. What was still more important, however, was that the Quran was composed in *ᶜarabīya*, the code of poetry at that time. That was the reason why, in spite of the differences in form and content between his recitation and poetry, many Meccans initially took Muhammad for a poet.

No other revealed text documents its own reception as the Quran does: it records the reactions of the faithful and the unbelievers, quoting them and commenting on them. We learn from the Quran itself that no other reproach troubled the Prophet as much as the assertion that he was 'just' a poet. In the later surahs, the rebuttal to that accusation becomes formulaic, but the thoroughness of the early instances is evidence that the danger was genuine. We must conclude that Muhammad found himself compelled, especially in the initial phase of his prophecy, to struggle against being mistaken for a poet because of certain of his acts, behaviours or speeches. If there had been nothing in his ministry to suggest that identification, his opponents would never have thought of calling him one in the first place. They would have found other arguments to challenge his claim to divine revelation. They could have said, for example, that he was a liar, a thief or a charlatan. 'But they said: He is just making up verse; he is a poet' (21:5).

Muhammad's opponents' assertion that the Quran was poetry cannot have been merely polemical: it must have reflected many people's actual impressions – not because the Quran was identical with poetry in the minds of the community that received it, but because poetry (and the other genres of inspired oratory) was the only point of reference they could compare it with; it was the thing that was least different from the Quran. The Muslim tradition documents this, reporting again and again that the Meccans went to poets and other masters of the literary language and asked them what to call Muhammad's recitations. In answering – with fascination and amazement – that the Quran was neither poetry nor rhymed prose, they outlined the horizon of their expectations. 'I know all kinds of qasidas and the *rajaz*; I am familiar even with the poems of the jinn. But, by God, his recitation is like none of them', Muhammad's famous contemporary Walid ibn al-Mughira confessed – to quote just one of many similar opinions.[3] And in its consistent reports that the poets and rhetoricians were aware of the Quran's stylistic uniqueness, the tradition mentions conversely that it was not easy for simple people to distinguish clearly between poetry and the revelation. The story is told, for example, of one of the Prophet's followers, the poet Abdullah ibn Rawaha, that his wife surprised him leaving a concubine's chamber and demanded an explanation. She had long suspected him of having secret affairs. Knowing that Abdullah had once sworn an oath never to recite the Quran except in a state of ritual purity – and, if he had lain with the concubine, he would have been unclean – she challenged him to recite something from the Quran as a way of exposing him. The poet immediately recited three lines of a poem that sounded so similar to the Quran that his wife was persuaded of his innocence: she 'thought it was a *qurʾān*'.[4]

Since it was in danger of being confused with poetry, the Quran was compelled to repudiate poetry: 'And the poets – the perverse follow them.'[5] Only the awareness of these circumstances allows us to understand the polemics against poets contained in the Quran, especially in the 26th surah. The Quran was not taking part in a literary competition. Poets might vie for the leadership of a single tribe, but the Quran radically challenged the whole tribal structure of Arab society and its polytheism by proclaiming the principle of unity – both the unity of God and that of the community. The poets meanwhile, more than any other group in that society, were protagonists of the tribal order of the *Jahiliyyah*. To read into the Quran a blanket condemnation of poetry, as people often do, is not defensible. The Quran criticizes the poets only where they cling to their leadership role and take inspiration from devils, and it makes an explicit exception for those poets 'who believe, do good, and are mindful of God' (26:227).

Evidently the Prophet was victorious in his conflict with the poets, otherwise Islam would not have spread so rapidly. The Quran itself only hints at the reasons for that success. Although it reflects the situation at the time of the revelation, referring to specific events and developments, it does so for an audience that is already familiar with those events. It does not recount, as a history book would, what happened on this or that specific day, but instead alludes to the events by isolated cues that stimulated the memories of its immediate audience. To understand the historical context, later readers often have to rely on secondary sources such as the biographies, the history books and the traditional texts on the 'occasions of the revelations' (*asbāb an-nuzūl*).

In the European view of Islam's early history, Muhammad's success is attributed to social, ideological, propagandistic or military factors; writers emphasize the Prophet's charisma or his egalitarian message. Muslim sources draw a different picture. According to them, Islam triumphed primarily by the verbal force of the Quran, by the sheer aesthetic power of its melodic recitation. Only here, in the history books, biographies and theological compendia, in the Muslim community's retrospection on its salvation history, Muhammad's conflict with the poets coalesces into a struggle with a literary aspect, fought, to a certain extent, after the model of the ancient poets' duels, as in the anecdote about the greatest of Arabia's poets, Labid ibn Rabia. The pages of his poems were hung on the doors of the Kaaba as a symbol of his supremacy. None of his fellow poets dared accept the challenge by hanging his own verses beside Labid's. One day, however, there came some followers of Muhammad, who at that time was reviled by the heathen Arabs as an obscure sorcerer and a mad poet. They hung an excerpt from the second surah of the Quran on the door and challenged Labid to read it aloud. The prince of poets laughed at their presumption. To pass the time, or perhaps in derision, he acquiesced and began to declaim the verses. He was overpowered by their beauty and professed Islam on the spot.

Conversions of this kind are one of the most frequent topoi in Islamic salvation history. The tale is also told, for example, of a scout who came to Mecca from Yathrib, the future Medina, to investigate the mysterious rumours about the appearance of a new prophet. Sternly warned against the prophet's magic tricks, the man had been urged to plug his ears before encountering people who recited his prophecy. So the investigator walked along the streets of Mecca and encountered a group of the faithful listening to a Quran recitation. He thought to himself, 'I am a man of reason and experience. Why make a fool of myself by plugging my ears just because someone is reciting something?' He took the wadding out of his ears, heard the sound of the Quran, and professed Islam then and there. The famous sirens in book twelve of Homer's *Odyssey* cannot have been more enticing.

These conversion stories, which always have the same structure, reveal their unique character when we look for an analogous theme in other religions. The phenomenon of a conversion effected by an aesthetic cause, which is frequently claimed in Islam even in later centuries, is scarcely attested in Christianity, for example. Neither in the Gospels nor anywhere else are there corresponding accounts in any comparable density. The great conversions and initiation experiences in Christian history – those of St Paul, St Augustine, Pascal and Martin Luther, to name just a few – were triggered, as far as we know from the autobiographical testimony, by experiences which, while no less remarkable to the onlooker or the reader, are not primarily aesthetic: it is not the beauty of the divine revelation that stands out in the subject's consciousness but its moral and ethical message to the individual. That does not mean that the development and the religious practice of Christianity, or any other religion, would be conceivable without the aesthetic fascination of certain spaces, texts, chants, shapes, smells, acts, gestures, vestments – or that Protestantism, for example, would have spread so rapidly in the German-speaking countries without the verbal power of the Luther Bible. Yet, in the picture that the Christian or, more specifically, the Protestant community forms of its own past, the aesthetic impulse, however relevant it may be to religious practice, has only secondary importance. Few Christians would claim that Jesus' disciples were drawn to him because he seemed particularly handsome or because his oratory struck them as formally perfect, and no Christian catechism teaches the linguistic perfection of the Gospels as a cause of the triumph of Christianity.

While there are conversions to Christianity that are caused by the beauty of the scripture, accounts of such conversions do not make up any significant part of the total corpus of Christian documents on the spread of the religion; they are not a recurring motif in the literature of Christian salvation history or part of Christians' cultural memory. In the Muslim identity, however, the aesthetic fascination that the Quran exerts is a fundamental part of the religious tradition. It is not the experience of beauty per se, but this act of collective awareness and interpretation that is specific to the religious world of Islam. Only in Islam has the rationalization of aesthetic experience produced a theological-poetological doctrine, namely the doctrine of *iᶜjāz*, the unsurpassability and inimitability of the Quran. To a Christian, the argumentation of *iᶜjāz* could hardly be more strange: I believe in the Quran because its language is too perfect to have been composed by a human being. Indeed, the doctrine amounts to an aesthetic proof of God, or of truth. Nothing analogous in the religious sphere is found in any Western culture. At best, one might think of the subjective impressions that some musical compositions, by Bach or Mozart perhaps, can produce. It is no coincidence that listeners tend to call them 'divine'.

The relationship between the revelation and poetry in the history of Arab culture could hardly be closer. Arabic literary scholarship, for example, owes its development to the study of the Quran. If the miracle of Islam was the language of the revelation, then scholars had to analyse that language to prove its primacy – and hence had to compare the Quran with poetry. Thus the study of literature was an early spin-off from theology. In the ninth century, Muslim scholars began to collect exemplary passages of Arabic poetry to contrast them with the Quran. The primary goal was to develop a poetics, to define criteria that could be used to identify a verse as excellent, exemplary, effective and beautiful. Their motivation was at first apologetic, but their literary interest increasingly became detached from its theological agenda. For Arabic literary scholarship, the Quran is more than just a central text: the discipline originated in large part in efforts to analyse, and not merely describe, the experience of the Quran's beauty and poignancy on the basis of understandable, empirical evidence. From the tenth to the twelfth century, great works on Arabic poetics were written which anticipated numerous insights of modern linguistics and literary studies – for example, by transcending the ancient dichotomy of form and content with the concept of *naẓm*, the 'order' or 'structure' in which a poetic idea is expressed. The Arab rhetoricians discussed the Quran and poetry in the same breath, yet without playing one against the other. A high-ranking theologian of the eleventh century, the Iranian Abdulqaher al-Jurjani, who was also, quite naturally one might say, the most important scholar of poetics of his time, was persistently concerned with the specific quality that constitutes the excellence of a line of verse, whether from the Quran or written by a poet. And he analysed that specific quality with constant comparisons between the Quran and poetry – an interleaving of theology and literary study that could not be taken for granted in the Arab world of today.

While literary scholarship was first brought into being with the Quran and became an autonomous discipline soon afterwards, the Quran, paradoxically, also had a certain secularizing effect on poetry. With the triumph of Islam, poetry at first gave up its metaphysical pretensions and concentrated on secular motifs: love; courtly and urban life; the virtues. Later, in the eighth and ninth centuries, poets at the Abbasid courts and cities repositioned themselves, setting themselves apart from Islam. In deliberate competition with the prophetic revelation, they invoked other sources of inspiration besides the One God, including the jinn and the satans. The most famous satanic verses are those of Abu Nuwas, perhaps the best-known poet in the history of Arabic literature. As in the modern period in Europe, the invocation of supernatural powers is more a literary motif than a reference to real experience. The important thing was to break Islam's monopoly on inspiration. The poets were in competition with the Quran, striving to surpass it as a stylistic monument. In the eighth century, poets and men of letters who met in literary circles told one another, 'Your poem is more beautiful than this or that verse of the Quran', and, 'That line is more beautiful than this Quran verse.' Intellectuals such as al-Mutanabbi and al-Maᶜarri disputed the unsurpassability of the quranic language far into the eleventh century. But, at the same time, the Quran remained the paragon and the standard even to those who sought to disprove the miraculous nature of its language. When Bashar ibn Burd, a free-thinking poet of the time, called one of his favourite poems more beautiful than the 59th surah, he must have thought the surah was not bad.

As a direct competitor to the Quran, poetry was in a way much more dangerous than other religions, which were accorded their place in the world of Muslim faith. Even today, the relationship between the Quran and poetry is in some ways highly ambivalent: in the Arab tradition, poetry was the only medium besides the revelation – and, later, mysticism – to which was ascribed, and which claimed for itself, a connection, however limited, to a transcendental reality, an access to supernatural inspiration. Even those who reject poetry do so because they recognize that connection and consider it dangerous – otherwise they could ignore poetry as meaningless. The conception of the poetic act as one of rivalry with God, and hence as potentially sacrilegious, became a fundamental theme of Arabic literature. As long as it remained secular, literature in Muslim cultures was subject to few restrictions, or at most to political and moral ones. But where the poets competed directly with religion, whether by referring to a celestial source of inspiration or by trying to imitate and surpass the style of the Quran, they faced religiously motivated criticism and occasionally persecution. From a contemporary point of view, Arabic literature combines the contestation of orthodoxy, or even of simply traditional faith, with 'the Promethean thrust of modern poetry', which Octavio Paz has outlined as the 'will to create a new "sacred," in contradistinction to the one that churches offer us today.'[6]

Among those in the Arab world who are committed to this old and new endeavour, the Syrian poet Adonis holds a special position. His work can be read as an impassioned struggle, sometimes violent, sometimes bordering on tender, with his own intellectual and aesthetic tradition. The religious streak that permeates his writing makes it impious. For the poetry with which Adonis has made his mark is not religious in the sense that it serves religion; it is a poetry that vies to supplant religion. Adonis harks back to the role of the poet in the *Jahiliyyah*, whose prophetic aspirations were rejected by Islam, and he also refers to the mystic poets of the tenth century, such as al-Hallaj and an-Niffari: after the victory of Islam had virtually secularized poetry, leaving its invocations of demons, angels or Satan more formulaic than expressive, the mystics had once again given it metaphysical weight. Their poetry became prophetic. They also broke with the Arabic poets' traditional canon of rules to create their own verbal and spiritual reality – just as the Quran had done before, in Adonis's interpretation, and as he now does in turn in his own poetry. Unlike the mystic poets, who saw themselves as Muslims, with a religious justification for their violations of aesthetic and religious norms, Adonis refuses Islamic associations. He casts off religion; he does not ignore it, as most poets of his time do, but directly addresses this process of moulting.

> Today I burned up the mirage of Saturday,
> The mirage of Friday.
> Today, I cast off the house's mask.
> I exchanged the god of blind stone,
> And the god of the seven days,
> for a dead one.[7]

In Adonis the ambivalent relation between the Quran and poetry is ideally clear. He replaces the God of the seven days with a dead God, yet he is the same poet who praises the Quran as the source of the modern in Arabic poetry. And in fact the Quran has enriched Arabic poetry as no other text. It liberated poetry from the narrow confines of the known genres and revealed new ways of treating language, metaphor and themes. There were no written standards, no theoretical study of language and literature, until they arose from quranic hermeneutics. Just as theologians referred, as if instinctively, to poetry in analysing the language of the Quran, the inverse took place and continues to take place again and again: poets and literary scholars refer to the Quran in making statements about poetry. An example is the movement in Arabic poetry known as the 'moderns' (*muḥdathūn*), who dominated the discussion of literature in the eighth and ninth centuries. The 'moderns' felt motivated and authorized by the imagery of the Quran and its stylistic deviations from the strict formal rules of poetry to incorporate ever new rhetorical figures in poetry, and so to modernize the norms that had been handed down. In their purely literary-aesthetic discussion of modern poetry, the Quran as a poetically structured text was the natural and central point of reference.

Adonis himself is, moreover, an example of the literary productive power of the Quran. The language of his poetry has assimilated that of the Quran to transform it again in turn – to demolish it from the inside out. And that language is none other than the *ᶜarabīya*, the 1500-year-old literary language of the Arabs. It is both a curse and a blessing: crystallized in pre-Islamic times into a structure of breathtaking complexity, regularity and semantic density that differed substantially from the colloquial language in its dozens of dialects, classical Arabic has changed little in its morphology since then, and its ancient metrical principles are still taught today. Its permanence is due primarily to the Quran, which, composed in the idiom of ancient Arabic poetry, gave that idiom a unique normative power. Arabic is probably the only language besides Sanskrit whose grammatical rules were historically devised, not on the basis of current linguistic practice, but – in principle and to a high degree in practice – on the basis of a single book whose grammatical reality was, regardless of day-to-day communication, enshrined as a standard and made, in the truest sense of the word, absolute.

Roman Jakobson once asked, 'How would the norms of the Russian literary language ever have been relaxed had it not been for the Ukrainian Gogol and his imperfect Russian?'[8] The Arab world could have had a Gogol too, but, faced with the existence of a divine paradigm, it would have been harder for him to provoke a shift in the norms. In other cultures, the grammar rules and the aesthetic norms adapt to the inevitable changes of the times, but, in Arabic, education, literature, science, religion and politics have remained bound for centuries to a historic manifestation of the language as a fixed ideal which grammarians only study and describe in ever greater depth and detail. Although it is considered unattainable, that ideal is nonetheless prescribed as the model which every writer and orator must emulate. Arabic illustrates in the extreme the tendency to keep sacred languages intentionally static: although they do not bring the natural evolution of language to a complete standstill, sacred texts can slow it considerably.

Yet, at the same time, the colloquial language of Arabs continues to change, like that of any other people, by incorporating outside influences, for example, and because otherwise its speakers' faculties of perception and representation would stagnate as the world continues to change. This situation, in which a formal language is considered the real, true language even though it has less and less in common with day-to-day linguistic practice, and has to be learned almost as a foreign language, has been called a 'linguistic schizophrenia'.[9] None of the dialects has been able to develop into a formally autonomous language, as Italian did, and even where the dialects are practically separate languages, as in the Maghreb, they are not accorded that status. Although the idioms spoken in the Maghreb are more different from classical Arabic than Italian is from Latin, they are designated as dialects, because the Arabs – Muslim, Christian and, until the mid-twentieth century, Jewish Arabs alike – identify themselves as a community, a community defined by nothing but a common language, namely the language of pre-Islamic poetry and of the Quran. In the Arab *nahḍa*, the early modern movement of secular awakening, it was the non-Muslim intellectuals who stressed the standard language as the one bond uniting Arab society: in defining Arab culture by its language rather than by Islam, the religious minorities asserted their claim to equal participation. To that end, paradoxically, the secular powers resorted – often quite explicitly – to the Quran as the highest manifestation of the Arabic language.

In this way, classical Arabic has remained, unlike Latin, a living language to the present day, and it continues to be spoken alongside the dialects. It is the language of all public occasions, of learning and of poetry – and one is seldom aware that the standard language of today is by no means congruent with the language of the Quran, but much simpler, grammatically, morphologically and phonetically. In the listener's mind, modern standard Arabic is perceived as an old, venerable language and is instinctively equated with *ᶜarabīya*. Consequently, an Arab poet who masters classical Arabic and can recite it skilfully can easily conjure up a mythic aura. What is much more difficult is to imbue the language with a contemporary spirit. Modern Arabic poetry has taken up this challenge again and again, with magnificent success in quite a few of its texts.

There has always been poetry in dialect as well, of course, by poets and singers who often compose their verses spontaneously, in performance, and have a tremendous impact in broad segments of the population, including those with little education. These poets have always been ascribed to the folk cultures of their respective countries, however, which are relatively strictly segregated from the high culture. Only in recent years have younger poets appeared who use a more colloquial, contemporary language. Rather than consciously violating the classical standards, they simply ignore them. As an intellectual position and a cultural policy, that is innovative and frank; aesthetically, however, I perceive it – perhaps because I am not familiar enough with contemporary Arabic poetry – mostly as a loss. Many younger poets seem not to care about the rules and the phonetic diversity of literary Arabic, which one would have to master if one would transcend them. Their poems are closer to the colloquial language; their recitation is as expressionless and interchangeable as the poetry readings we are familiar with here in Germany. The young poets' flippant attitude could be appreciated as candour in a linguistic context in which false pathos is a particularly frequent annoyance, but often what promises directness turns out to be simply shallow. It has neither the immediacy of folk poetry, which responds spontaneously to an audience, nor the aura, the phonetic range and the rhythm of the classical literary language.

The Arabic language has a certain magic: the mere sound of its precisely accentuated words can create a strangely solemn, almost sacred and, at the same time, energetic atmosphere, which is communicated over and above the semantic meaning, as listeners can experience both in Quran recitation and in the recitation of a great contemporary poet. Both preserve the wealth of nuances in phonetic articulation and the sometimes extravagant length of the vowels; both are concerts of sound and rhythm. The fascination they exert even on listeners who do not understand Arabic can be explained, to a certain extent: it lies, among other things, in the alternation of very demanding, often strained consonants formed deep in the chest and extremely long, almost sung vowels that erupt in semantic-acoustic bursts. Both the sophistication of the consonants and the melody of the vowels are alien; they are not heard in everyday Arabic. The varieties of colloquial Arabic have levelled out the rich nuances of the classical sounds and trimmed the vowels to a normal length, which is natural. The full phonetic range of Arabic has been preserved only in poetry and, still more completely, in recitations of the Quran, which are among the great artistic events of traditional Arab societies and are attended by Muslims and Christians, believers and aesthetes alike. The best Quran singers win honours in competitions and are admired throughout the land. They even have their own fan clubs, whose members often include Arab Christians who revere the Quran not as revelation, but as the poetic touchstone of Arabic culture. I asked Egyptian taxi drivers why, in the middle of a traffic jam in sweltering heat, they put on a cassette of Quran recitation, and their answers always amazed me. The reasons they gave did not include the text's inspiring words or its profound meaning, nor did they profess fervent faith; instead, the answer I heard again and again was: 'It's so beautiful!'

But this fascination that the Quran has exerted for centuries also brings with it a danger. Because, according to the Muslim conception, God addressed humanity in marvellous Arabic – chose Arabic among all languages – that language took on a status which many speakers down to the present perceive as compelling, elevating and sometimes oppressive. That makes Arabic uniquely susceptible to stagnation, to mythification, formalism, kitsch – susceptible, too, to ideological exploitation, to demagogy. Anyone who has experienced a well-phrased, stirringly delivered public speech in an Arab country will have observed the powerful, 'magical' effect the language has on an audience. To realize what that means, perhaps we must imagine what such a thing would sound like in English: the constant presence of a 1500-year-old form of expression – and moreover, one charged with sacred associations – in the society, in its religion, its literature, its politics. Then we can see the seemingly 'mythic' power that the language has an Arabic context. A politician, a preacher or a poet who lifts up his voice to speak in classical Arabic is using an instrument that is sufficient in itself, if he masters it adequately, to captivate his listeners. His language works as a kind of time machine, transporting the audience back to a mythical past. Even a televised excerpt of a speech by, say, Arafat, Gaddafi or Saddam Hussein conveys an impression of that power – recordings of the great speeches of Nasser still more; Nasser's rise to power would have been unthinkable without his magnificent rhetorical talent.

In the film *Nasser 56*, which was shown everywhere in the Arabic-speaking world some years ago, we can observe how perfectly the great orator (or the actor Ahmad Zaki who portrays him) was able to play on the different levels of Arabic, switching between the popular and formal registers, achieving persuasiveness and attention simply by his linguistic manner. The film illustrates how, by ostentatiously pronouncing standard Arabic sentences at the right moment, even by flinging an 'archaic' formula such as *yā ayyūhā l-ikhwa* ('O ye brethren!') at the audience, the speaker can electrify his listeners and claim a lineage that goes back one and a half millennia. Even the packed Beirut cinema where I saw the film was filled with that incomparable suspense, and in the final scene, every time Nasser addressed his audience with the classical vocative particle, blasting it out with his face hardened to a mask by the tension, I could feel how the audience held their breath. And at the end of that speech, when the socialist Nasser at a lectern at Al-Azhar University cries *Allāhu akbar* four times, with brief, significant pauses, he comes full circle, returning to where his own history began: he becomes a prophet.

The statesmen of today, the generals, prime ministers and young kings, and the recently deposed Arab dictators, do not possess Nasser's rhetorical skill. Accordingly, they are less effective. Rival leaders are driven all the more to resort to the *ᶜarabīya*, the ancient language of the poets, the language of the Quran, which is both a jewel and a weapon. The fascination that fundamentalism exerts is also bound up with language. The fundamentalist leaders take pains to speak a pure Arabic untainted by popular idioms or foreign words. In spite of its superficial similarity, their language usually has little in common with the Quran and its power, since the appeal of the quranic language lies in its violation of norms, in its surprising grammatical figures and its extraordinary images. The Arabic spoken by modern fundamentalists is often appallingly trite, puritanical, conformist – in a word, artificial. Yet it is perceived nonetheless as pure and religious, mythic and, in a blunt, banal sense, exalted. The code of the language itself becomes a tool used to legitimize the speaker's claim to sacred authority.

On the first day of the American air offensive on Afghanistan, Osama bin Laden published his first video. What baffled me was that bin Laden spoke exquisite Arabic. Not once did he slip into dialect, as the modern generation of Arab leaders often do, nor did he confuse the complicated inflectional endings, which even intellectuals sometimes mix up. He chose antiquated vocabulary, familiar to educated Arabs from religious literature and classical poetry, and avoided all neologisms. In a way it was the puritanical, conformist Arabic of the fundamentalists, artificial in its stiffness. But, for the first time, I was hearing someone whose speech made the puritanical form sound perfectly natural and surprisingly spellbinding, even to me. The crucial point from a rhetorical point of view was not the eloquence of the speech itself: Osama bin Laden was appealing to a primordial language, one of unadulterated purity. It sounded like a traditional speech, but in reality, it represented a complete break with the tradition of Arabic rhetoric. The real heirs of this tradition, the Arab theologians of today, speak very differently, with – if they are well trained – their breathtakingly rich articulation of the classical Arabic consonants, their precisely modulated and sustained vowels. Osama bin Laden lacked the theological training, the years of learning Quran recitation and Arabic elocution, and, although he seemed to speak an antiquated Arabic, it sounded simple, clear, even modest. His rhetoric worked precisely because of its lack of ornament, by a conscious modesty of expression that has no precedent in the rhetorical tradition of classical Arabic. This linguistic asceticism signalled a rejection of the burden of tradition, a return to pure roots, just as bin Laden's robe and the setting of the video – a cave, an allusion to Muhammad's first revelation! – were designed to lend him a prophetic aura. Even the lack of accentuation in his rhetoric attested to the puritanical Wahhabi spirit, which purports to be identical with the spirit of God's messenger. The break with the dominant tradition is most distinctly noticeable when bin Laden cites phrases from the Quran: while other speakers grotesquely raise and lower their voices as soon as they quote the revelation, bin Laden proceeded in the same solicitous tone, as if he would level out the difference between his own speech and the Word of God.

Osama bin Laden rejected the facts of Muslim history to return to the supposed origins of Islam, but at the same time he turned his back on tradition. He rejected ornamentation of any kind, all rhetorical devices – the whole history of Quran exegesis – to return to the bare, original text, the pure unadulterated scripture. It is no coincidence that, in Christianity, such an explicit abstinence from aesthetic grandeur is characteristic of Protestantism. The new Muslim puritans' rejection of excessively musical Quran rectitations, as in Saudi Arabia, signals a profound conflict. A fundamentalist reading of a source text could be defined in literary terms as the assertion of a single, eternally valid, literal interpretation. A fundamentalist exegesis denies the source's ambiguity, which was always seen as praiseworthy in the theological tradition of Islam – as in that of Judaism. The classical Muslim commentators agreed that no verse of the Quran can be reduced to a single, absolute meaning: the Quran is said to be *dhū wujūhin* – that is, it has many faces, like the many *pānīm*, the manifold faces that Jewish scholars find in the Torah.

Today virtually all secular and all mystical interpretations in modern Muslim Quran scholarship build on this fundamental principle of Muslim exegesis: they insist on the ambiguity of the text, and hence on the poetic nature of the Quran, its poetically structured language. For every poetic text can be read and interpreted from many perspectives, without diminishing its singularity and its originality. The ambiguity itself defines the text as poetic; indeed, it stops being poetic if it is made unambiguous. That reduces it to a mere treatise, an ideological manifesto or – in the case of a revelation – a mere legal text. For scholars such as the Iranian Abdolkarim Soroush and the Egyptian Nasr Hamid Abu Zayd, the insistence on the ambiguity of the text, on the inexhaustibly varying act of interpretation, goes hand in hand with an emphasis on its beauty, its poetry and its musicality. They know that, if the Quran is accepted as a revelation and at the same time as a literary monument and an acoustic structure, it becomes a whole cosmos of signs, meanings and interpretations, readable in a multitude of different ways. Such an approach to the revelation would be diametrically opposed to the kind of monopoly on interpretation that fundamentalist currents claim almost by definition. That is why they warn against arbitrariness, emphasize the clarity of the divine word, and turn their backs on its beauty. The intellectual and often physical dispute over the Quran that is carried on in the Islamic world today can also be understood as a contest for its aesthetic dimension, which some see as endangered. 'Now the sirens have a still more terrible weapon than their song', Franz Kafka wrote, 'namely their silence.'[10]

— 2 —

REVOLT AGAINST GOD

Attar and Suffering

When the great tenth-century mystic Abu Bakr ash-Shibli visited a madhouse in Bagdad, a young inmate begged a favour of him: in his next prayer, would Shibli ask God why He so tormented this madman; why He held him, bound and shivering, in a strange place, far from his parents, hungry and cold, dressed only in rags; why He was so merciless, so devoid of magnanimity; why He had started a fire in this man's heart but provided no water to extinguish it; why God did not even allow the madman to escape Him? The holy man promised the insane sufferer that he would pass on his message, and turned away, weeping. When he had gone out the door, the madman suddenly called after him:

> No, no, please don't tell God any of what I asked you, not a word. If you tell Him, He'll make it a hundred times worse. I won't pray for anything; He doesn't listen anyway. He is sufficient unto Himself.[1]

The Persian poet Fariduddin Attar, who lived at the turn of the thirteenth century in Nishapur, a city in the northeast of modern-day Iran, tells this story in his *Book of Suffering*, probably his last and certainly his gloomiest work. In forty chapters, an allusion to the forty-day ritual retreat still practised in Islamic mysticism today, Attar traces the soul's journey through the cosmos. Disaffected with himself and the world, the 'philosophical wanderer' sets out in search of redemption, hope or, at least, consolation. He comes to the archangel Gabriel and laments that he has been thrown helpless into the world without head or foot; he asks Gabriel whether he knows any remedy for the pain that torments him. Gabriel imparts to the wanderer that his own lot is much worse and sends him away without an answer: 'We have enough pain of our own!'[2]

The other angels, and after them all the other celestial beings, likewise turn the wanderer away. No one can help him; everyone else is more desolate than he on the unbounded scale of affliction. Even Paradise complains: as if it were the just who entered in! But no, the wrong people had that good fortune. Paradise, in its own eyes, is really nothing but a vale of tears inhabited by the simple-minded. Appearances are deceiving: 'You see the beauty of the candle, but you don't see that the candle burns itself up in solitude.'[3]

And so it continues, on and on: the animals, the Devil, the spirits, Hell, humans, flowers: all of them answer the wanderer's hopeful, woeful lament with a heart-rending elegy on their own specific miseries. Attar develops a comprehensive and radical cosmology of pain in which every being in the world and in the higher spheres is a sign – just as in the Old Testament or in the Quran – not a sign of God and His mercy, however, but a sign of despair, a sign of God's absence and the painful meaninglessness of the world's way, which admits being only in destruction. Attar inverts the quranic creation story in particular, according to which God created all life on earth, all the phenomena of nature, history, human perception and sensual pleasures, so that they might bear witness to their Creator: Attar maintains the emblematic character of creation but reads the signs as negative.

In three darknesses, a seed without heart or religion,
Compressed mud dunked in brackish water,
Beaten back and forth like a ball in a game,
That from the beginning he might learn confusion. Drenched in blood, nine months long,
He had no other food but blood. What befell him there – better not to ask.
I told you of his body; of his soul – better not to ask. Head down he fell from his mother's womb,
Only to land in blood again. As his beginning was of filth,
Save your hopes of cleanliness. A shuttlecock, he came to love the blows,
That is to say, confusion became natural to him. Nine months he spent in the womb's blood,
That is to say, feeding on blood is how everything begins. Fallen head down on the earth, drenched in blood,
That is to say, it begins with parting and a topsy-turvy world. In tears his lips sought milk,
That is to say, weep, for you are of the mammal kind. Clawing fast to the breast, he saw nothing but blackness,
That is to say, live now, in bitterness and darkness. As a child he ran, stopping never,

That is to say, far are the children from the soul's rest. In youth he strayed, so strange he felt,
That is to say, naught is youth but an errant path. Soon age thwarted his wits,
That is to say, look not to the dotard for beatitude. Bewildered at the end he sank into his grave,
That is to say, never a trace of soul, of purity he found.[4]

The wanderer slogs on to the prophets – to Adam, Noah, Abraham, Moses, David and Jesus – but only Muhammad has a hint for him: he should seek not in the world but in himself. So the wanderer now travels on within himself, via the senses, the imagination, the mind and the heart, and finally arrives at the soul. 'What you have sought is within you', says the soul, and invites the wanderer to sink into its ocean. Thus far, the journey was to God, the poet concludes; now begins the journey in God.

That is the framing plot of Attar's 7539-line epic, which is strewn with countless embedded stories in an arrangement familiar from the *Thousand and One Nights*. Weaving individual threads of other colours into the main fabric of the story is a fundamental narrative strategy of Middle Eastern literature, and it makes no effort to hide its origins when it reappears in Europe, in *Don Quixote* or the *Divine Comedy*, in the *Decameron* or even in Lewis Carroll's *Alice* stories. But Attar's *Book of Suffering* recalls the *Divine Comedy* in more than just its structure. The two poems are both logbooks of the soul's stations on its journey through the cosmos. This motif is a very old one, much older than Attar and Dante. The soul on its flight through Heaven and Hell is one of the most important and most fascinating topoi in the literature of antiquity and of the Middle East. The first Islamic journey to Heaven is Muhammad's night journey (*miᶜrāj*), mentioned in the Quran and portrayed in folkloric colour in the anonymous *Book of the Ascension* (*Kitab al-miᶜrāj*). Variations on Muhammad's heavenly journey are found not only in Attar's *Book of Suffering* but also in many other works of Arab-Persian literature, including those of the poet al-Maᶜarri, the mystic Ibn Arabi and the philosopher Avicenna. European literature takes up the conceit of the cosmic journey of the soul in Dante's *Divine Comedy*. From there, the theme continues in Milton's *Paradise Lost*, in Part II of Goethe's *Faust*, and also in the description of Joseph's dream journey to Heaven in Thomas Mann's *Joseph and His Brothers* and Gerhart Hauptmann's *Der Grosse Traum* [The Great Dream]. And the tale in Georg Büchner's *Woyzeck* of the solitary child travelling alone through the universe and finding every place deserted reads almost like a miniature version of Attar's *Book of Suffering*.

The paths travelled by this topos, a highly productive one for Europe as well as for the Middle East, have at least in part been brought to light, although some Romance scholars have responded with scepticism to the discoveries of the Arabists – with scepticism, and often with the blindness of those who will not see. In the *Divine Comedy* of all places, a pivotal text in the search for European identity, they find Arab-Islamic culture only as a footnote, if at all – by no means as a central source. But in fact, Dante plainly drew on *The Book of the Ascension*, which was available to him in a number of translations, in writing his *Divine Comedy* (although that did not stop him from assigning Muhammad a place in Hell); another source he may have used is an Italian translation from the Hebrew of Avicenna's account of the soul's cosmic journey, which is itself nothing but a variant of Muhammad's ascension. Even if Dante could not have read Attar, the many similarities between his *Divine Comedy* and *The Book of Suffering* are not coincidental, since both poets – the Persian Attar and, a hundred years later, the Italian Dante – refer to a common literary topos and, in part, to the same sources. Just as Attar appropriated the ascension motif for Sufi purposes, Dante gave the Islamic material a Christian interpretation, down to its details. And, where its Eastern elements are concerned, Dante's work is more than a mere appropriation. The *Divine Comedy* can be read as a reaction to those elements of Arab culture whose influence Dante felt to be particularly dangerous: the heretical rationalism of the Averroists and the overly permissive poetry of courtly love. Dante's celestial journey is virtually an anti-*mi*ᶜ*rāj*, a rebuttal to the account of Muhammad's ascension, intended to demonstrate the falsity of Islam and the superiority of the Christian faith. Like no other work, Dante's *Divine Comedy* is hence an interface both for the acquisition of Arab-influenced culture in Europe and for its repulsion.

The comparison of *The Book of Suffering* with the *Divine Comedy* is the more enlightening because it brings to the fore Attar's critique of what exists on earth, his doubt of what is theologically foretold and, at the same time, his humanism. Dante appears altogether sanctimonious when we discover his predecessor, whose book is not only an explicit criticism of God's plan of Creation but also a vehement polemic for religious tolerance and against the dogmatic Muslim orthodoxy, bristling with a broad critique of the social and political conditions of his time. While the *Divine Comedy* criticizes the divine order at most indirectly – as, for example, in the tenderness with which Dante describes the lovers Paolo and Francesca, damned to Hell for their sin of lust – *The Book of Suffering* displays the extremes of despair in which Man openly turns against his Creator. God, who is supposed to be closer to believers than their own jugular vein, is far away in *The Book of Suffering*. He exists, but He is remote. At best. For, while the remoteness and the concealment of the Creator are among Attar's recurring afflictions, in many episodes he suffers from the exact opposite: the cruel proximity to God. A fool wandering in the desert is surprised by a severe thunderstorm. Lightning threatens to incinerate him, rain threatens to drown him; he is sore afraid. Then a voice calls to the fool from the storm-lashed heavens (and we may well read this as a caricature of scenes from the Old Testament and smile):

> 'God is with you, have no fear.'
>
> 'But that is why I am afraid,' the fool cries; 'I am afraid *because* He is with me.'[5]

God torments humans simply to pass the time, out of self-indulgence and vanity. God is the potter who shapes vessels with great skill, only to smash them for pleasure, to enjoy the crash of mortal woe. 'But we're the poor musicians and our bodies the instruments', as we know from a related image by Georg Büchner, the chief prosecutor of God among German poets: 'Do we wring these awful yowlings from them only to have them rise higher and higher and fade away into a voluptuous sigh in the ears of heaven?'[6]

Perhaps Büchner's Valerio is right, and almighty God was only bored: Sultan Mahmud of Ghazni, who often symbolizes the Almighty in Attar, sits alone in his palace. No one comes to visit him, no one wants anything from him, not even the beggars request an audience. Alone, he – read: God – roams through the vast halls of his palace. He is bored; he is lonely. What is the matter, he asks his vizier; why does no one come to him any more? Because justice reigns, the vizier answers. Then Mahmud sends out his soldiers to attack the villages; he foments animosity among the people, and extorts rapacious taxes and duties. Directly the royal halls are filled with people craving boons, seeking advice, begging for mercy. Sultan Mahmud leans back, content.[7]

Only by resistance is it possible to survive in the face of God. A hermit in a barren place who devoted himself entirely to God, without a care for his own sustenance, receives a visit one day from two hungry guests. He waits until evening before worrying whether he should get them something to eat, and then finds nothing, and is ashamed before his guests. Then he lifts his voice to Heaven and cries, 'If You send guests to me, of all people, then at least send me something for me to feed them! If You send me some food, I'll let it rest; but otherwise I'll take this club and knock all the chandeliers in Your mosque to bits!' Instantly a servant appears bringing a rich platter of food. The two guests are horrified by their host's monologue, however. He growls, 'You have to show God your teeth; nothing else does any good.'[8]

The holy men and the fools in *The Book of Suffering* accuse God; they refuse or resist Him; or they are at war with Him, like the mad holy man Luqman Sarakhsi: he mounted a hobbyhorse, took a stick in his hand, and rode out of the city to do battle with God. Out in the field, a mighty Turk caught him, beat him bloody and took away his stick. Discouraged and bleeding, Luqman returned to the city.

> 'Well, how did the battle go?' asked a gawker in the crowd.
>
> 'Don't you see my bloody shirt? God didn't dare take me on Himself, but He summoned a giant Turk to His aid. Naturally I didn't stand a chance against him.'[9]

The Book of Suffering is a little-known work of universal literature but a terrifying and a disturbing one. Insight is limited, as in Schopenhauer, to the recognition of absurdity. It speaks to us not only in its hopeless pessimism but also in its pitch-black humour, as when Attar relates the story of a fool who must have known Beckett's saying that we are born astride a grave. After a funeral, the fool remains sitting beside the grave and makes himself comfortable. When they ask him why he does not return to the city, he says he doesn't want to make any more unnecessary detours. 'Woe if I go; a pity that I came', says the fool, turning away from his questioner.[10]

Probably because the God that he portrays is so unreliable, many of Attar's verses reveal an attitude that, to a present-day reader, oscillates between Enlightenment and existentialism: the individual's responsibility for himself is emphasized constantly, and the psychological process of creativity in writing is discussed more explicitly than in any other work of classical Persian literature; there is a whole chapter against fanaticism and there are dozens of pleas for mercy, forbearance, brotherly love and virtues considered modern, such as religious pluralism, which is not merely accepted but praised as a treasure. In view of Attar's time and culture, it is remarkable, perhaps even unparalleled, how resolutely he insists on the individual's responsibility to experience the Creator's reality for himself and not to follow His commandments blindly, but by his individual will. Imitation, *taqlid*, is almost as bad a word to Attar as dogmatism, *ta*^{c}*assob*: the offspring of asses, he writes, are not made to follow the path of sharia; if they walked that path, we would know they were blindly following their mother. Because the law of religion is not given to Man as his nature, no compulsion can free him of the choice to follow it. Such positions, and the whole individuality of Attar's writing, perceptions and convictions, are like precursors of the modern age. That they have found their way so explicitly and insistently into an early thirteenth-century text is primarily an indication that the Sufis disseminated and adopted the humanism that had already taken shape under the Buyids in Baghdad – a humanism that Attar must have seen as endangered, however, otherwise he would hardly have expounded it so angrily. The Mongol invasion, which levelled the cities of the eastern Islamic world and cost the lives of most of its inhabitants, the septuagenarian Attar probably among them in the massacre at Nishapur in 1221, brought final confirmation of the fears that he had expressed, poetically and religiously, in *The Book of Suffering*. Islamic culture never really recovered from that onslaught.

Yet the period in which Attar lived was not only the last days of his world: it was also the period in which Europe absorbed the ideas of the Orient in every field and began to discover Man as subject. In the West, too, as research shows with growing clarity, the twelfth century has a special status as a time in which religious concepts of the world were shaken and the transition to more rational structures of consciousness took place (contrary to the traditional notion that this process began only with the Italian Renaissance of the fourteenth century). The humanism that Attar saw as endangered continued to develop in a different culture.

By interpreting the whole world as a single utterance of God addressed to humanity, the Quran profoundly elevated Man: no longer merely a part, even the crown, of Creation, Man was now its meaning and purpose, its cause and telos. Man in the Quran is therefore not a 'likeness' but a 'successor' or 'viceroy' (*khalīfa*, caliph). This is a fundamental distinction, although one that is rarely thought about, as far as I can see: Man is not merely created in the image of God; he is given responsibility for completing Creation. The Quran declares Man an autonomous being and, at the same time, expects him to give up his autonomy voluntarily. The word *Muslim* ('surrender, submit, make peace') indicates the active sense of that surrender: even if the result of this act were an abdication of free will, as Western descriptions of Islam often claim, still the act itself necessarily takes place on one's own initiative – unless we read into the Quran a strict predestination, declaring that human will is automatic. The range of actions is extremely restricted, it is true: if Man turns towards God, the sense of Creation is fulfilled. If Man turns away, he commits evil and brings damnation upon himself. The case that Man turns to God but does not surrender to Him – that he recognizes God's power and yet defies it – is not envisaged in the Quran. A fool comes across a meeting of scholars. They are talking about Creation and mention that God made Man out of mud and heart. The fool is scandalized by the devout words: 'If even the mud and our hearts come from Him, what in this world belongs to us? Do we really possess nothing but our appetites? If everything comes from Him, who then am I?'[11]

In a certain sense, the first truly autonomous, Promethean act that would elevate Man to make him God's successor, the one who follows Him and the one to replace Him, would be this: Man does something that is not foreseen in God's plan. His revolt would consummate his individuation; it would presuppose that he promotes himself to God's viceroy. In renouncing hope, he would have his reason to go on living. In his poem *Hiob* [Job], Yvan Goll writes,

Why I'm still alive?
Insecure God
To prove You to Yourself.[12]

Attar's Prometheus, however, far from hating the gods, is transformed into a fool whose love of God is unrequited, who replays the tragedy on the world's rear stage, where no one takes him seriously. A fool sees people walking out adorned with new clothes on a feast day while he has only rags to wear. 'You Knower of the secrets', he cries to Heaven, 'Please give me shoes, a shirt and a turban, and I won't bother You again until the next feast day!' When nothing happens, the fool tries humility: 'At least give me a turban. I'll do without the shoes and shirt.' A joker hears the fool's prayer and throws down an old lousy turban from a rooftop. The fool flies into a rage and throws the turban back up to the roof, crying, 'I'm not wearing a rag like that! You can give that to Your angel Gabriel.'[13]

The notion that Man can morally surpass God is one of many concepts that Attar could not have found in the Quran. It is conceivable in the Hebrew Bible, however, a much more frequent source of motifs that are found in Attar's *Book of Suffering*: Yahweh is inferior to humankind in many biblical passages, except in power. Job says so explicitly when he protests his innocence and God's injustice. In the face of God's acts of violence, which pervade the whole Bible right up to the Revelation of John, in which only 144,000 people escape His destruction – in the face of this history of rage Job adheres faithfully to the law, to the sincerity and charity that the same God has imposed upon him:

If I have seen any perish for want of clothing, or any poor without covering;
If his loins have not blessed me, and if he were not warmed with the fleece of my sheep; . . .
This also were an iniquity to be punished by the judge: for I should have denied the God that is above.[14]

The biblical Book of Job is testimony of human self-awareness. 'A man has overtaken, has enlightened his own God. That . . . is the abiding lesson of the Book of Job', Ernst Bloch writes.[15] By the same logic, and in a complete reversal of the quranic view, Attar's fools cry out that God should follow Man's example; He should behave Himself; should learn from humanity how to love. Very similarly, Büchner's Lenz says, 'As for myself, were I almighty, you see, if I were, if I could no longer put up with all this suffering, I would just save, save everyone.'[16] And Schopenhauer, putting himself in God's place, shudders, 'If a god has made this world, then I would not like to be the god: its misery and distress would break my heart.'[17] When they appeal to God's mercy, the holy men and the fools who rebel against God in *The Book of Suffering* and other Sufi texts are true to God's word in the face of God Himself. Emmanuel Levinas has characterized such an attitude among Jews as 'loving the Torah more than God'.[18] A fool cries out to Heaven: 'If Your heart is not moved by what goes on down here, take mine. Is Your heart really so obdurate?'[19]

Such thoughts are not permitted ordinary humans, and, in Attar's world, the unbelievers and the indifferent are benighted anyway. Rebellion against God is the prerogative of saints, prophets and fools; it is by no means recommended as a general course of action. Only lovers are forgiven their sin; only fools are exempt from the law; only Moses himself may – out of love, as Attar repeatedly emphasizes – break the tablets of the Law. A mother, in frantic lamentation over her slain son, uncovered herself and blasphemed against God:

> Her back was bent like an bow,
> Shooting the arrow of her sorrow to Heaven.

When someone remonstrated with her and told to put her veil back on, the woman answered,

> If the fire burned in your liver as it burns in mine,
> My actions would not only be permitted you, but required of you.
> Before my fire kindles your heart,
> Do not set yourself up as judge. You are not the mother of a dead child;
> How dare you prescribe me how to mourn? I see you are one of the free;
> You know nothing of those who are bound to suffering.[20]

Attar is not instigating heresy – and this is crucial if we are to avoid misunderstanding *The Book of Suffering* as a negation of religion. He is describing a specific affect on the part of those who are close to God: 'He who burns with love for Him is pure.'[21] Complaint and rebellion are incorporated in faith itself; they become a theological, spiritual and – when seen against the backdrop of the mystic rituals – quasi-liturgical theme, such as we know from the Hebrew Bible. It is psalmists who censure God in their prayers; it is Job, the most faithful of God's servants, who rebels against God. And this same Job is not punished for his protest – he is richly recompensed, even though he does not forgive God but only submits to Him, recognizing His power. God Himself sanctions rebellion by rewarding not Job's three friends but Job himself – and, while He does not answer Job's complaint, neither does He reject it; He lets it stand. Just as Job is rewarded without receiving any answer to his questions, so Attar implies that, if any mortals find redemption, it is most likely the rebellious fools and the blasphemous saints who do so. The mystic Bayezid Bestami, who, after completing his threescore years and ten, calls God to account for His seventy thousand years, hears a voice on finishing his tirade against Heaven:

> Wait for the Day of Reckoning, then I will turn your seven limbs into atoms and turn every atom into an eye, and I will grant you an audience for every eye. That will be your reckoning for four thousand years, and you will see more than you can look at. Whosoever sees this Sun will find here what was promised him.[22]

And Attar himself says that the same God who torments man also teaches man the complaint to assuage the torment.

> When You press me into the ground of Your wrath,
> You scatter a hundred treasures of kindness over me.
> And when the sword of Your justice wounds me,
> The salve of Your mercy shall heal me.[23]

God is the both the tormentor and the healer, the sword and the salve. Attar's verses translate into human terms what Yahweh says in these: 'I kill, and I make alive; I wound, and I heal: neither is there any that can deliver out of my hand.'[24] Neither the Bible nor Attar advocates blaspheming God; rather, they depict rebellion against God as an intimate, perhaps the most intimate moment of faith: 'How shall the sane man dare to say what the lover says?'[25] On the way to Mount Sinai, Moses meets an enlightened ascetic. The hermit says, 'O Moses, tell the Creator: "Thy commandments are carried out, therefore be merciful."'

As Moses continues on his way, he meets a man who has been driven out of his senses with the love of God. The man says, 'Tell the True God, "This piece of skin and bones loves You – do You love it too?"'

Moses goes on and finally meets a bareheaded, barefooted fool. The fool says boldly to Moses, 'Tell the Creator, "How much more misery have You yet in store for me? I have no more strength to bear it. Sorrow has eaten away my soul; the bright day is night to me. I will renounce You – but will You finally leave me alone?"'

When he arrives at Mount Sinai, Moses dares to give the Lord only the first two messages. God grants the prayers of the ascetic and the lover. When the prophet turns to go, God says,

> 'You have kept the fool's message from Me.'
>
> 'O Lord, I thought it better not to repeat to You his indecent speech. Although You have already heard it, it is not fit to be pronounced again.'
>
> 'Tell the fool: "Even if you renounce Me, I will never renounce you."'[26]

Attar avoids suggesting that fools and holy men who question God's righteous order might receive an explanation. He praises them as God's intimates but lets their accusations go unheard. God is not justified in Attar any more than He justifies Himself in the Book of Job. When Bayezid demands that God give an account of Himself, he is not refuted, but rewarded. This is the paradox of heretical piety in which Attar follows in the footsteps of the Bible: clinging to God, at the same time denying Him the attribute of kindness, and ultimately being rewarded for this ire against God – all this together makes up the theme of Job; it does not consist of pure accusation or pure acquiescence. The theme is found in all of Attar's epic poems but in its most pessimistic shading in *The Book of Suffering*, where he describes suffering and the rebellion that arises from it more drastically than in any book of Islamic literature while only hinting at redemption and the possible commendation of rebellion.

Ernst Bloch and other modern interpreters concluded that the motif of submission was a later emendation to the Book of Job. Textual criticism aside, there are thematic and dramaturgical arguments to the contrary. *The Book of Suffering* allows us to see more clearly that rebellion against God presupposes a nearness to Him. In this scheme, rebellion arises from piety itself, as the story of Dhu n-Nun's disciple illustrates. The disciple undergoes forty forty-day retreats; he prays ceaselessly, fasts, keeps vigils and is silent for forty years without attaining enlightenment or even the hint of a spark of hope. He doesn't want to complain, he says to his master, but he just doesn't know any more what else he can do to obtain a sign. Dhu n-Nun answers that, if God will not look down on the disciple in kindness, then perhaps He will do so in wrath, and recommends that he take a break from praying and fasting and indulge himself to his heart's content. The disciple gorges himself and goes to bed. Immediately the Prophet appears to him in a dream to give him a message from God: 'How can a person lose who consorts with Us?'[27]

Job and the fools, holy men and dervishes in *The Book of Suffering* do not lose their faith in God when they rebel against Him: in their desperation they are more religious than the faithful who praise God but close their eyes to the real state of His creation. Those who love above and beyond the usual measure dare to demand that God fulfils His own revelation. After all, God did not lose His bet with Satan: Job's rebellion against God does not imply that he denies Him. Disobedience here becomes an act of submission, for, by emancipating himself from God, man becomes pleasing in God's sight.

> The eye of your forgiveness sought a rebel,
> So I took the field of resistance.[28]

Even when they do confront suffering, the orthodoxies of all three monotheistic religions push it away when they look for an explanation of it. Their answers are confined to canonical persuasions and traditions, regardless of the subjectively felt depth, sorrow and sincerity of their phrases. Their whole struggle is aimed at remaining within traditional bounds, even though they recognize the calamitous condition of reality. By attributing some kind of sense to injustice, or by giving up hope of any explanation of it in this world, they cling to the moral perfection of the Creator – although, or because, they realize that reality is full of calamity – for fear of falling into unbelief. Other than the denial of God in atheism and the defence of God in the many varieties of theodicy, it rarely occurs to them that another human reaction is conceivable, one that is probably even older historically: there is a God, but He is neither loving nor just; there is a meaning, but it is baneful. In all religions, no doubt, there have been individuals – poets, mystics, theologians – who have found words to express man's suffering under God or who have upheld it with dogma. Outside monotheism, it is almost natural to do so, as in Greek antiquity and, still more commonly, in Hinduism. That is, the piety that rages against the gods leads to a complete reversal of values and beliefs only in the case where there is just one God.

In monotheism, rebellion against God is rebellion against the whole religion, which teaches an opposing idea of God as more just. It is in a sense a counter-theology, one which does not abolish the boundaries against atheism but does make them permeable. The Jewish tradition in particular – to a greater extent than Islamic culture, in which the religiously sanctioned incrimination of God is limited largely to mysticism – seems to allow some people to revolt against God: throughout the centuries, down to the Jewish reflections on and descriptions of the Shoah, there have been numerous expressions of rebellion which have remained, in their conception and their self-conception, within the religious tradition. In Judaism, quarrelling with God often takes the form of pleading in a court of justice. The story is told, for example, that the surviving members of a rabbinical court met in one of the barracks of Auschwitz, as witnesses of the terror that was being visited on the Jews, to put God on trial. At dawn they announced their judgement: because He has been guilty of outrageous neglect towards His children, the Most Holy, praised be He, is expelled forthwith from the community. It was as if the cosmos held its breath. 'Come', sighed the rabbi at last, 'it's time to go and pray.'

God is praised and condemned in the same breath. The rabbi repudiates God, then says, 'Let's go and pray.' That is essentially what concerns Attar, and what concerned the lamenting prophets and the psalmists before him and the dying Heinrich Heine centuries after him: 'The tears of the wronged cry out to God!' Heine writes from his 'mattress grave', and in the next sentence says he bears his 'misery with submission to the ineffable will of God'.[29] Heine condemns his Destroyer and, without lifting his pen from the paper, reveres his Creator: 'O God! You wanted me to perish, and I perished. Praised be the Lord!'[30] The same Jeremiah who decries God's injustice also speaks of Him as the righteous judge. Even the gloomiest psalms address God as a beloved Father. Levi Yitzchak of Berdichev interrupted worship on Yom Kippur to protest against God's failure to protect the people of Israel – whereas any king of flesh and blood would take care of his people – then went on to recite Kaddish, beginning with the words, 'May His great name be exalted and sanctified in the world.'[31] On another occasion, he prayed, 'Master of the world! I do not ask that You reveal to me the mysteries of Your ways – I could not comprehend them. I do not want to know why I suffer: my only desire is to know that I suffer for Your sake.'[32]

The twentieth century, however, has visited on humanity and on the Jewish people in particular an atrocity that left even protest impossible – for protest requires the very self-awareness that was replaced in the concentration camps and gas chambers with a mere number. The prayer of Levi Yitzchak, 'I do not want to know why I suffer', was adapted by Rabbi Judah L. Magnes, the mentor of Hannah Arendt: '. . . but only if You know that I suffer.'[33] In Attar, Majnun's mad love for Leyla brings misery and contempt upon him. At one point his father says to him,

> 'You simpleton! You have made yourself contemptible. No one would sell you so much as a loaf of bread now.'

'I suffer these torments only for the sake of the one I love. Does she know that I suffer for her sake?'

'She knows.'

'That is enough to keep me breathing until Judgment Day.'[34]

As recently as the twentieth century, the motif of quarrelling with God – that is, the Job motif in all its forms as it runs through all three Abrahamic religions, usually near the margins, often pushed beyond them, lost from sight for centuries – is characterized by this component: it includes its apparent opposite. 'Though he slay me, yet will I trust in him', says Job.[35] At the end of Zvi Kolitz's oppressively beautiful story about the fate of a Jewish father in occupied Warsaw, the first-person narrator recites the prayer of a Sephardic Jew. It seems to be a variation of Shibli's cry, 'My God! If You made the whole sky my yoke and the earth my hobble, and if You made the whole world thirst for my blood, still I would not renounce You.'[36] Indeed it could be a variation, through convoluted but not overly long historic paths, of Shibli's exclamation, if we remember how Jewish mysticism is involved in Sufi literature:

> 'God of Israel,' he said, 'I have fled to this place so that I may serve You in peace, to follow Your commandments and glorify Your name; You, however, are doing everything to make me cease believing in You. But if You think You will succeed by these trials in deflecting me from the true path, then I cry out to You, my God and the God of my parents, that none of it will avail You. You may insult me, You may chastise me, You may take from me the dearest and the best that I have in the world, You may torture me to death – I will always believe in You. I will love you always and forever – even despite You. Here, then, are my last words to You, my angry God: None of this will avail You in the least! You have done everything to make me lose my faith in You, to make me cease to believe in You. But I die exactly as I have lived, an unshakable believer in You.'[37]

A man turning to God in his hour of need calls for no explanation; Man indicting God in his desperation is illustrated many times over in the history of literature. But Attar describes in many verses how the two acts go together and how they culminate: how creatures, faced with their own destruction, clutch at God with love – not *in spite of* His guilt, but *because* of it. When the fools and the holy men feel they are being tormented by God Almighty in person, their moans take on the presumptuous tone of intimacy in which they can tell Him anything: accusations, blasphemies, wisecracks, taunts, haggling, threats and curses – like the hermit in *The Book of Suffering* to whom God sends guests, but nothing for them to eat, they would smash to bits the chandeliers in His mosque. It is the tone that both Job and Jeremiah raised, and the tone heard loudest in the history of both Judaism and Islam in times of oppression, persecution and slaughter. In Angel Wagenstein's autobiographical novel *Isaac's Torah*, a picaresque narrative of a Jewish life through 'two world wars, three concentration camps and five motherlands', Rabbi Shmuel says in a sermon:

> Well, I'm asking you, is the Lord not seeing all this? Or is He drowsing and picking His nose? Or is God too, glory to His name for the eternity of time, a senile old man who is flattered by the fact that people are dying in His name? I don't know, my dear brothers, I cannot give you an answer. In any case, I'm thinking: If the Lord had windows, they would long ago have smashed His panes![38]

I began by telling the story of Shibli's visit to the madhouse and the fool who called after him not to tell God of his complaints for fear He would make his fate a hundred times worse. Elie Wiesel tells of a little group of Jews praying in a synagogue during the Nazi occupation. Another Jew appears at the door who is very devout but has gone mad. He listens to their prayers for a while, then he says, softly but urgently, 'Shh, Jews! Do not pray so loudly [or else] God will hear you. Then He will know that there are still some Jews left alive in Europe.'[39]

In Christian Europe, the Job motif takes a completely different course from that in the Jewish and Islamic traditions. A comparison of early commentaries on biblical stories – such as that of Job or of Jonah – reveals that the Christian exegesis almost completely ignores human resistance against God's will, while the Jewish commentators at least treat it as a religious phenomenon, and sometimes with approval. Immanuel Kant remarked that Job, 'before any court of dogmatic theologians, before a synod, an inquisition . . . would have likely suffered a sad fate.'[40] Throughout the whole history of Christian theodicy, from the Church Fathers until well into the twentieth century, the dimension of rebellion against God has received next to no consideration.

There is protest against God in Europe, too, but it is articulated only very late, and then mainly outside religion. Not even Christian mysticism has incorporated the Job motif in its full breadth, because the mystics primarily sought compassion with God's human incarnation. Man's rebellion against a transcendental authority became a literary theme in the strict sense only during the Enlightenment – or, more precisely, as a part of the disappointment and disquiet of rationalism on realizing that there was no rational proof of God's wisdom and goodness. In her book on the problem of evil, Susan Neiman takes as the beginning of this rebellion in Europe the statement of King Alfonso X of Castile, which was censured for centuries: 'If I had been of God's counsel at the Creation, many things would have been ordered better.'[41] That this remark situates the 'first Enlightenment hero'[42] precisely at Europe's junction with Middle Eastern culture is logical in a way that has been almost completely disregarded in contemporary Western histories of philosophy – including Susan Neiman's. In these cultural histories, the revolt against the Creator seems to have appeared out of thin air.

The myth of Western culture's virgin birth out of the spirit of classical antiquity has its origins in the Renaissance; it was shaped to a great extent in the nineteenth century, when the Orient was conceived as the absolute Other of Western culture. In literary scholarship more specifically, the paradigm of an exclusive Occidental literary history, still dominant today, can be traced to two German-language studies of great brilliance and equally great influence which appeared after the Second World War: Erich Auerbach's *Mimesis* of 1946 and Ernst Robert Curtius's *European Literature and the Latin Middle Ages* of 1948. In these interpretations of European literary history, both of which became canon, non-European names, works, titles, genres, styles, themes and narrative forms are virtually non-existent, even though a work such as the *Decameron*, in its form and in many of its stories, is so deeply saturated with the literature of the Middle East that the word 'influence' hardly does it justice: it would be more accurate to call Boccaccio an author of the Orient, in the same way that we now classify some Japanese or Middle Eastern authors as belonging to modern literature, the paradigms of which were formed in the West. Even in his long chapters on Dante, Curtius mentions no Arabic precursors, contacts or sources, although studies of them had long been available. He ignores the Arabs' 700-year presence in Spain by beginning the history of Spanish literature with the sixteenth century, without wasting so much as a thought on why Cervantes, for example, passes off his *Don Quixote* as a translation from the Arabic that he bought in the Toledo marketplace. Curtius's work, in itself of course magnificent – and a standard reference whose influence is felt in the school curricula of the German-speaking countries to this day – is an especially striking and significant illustration of the exclusionary mechanism by which Europe constructs its history.

Europe not only shares with the Middle East its two essential intellectual roots – Greek antiquity and ancient Israel – but it was able to take shape, intellectually and historically, as an independent identity only by distinguishing itself from something other: from Islam, and from the whole sphere of Arab culture, which in the twelfth century set the standards for intellectual and academic life, not just in southern France and southern Italy but as far north as Bologna, Paris and London – a cultural sphere whose composition included the various Muslim traditions alongside Judaism and Eastern Christianity, and one which, in the cities at least, gave rise to an intellectual attitude that was in some parts firmly areligious. As the texts of Christian scholasticism show most distinctly and symbolically, however, Europe's self-definition by contradistinction was at the same time an assimilation of what had originally been considered Arabian. The Arab cultural sphere was far more important to Europe's cultural history than a mere mediator of ancient knowledge. In their European manifestations, both of the major intellectual movements of the Middle Ages – dialectical theology and humanism – still bear distinct traces of Middle Eastern culture today in their substantial and fundamental elements. Arabic-language philosophy is 'one of the source areas of our Enlightenment', Ernst Bloch remembered, 'of an extremely idiosyncratic, materialistic vitality, one developed in an un-Christian way out of Aristotle';[43] and modern European literature begins on the borders of the Arab world, not just geographically – in Renaissance Italy, in southern France at the time of the troubadours, in Spain after the Reconquista. Europe absorbed the intellectual currents of Islam and of Arab Judaism, assimilated them in order to transform them, Europeanize them – or, rather, to attain an independent European identity in the first place. This dual process of assimilation and differentiation has played a key role in the creation of a secular modern age which abolished, not Christianity, but the medieval primacy of theology.

Since the scholarship of the German-speaking Jews, there has been no lack of proposals to treat the Arab-influenced cultures of the Middle Ages, and especially that of Andalusia, not just as mediators of Greek sources but as a part of Europe's history of ideas. Yet some in European medieval studies, Romance philology and the history of philosophy, and especially scholarly journalism, refuse today to recognize the clearest philological or historical evidence (such as the etymology of the word 'troubadour') of the Eastern origin of European philosophical concepts and literary genres. As the American literary scholar María Rosa Menocal noted, this resistance to a specifically Islamic–Jewish lineage of European modernity, which still resonates in day-to-day politics – for example, in the controversies over Turkish membership of the EU and over whether 'Islam is part of Germany'[44] – recalls the objection to Darwin's findings that man couldn't possibly be descended from apes.[45] Criticism of the Creator in particular was far advanced in the Orient's Jewish and Islamic history of ideas; this should be plain enough. It is therefore by no means coincidental, but of emblematic importance, that the Castilian Alfonso X of all people should have hit upon God's ineptitude – and that he did so as an immediate reaction to his study of Arabic sciences, for which he had summoned Jewish scholars from nearby Toledo.

In Europe, Man's rebellion against God is closely connected with secularization. Shakespeare and Gryphius are early witnesses to the fact. What has been forgotten is that Leibniz's famous apology for creation as the best of all possible worlds was a rebuttal to the doubts as to the meaning of creation that the French philosopher Pierre Bayle had raised in his *Dictionnaire historique et critique*. Bayle describes God as a father who placidly looks on as his children break their bones, just so he can demonstrate afterwards what a good doctor he is. David Hume, too, invokes images of this sort: God as an ostrich; as a dilettante shipbuilder; as a vain fool. Both authors, however, use such similes primarily to refute positive definitions of God altogether. Taking the figure of Prometheus as an example, Hans Blumenberg has shown how the rebellion against God took shape in the eighteenth and nineteenth centuries and merged into the emancipation of Man. A key stanza in Goethe's poem 'Prometheus' reads as follows:

> I should respect you? For what?
> Have you ever soothed
> The pain that burdened me?
> Have you ever dried
> My terrified tears?
> Was I not forged into manhood
> By almighty Time
> And everlasting Destiny,
> My masters and yours?[46]

Dostoevsky established the model of the rebel against God in modern literature in Ivan Karamazov, who rejects the Christian impulse to forgive outrageous injustice. Ivan Karamazov does not deny God by any means, but he wants nothing more to do with a Truth that is responsible for the tears of a suffering child: 'It's not that I don't accept God, Alyosha, I just most respectfully return him the ticket.'[47] Likewise Camus' Dr Rieux, after having attended the agony of a child with Father Paneloux, refuses 'to love this creation in which children are tortured'.[48] Although Rieux takes the next step and renounces his religion, like Büchner's Danton before him, his basic religious disposition is unchanged: it is the source of the problem in the first place. Even Camus' atheism conceives the world as the object of a higher power. Following in Dostoevsky's path, he calls that atheism a 'metaphysical revolt' in itself, one which presupposes the personified God of the Hebrew Bible as responsible for 'mobilizing the forces of rebellion'. When Rieux begins to doubt God, it is because he conceives Him to be just. 'The history of metaphysical revolt cannot be confused with that of atheism', Camus writes. 'The rebel defies more than he denies.'[49]

By lending a voice to the protest against God, European literature was also in large part responsible for what was at least an occasional return of the Job motif in Christian theology, in Dorothee Solle and Friedolin Stier, and also in Karl Rahner and Johann Baptist Metz. Karl-Josef Kuschel calls it a 'theohistorical tragedy that these traditions of protest against God had to be escalated by atheists before they were heard within the Church.'[50] In Attar's own culture, on the other hand, protest against God finds a voice almost exclusively outside the religion. It is an external critique. It is important to remember again and again, when talking about the deep-seated crisis and the loss of creativity, tolerance and freedom in the Arab world today or under the political dictatorship in Iran, that most of the poets and mystics who attacked the dominant concept of the world and the traditional norms of their time saw themselves as devout Muslims. And not only that: they were consistently present in their own culture. That is what I am talking about: a vital, dynamic and creative society is one which does not leave radical criticism to the outsiders but undertakes it itself; that is, it is one which allows and even institutionally encourages self-criticism – just as kings kept professional scoffers and fools and contemporary states give prizes to their critics; just as cities support avant-garde theatre. How else could religious and political conditions progress if their truths were not attacked anew, over and over again, if they were not pressed by criticism to find new answers, over and over again? And self-criticism means, ultimately, that the critic still belongs to the self in question, just as the greatest critics of Western culture have been a brilliant, outstanding feature of that culture.

Criticism of other cultures is always affirmative towards one's own culture and, hence, the opposite of literature's motive and purpose. Literature – all art and intellectual activity – is in essence a self-critical act. Faridoddin Attar is the best evidence of that: he is not a heretic but a classic of Persian literature and an example of what Islamic culture was capable of – which always included the opposite of what the religious elites defined as Islamic. Rationalistic and mystical understandings of religion, the radical liberality of erotic narratives, the acceptance of both political and religious critique, and even open heresy, no longer have a place either in Attar's country or in the Arab world, with the exception of individual countries such as Lebanon. 'I am greater than

God', the mystic Bayezid Bistami cried out. Bistami is one of the great saints of Islamic mysticism. Today he would be branded a heretic if people remembered his sayings, as Kant once observed that Job would be in the Christian world. The greatness of a culture is apparent where it admits ire against its greatest authorities, and even ire against God.

— 3 —

WORLD WITHOUT GOD

Shakespeare and Man

In pre-Christian times, on the soil that is now English: enter an old man, a greybeard, by his own account over eighty years old; in proportion to modern life expectancy he would certainly be over a hundred. For months, perhaps for more than a year now, he has been travelling on foot, accompanied at first by foolish companions, but now alone. With no destination, orientation or hope, he has wandered barefoot through forests, marched over heaths, waded through rivers, climbed over mountain ridges. His mind has long since grown dim; without respite he talks incoherently to himself; he sees horsemen and mice where other people see trees and herbs. He has spent not only the days but the nights too out of doors, we must assume, in the rain, in the snow, and once in an open field under the worst thunderstorm that ever broke upon England. He has no money and no one in the world; he probably feeds on berries, nuts, mushrooms, grasses or, in winter, nothing at all for days at a time, scratching the bark off the trees at best, or beating the frozen earth with a stone to dig for a root or a worm. He has knotted himself a garment of wild flowers that barely covers more than his genitals. 'O ruin'd piece of nature!' cries his old companion the Earl of Gloucester, whom Lear no longer recognizes.[1]

We have to imagine this physical dimension, the nearly naked body, emaciated to skin and bones, the layer of dirt on the wrinkled skin; probably, after such a long time without shelter, with abrasions, chilblains, scars, open sores, abscesses and insect bites; calluses visible not only on the soles of his feet but on his elbows, buttocks and back; the white, matted, long hair sticking out in all directions; the equally unkempt beard down to his chest; the sagging eyes; the cheekbones jutting out of his face – we have to envision the misery, neglect and exhaustion of an already age-worn body to picture Lear, the former king, as he re-enters the stage in the sixth scene of Act IV. Even as spectators, we have to imagine it: it's not possible to see it on the stage. A realistic performance is impossible for the simple reason that an actor, in the course of a performance, can imitate perhaps the mental but not the physical transformation that Lear undergoes in the course of the play from the greatest possible wealth, prestige, luxury and ease to a state that implies in every respect the most extreme distress, abandonment, pain. And even supposing two actors were to divide the role between them, the Lear of the fourth and fifth acts would thwart any attempt at mimesis; his physicality at all events would inevitably be recognizable as a pretence. A man who looks like Lear in his downfall can no longer stand up on a stage. He no longer belongs to any community, to say nothing of a theatre company.

And yet Shakespeare must have done more than simply imagine Lear. Born during the imposed Reformation of mid-sixteenth-century England, but in a Catholic family, he knew naturalistic images of a cadaverous body, racked with pain, exposed to wind and weather, from his childhood – perhaps also from a journey taken as a young man to remote Lancashire, where Catholicism was still tolerated. He knew them from pictures of the Passion of Christ; he knew them from crucifixes. Of course I don't know what the Jesus looked like that may have been secretly harboured in Shakespeare's parents' house in Stratford, or the one that hung in the home of his Catholic hosts in Lancashire. But I do know the crucifixes that were carved everywhere in Catholic Europe on the threshold from the Middle Ages to the modern era, in the fourteenth and fifteenth centuries; I know the images of Jesus in my own city, Cologne. Only a few hundred yards from my office, for example, in the church of St Kunibert, in the neighbourhood named for it near the central station, stands a *pietà* from the late fourteenth century which shows the physical torment of the Saviour in harrowing severity, His body nothing more than a skeleton over which the skin is stretched so that the hollows between His ribs form deep furrows; His lips pressed together; the wound in His side open a finger's breadth, the brown blood mixed with dirt spattered over His whole body.

Perhaps you have to have grown up in a non-Catholic environment today in order to imagine the amazement mixed with fright that beset a Catholic of the late Middle Ages on seeing the suffering of the Saviour exhibited so naturalistically. Until the thirteenth century – and until the present in Orthodox church painting – Christ's agony is portrayed symbolically; the intention was not to reproduce His physical pain, to make its pictorial representation as true to life as possible so that the viewer might sympathize with it, but to point to that pain as the absolute

Other, the unrepresentable. The art of the early Church not only avoids but, by its strict formalism, prevents the illusion that Jesus could really have looked like that, could really have been so scourged and nailed to the Cross, could really have died in that way. Like the medieval passion play or the narrated lives of the saints with their indirect speech, medieval painting is based on the principle of alienation. One might draw an analogy with the great substantial difference between epic and dramatic art as defined by Goethe and Schiller in their joint essay: 'that the Epic poet presents the event as *perfectly past*, and the Dramatic represents it as *perfectly present*.'[2]

Naturally the transition, the turn of the artistic era in fact, did not take place simultaneously in all of Europe's Christian cultures, but, when it happened, it was always remarkably rapid. Within a few decades, the painters and sculptors who decorated churches discovered, along with perspective, the physical dimension of the Passion, which Shakespeare evokes in *King Lear* as in no other drama, and indeed twofold: not only in the pitiful wandering king but in the likewise wandering Earl of Gloucester, who has had his eyes gouged out on stage. And if you are not inclined, at the sight of these two sufferers, to think first of Jesus, whose passion is moving in part because of the beauty and youth of His tortured body, many other martyrs may come to mind whose suffering is represented with ever stronger illusion as the Renaissance gives way to the baroque in Christian art. Shakespeare, the founder of modern dramatic literature, was not only a contemporary of Cervantes, the father of the modern novel; he was at the same time a contemporary of Caravaggio, who like no other painter lent physical horror, and at the same time the banality of reality, to the suffering of the saints. At the time when Shakespeare created his *King Lear* in London, probably in the autumn of 1606, Caravaggio was painting *The Crucifixion of St Andrew* in Rome, in a way that visualized the physicality of a tortured old man in shocking naturalism. Except for the fact that Lear of course does not die on the cross, we must imagine his naked, weakened body as something like Caravaggio's St Andrew, down to the ribs with the skin stretched over them, the pupils rolling up under the nearly closed eyelids, the pain-stricken expression of the face, the dirt under the toenails, the gawking faces of the onlookers:

> I am bound
> Upon a wheel of fire, that mine own tears
> Do scald like molten lead,[3]

Lear cries. In any case, there is nothing in the history of premodern Occidental culture that corresponds to the extreme of distress, neglect and pain that Shakespeare presents twofold, in Lear and in Gloucester, except the testimonies, portraits, narratives and passion plays of the Christian martyrs, which must have been familiar to Shakespeare from his upbringing. 'I am worse than e'er I was',[4] moans Gloucester's faithful son Edgar in the play, as early as the beginning of Act IV. But Edgar, who plays the fool to avoid detection by his diabolical brother's henchmen, immediately corrects himself with the wisdom of a true fool:

> And worse I may be yet. The worst is not,
> So long as we can say 'This is the worst.'[5]

And, in fact, Shakespeare sends his two heroes on a *via dolorosa* on which the pain increases exponentially, with mathematical relentlessness, from each station to the next, from the fifty knights that are deducted from Lear's retinue of one hundred to the twenty-five that suddenly must suffice, then only ten, then five, until finally the king has only a single fool for all his court – 'Now thou art an O without a figure', the fool mocks him,[6] – beginning with the betrayal of first the one, then the other daughter, ending with the father's guilt in the death of the third, his only faithful daughter. 'And these same crosses spoil me', says Lear himself.[7] Only Lear is not a martyr, nor is Gloucester. Shakespeare equips his dual heroes with all the insignia of a Christian hagiography, in the course of which desperation, betrayal, repudiation and, most of all, physical torment escalate – with the difference that, in Shakespeare, there is nothing holy about the process. Lear and Gloucester do not sacrifice themselves for God, for their faith, for any community. On the contrary: out of a sheer need for power and prestige, they sacrifice others – and in fact they sacrifice the only people who credibly show their affection: Lear his daughter Cordelia; Gloucester his son Edgar. And when Lear and Gloucester so dramatically do penance in the play, they do so not vicariously for other people, or for humanity, but only for their own vanity, their stupidity and immoderation. Lear and Gloucester suffer not for too much love, but for too little.

I have always been amazed that Lear gets off so lightly in most performances and film productions – that he is celebrated for his tragic greatness, mourned for his heroic downfall. Harold Bloom in his famous interpretation goes so far as to set Lear's magnificence, majesty and greatness above that of the biblical Solomon, ascribing to Lear a 'magnificent generosity of spirit, which makes him love too much';[8] it is the superhuman greatness of Lear's feelings for his fellow man that make him 'almost apocalyptically needy in [his] demand for love'.[9] Bloom writes that, when he discusses *King Lear* in lectures or seminars, he always reminds his students of the fact that Lear is much loved by all the benign characters in the play: Cordelia, the fool, Albany, Kent, Gloucester and Edgar. That may or may not be true, but in any case it is not a demonstrable fact: the protagonists' sympathies are not nearly as prominent in the first act as the social hierarchy underlying their actions. When Cordelia answers the question as to how much she loves Lear by saying that, while she loves her father, her love will belong to her spouse as well as soon as she marries, that is certainly worth more than her sisters' oaths of love – yet there is nothing here that visibly exceeds the ordinary measure of filial affection; rather, we see sensibility and radical honesty. Nowhere is there any suggestion that the fool, Albany, Gloucester and Edgar feel more than simply loyalty, friendship or sympathy for their king – that they are devoted to him, as Bloom claims, in great love. The fool conceals any feelings he may have under his mockery; Gloucester meets Lear only later; Edgar's relationship to Lear doesn't even come up; and Albany as Lear's son-in-law shows only a certain sympathy – and even then it is overlaid with his guilt feelings – when his wife's cold-heartedness exceeds all bounds. Even in Kent's case, it is uncertain whether his courage in opposing Lear's older daughters arises from his sense of duty as the king's vassal or from a deep love for an old man who seems to love only himself. An actor may play Lear's vanity as the need for love, his egoism as insecurity, his blindness as eccentricity, but the text itself supplies no reason why we should like Lear, or even feel pity for him. On the contrary: what should we think of a father who forces his daughters into a public test of love to determine their shares in his inheritance; a father who knows so little of his daughters that he believes the obviously hypocritical flattery of the older two while rejecting the realistic declaration of the youngest as insufficient; a father who then tells the same youngest daughter he will love her no better than people who devour their own children; a father who disinherits and repudiates this daughter and then, in cursing her, displays an egotism that leaves us speechless: 'Better thou hadst not been born than not to have pleased me better.'[10] Such a father would be a case for the child protection authorities, a psychiatrist or even the police, but not for a tragedy – not by the classical definition of tragedy as caused by man's ineluctable entanglement in a fate not of his making. And a king who insults his most faithful, his oldest retainer as vassal, miscreant and recreant, who banishes the retainer just because he tries to deter him from an unjust and disastrous decision – such a king has more of the tyrant than the hero and should look for the cause of his fall in himself rather than invoking fate.[11]

The Earl of Gloucester's guilt is little less than Lear's when he condemns his older son, so well beloved up to then, as a traitor and outlaws him without verifying the evidence against him, without so much as hearing him in person. The brutality of his very first words is absolutely inappropriate to a person whose character is supposed to be as noble as he is often portrayed to be on stage. In the first scene of the play, Gloucester confesses to the Earl of Kent how ashamed he is of his own son: 'I have so often blushed to acknowledge him, that now I am brazed to it.'[12] But this son, Edmund, is standing by and listening as his father maligns him. And as if that were not insulting enough, Gloucester goes on to make fun of Edmund's conception:

> though this knave came something saucily into the world before he was sent for, yet was his mother fair; there was good sport at his making, and the whoreson must be acknowledged.[13]

When a father *thinks* such things about his son, that is bad enough for the son, who can't help noticing his father's contempt; but when the father has no qualms about *speaking* his contempt openly to a third party, that explains and almost justifies the son's feelings of inadequacy that set the crime in motion and seal the father's doom. Although Lear and Gloucester suffer like martyrs, and act like martyrs – as, for example, when Gloucester announces he will bear his affliction 'till it do cry out itself / "Enough, enough," and die'[14] – although, when Lear promises to be 'the pattern of all patience',[15] they die like martyrs, they are perpetrators, not victims. If anyone in Shakespeare's drama testifies by their own blood, it is Cordelia, whose loyalty to her father costs her her life. That is why Lear's presumption reaches its pinnacle when he places himself on the same moral level as his daughter, appointing himself, together with her, 'God's spies':

> Upon such sacrifices, my Cordelia,
> The gods themselves throw incense.[16]

The comparison of Lear's sufferings with those of Job, which has become a platitude in literature on Shakespeare, also fails at the critical juncture. The play itself is full of allusions to the book of the Old Testament, starting with the macabre wager in the exposition, then more distinctly with almost literal quotations, such as the comparison of humanity with worms and dust and the complaint against God, and, just as Lear and Gloucester are led step by step, scene by scene into ruin, so too is Job's life destroyed not in one blow, but piece by piece, until it is reduced to the naked piece of flesh incessantly scratching at a hill of earth:

> As flies to wanton boys, are we to the gods.
> They kill us for their sport.[17]

But when Lear sees himself as Job, when he declares his silent submission to the misfortune that breaks over him like a force of nature, like a tempest – that is merely his own perception. For unlike Job, who at the end of his book puts his hand over his mouth, Lear still revolts, literally with his last breaths, against the death of his daughter and hence against his own lot:

> Had I your tongues and eyes, I'd use them so
> That heaven's vault should crack.[18]

In the logic of the play, Lear's self-styling as a martyr demonstrates the hubris that brings him low. Job, we recall, suffers his misfortune as the most righteous and most pious of all men: the whole sense of the biblical book lies in his suffering without cause, in the rupture between cause and effect, crime and punishment. The Book of Job casts grave doubt on God's goodness. Shakespeare introduces Lear, on the other hand, not as a righteous and God-fearing man but as a deterrent example of extreme capriciousness and vanity. Job in the Bible is tested, whereas Lear bears the consequences of his own actions, just as Gloucester is explicitly said to be doing penance for his own sins:

> The dark and vicious place where thee he got
> Cost him his eyes.[19]

The audience may be moved to pity by the magnitude of their suffering, but the responsibility for it lies with themselves – not with the gods, but with human beings. 'This is the excellent foppery of the world', says Edmund, Gloucester's bastard, rejecting the medieval theocentric cosmology:

> that, when we are sick in fortune, – often the surfeit of our own behaviour, – we make guilty of our disasters the sun, the moon, and the stars: as if we were villains by necessity; fools by heavenly compulsion; knaves, thieves, and treachers, by spherical predominance; drunkards, liars, and adulterers, by an enforced obedience of planetary influence; and all that we are evil in, by a divine thrusting on: an admirable evasion of whoremaster man, to lay his goatish disposition to the charge of a star![20]

No other appreciation of Shakespeare is read more often than this: that his work lays the cornerstone of the modern individual, the foundation of human autonomy or, as the subtitle of Harold Bloom's book has it, 'the invention of the human'. And no other drama is cited more often as evidence of Shakespeare's founding role in world literature than *Hamlet*. And it's true: never before had the human individual been described more precisely, more profoundly, hence more coldly and ruthlessly, in his ambivalence and inscrutability, his splendour and subtlety, his fears and desires. That is what continues to amaze us in every new performance of Shakespeare's dramas today: not the construction of his plays, not the dialogues, not the suspense – however well devised they may be. What amazes us even today – and, analogously, what amazes us in Shakespeare's contemporary Caravaggio – is their knowledge of human nature. Shakespeare's gift to theatre and Caravaggio's to art is not this or that plot, this hero or that villain: it is the 'I', or, to be more exact, it is the collision of many real, contradictory, fascinating, repulsive 'I's. Hegel hits the new quality of Shakespeare's representation of people on the head in his lectures on aesthetics when he says that even the formal passions, such as ambition in *Macbeth* and jealousy in *Othello*, are portrayed as the pathos of absolutely individual characters:

> Indeed the more Shakespeare proceeds to portray on the infinite breadth of his 'world stage' the extremes of evil and folly, all the more . . . does he precisely plunge his figures who dwell on these extremes into their restrictedness; of course he equips them with a wealth of poetry but he actually gives them spirit and imagination, and, by the picture in which they can contemplate and see themselves objectively like a work of art, he makes them free artists of their own selves, and thereby, with his strongly marked and faithful characterization, can interest us not only in criminals but even in the most downright and vulgar clouts and fools.[21]

King Lear epitomizes the step, observable in all of Shakespeare's works, that presages the postulate of the autonomous 'I': God is – I will not say abolished – but He is ignored, treated as absent or even irrelevant. If we review the great comedies, histories and tragedies in our mind's eye, there is hardly any human quality that Shakespeare does not treat. But where is God in Shakespeare's dramas? His name comes up repeatedly in the characters' supplications, whether in the singular of the Christian religion – in spite of the Bishops' Ban – or, more often, in the plural of the classical religion. Preachers also appear in many plays, sympathetic monks such as Friar Lawrence in *Romeo and Juliet*, thoroughly unpleasant dignitaries of the Church such as the papal legate in *King John*, and true believers such as Isabella in *Measure for Measure*. But in contrast to classical, medieval or Renaissance theatre, God – or, in more general terms, Fate, the Higher Power – is no longer a subject; God is not involved in the plot. This is true of all Shakespeare's works, or at least all the tragedies. But God's absence is most striking in *King Lear*, because Shakespeare consciously composed it as a passion play. The set pieces of religion – its motifs, allusions, situations – are still there, lying around like cast-off clothes, and the active characters too still consider themselves characters in a religious spectacle – but the play itself makes it quite clear from the beginning that only mortals are at work here: good and evil, magnanimous and resentful, devout and egotistical humans, even the mightiest of them foolish, even the strongest ephemeral. Lear experiences his finiteness in the elemental plane as physical vulnerability, protesting, 'They told me I was every thing; 'tis a lie, I am not ague-proof.'[22]

In no other play did Shakespeare construct his own world so much like the world of the Bible as in *King Lear*. That is why the difference between Shakespeare's world and that of the Bible is more distinct than in any other play. Not only does Lear's and Gloucester's suffering externally resemble martyrdom, while in its essence it is the opposite. Nature too appears in *King Lear* as something powerful and violent, as in the Book of Job, except that it is not controlled by God, but self-propelled:

> Blow, winds, and crack your cheeks! rage! blow!
> You cataracts and hurricanoes, spout
> Till you have drench'd our steeples, drown'd the cocks!
> You sulphurous and thought-executing fires,
> Vaunt-couriers to oak-cleaving thunderbolts,
> Singe my white head! And thou, all-shaking thunder,
> Smite flat the thick rotundity o' the world!
> Crack nature's moulds, all germens spill at once,
> That make ingrateful man![23]

Where God in the Book of Job resorts at length to Nature as an instrument, a creature, for demonstrating His power, Nature itself takes the place of God to the modern, Shakespearean man: Edmund sloughs off the religious world order with the words 'Thou, nature, art my goddess', and vows, 'to thy law / My services are bound.'[24] The boost that human autonomy receives in Shakespeare and through Shakespeare is due not only to his individual genius but of course to the time and the place in which he lived. Still more directly than a painter in his studio or a poet at his desk, a dramatist absorbs the urges, desires and expectations of his audience, especially if he treads the stage as an actor himself, so that his art is immediately aimed at making paying customers applaud. Accordingly, what Adorno called 'Shakespeare's . . . breakthrough into mortal and infinitely rich individuality'[25] can also be observed in other dramatists of Elizabethan theatre, especially in Christopher Marlowe. *The Tragical History of the Life and Death of Doctor Faustus* also tells, in a different way than *The Tragedy of Hamlet, Prince of Denmark*, of the drama of human free will amid the political, intellectual and social upheavals of the early modern period. Both plays allude explicitly to the reformer Luther in attributing to their hero a sojourn in Wittenberg. And both plays rework medieval motifs, such as Purgatory and the pact with the Devil, just when the Reformation, humanism, materialism and modern science are tangibly transforming everyone's reality (the novelty of the new becomes apparent in their recourse to the old or the archaic, just as in their contemporaries Cervantes and Caravaggio).

Yet it is remarkable that the quasi-Copernican revolution that takes place in theatre at the turn of the seventeenth century does not occur simultaneously in the other genres of literature or in philosophy. God is perfectly present in John Milton, for example, the most important poet of the generation after Shakespeare, or in Andreas Gryphius in the German-speaking countries, even if their works do not conform to any orthodoxy, even if they question God's justice, even if they indict God. Similarly, the early Enlightenment philosopher Pierre Bayle takes God seriously precisely by making him the object of his indictment. Even a hundred years later, David Hume still describes God in gloomy images – yet he does discuss him; God is still worth thinking about, even if Hume's aim in his philosophy is a morality that does without God. But, in Shakespeare, God is out of the picture.

I am not sure whether I would subscribe exclusively to Jan Kott's brilliant interpretation of *King Lear* as endgame. The emphasis on responsibility for determining one's own fate, the link from crime to punishment, and the abstinence from ideas of grace can also be seen in the context of the Reformation and its world view, which may have reflected Shakespeare's own, in spite of his Catholic parents, and which in any case must have reflected that of the London public of the early seventeenth century. The new King Edgar, whom Shakespeare depicts in an altogether positive light, explicitly insists in the last scene of the drama that the divine order is just and that evil is solely man's responsibility, and even the wise fool formulates in the first act, where he expounds his doctrine of right living, an admittedly very simple, early version of the Protestant ethics of hard work and frugality:

Have more than thou showest,
Speak less than thou knowest,
Lend less than thou owest,
Ride more than thou goest,
Learn more than thou trowest,
Set less than thou throwest;
Leave thy drink and thy whore,
And keep in-a-door,
And thou shalt have more
Than two tens to a score.[26]

Yet at the same time – since a play after all is not a philosophical treatise but a symphony of different, contradictory and self-contradicting voices – the text returns with such conspicuous frequency to the idea of nothing – 'That is nothing, fool',[27] 'nothing can be made out of nothing',[28] 'I am a fool, thou art nothing',[29] and so on – that one wonders whether Shakespeare is not consciously resisting the doctrine of late medieval Christianity which denies an independent existence to both nothing and evil. The important thing, however, is this: no matter whether we read the play as nihilistic or as Reformational – in either interpretation, God is irrelevant. If He exists, the issue of theodicy that *King Lear* seems to raise is answered with human free will as the only cause of evil: God is then exonerated but at the same time dethroned. If He does not exist, the issue does not arise.[30] Whichever we choose of the options Shakespeare leaves us, his play blatantly refutes all the excuses that God's medieval Christian apologists offered.

I can well understand that Leo Tolstoy cited the much praised *King Lear* to explain his 'complete disagreement'[31] with the universal adulation of Shakespeare. Tolstoy's diatribe was rarely given serious treatment (except by George Orwell, who discussed it in two eye-opening essays),[32] even in the reception of his own works, much less in the literature on Shakespeare. As far as I can see, it was never republished in Germany or in England after its first appearance in 1906. Nonetheless, Tolstoy identifies something essential about Shakespeare, whether or not we are glad to see it held against him: namely, that his plays rejected 'the religious essence of art'.[33] Tolstoy sees this rejection, and not just the desire of Lessing and others for something more lively, free and popular than French theatre, as the principal reason why the Germans rediscovered Shakespeare in the late eighteenth century, that is, in the course of the Enlightenment:

> The fundamental inner cause of Shakespeare's fame was and is this: that his dramas were 'pro captu lectoris', i.e., they corresponded to the irreligious and immoral frame of mind of the upper classes of his time.[34]

But, for Tolstoy in his late period, drama without a fundamental religious element is 'the most trivial and despicable of things':[35] 'That is why I think that the sooner people free themselves from the false glorification of Shakespeare, the better it will be.'[36]

Fortunately for us, the audience, theatres have not followed Tolstoy's appeal. Yet we may observe that Tolstoy, in his indignation, understood Shakespeare better than generations of critics who have squeezed *King Lear* into a pattern of Christian redemption, a schema in which the two protagonists, through their suffering, gradually attain self-knowledge, repentance and the affirmation of divine providence. Even interpreters who do not follow an explicitly Christian reading have referred to the Aristotelian concept of catharsis to point out the connection between suffering and redeeming insight. Yet there is nothing redeeming about Lear's insight; his suffering has no positive meaning. He is wiser than before, it is true – but not happier, and he is far from being freed, relieved, redeemed. On the contrary: only with his newfound sight does Lear take in the whole extent of his, and man's, misery, which Kent puts into words: 'All's cheerless, dark and deadly.'[37] Edgar's summation in the last words of the play is likewise damning: there is no prospect of relief, no hope – 'The weight of this sad time we must obey.' At the same time, Edgar's appeal, recalling the state of man's existence, contrasts with Job's behaviour in the Bible: Job puts his hand over his mouth, never again to say what he feels. Edgar for his part calls for – what exactly? Not resistance: it is not even resistance; it is really only a lament that goes unheard, a cry of anger perhaps, or a sigh. It is what literature does when it no longer serves a higher purpose:

> The weight of this sad time we must obey;
> Speak what we feel, not what we ought to say.[38]

Why do we still read Shakespeare; why is he still performed? If it were true that his work stands *only* for the foundation of the modern individual, if it marked *only* the beginning of human autonomy or the invention *only* of the human, we would be interested in it today only as a milestone in the history of ideas. There is something more, something prophetic, that raises Shakespeare above his own time: in his plays Shakespeare anticipates the drama of the modern individual, the disaster of man's autonomy, the doom of being human. Lear behaves as if he were an omnipotent God who needs only to *will* something to bring it about. He is commensurately shocked when he finds himself demoted to a mere mortal. Inversely, the villainous Edmund in the play ascends to become his own God by taking his destiny into his own hands, overcoming his impotence – he *does* something to bring it about. Edmund is not inclined to submit to 'the plague of custom'[39] that disinherits him as a bastard and a second son: 'Let me, if not by birth, have lands by wit.'[40] The echoes of Macbeth, Richard III, Iago are no coincidence; it is the credo of the new, the Shakespearean man: the choice is mine.

> What is a man,
> If his chief good and market of his time
> Be but to sleep and feed? A beast, no more.[41]

Thus the morally positive formulation of such a sympathetic character as Hamlet.

> Sure, he that made us with such large discourse,
> Looking before and after, gave us not
> That capability and god-like reason
> To fust in us unused.[42]

Only in a world without God is man truly free. The only question is whether that is good. The anthropology Shakespeare develops in his plays suggests it is not. All too often, the rationality that questions, influences, moves to overthrow the order of the world is instrumentalized – 'All with me's meet that I can fashion fit', as *King Lear* has it.[43] And so the mortal who serves no God or earthly lord all too easily serves only himself: 'We have seen the best of our time', Gloucester describes the age, 'Machinations, hollowness, treachery, and all ruinous disorders, follow us disquietly to our graves.'[44] The many descriptions, similes and images of a world in which everything is upside down – more frequent in *King Lear* than in all the other plays – do not suggest that Shakespeare believed in the progress that his work diagnoses. Before the Enlightenment, he already knew its dialectics: 'Love cools, friendship falls off, brothers divide. In cities, mutinies; in countries, discord; in palaces, treason; and the bond cracked 'twixt son and father.'[45] When nothing is in its place, when the world is literally deranged, deranged people are suddenly the only ones who seem normal. Among all of Shakespeare's great clown characters, Lear's fool is the only one who disappears in the course of the play. From the fourth act he is simply no longer present, with no explanation or leave-taking. He has simply become dramaturgically redundant; his mission has been accomplished since the others have gone mad – Lear and Gloucester – or are acting mad, in Edgar's case. Intentionally or otherwise, they have taken the advice the fool gave his king in the beginning: 'Sirrah, you were best take my coxcomb.'[46] And, indeed, Lear speaks wisdom only when he has lost his wits; Gloucester achieves insight only when he thinks he has thrown himself off a cliff; and it is wisdom that inspires Edgar to act the fool. The other founding figure of modern literature, Don Quixote, likewise sees horsemen or mice where other people see trees and herbs. And so the 'I' that thought it was winning emancipation from God may only have been tilting at windmills.

> When we are born, we cry that we are come
> To this great stage of fools,[47]

Lear realizes on returning to the stage in Act IV, scene 6. 'Reason in madness', murmurs Edgar in dismay as he listens to the former king.[48]

At his last entrance, King Lear carries his dead daughter in his arms. 'Thou'lt come no more', he wails, as Mary seems to wail, bearing her dead son in her arms in the church of St Kunibert near my office. And as if he would declare an end of days, an eschaton devoid of faith, of hope, of peace, Lear adds five times: 'Never, never, never, never, never!' Then he asks one of the gentlemen about him to 'undo this button': whether he means a button on Cordelia's gown or one of his own – we must imagine Lear is dressed again in this scene – is not clear, nor do the commentators agree. And then something strange happens, another thing the commentators must leave up to the performer's interpretation. 'Do you see this?' Lear asks the assembled lords:

> Look on her, look, her lips,
> Look there, look there! (*Dies*)[49]

What should the bystanders see? Is Cordelia regaining consciousness? But then they would react to her awakening, to her survival; they would say something or bend over her. The text suggests, rather, that Lear fools himself into thinking he sees his daughter breathe; perhaps he only imagines it, dreams it, wishes it; but perhaps he says she is alive although he knows better, says so in spite of the evidence; perhaps, by denying the reality, he dies – like Gloucester after his imagined fall from the cliff – in a moment of joy or relief.

Again, the text does not permit a clear decision as to which of the possible events Shakespeare intended – most likely Shakespeare intentionally chose an ambiguous wording here. So I can only wish, and not contend, that, in Lear's last moment, delusion triumphs over reality. In becoming foolish, Lear became happy. And if I understand the fool simply as a character who ignores the factuality of appearances, who suspends the power of reality, then the play's eschatology still offers a way to prevail on this stage that is the world. We are not eternal; our imagination can be.

— 4 —

HEROIC WEAKNESS

*Lessing and Terror**

About noon on 4 November 2011, according to the police reports, Uwe Mundlos and Uwe Böhnhardt set fire to a mobile home in the Stregeda district of Eisenach and then shot themselves in it. One hundred and eighty kilometres away, in one of the better neighbourhoods of Zwickau, the two young men's companion Beate Zschäpe searched the Internet for a remedy against nausea, then spread a combustive agent in the flat they had shared and set it on fire. Just as she went out of the door with her two cats, Lilly and Heidi, an explosion blew the façade off the house. Beate Zschäpe left the cats with a neighbour and fled, before turning herself in to the police a few days later. In the rubble, investigators discovered the 7.65 millimetre Browning pistol, a Česká model 83, with which eight immigrants from Turkey, one from Greece and a police officer had been murdered since the year 2000.[1] They also found a DVD containing a fifteen-minute film in which the cartoon figure of the Pink Panther makes a 'tour of Germany', visiting the scenes of the ten murders and of two bombings in Cologne. The photographs of the murder victims lying in their own blood are labelled 'Original'. The murder series is titled 'Operation Kebab Skewer' [*Aktion Dönerspieß*]. An organization called 'National Socialist Underground', abbreviated NSU, claims authorship of the video, introducing itself as a 'network of comrades with the principle "less talk, more action"', and announces, 'Until radical changes take place in politics, the press, and freedom of opinion, the activities will continue.' The film's background music is the Pink Panther theme.

We must assume that Uwe Mundlos and Uwe Böhnhardt had reckoned with the possibility of their own death and taken precautions to

* Speech at the opening of the Lessing festival, Thalia Theatre, Hamburg, 22 January 2012.

escape arrest. Their flat in Zwickau was equipped for a final battle, with numerous motion detectors and surveillance cameras and nine firearms kept ready to hand, including a repeating rifle with a sawn-off stock and a submachine gun. And at noon on 4 November, they hardly had time to think: a police patrol car had followed them after a bank robbery and was about to arrive, and the whole operation – setting the fire, arranging who would shoot whom first, coordinating with Beate Zschäpe, who would set fire to the shared flat and flee after bringing the cats to safety – depended on so many individual decisions, each of which was momentous in itself, that they could not conceivably have been acting spontaneously. And even if, in spite of all appearances to the contrary, Uwe Mundlos and Uwe Böhnhardt panicked and killed themselves spontaneously at noon on 4 November, out of desperation, fear of prison or shame, they still made a sacrifice, from a subjective viewpoint, by committing themselves totally to armed political struggle, and hence to the life of outlaws, to isolation from their own families and condemnation by society, to renouncing a conventional career, to the insecurity of life in the underground and the constant danger of arrest, injury or death.

There is a play by Gotthold Ephraim Lessing written in 1759, little known and seldom performed, in which a young man sacrifices himself for his country. *Philotas* is the title of the one-act play, and also the name of the prince who is taken prisoner in his first battle against the army of King Aridaeus. Philotas must fear that his capture will cost his country the war, for his father, he knows, will do anything to bring him home, ransom him, redeem him. His father will lose the war for love of his son. The son blames himself: 'Through me, wretched youth', he says, his father will 'lose in one day more than he has gained in three long toilsome years with the blood of his noble warriors, with his own blood.'[2]

But then Philotas' fate seems to take a surprising turn for the better. It is not only he who has been taken prisoner during the battle: so too has the son of Aridaeus, the enemy king. Aridaeus announces to Philotas that the two princes will be exchanged, which will restore the balance between the two warring parties and perhaps even bring about a reconciliation. Although at first Philotas is relieved that he will be able to return home without bearing responsibility for his country's defeat, the drama soon takes another turn – the crucial one. During a two-page monologue,[3] the prince realizes that his death would give his country a decisive advantage: 'For my father', Philotas argues, 'would then have a prince as his prisoner, for whom he could make any claim; and the king, his enemy, would have the body of a captive prince, for which he could demand nothing.' What must he do? Die, Philotas realizes, and is surprised: 'nothing more? – O truly the man is mightier than he thinks, the man who knows how to die!' We are accustomed, from the statements of statesmen and the commentaries of television, to hearing terrorist attacks and especially suicide attacks called cowardly. That always strikes me as a bit strange, and also helpless. The act of a terrorist, and in particular a suicide attacker, is immoral, unjust, inhuman, and so on – but it is not exactly cowardly; on the contrary, one would have hoped the attacker, instead of risking or even sacrificing his own life for his convictions, would have been overcome by fear before the end. Not only in their own eyes, but also in the eyes of many like-minded people who commemorated them as heroes in public celebrations, Uwe Mundlos and Uwe Böhnhardt also sacrificed themselves for their country.

The statement may sound absurd to those who associate patriotism with different, more peaceful ideas than a pair of far-right-wing terrorists did. But those who would combat political violence must try to understand its motives, examine its history – and that includes its biographical histories – and study the thinking of its protagonists. A criminal may or may not consider his acts reprehensible, but a politically motivated criminal who is prepared to die necessarily acts – in his own opinion – justly, even when he kills people who are completely innocent by his own standards, such as bystanders, children or, in the case of the Zwickau trio, a police officer of irreproachable nationality; the terrorist may, as many instances in the history of political violence attest, count his pangs of conscience as an additional and especially heavy sacrifice which he has resolved to bear with utmost dedication. This holds equally for murders committed in the name of Islam and for murders committed in the name of Germany. Any thing, Philotas continues, as if he were holding a philosophical seminar, any thing is perfect if it fulfils its purpose. And what is the purpose of a patriot, however weak he may be, even a captive one who has failed on the battlefield?

> I can fulfil my end; I can die for the welfare of the state; I am therefore perfect, I am a man. A man! although but a few days ago I was still a boy.

The will to heroic self-sacrifice carries to its extreme the principle that the video of the Nazi underground advocates: 'Less talk, more action'. Or, in the words of the best-known slogan of the terrorist network al-Qaeda: 'You love life, we love death'; or, in Lessing's 'He who has lived ten years has had ten years' time to learn to die.'

Are Uwe Mundlos and Uwe Böhnhardt suicide assassins? No, certainly not. Their crimes were in fact cowardly in that they shot their victims from ambush or from a safe distance. But let us remember that, after 11 September 2001, public opinion was dominated by a helplessness very similar to that which was seen in Germany after 4 November 2011.[4] Both the head of the Zwickau terrorist cell, Uwe Mundlos, and the head of the Hamburg terrorist cell, Mohammed Atta, were from educated families which were not characterized in the slightest by national or religious extremism: Mundlos's father had been, even under the East German regime, somewhere on the scale from free-thinking to critical of the political system; Atta's parents had a secular orientation. In 2011, magazines such as *Der Spiegel* and *Stern* were surprised to discover that, before he became an Islamic terrorist, Mohammed Atta seemed to have been ideally integrated in Germany, studying ecology and the renovation of historic city centres; he had a German girlfriend, occasionally rolled a recreational joint, and on weekends joined the pilgrimage, not to the mosque, but to Millerntor Stadium and FC St Pauli. One day, to the surprise of his teachers and fellow students, he returned from a holiday in Egypt with a beard and the traditional gellabiya, which no one in his family had worn for at least two generations. The question was heard on all sides: How could a broad-minded, socially involved student have become a mass murderer? Yet the journalists who researched the biographies of the suicide attackers were unable to find a plausible answer. Uwe Mundlos, the son of a professor, also read a great deal, earned good grades and was partial to scientific subjects. His former classmates and friends described him as an intelligent but inconspicuous boy; his favourite band was AC/DC, but he also liked the soft-rocker Udo Lindenberg; Uwe Mundlos had worn his hair long. One day, to the surprise of his teachers and classmates, he came to school with short hair parted on the side and jump boots on his feet.

The ordinariness and probably the comfort that are likewise known to have characterized the family backgrounds of most members of the Red Army Faction are not at odds with their later conversion to political extremism but seem, in fact, to increase the attractiveness of a lifestyle that radically rejects and even opposes bourgeois norms. Nor did Lessing neglect to mention the thrill that the prince felt at the thought of exploding the secure, predetermined path of his existence:

> What fire rages in my veins? What inspiration falls on me? The breast becomes too narrow for the heart! Patience, my heart! Soon will I give thee space! Soon will I release thee from thy monotonous and tedious task!

The monologue also expresses the external coolness that correlates with the inner fire, the prudent planning and the cold-blooded execution, when Philotas himself remarks that, in view of the grand prospect of winning the war by his death, he suddenly becomes completely calm, and in the scenes that follow he coolly carries out his plan to obtain a sword, lull King Aridaeus into confidence, and prevent the offer of a prisoner exchange from reaching his father.

In the terrorists' biographies, however, there is more that is conspicuous besides their inconspicuousness, to paraphrase the press reports that followed 11 September 2001 and 4 November 2011. Both Mohammed Atta and Uwe Mundlos were described by their former associates as especially amiable and sensitive. 'Kind, Nice, and Never Angry' was the title of an article in *Der Spiegel* about Mohammed Atta's past.[5] 'Kindness [*Menschlichkeit*] is the word heard again and again when Atta's former fellow students talk about him', a puzzled *Stern* reporter commented.[6] Similarly, some neighbours remember that Mundlos lovingly took care of his disabled brother, regularly accompanying him to the doctor and taking him for walks in his wheelchair, and never failed to greet the elderly lady watching from her window. As it had speculated about the head of the Hamburg terrorist cell ten years previously, the press wondered in late 2011: 'How could a friendly professor's son turn into a hate-driven right-wing terrorist?'[7]

It is as easy as it is inoffensive to call young men like Mohammed Atta or Uwe Mundlos beasts, madmen, Nazi killers, as the tabloid reporting of *Bild*, for example, does constantly, to distance the perpetrators as far as possible from society and, most of all, from the agitation of the paper's own opinion pieces and campaigns – to dismiss the perpetrators as pathological. But the disturbing thing about such political violence becomes visible in its full magnitude only when we put together those pieces of the puzzle that don't seem to fit the picture: the bourgeois conventionality, the education, the intelligence; the kindness, the idealism. Two hundred and fifty years ago, Lessing wholeheartedly rejected Philotas' attitude, and his dramatic aesthetics is consistent with his numerous invectives against the cult of heroism and patriotism when he writes about tragedy, in the nineteenth instalment of his *Hamburg Dramaturgy*: 'To make it a mere panegyric of famous men, or to misuse it to feed national pride, is to degrade it from its true grandeur.'[8] Lessing nevertheless did not present the prince as a madman: in the great monologue of scene 4, he followed the train of thought, step by step, that leads a young, pensive, and all too enthusiastic person to sacrifice himself for a political goal – just as Uwe Mundlos and Mohammed Atta are not described as muddleheaded even after their conversion to political extremism; on the contrary, it is striking in both the biographies that they were known among their comrades-in-arms for their clever arguments and their erudition, not for crude slogans. 'Who is a hero?' Philotas asks, and remembers his father's sentence that a hero is a man who knows higher values than life: 'A man who has devoted his life to the welfare of the state; himself, the single one, to the welfare of the many.' Philotas pauses briefly and asks himself whether he is not too young to die a hero's death, just as Mohammed Atta and Uwe Mundlos may have asked themselves whether they as individuals were not too powerless to confront an enemy as abstract and at the same time as superior as the West, capitalism or a state. But then Philotas reflects that what matters is not the actor, but the act, not the words of explanation, but the deed itself: 'How old must the pine-tree be which has to serve as a mast? How old? – It must be tall enough, and must be strong enough.'

Less talk, more action – to the National Socialist Underground, that meant only action, no talk at all. Many commentators were puzzled by the fact that none of their murders and bombings was followed by a communiqué claiming responsibility. After all, it had been customary in the conventional form of terrorism – that of the Red Army Faction, the Basque separatists and militant Palestinian groups – for violence to be used towards specific political goals laid out on paper: the overthrow of a system of government, the release of prisoners, national autonomy, or the end of an occupation. But is the absence of a statement of purpose really so unusual? In the last two decades, a new type of terrorism has taken shape worldwide, a terrorism which draws its terror from wordlessness. The attacks of 11 September 2001 were at first free of all statements, unaccompanied by any political demands, not based on any documented ideology. Osama bin Laden claimed authorship of the attacks only much later and, even then, was intentionally vague about the exact connection between the aircraft hijackers and al-Qaeda. In the ping-pong between the international media and the American government, which willingly reinforced the eerie, anti-political atmosphere, Osama bin Laden styled his organization as a huge, ethereal power that might strike anywhere, any time: never again would an American live in safety, he ominously announced in the closing sentence of his first video message. Isn't it possible that the National Socialist Underground wanted to create the same feeling among Turkish immigrants by choosing victims scattered all over West Germany: the feeling of facing an abstract, intangible power, of danger to every foreigner in Germany everywhere, all the time?

The anthrax attacks, too, which had America up in arms shortly after 11 September 2001, and the Unabomber before that, the Aum cult's poison gas attack in the Tokyo metro, the acts of violence of

Charles Manson and American Christian cults such as 'Heaven's Gate' and 'People's Temple', and the Oklahoma City bombing for which Timothy McVeigh was later sentenced to death – all took place without any written statement of responsibility. This relatively new type of political violence draws its power from the rejection of political discourse, the renunciation of all argumentative contest. Its enemies are conceived no longer as specific states, governments or parties but as systems of government, ethnicities or cultures. Accordingly, for this kind of terrorism, which is neither accompanied by specific demands nor aimed at bombing the rulers into negotiation, there can be only total victory or none at all; the terrorists' own annihilation or the complete destruction or expulsion of the enemy – that is, of the dominant system, the other race, the unbelievers, the inferior culture.

Yet the response to this kind of undeclared terror cannot be to conform to its mentality, to perpetuate its eeriness and to declare war, as the terrorists do, on a system, a race, a religion or a culture. Terrorists have an ideology, pragmatic goals, a support network and ideological backing in parts of the society, even when they appear with no manifesto, no demands and no name. With the suicide of Uwe Böhnhardt and Uwe Mundlos and the arrest of Beate Zschäpe and other helpers, the National Socialist Underground has probably disbanded. But the conditions that led to its formation and, more alarmingly, to the length of its bloody career still exist.

Just as learning about Islam is unavoidable if we want to understand Islamic extremism, it will also be impossible to understand nationalist extremism without learning about nationalism. And the more so since the European project, which seemed to have definitively overcome nationalism on this continent, ran into a crisis of legitimation long before the financial crisis – let us only recall the failure to ratify a European constitution – and national identity witnessed a revival all over the continent. In Germany, people still lean back and point to countries such as the Netherlands, Austria, Switzerland, Hungary, Italy, Denmark, Finland and Poland, where parties called 'right-wing populist' already have or have had a share in government and, in some cases, have even won parliamentary majorities. The phenomenon that is designated by the neologism 'right-wing populism', as if it were something novel, perhaps even a kind of political fad that may soon be gone again, actually has a very long history. In its essential characteristics, right-wing populism, as an anti-European, xenophobic, anti-egalitarian movement whose rhetoric uses the vocabulary of defensive war, stands for nothing other than the nationalism of the nineteenth and early twentieth centuries. It has not yet found an effective political forum in

Germany, in part because the established parties have so far, in spite of deviations, proved to be relatively immune on the whole to nationalistic tendencies. However, a look at the society at large – by means of empirical surveys, for example – yields an entirely different picture. Here there is no significant difference between the Germans and other European societies. Bookshops are full of best-sellers, whether on issues of migration, the economy, culture, history or the European Union, which once again see the world strictly from the point of view of the German nation, and the two publications with the highest circulation in the country, *Bild* and *Der Spiegel*, spread a degree of mistrust against the European project that is worthy of the influential media of Britain or, more recently, Hungary.

Since reunification, there is in Germany the hope and, at least since 2006, when the country hosted the football World Cup, the firm opinion that joyful, peaceable and xenophile patriotism can be separated from the nationalism that plunged the country into ruin twice in the twentieth century and annihilated whole ethnic communities. Like the other peoples of the earth, in this opinion, the Germans too must finally find a normal, relaxed attitude towards their nation. In fact, people have from time immemorial defined themselves as belonging to a 'we', as members of a community distinct from other 'we' communities. From time immemorial people have sung the praises of the cities, regions and territories in which they were born, in which they grew up, which they call home. From time immemorial people have also felt a special connection to their own language. Not only is there nothing wrong with that – the appreciation, cultivation and love of our familiar surroundings, our own culture, is as natural as love for our own parents. In those same years in which he vehemently repudiated patriotism as a political position, Lessing defended Germanic traditions against the French affectations of contemporary literature.

Love of one's nation, on the other hand, is by no means as natural as it would seem since the World Cup in Germany – because the modern concept of the nation as a largely uniform linguistic, religious, territorial and ethnic community was invented only as recently as the nineteenth century, for one thing. Younger still is the belief that political and national unity should coincide and that the whole planet should be divided into states that conform to the same criteria as nations. The concept of the nation-state that arose in the course of the American and French revolutions and was adopted by the bourgeois liberalism of the nineteenth century was based not on ethnic or cultural *conformity* but on the political *consent* of its citizens; hence the beautiful term that denotes the rediscovery of the concept in the Federal Republic of

Germany – *Verfassungspatriotismus*, 'constitutional patriotism'. There is a violence inherent in the aspiration towards an ethnically, territorially and linguistically uniform state and towards a world order constructed of nations inasmuch as the presumed homogeneity rarely, and in the German-speaking countries never, coincided with the ethnic, linguistic and religious diversity of real life; yet that violence has almost been forgotten today since, fortunately, the concept of the nation has been largely defused, not only in Europe but also in other parts of the world, whether by integration in international organizations or by increasing economic and cultural interdependence and the immense migrations of peoples, and in any case by the multinational fantasy images of the culture industry and the alternative world of sport. Those who wave the German flag at a football match are generally not intent on world *domination*, only on world *championship*.

However, to take just this obvious example from day-to-day experience, those football fans who, screaming, cheering, bellowing in the heat of an important tournament match, have felt for themselves that their team is always right when they protest a foul or an offside by the opponents, while the other team is always wrong when they claim the ball bounced completely past *our* goal line – those fans should sense how dangerous it would be to idealize collective belonging if it were transferred back from the sphere of games to that of politics and social action. Lessing describes that danger in his tragedy, as Philotas, his resolve unshakeable, refuses to talk with the enemy king, Aridaeus:

> I know nothing else, but that you and my father are involved in war; and the right – the right, I think, is on my father's side. This I believe, king! and will believe, even though you could prove the reverse indisputably.[9]

That final sentence – 'and will believe, even though you could prove the reverse' – exactly describes the dynamite that lies in ideologizing the feeling of belonging: the collective truth's immunity against individual experience and discernment.

Of all the aspects of the murder series for which the Zwickau trio and their helpers are responsible, this is the most shameful: that no one, over a period of more than ten years, and in spite of glaring facts, believed the victims' families and the few activist groups and dedicated journalists who suspected racist motives. Worse still, one after another the victims themselves were declared the guilty parties, presumed to be involved in drug deals or protection rackets, supposed victims of a vendetta or a crime of jealousy, an 'honour killing'. Those directly responsible for this failure are the German law enforcement agencies: the police, the investigating prosecutors and, most of all, the *Verfassungsschutz*, the state and federal constitutional defence agencies, which not only failed to solve the crimes but actively prevented their investigation, according to Heribert Prantl's summary in *Süddeutsche Zeitung*. Siegfried Mundlos, for example, the terrorist's father, described to a reporter the mutual mistrust between the *Verfassungsschutz* and the police: at one point, two men at his door advised him to use a public telephone when he talked to his son to avoid police eavesdropping. The *Berliner Zeitung* reported that the *Verfassungsschutz* constantly informed Tino Brandt, the leader of a neo-Nazi group in the state of Thuringia, of police surveillance activities. And on occasion the *Verfassungsschutz* agents in their cars even pursued the police cars following Brandt.

It would be nice to be able to attribute such debacles to the amateurishness of the investigating agencies. But, in fact, week after week, new evidence came to light of the security forces' bias and negligence in dealing with right-wing violence. In hindsight, there is simply no explanation for the *Verfassungsschutz*'s denial that right-wing extremists were behind the serial murders. As just one example, let us recall the song recorded by the notorious band Gigi und die Braunen Stadtmusikanten to celebrate the murders: 'Fear and terror rule in all the kebab shops / The sandwich sticks in their throats, / for he comes often unannounced / to the kebab stand, because nine are not enough.'[10] This song, which clearly indicates insider knowledge of the crimes, was not anonymously uploaded but played at concerts and sung by hundreds of enthusiastic fans. It was a regular hit in the neo-Nazi scene, which is infiltrated by confidential informants. And yet the band went unchallenged, and the singer Gigi, alias Daniel Giese, was not a subject of investigation until after 4 November 2011. The *Verfassungsschutz*, to paraphrase Lessing's *Philotas*, would not believe the perpetrators were German, even though it had long been shown indisputably that they were.

Since 1989, anti-racist initiatives in Germany have counted 182 deaths as a result of right-wing and racist violence. The German press reports at least 150. The federal government insists even today there have been 'only' forty-seven such deaths. That indicates that the structural repression continues. It is one reason why Uwe Mundlos, Uwe Böhnhardt and Beate Zschäpe remained underground for thirteen years even though there were numerous indications of their whereabouts, even though they were apparently by no means isolated, even though they had a broad network of supporters and sympathizers who canvassed and collected money for them at meetings. This structural repression is one reason why the investigators were set on the mafia murder theory to the very end. From 2001 to 2011, extreme right-wing crime increased by 50 per cent. Yet the federal *Verfassungsschutz* agency closed down its section on right-wing extremism in 2006. In 2009, the youth minister, Kristina Schröder, drastically cut funding for initiatives to combat xenophobia, and she would have made another cut at the end of 2011 if the National Socialist Underground's crimes had not come to light.

There is no one in German politics today, not even the *Verfassungsschutz* itself, who would dispute the massive, heretofore unthinkable failure of the law enforcement system. But there is also no evidence to date that the Zwickau terrorists were protected by *Verfassungsschutz* agents. More probably, the serial failures in the investigation were not intentional but the expression and the consequence of a social attitude. After all, the general public was all too willing to see its own stereotypes and prejudices confirmed, and refused to empathize with the victims' families. The expression 'döner-kebab murders'[11] was introduced into public usage not by the *Verfassungsschutz*, but by reputable newspapers; it is not far removed from the perpetrators' own term, 'Operation Döner Kebab Skewer'. What does the word 'döner murders' tell us except that the crimes were a cultural phenomenon, inaccessible to Western rational thinking, and hence yet another reason to view Turkish immigrants with suspicion? As late as 2005, when the signs of a racist motive had long since begun to multiply, *Bild* claimed that all six victims of the murder series to date had done business with an import/export company in Istanbul, investing mainly in the drug trade. A year later, *Der Spiegel* made bold to publish the thesis that 'the Turks' impenetrable parallel world is protecting the killers'.[12] In 2009, the same news magazine blamed the betting mafia, and then in 2011, a few months before the suicides in Eisenach, it suspected that 'an alliance between right-wing nationalist Turks, the Turkish secret service, and gangsters'[13] was behind the murders.

To see what this kind of rush to judgement means for the victims, we can turn to the murder that took place in Hamburg: the father of the greengrocer Süleyman Taşköprü was holding his son's body in his arms when he was escorted out of the shop and interrogated at the police station for several hours. Although neither that first nor any subsequent interrogation yielded anything to substantiate suspicions, the Hamburg newspapers soon reported that Süleyman Taşköprü had probably been involved in criminal activities. Neighbours withdrew; friendships were broken off. The murder of their son was followed by a character assassination of the family. This happened not just to the Taşköprüs but in similar or more drastic form to the families of almost all ten murder victims: until 4 November 2011 they were left alone with their suspicions that their father, their husband, their son had been the victim of a racist crime. To be fair, I must add that the editors of *Der Spiegel* and some other publications have since taken a critical look at the orientation and the vocabulary of their own reporting.

Lessing is rightly praised for his knowledge of foreign cultures and his pleas for tolerance. He was one of the first German authors to use the term 'cosmopolitan' and its German counterpart, *Weltbürger*, citizen of the world. It is more rarely noted that his cosmopolitan outlook was accompanied by a consistently critical relation to his own society.

> I have absolutely no concept of love of country (I am sorry to have to confess to you my shame), and it seems to me most decidedly a heroic weakness that I am quite happy to do without.[14]

In the mid-eighteenth century, of course, patriotism meant something very different than it did in the late nineteenth century. The fatherland that it implied was not a nation but one of many states within a language area that was only gradually building a common consciousness thanks to the printing press, Bible translations, increasing literacy and German literature. To Lessing, patriotism would mainly have meant choosing between Saxony and Prussia, which were at war with each other, or between Berlin and Leipzig, both of which were home to him, just as today it is quite natural for someone to feel a sense of belonging both to Germany and to Turkey. To use a term common in today's discussions of migration, Lessing was caught in a severe identity conflict. Of course, he himself saw it quite differently: he saw not the conflict but the richness of a twofold and, as a citizen of the world, even multiple belonging. He was 'one of the most impartial people in the world', he once said cheerfully in response to an accusation of insufficient loyalty.[15] And since, like all children of immigrants who speak critically about German affairs, I am accustomed to hearing the objection that I should first put my own house in order, I would like to point out that, at least in connection with the topic at hand, Germany – Germany *too* – is my own country, my own culture.

Yet the fact that Lessing belonged to different states at different times was not the reason, or not the only reason, for his rejection of patriotism. If it had been, he would have been able to integrate in the Prussian majority society in his Berlin period and in the Saxon majority society in his Leipzig period. But the opposite was the case: as he said himself in his later years, people in Leipzig took him for an arrant Prussian, and in Berlin they took him for an arrant Saxon, and his writings furnish evidence for both views.[16] Lessing always rejected patriotism with reference to the state to which he was closest at the time. He was a staunch believer in fouling his own nest, a 'virtuoso of trouble-making', as Daniel Kehlmann calls him.[17] His self-criticism is by no means merely politically or ideologically motivated. Lessing, who is introduced to us in school as worldly-wise, had a fundamental inclination to revolt against whatever presented itself as received opinion. 'The spirit of contradiction is so characteristic of him', his old friend Christian Felix Weisse once said, 'that he would be the first to oppose his own opinions as soon as his paradoxical assertions met with general acceptance.'[18] Lessing's invectives against the dominant theology of his time are legendary, and his most famous play, *Nathan the Wise*, was in its time an intentional and, moreover, an unprecedented provocation, bringing to the stage Jews and Muslims who were superior in wisdom and charity to the Christian protagonists. Note that Judaism had only secondary importance in the play and Islam almost none at all: although Lessing had studied Islamic culture intensively, and had analysed and refuted the European polemic against Muhammad in his *Vindication of Hieronymus Cardanus* twenty-five years earlier, in *Nathan* he did not display his surprising knowledge of Islam but was content with allusions, as in his version of the 'ring parable' on the question of the true religion, for example, when the wise judge, refusing to decide which of three similar rings is the authentic, beneficial one, pronounces the parable's central motif:

> To match the rest in bringing to the fore
> The magic of the opal in his ring!
> Assist that power with all humility,
> with benefaction, hearty peacefulness,
> And with profound submission to God's will![19]

'Profound submission to God' is nothing but a translation of the word 'Islam', and of course Lessing knew that. But in the dramatic text he does not expatiate on the fact, because he was not writing *Nathan* as a didactic play about Islam or about the Arab empire of Saladin's time; he only wanted to show that it was possible to act humanely without being a Christian. Lessing used the Orient as a screen on which to project the positive opposite of his own culture. In imagining a possible peace between the religions, he was criticizing the actual violence of Christianity. But the state he lived in was too intolerant to receive his play about tolerance: Lessing never saw his *Nathan* performed.

Lessing was an acerbic polemicist not only on political and religious issues but also on aesthetic questions – a notorious contrarian and a master of insult when addressing someone as widely admired as a Klopstock or a Wieland. The opening of his tirade against Johann Christian Gottsched, the highest authority in German literature of his day, is both famous and characteristic:

> 'Nobody,' say the authors of the Bibliothek, 'will deny that the German stage has Professor Gottsched to thank for a great part of its improvement.' I am that nobody; I deny it outright.[20]

At the same time, Lessing movingly took the part of social pariahs all his life; he defended his Jewish friend Moses Mendelssohn, fed beggars, sheltered vagabonds in his home for weeks at a time, and helped former prisoners, prostitutes and difficult personalities who had brought trouble on themselves or got into a jam. To learn from Lessing means not just making a principle of self-criticism, of contradicting received opinion. It also means holding strangers in esteem, coming to the aid of the weak. Today too, in my estimation, that is a fundamental responsibility of all intellectual activity and literature: to show respect for the other and rigour towards one's own; to defend the marginalized and to contest the dominant.

The dominant discourse has always taken the opposite orientation, whether in Lessing's time or in our own; whether in Germany or in other countries. It is apologetic towards itself and critical towards others; it extols the prosperous and denounces the weak. We can take almost any best-seller on the topic of Europe in recent years, any talk show on the topic of migration, any tabloid headline on unemployment benefits – serious or frivolous, well intended or sensational. Regardless of the position taken, the structure of the discourse is the same: the 'we' that appears in it is always the party threatened. The alien, meanwhile – the immigrant, the Muslim, the Eastern European, the asylum-seeker, the European institutions and, most recently, the Greek – always stands for the threat. The only difference in the positions of the best-sellers, talk shows and headlines is whether they represent the problem as soluble or insoluble. Lessing's conception of the state, on the other hand, was egalitarian to the core, and two decades before the French Revolution, two centuries before the inalienable fundamental rights of the German constitution, it was anti-populistic.

He resists the dichotomy between own and other, between majority society and minority, between dominant and dominated. To Lessing, 'we' is everyone. He judges the state not by its majority, but by the status of the minorities.

> The sum of the individual happinesses of *all* members is the happiness of the state. That is the only happiness the state can have. Any other happiness of the state in which individual members suffer, and *must* suffer, however few, is a veneer covering tyranny. Nothing else![21]

That was more than two hundred years ago, and since then the majorities in the world have certainly not treated their minorities more humanely. Opinions, however, have changed. To take just the word

'Enlightenment': as early as the dawn of the Romantic period, a decade or two after Lessing's death, it had become a catchword used not so much to combat the elites as to scoff at them. Lessing's concept of tolerance was so completely absorbed, first by the bourgeois conscience and later by the churches, that it has completely lost its force as a critique of authority. Two hundred years ago, the Protestant orthodoxy considered Lessing an extremist; today, any political, religious or social movement that proclaims the inferiority of people of other faiths, other races or other political opinions would be considered extremist. Intolerance as a basis of political thought and action in the twenty-first century must first be passed off as tolerance. The simplest way to do that is to claim that one's own tolerance needs to be vigilantly defended against intolerance. Those who would bring Lessing's message to the stage today, the message concentrated in the parable of the rings, must take into account the reason why it has so few supporters: namely because it has become a commonplace – and therefore invites all the more contradiction from those whom we label extremists today. A theatre that would take Lessing's message seriously must ask itself why that message has become so empty that, although the orthodoxies of all religions, the heads of state and the participants in world economic meetings recite it as a mantra, the cultures, the religions and the other identity machines nonetheless grow more aggressive with each passing day. To believe in Lessing's utopia today, we must negate it, lest it become an affirmation of the status quo and hence the opposite of what it was in 1778.

Lessing himself mentioned the material exploitability of talk about tolerance, although that has been and continues to be overlooked in his reception, which is blinded by its concern with edification. Nathan says, when he hits on the idea of telling Saladin the parable of the rings, 'That's it! And that can save me! Not only children can be quieted with fables.'[22] That is the parable in the late eighteenth century, and that is what it would be in the early twenty-first century too: Saladin, set upon by Crusaders and an economic crisis, longs for a little peace; he can be quieted with a fable and likes it so well that he rewards Nathan richly: tolerance has become a sales pitch. Few interpreters have noticed that Lessing created in Nathan the first broker of humanitarianism. Yet in doing so he neither discredited the parable of the rings nor repudiated its message. It is not invalidated just because Saladin, who is introduced as a despot, is enchanted by it. But Lessing purposely referred to the despot's predilection for basking in his own benevolence between his affairs of state. Such a predilection is still found with conspicuous frequency among the heads of countries, corporations and theatres. Lessing himself foresightedly noted the ambivalence of his beautiful utopia and was ahead of the greater part of his own reception history: for if we are content, as all four of the productions of *Nathan* have been that I have seen in German theatres – productions which were certainly not representative but in their intentions probably typical – if we are content with general good intentions, then we are going along with the racket being run with the message of the ring parable. This racket is the opposite of progressive art: it is a testimonial to ourselves; it is the self-affirmation 'We are so good; the world may be bad, racist, violent, intolerant; but *We Understand*; *Come Together*.'

It is no coincidence that the intellectual discourse of commercialized rapprochement is composed of advertising slogans. No major enterprise has failed to espouse tolerance in lavish conferences; no academy and no foundation can do without its tolerance programmes, no ad campaign for soft drinks or cigarettes would abstain from the united colours reconciling the world, no tabloid is so xenophobic that it does not pledge support for cultural, ethnic and gender diversity, and it is hard to find a municipal theatre today that does not promote intercultural understanding: *we're doing our bit*. But notice the costumes: while Saladin, the addressee of the message of tolerance, customarily represents the foreign by his Oriental robe, Nathan as the ambassador of tolerance most often wears a Western lounge suit. But really Nathan is just as Middle Eastern as Saladin, and Lessing portrayed only the Templar, the representative of his own religion, Christianity, as a religious fanatic. The play Lessing wrote against the intolerance of the West is used in today's theatre to Westernize tolerance. Its protagonist is no longer one of *them*, as Lessing made him, but *one of us*: Nathan the White.[23]

After 4 November 2011, the sociologist Wilhelm Heitmeyer said he was shocked at the impression still conveyed by many politicians and some of the media that the National Socialist Underground are 'a few misfits in an otherwise intact, humane society'; he said the right-wing terrorists had legitimized their violence by drawing on 'a stockpile of misanthropic attitudes in the population'.[24] In his long-term empirical study *Deutsche Zustände* [German conditions], of which the tenth instalment was published in autumn 2011, Heitmeyer's own findings are more nuanced. The number of potential supporters of a right-wing populist party in Germany is declining significantly; at the same time, however, right-wing populist views are increasing significantly among all respondents. Every tenth German now agrees with the sentence 'The use of force can put a stop to contention.' Every fifth believes, 'If others come here, they may need to be shown who's boss here, by the use of force if necessary.' More than two-thirds of the respondents agreed with the sentence 'To preserve law and order, we should crack down on misfits and troublemakers.' A study on extreme right-wing attitudes in Germany by the Friedrich Ebert Foundation yields similar findings. More than one in ten Germans, the study discovers, wishes for a 'leader who would govern Germany with a firm hand for the good of all'. The same proportion of Germans consider dictatorship a better form of government. Heitmeyer concludes that an 'ideology of unequal worth' is spreading through the whole society, and, while he sees right-wing populism currently declining as a political power, he finds evidence of a growing acceptance of nationalistic, xenophobic and anti-egalitarian attitudes in the established forums of public opinion, from political parties to the talk-show democracy of public television, from the cultural supplements to the best-seller lists. It is more than a coincidence that the most successful book of recent years, and in fact of post-war German history, was one that explains 'our' superiority and the threat 'they' pose to us, not by cultural differences, as the right-wing populists do, but by anchoring the argument in genetics. It is the writing on the wall.

In 2011 I did not take part in the controversy over Thilo Sarrazin and his book *Deutschland schafft sich ab* [Germany's self-destruction] because I was busy finishing the novel *Dein Name*, which the Thalia Theatre and the Hamburg Schauspielhaus transformed into such a marvellous event for the Lessing festival. Of course another motive was the one I have already mentioned: the urge to criticize and not defend my own. After all, Islam – Islam *too* – is my own culture, my religion. But, in preparing this speech, I asked myself what words it was that the National Socialist Underground replaced with actions, and, to answer that question, I studied the programme debates in the NPD and the theoretical journals of German right-wing extremism. There I encountered the idea of Germany's demise so often that I couldn't avoid reading the book myself – no other author in recent years has electrified nationalist thinking as Thilo Sarrazin has. And when in the next few minutes I discuss his assertions, even he must accord me a certain authority: after all, he cites me as a witness for his prosecution and so appears not to count me among the do-gooders, Islam glorifiers and tolerance preachers – and anyway, if they are to stand trial, Gotthold Ephraim Lessing must also be accused as their most radical proponent among German poets.

When asked about the broad reception and the overwhelming approval that his arguments have found among Germany's far right wing, Sarrazin himself shrugs his shoulders and says that the earth would not stop being round if Nazis declared it round. The problem is that the common ground that the neo-Nazis have discovered between themselves and Sarrazin is by no means limited to undisputed facts:

it turns upside down the whole civilized concept of the world that has developed in the West out of classical antiquity and monotheism, through the French Revolution and the Enlightenment, and after two world wars and the disasters of European nationalism. And I am referring not so much to Sarrazin's statements about Islam and his call for a restrictive immigration policy, despite the vehemence with which he renounces the consensus that has developed among the democratic parties since the CDU began to take an active part in shaping a society with immigration. For there are many books in which we could read such objections, and much more aggressive ones. Nor am I referring to Sarrazin's plea for an explicitly nationalistic conception of politics, which stands in fundamental opposition to the project of European unity. Nor yet am I referring to Sarrazin's conception of the family, in which the mother exists primarily to give birth. No, what I am referring to is Sarrazin's emphasis on the inequality of human beings and his views on demographic policy; I am referring to his statements on the connection between evolutionary pressure, ancestry and intelligence; I am referring to the authors Sarrazin cites in his notes, to scholars such as Kevin B. MacDonald, who appeared as a defence witness at the trial of the British Holocaust denier David Irving, and the Leipzig researcher on intelligence and genealogy Volkmar Weiss, who was appointed by the NPD group in the Saxon state parliament to an expert commission on demographics. I am referring to the biological concept of Judaism that Sarrazin expresses when he praises the 'Jew gene' and his analytical basis of 'racial hygiene' when he bemoans 'the proportion of congenital disabilities among Turkish and Kurdish immigrants'.[25] And, not least, I am referring to the derogatory language with which Sarrazin reduces whole segments of the population to their – very dubiously estimated – economic utility, without concealing the resentment that underlies his pseudo-rational argumentation.

As just one example of his many such formulations I may cite Sarrazin's adage, from a now famous interview with the cultural magazine *Lettre International*, which won him several front-page appearances in *Bild* a year before his book's publication: he is not required to acknowledge anyone, he said, who 'continually produces new little head-scarf girls'.[26] In the analysis of the Berlin sociologist Achim Bühl, 'the word "produce" here expresses first of all the speaker's psychopathological disgust with the sexuality of the so-called underclass, combined with sexual fantasies, and at the same time it represents a drastic form of dehumanization, since the term is normally used only for things, not for persons.' On the term 'head-scarf girls', Bühl comments that it is aimed at 'depersonalizing' an entire segment of the population: 'Reducing them to the singular attribute of "wearing a head scarf" – especially in the context of deploring their existence – goes hand in hand with the loss of personal dignity and human rights.'[27] And Sarrazin is by no means content to calculate the negative utilitarian coefficient to be applied wholesale to this or that population group; he also demands, starting in this first interview, specific pro-natalist policies so that the Turks do not conquer Germany the way the Kosovars conquered Kosovo:

> the lower the class, the higher the birth rate. The Arabs and Turks account for a proportion of births two to three times higher than the proportion of the population they make up. Large parts are neither willing nor able to integrate. The solution to this problem can only be: no more influx, and those who want to marry should do so abroad. Brides are constantly being shipped in.[28]

The programme of 'soft' eugenics driven by social benefits and immigration laws that Sarrazin expounded more specifically a year later in his book – with the explicit goal of preventing the extinction of the German people – is even more drastic than the party programme of the NPD: 'The goal of all measures must be: those who, on the other hand, are supported by the state should not be induced to increase that support by means of children.'[29] Protecting one's own national community, conceived as natural and homogeneous, against excessive immigration by genetically inferior peoples, while denying not only their willingness but also their ability (!) to integrate on the basis of their biological predisposition and cultural character – this kind of thinking is more than just right-leaning or populist. It meets, down to the details, the common definitions of ethnic nationalism. It openly professes to hold members of other religions and other races, and – if we examine Sarrazin's responses to his critics – people of other opinions, inferior. In the words of a leading medium of extreme right-wing theory, the periodical *Hier & Jetzt* [Here and now], which devoted a special issue to his book, 'Sarrazin has said what we nationalists . . . feel in our *völkisch* [i.e., ethnic-nationalistic] hearts.'[30]

Of course, the serial murders of the National Socialist Underground began many years before Thilo Sarrazin's book was published. The 'self-destruction of Germany' is not the cause but, rather, the most spectacular expression of that 'ideology of inequality' whose spread in many levels of society can be observed and empirically measured, whether in regard to foreigners, the poor, the concept of democracy – spectacular because Sarrazin's sweeping success established as at least worthy of discussion a philosophy that up to then had been enunciated only among right-wing extremists; spectacular also because that success is due to the collaboration – one might also say the propaganda pool – of the country's two largest media groups, Bertelsmann AG, who published the book, and the newspaper publisher Springer, who in an unprecedented campaign put it on page 1 of their newspapers for weeks; and spectacular, finally, because editors of every political stripe gave the biggest forum imaginable in Germany – in the form of advance excerpts, major reviews, magazine features, along with talk shows in public networks and even a completely unchallenging interview in such a reputable and sophisticated periodical as *Lettre International* – to an author whose statements have turned out to be a 'treasure trove for the political work of the nationally identifying right', to quote *Hier & Jetzt* again, 'whether in the struggle for minds or in day-to-day legislative business'.[31] Or in the words of the sociologist Achim Bühl: 'Core elements of Nazi ideology mutate into provocations that stimulate major controversies.'[32] Neither Thilo Sarrazin nor his publisher Bertelsmann AG, nor Springer, and least of all *Lettre International*, bears the responsibility for the murders of eight Turks, one Greek and one German police officer. Nonetheless, they have done more to popularize the ethnic nationalism that Uwe Mundlos adhered to than the National Socialist Underground. They have given mass distribution, extending far into the middle-class and even intellectual milieux, to a philosophy that just a few years ago would have been considered extremist by the general public; they have lifted the taboo from its derogatory diction and brought it into the mainstream of society.

In 1959, when the historian and philosopher Hannah Arendt received the city of Hamburg's Lessing Prize, she contradicted Lessing at just one point in her brilliant acceptance speech. It was the point at which the sultan Saladin tells the Jew Nathan to approach the throne. Arendt said in 1959 that, to her, Nathan's reaction to the command 'Step closer, Jew', saying in effect, 'I am a man', betrayed an attitude of 'grotesque and dangerous evasion of reality'.[33] For many years, she said, she considered the only adequate answer to the question 'Who are you?' to be: 'A Jew.' Hannah Arendt said that with visible regret – indeed, with a sadness that is still moving half a century later. She stressed several times that, by the expression 'a Jew', she did not mean to imply any special or exemplary kind of human being. Nor did she mean to invoke a historic reality; she was 'only acknowledging a political fact through which my being a member of this group outweighed all other questions of personal identity or rather had decided them in favour of anonymity, of namelessness.' And she recalled the 'basically simple principle . . . that is particularly hard to understand in times of defamation and persecution: the principle that one can resist only in terms of the identity that is under attack.'[34] Certainly Arendt remained in the United States after the war in part because she was better able to live and write there as a human being and not as a member of a certain people.

In the same year in which Hannah Arendt accepted the Lessing Prize of the city of Hamburg, my parents emigrated from Iran to Germany. Eight years later I was born in the Westphalian city of Siegen. When I read Hannah Arendt's acceptance speech recently, because I was supposed to receive a prize named for her, I asked myself what I would have answered in Nathan's place. It was shortly after 4 November 2011, the day that shed light on the murders that had claimed the lives of nine people simply because they belonged to different peoples: one simply because he was a Greek, the others simply because they were Turks. One of the NSU attacks, I read in the newspapers, had taken place in our immediate neighbourhood, a few doors away from the Cologne day-care centre where I picked up my daughter every day about 4 p.m. There was a little grocery in the street, not outwardly recognizable as foreign, just a rather larger corner shop that an Iranian family had taken over, without changing the decor or the selection of goods. I often went there, not for the weekly shopping I admit – the prices were relatively high – but for immediate needs, and then I chatted with the owners or their daughter, a grammar-school student, apparently, who did her homework sitting behind the counter, and I was glad that my own daughter had the chance to hear and speak Persian for a few minutes. One day the shop was closed, the shutters down. I thought, well, probably most customers had only shopped there for their immediate needs, and it wasn't enough for them to get by. After 4 November 2011, I learned that one of the terrorists from Zwickau, from the description probably Uwe Mundlos, had entered the shop with a shopping basket containing a tin Christmas box painted red with a star pattern. The unknown customer took a few items from the shelves, then said at the counter he had forgotten his wallet. He promised to come back with money and went away, leaving the basket. When he didn't return, the owner put the basket in a back room. Four weeks later, his daughter opened the Christmas box, which contained explosives. She survived with severe injuries, her pretty face marred for life. The family moved, leaving no forwarding address. Who had informed the Zwickau terrorists that the shop, whose sign still bore the previous owner's German name, along with those of two Cologne beers, had been bought by immigrants? The National Socialist Underground must have had supporters in Cologne, still undiscovered today; in any case, the schoolgirl was attacked not as a human being, but as a foreigner, an Iranian, a Muslim, about eighty yards from my daughter's day-care centre. So I asked myself how I would answer when addressed as a foreigner, an Iranian, a Muslim. Would I insist on being called a human being, a human being above all else? Or would I, after 4 November 2011, consider Nathan's answer a grotesque and dangerous evasion? I didn't need to think it over long. Half a century after Hannah Arendt's speech and my parents' immigration, I would once again be able – I would *still* be able – to answer in Germany that I am a human being.

None of us – not my parents, not my brothers, no member of our numerous family – has experienced in Germany what Hannah Arendt experienced. In spite of all the friction of isolated incidents, they are outweighed for every one of us by gratitude for the freedoms this country has given us, for the opportunities it has offered us, for the rights it has granted us. I often think, as I travel around the country, and more often still when I return from other countries, that Germany has developed in the fifty years since Hannah Arendt's Lessing speech and my parents' immigration into a surprisingly tolerable country, and even a humane and lovable one. Perhaps I don't talk about this love so often, but I think it is perceptible in my books. If I don't talk about it, the reason is the one that Lessing teaches me when he remarks that the patriot in him may not be altogether smothered – but 'the title of a zealous patriot, to my way of thinking, is the last thing I would covet; a patriot, that is, who would teach me to forget that I ought to be a citizen of the world.'[35]

Perhaps you find these last sentences surprising, especially at the end of this particular speech. Perhaps they sound too conciliatory to you; yet they are meant in a combative spirit. For those who espouse nationalism do not stand for the Germany I am glad to live in. They are rebelling, whether violently or otherwise, whether with the means of an extremist party or a media group, whether from the margins of the society or from its middle, against a degree of pluralism and cosmopolitanism that neither Hannah Arendt nor my parents would have thought possible in 1959. I find my Germany today represented by Aridaeus rather than Philotas.

When Lessing wrote his tragedy on patriotism, Philotas embodied the society's ideal of enthusiastic patriotism. Lessing, however, evidently loved Aridaeus, the king of the others, the enemy, who asks Philotas what a hero would be without philanthropy and surrenders without fighting when Philotas kills himself out of love for his fatherland:

In vain have we shed our streams of blood, in vain have we conquered lands. There he departs with our booty, the greater victor! – Come! Get me my son! And when I have him, I will no more be king. Do ye believe, ye men, that one does not grow weary of it?[36]

— 5 —

GOD BREATHING

Goethe and Religion

Imagine we were to do nothing. We would lie comfortably, our hands beside our body, our eyes closed, hearing no noises anywhere about, feeling no pain, or even the tension of this or that muscle, neither shivering nor sweating. Straight away we would notice that we cannot do nothing. We would still be breathing. We would hear the stream of air whispering into our nostrils or softly hissing between our lips and teeth; we would notice, if we paid careful attention, the tingling in our windpipe as the air flowed through; we would feel, depending on how we drew our breath, our chest or our abdomen expand, until the breath returned and flowed back up our windpipe and out through our mouth or nose, and our chest or our abdomen contracted again. We could hold our breath, but only for a few seconds, a little longer if we were in good physical shape – a minute, maybe two. Then we would exhale again all the more forcefully. We cannot command our own breathing – not even our own breathing is under our command. Over the most elementary activity of our lives we have – I won't say no control, but – only minimal control, only a few seconds or a minute or two of control. Is it we, then, who are doing the breathing in the first place?

The difference between a religious frame of mind and one which explains the world as purely immanent can probably be linked to no other question as precisely, vividly and radically as to the question of our own breathing. God by comparison is a secondary and, more to the point, an abstract concept, one that is ultimately inexplicable: you can be religious without mentioning God; you don't even have to know the word, or you can banish it from your speech. All the other terms that the monotheistic tradition attributes to religion are even more amorphous: the revelation, the holy, creation. Even if we think we know precisely what we mean by them, perhaps after years of speculative inquiry or a spiritual epiphany, we would have no way of knowing that others use them in the same sense, or used them in the same sense two hundred or two thousand years ago. They are rich terms whose long history is specific to each religious community, and still more specific to each language community, and they are therefore anything but adequate to designate something immediately perceptible, as one could say of the word 'wood', for example, or of 'milk', or even of the word for the cultural artefact 'bread'. We could show any person in the world a loaf of bread, a piece of wood, a glass of milk, and he or she would, as a rule, be able to translate it precisely into his or her language – but it is not so with the revelation, the holy or creation, much less with God. Breath, however, is something we can perceive in our nostrils or between our lips and teeth, as a tingling in our windpipe, as an external force acting on our chest and our abdomen, on which our life depends – on which we depend. Breath is the fundamental religious experience, which we can either deny or accept:

Im Atemholen sind zweierlei Gnaden:
Die Luft einziehn, sich ihrer entladen.
Jenes bedrängt, dieses erfrischt;
So wunderbar ist das Leben gemsicht.
Du Danke Gott, wenn er dich preßt,
Und dank' ihm, wenn er dich wieder entläßt.[1]

In drawing breath are graces twain:
Inhaling air, discharging it again:
The former crushing, the latter relieving;
Such a wondrous mixture is living.
Thank thou God when He presses thee,
And thank Him when He releases thee.

Who is breathing? The immanent frame of mind would explain breath as the consequence of purely physiological causes. It would also put human autonomy into a certain perspective, but it would attribute the cause of the intake and outflow of air to bodily functions: muscles, metabolism, brain waves, blood vessels, heartbeats, and so on. At the same time, breathing – indeed nothing so much as breathing – can metaphysically unsettle even the most prosaic mind.

Perhaps most people take their own breathing too much for granted to be disconcerted by it – but let us imagine we are a mother, or a father, in a delivery room. We would see our own child gasp for air for the first time, see the swelling and subsiding of his or her little abdomen, smeared with blood and brownish tissue as if with wet clay, see the umbilical cord, which no longer needs to supply the child, and in our euphoria, admittedly stimulated by our own hormones, we would spontaneously perceive that breath not as a mere physiological pattern but as a gift – a grace, as Goethe calls it in his 'Talismans' – a gift of nature if you prefer, or fate, or chance. Without resorting to theological systematic terms, I am sure that man's belief in God had its origin in situations, such as the birth of one's own child, in which a person is overwhelmed by the need to give thanks. For expressing gratitude means giving thanks *to* someone or something. In *Wilhelm Meister's Apprenticeship* we read:

> Happy was I, that a thousand little incidents in combination proved, as clearly as the drawing of my breath proved me to be living, that I was not without God in the world. He was near to me: I was before him. This is what, with a diligent avoidance of all theological systematic terms, I can with the greatest truth declare.[2]

Or when a person is overcome by the urge to plead for something: we see our own mother, our own father, breathing on her or his deathbed, see her or him grown pale, wasted, eyes closed, unresponsive; see her chest, in spite of her exhaustion, swelling and collapsing as rapidly as a baby's, hear her pulse perhaps amplified by the beeping of the heart-rate monitor, realize that her pulse is slowing, blanch at the long and lengthening silences after each inhalation before her breath returns, tenths of a second or whole seconds of complete inertia during which we ask ourselves each time in alarm – no: during which even the toughest of us plead and beg that the air drawn into her chest might flow back out again. In our need we turn to our mother, our father, and yet we realize at their deathbed, if not before, that they don't have – that not even our own parents, who seemed so powerful to us as children, have power over their breathing. Who or what does, then? I am certain that man's belief in God originated in part in the need to turn to a mother, a father, who is immortal. Goethe prefaced his 'Marienbad Elegy' with the following lines from his play *Torquato Tasso*:

> When man had ceas'd to utter his lament,
> A god then let me tell my tale of sorrow.[3]

Goethe himself strictly avoided the sight of people he was close to when they were dying or dead. When his wife Christiane lay dying, he fell ill himself, only to rise again promptly once her body had been carried out of the house. He likewise followed the progress of Schiller's demise from the excused remoteness of his own sickbed. After the death of his beloved sister, he was silent for days; against all etiquette he stayed away from the funeral of Grand Duke Charles Augustus;

and death notices were often delivered to him with the retardation that relatives have always misconceived as kindness. Goethe's dread of the encounter, especially the physical encounter, with death, which scholarship has diagnosed as a death neurosis, seems all the stranger since he had exact knowledge of anatomy and as a student had attended several autopsies. Yet on reading the corresponding passage in his autobiography, *Dichtung und Wahrheit*, we see clearly that the anatomy lessons were intended not only to increase his knowledge but in at least equal measure to free him 'from all apprehension as to repulsive things'. In the dissecting room Goethe hoped to make himself insensitive to death – and he was successful to the extent that 'nothing of this kind could ever put me out of my self-possession.' The term 'apprehension' can be understood here not only in the superficial sense Goethe intended of an 'uneasiness' or 'aversion' but also literally, as a 'sensory impression'. Looking at unknown, anonymous cadavers, he may have been able to steel himself 'not only against these impressions on my senses, but also against the infections of the imagination.'[4] Seeing a loved one die was a completely different matter, and remained so into Goethe's old age. Precisely because his faith in God was grounded in empirical experience, Goethe must have feared the agitation that the sight of death causes.

His religious awakening, Goethe recalls in *Dichtung und Wahrheit*, began with two awe-inspiring natural events. One was far away, but unprecedented in its destructive force: the earthquake of Lisbon on 1 November 1755, which 'spread a prodigious alarm over the world, long accustomed to peace and quiet': 'In vain the young mind strove to resist these impressions. It was the more impossible, as the wise and scripture-learned could not themselves agree as to the light in which such a phenomenon should be regarded.' The other event, the following year, seems comparatively ordinary in the sixty-year-old's hindsight but pierced the child's senses with roaring noise and blinding light, with cold, wet and the sweat of fear:

> A sudden hail-storm, accompanied by thunder and lightning, violently broke the new panes at the back of our house, which looked towards the west, damaged the new furniture, destroyed some valuable books and other things of worth, and was the more terrible to the children, as the whole household, quite beside themselves, dragged them into a dark passage, where, on their knees, with frightful groans and cries, they thought to conciliate the wrathful Deity.

The two experiences of an overpowering Nature haphazardly tossing humanity about – the hailstorm over his own house still more impressive than the disaster of Lisbon, which he only heard about – gave the child his first opportunities 'of knowing directly that angry God, of whom the Old Testament records so much'.[5] Almost as fast as the news had spread from Lisbon or the thunderstorm had swept away from Frankfurt, the child soon forgot God's 'manifestations of wrath' and saw 'the beauty of the world, and the manifold blessings in which we participate while upon it.' Goethe's earliest experiences of God are experiences of nature. But not only that: in nature God reveals Himself to the seven-year-old as someone, or something, that sometimes presses, sometimes releases. And finally, just as, in the *Divan*, Goethe, grown old, interprets that alternation positively, as dialectic – declaring the pressing itself as the miraculous, necessary precondition for the release – in the child too, trust outweighs fear:

> The God who stands in immediate connexion with nature, and owns and loves it as his work, seemed to him the proper God, who might be brought into closer relationship with man, as with everything else, and who would take care of him, as of the motion of the stars, the days and seasons, the animals and plants.[6]

Goethe's religious development took many turns and led him to make many statements about Christianity – and, indeed, about almost all religions that could be studied in his day – that either seem to be or actually are contradictory. In a letter to Herder, he called the 'whole doctrine of Christ' a scatological obscenity;[7] to the theologian Lavater, he openly admitted being 'a decided non-Christian';[8] he harboured a 'truly Julianic hatred' against Christianity.[9] Although it was important to him that his son August and his other children who died in infancy received the 'holy act' of baptism,[10] he called the Christian religion 'a last step to which mankind were fitted and destined to attain'[11] and answered his own question as to who today was still a Christian in the sense of Christ's own intention: 'I alone perhaps, though you may think me a heathen.'[12] His remarks on other religions appear no less paradoxical: characteristically, Goethe has been accused both of anti-Semitism and of philo-Semitism. He translated Voltaire's anti-Islamic play *Mahomet* and himself wrote a hymn to the Prophet of Islam; he loved the Vedas, but said the Indians had the 'most abstruse philosophy' and the 'most monstrous religion';[13] he wrote polemics against Spinoza and gradually approached pantheism. And, nonetheless, the basic contours of Goethe's religiousness show a remarkable continuity from the first to the last decade of his life: it is a religiousness of immediate perception and universal human experience, of precise observation and the obvious conclusions drawn from it – those that appear compelling even to a child. It is a religiousness without speculation and almost without belief, inasmuch as Goethe attributes it to the natural human instinct, buried perhaps under education and thinking, by which man sees himself as a creature and nature as creation:

> General, natural religion, properly speaking, requires no faith; for the persuasion that a great producing, regulating and conducting Being conceals himself, as it were, behind Nature, to make himself comprehensible to us – such a conviction forces itself upon every one. Nay, if we for a moment let drop this thread, which conducts us through life, it may be immediately and everywhere resumed.

Goethe wisely adds that particular religions behave quite differently, claiming God for just one proclaimer, one tribe, one people or one territory:

> This religion is founded on faith, which must be immovable if it would not be instantly destroyed. Every doubt of such a religion is fatal to it. One may return to conviction, but not to faith. Hence the endless probation, the delay in the fulfilment of so often repeated promises, by which the capacity for faith in those ancestors is set in the clearest light.[14]

Accordingly, Goethe's disparate statements about one religion or another do not always – indeed only very rarely – express discontinuities in his own religious development; they relate rather to the different manifestations, rites and doctrines of the religions concerned. In all religious traditions, to varying degrees, he recognized the general, natural religiousness that the child spontaneously felt, and the old man steadfastly upheld, on experiencing nature. Where the religious traditions differed, however – and, one might add, the more they diverged from man's anthropological religiousness, so to speak – Goethe judged differently. That is why he distinguished systematically and historically between church Christianity, which he considered a 'product of error and violence',[15] and a pure, original message of the Gospel; it is also why he felt, even in the last years of his life when he had long since turned towards Christianity again and even explicitly professed himself a Christian, that the doctrine 'that Three are One and One is Three' was 'opposed to the feeling of my soul for truth'.[16] Goethe considered Christianity 'eternal' to the extent that, in its biblical origins, he saw it as 'deeply anchored in human nature and its necessity'.[17] He rejected it to the extent that it had lost its 'original purity' soon after its origins and had deteriorated in the present day to 'muddled nonsense'.[18]

Faith is an altogether unfitting word for Goethe's religiousness. Subjectively, Goethe did not believe in God, he recognized Him; he saw, heard, smelled, experienced, breathed and felt – in both senses of the word – that there must be a single God:

> Critical reason has done away with the teleological proof of the existence of God; we put up with this. But what cannot be proved should remain valid to us as feeling, and we go back to all these pious notions from Brontotheology to Niphotheology. Should we not be allowed to feel in lightning, thunder and storm the closeness of a more than mighty power, in the scent of blossoms and the gentle stirring of a warm breeze a being that comes lovingly close to us?[19]

Where others derive their view of the world from religion, Goethe did the inverse, deriving religious principles from his perception of the world – 'for the singular is concealed in the multiple, and that is where belief begins for me; it is not the beginning but the end of all knowing.'[20] Goethe's piety does not stand in any contradiction to his scientific investigations, nor are they unrelated; on the contrary, faith and science, poetry and natural history depend on and complement one another. Albrecht Schöne has demonstrated this interdependence in reference to Goethe's *Theory of Colours*, which is clearly the attempt to bring a theological doctrine into harmony with empirical reality; Hendrik Birus has recently revealed it in individual lines of the 'Talismans' in his annotated edition of the *Divan*. Goethe drew the 'graces twain' of breathing, for example, directly from the 'Rose Garden' of the Persian poet Saadi (whose work he read in Olearius's baroque translation): 'Every breath we draw in helps to prolong life and, going out of us again, gladdens the spirit. Therefore in drawing breath are graces twain, and we shall thank God from our hearts for each.'[21]

At the same time, however, breath as a sign of life corroborates Goethe's own scientific observations: almost two decades before the *West-Eastern Divan*, Goethe wrote, in connection with Kant's *Critique of Pure Reason*: 'For me, the systole and diastole of the human mind were like a second respiration, never separate, always pulsating.'[22] Classical philologists will recognize systole from scanning ancient verse. In medicine, systole is the contraction of the heart, alternating rhythmically with its expansion, diastole: 'drawing in air, discharging it again' – or, as Goethe also described it in the historical part of his *Theory of Colours*, 'the pulsation in which life and sensation are expressed': 'contracting, expanding; gathering, releasing; binding, loosing; *rétrécir* and *développer*, etc.'[23] In other fields of empirical research too – meteorology, tone theory, epistemology, morphology – and in ethics, and in the creation myth, Goethe regularly discovered 'the alternating effects of contraction and expansion by which nature finally attains its goal'.[24] Even in connection with psychology, he found: 'There is a constant systole and diastole, a breathing in and a breathing out of the living organism; even if you cannot actually pronounce on this, you must observe it precisely and bear it in mind.'[25]

Gasping when we are startled and exhaling when we are relieved about something are reflexes that are immediately obvious to all of us. It is rarer for us to be aware of the opposite connection: that inhaling tenses the body, while exhaling physically relaxes us. Observe it closely: when we take a breath, only slight attention is needed to feel that the muscles in our ribcage or behind our abdominal wall – I don't mean to say they cramp, but they become firm, they contract. Ordinarily this tension is not unpleasant. Nonetheless, any inhalation can create the feeling that the breath drawn could become painful, even unbearable, if it did not immediately reverse and go back up the windpipe and out through the mouth or nose. And observe exhalation the same way: if we pay it even slight attention, we feel how the muscles – I don't mean to say they let go, but they yield, they expand. True, the relaxation is minimal. Nonetheless, we need only to hold our breath for a few seconds or, if we are in good physical shape, a minute or two to feel the relief that comes with exhaling. The escaping breath relieves us physically, by reducing the volume of air in our chest, as well as in the figurative sense, by dispelling the feeling that the air in our body could stop moving: 'Thus inspiration already presupposes expiration; thus every systole its diastole. It is the universal formula of life which manifests itself in this as in all other cases.'[26]

When Goethe read in Saadi about the dual graces of drawing breath, it cannot have given him any new insight – it must have been a reminder. Generalizing only slightly, we could say the same of his whole preoccupation with Islam: he was not persuaded by its basic tenets; they only confirmed what was already, more by feeling than by reflection, his religious conviction at the age of seven.

> 'I believe in one God!' This is a fine and praiseworthy dictum; but to recognize and proclaim God wherever and however he may reveal himself, that is actually bliss here on earth.[27]

Islam does not recognize the term 'profession of faith'. Strictly speaking, what is translated as 'profession' in reference to the Islamic profession of faith, for example, is a testimony, *shahāda*: 'I testify that there is no God but God.' The difference seems insignificant, but in substance it is most important: to profess is to declare one's belonging to a specific doctrine or a specific group; it is always a profession *of* something, or standing up *for* something, a public expression of an attitude, a belief. I can only profess something if there is an alternative, if it would also be possible for me to profess something else. To testify, on the other hand, is to make a factual declaration of a publicly recognized observation; it is based on an empirical perception or experience, which may perhaps be objectively deceptive but is subjectively as unequivocal as a loaf of bread I see before me, a piece of wood, a glass of milk. 'Am I not your Lord?' God asks mankind, in verse 7:172, on the day of its creation; 'Yes, we testify', the people answer. And God confirms that He is demanding testimony, a statement of facts before a judge:

Now We take you to witness,
So that you cannot say on the Day of Resurrection:
We were unaware of this!

Professing implies: among various possibilities, I profess this particular one. Testifying, on the other hand, is the affirmation of an occurrence or an experience which was thus and not otherwise. The alternative is not a different affirmation – the observation is too distinct, the Quran holds, to permit any ambiguity – the alternative to testimony is denial. Accordingly, the unbelievers in the Quran do not have the wrong belief among several possible ones; they are simply 'deaf, dumb and blind – so they do not understand', as a formula frequently repeated in the Quran puts it; and here 'not understand', *lā yaᶜqilūna*, actually means they do not perceive, do not receive through the senses, and therefore do not recognize. God says to the Prophet in verse 10:43 about the unbelievers:

Some of them listen to you,
But can you make the deaf hear,
Although they do not understand?
And some of them look at you,
But can you lead the blind,
Although they do not see?

The faithful, on the other hand, in the Quran are those who do the obvious things, namely see, hear, smell, feel, and use their reason in the sense Goethe meant when he wrote to Friedrich Heinrich Jacobi: 'When you say, one can only believe in God . . . I tell you, I attach great importance to seeing.'[28] In the Quran, people do not believe in God, they know of Him; they see, hear, feel and understand his existence as a manifest fact. 'He has provided sufficient signs', says verse 2:159 in Goethe's own version:

in the creation of Heaven and Earth, in the alteration of night and day . . . all of these are sufficient signs of the Oneness of God and of his benevolence for the nations if they regard them attentively.[29]

As a child Goethe had read in the Old Testament that nature is full of signs through which God reveals Himself to man, and he recalled it again and again, even as late as the *Maxims and Reflections*: 'If you want to deny that nature is a divine organ, you might as well deny all revelation.'[30] Islam takes up the biblical motif of God's signs, expanding it to form a truly semiotic theory, not only of creation but of all civilization. An extra-quranic word of God puts it most startlingly: 'I was a treasure and wanted to be discovered. That is why I created the world.' Not only through his prophets, but more widely still, manifest even to children and to primitive peoples, God reveals Himself in nature, in all of civilization, in history, in human experience, the sensory pleasures, especially love, in breath of course, in everything man-made:

> Surely in the creation of the heavens and the earth
> and in the alternation of night and day
> and in the ship that runs in the sea with profit
> to men, and the water God sends down from heaven,
> therewith reviving the earth after it is dead
> and His scattering abroad in it all manner of
> crawling thing, and the turning about of the winds
> and the clouds compelled between heaven and earth –
> surely there are signs for a people having understanding.[31]

Goethe likewise recognizes, not just in nature but in civilization too, in 'people's doings and dealings over thousands of years . . . the mysterious admixture of a higher Power in life'.[32] In both cases, the world is a medium or 'organ' through which God speaks to man. 'He hath set you the stars as a guide in the darkness by land and sea', says verse 6:97 in Joseph von Hammer-Purgstall's translation, which Goethe possessed. He appropriated the Quran verse as a poem of his own in the *West-Eastern Divan*:

> *Er hat euch die Gestirne gesetzt*
> *Als Leiter zu Land und See;*
> *Damit ihr euch daran ergötzt,*
> *Stets blickend in die Höh.*

> He hath set you the stars
> As a guide by land and sea;
> That you may delight in them,
> Gazing steadfastly on high.[33]

In Islam, Goethe did not find certain fundamental difficulties that caused him to struggle with Christianity. Religion and science do not need to be reconciled because the Quran derives faith directly from human reason – hence the rejection of miracles performed by

Muhammad (Islamic dogma acknowledges the miracles of the biblical prophets, yet degrades them to simple expressions of God's omnipotence, proving nothing further); hence too the designation of theology as a 'science', taught alongside the other humanities and natural sciences, in classical Islamic education. 'You take the Gospel as it stands for the most divine truth', Goethe writes in a letter to Lavater, objecting to all supernatural evidence of God's influence:

> an audible voice from Heaven would not convince me that water burns and fire quenches, that a woman gives birth without a man, and that a dead man rises again; I hold these rather to be blasphemies against great God and His revelation in Nature.[34]

In Islam, man is not born in sin, and therefore not dependent on any additional grace; he needs only to recognize his natural orientation towards God. 'The seven heavens and the earth, and whosoever in them is, extol Him', God says to the unbelievers in verse 17:44: 'Nothing is, that does not proclaim his praise, but you do not understand their extolling. Surely He is All-clement, All-forgiving.'[35] In emphasizing man's innate orientation towards God in connection with his theory of colours, Goethe alludes, intentionally or not, to the numerous comparisons of the divinity with light that he encountered in the Quran about the same time. That the seeker himself is a spark of the light he seeks is a basic teaching of Sufism. In the *Theory of Colours* we encounter it, by chance or otherwise, in an idea of Plotinus, who in turn had a strong influence on the Islamic mysticism of light: 'If the eye were not sunny, how could we perceive light? If God's own strength lived not in us, how could we delight in Divine things?'[36]

The anthropological orientation towards God follows from the rank the Quran assigns to mankind in creation when it explicitly calls man not the image of God, but His viceroy or successor – His *khalīfa* – and thereby confers on him the responsibility for completing creation. Hafiz, whom Goethe appointed his twin, points in several passages to man's Promethean burden.

> For Heaven's self was all too weak to bear
> The burden of His love God laid on it,
> He turned to seek a messenger elsewhere,
> And in the Book of Fate my name was writ.[37]

The tension found in the Quran between human dependence and human autonomy also pervades Goethe's work.

> None there are like these . . .
> Ever pressing onwards

With hungriness unspeakable
For the unattainable.[38]

In his later years, Goethe resolved the antagonism between divine providence and human free will, which was a dominant theme in Islamic theology, in the spirit of the rationalist school, writing:

> If we observe ourselves in every life situation, we find that we are externally determined from our first breath to our last; but that the highest freedom remains to us to form ourselves within our self, that we set ourselves in harmony with the moral order of the world, and so, whatever obstacles may arise, can attain peace with ourselves.[39]

Yet it was Islam's worldliness still more than its conception of man that Goethe emphasized: the appreciation of this world as the setting of an omnipresent revelation, the priority of active faith over merely correct faith, and the resolution of the dichotomy of sacred and profane. That immediately reminds us of pantheism, of course, and it reminded Goethe too of pantheism, which fascinated him just as much. Unlike Spinoza, however, Islam sees nature not as identical with God but as an 'organ' through which God speaks to man. As he grew older, Goethe took the difference between pantheism and monotheism more and more seriously. He saw in Islam the doctrine of God's omnipresence, which is what had drawn him to pantheism, reconciled with the belief in one God. So it is not paradoxical after all that Goethe's appreciation of Islam could have favoured a return to Protestant Christianity. Chancellor von Müller reports that Goethe said, in a conversation of 28 March 1819:

> Trust and humility are the true principles of every superior religion; subordination to a higher Will which regulates events, which we do not comprehend for the very reason that it is higher than our reason and our understanding. This is where Islam and the Reformed religion are most similar.[40]

I have not found any passage that would prove a causal relation between Goethe's Islamic studies and his rapprochement with Protestantism. In any case, that would be easier than what we should expect from such an unconventional, self-willed spirit. And yet the very thought contains what we could learn from Goethe in our time, and especially here in Germany, in a Europe that is increasingly diverse and at the same time increasingly ignorant of religion: that we have to contemplate the other to discover ourselves. How Goethe's reading of the Quran enriched his reading of the Bible is self-evident in view of the motifs they have in common. For the Quran by its own definition extends the tradition of the biblical religions, certifying them, yet at the same the Quran overcomes exactly what was hardest for Goethe, as a proponent of a universal religiousness, to accept: the claim to exclusivity. 'It is true, what God said in the Quran: We have sent no people a prophet except in their own language',[41] Goethe wrote, referring to the quranic concept of revelation, in which Islam is the last but by no means the only valid religion. In the thousandfold religions, Goethe saw 'a thousand expressions of this redeeming power':[42] 'In faith, I said, everything depends on the fact of believing; *what* is believed is perfectly indifferent.'[43] Although the divinity of Christ was particularly problematic to Goethe, who could not make it accord with his strict monotheism, as he grew older he increasingly saw in Christianity the familiar, personal form of a 'world-piety' (to use his term from *Wilhelm Meister's Travels*):

> The history of all religions and philosophy teaches us that this great truth, indispensable for man, has been handed down by different nations, in different times, in various ways, and even in strange fables and images, in accordance with their limited knowledge; enough, if it only be acknowledged that we find ourselves in a condition which, even if it seems to drag us down and oppress us, yet gives us opportunity, nay, even makes it our duty, to raise ourselves up, and to fulfil the purposes of the Godhead in this manner, that while we are compelled on the one hand to concentrate ourselves (*uns zu verselbsten*), we on the other hand, do not omit to expand ourselves (*uns zu entselbstigen*) in regular pulsation.[44]

Those of Goethe's expressions which seem to imply he professes Islam, as, for example, when he says he does not reject 'the suspicion that he himself is a Mussulman',[45] are always meant in the literal sense of submission to God – 'We all live in Islam, in whatever form we resolve to do so'[46] – not as an identification with the particular religion that was founded by the Prophet Muhammad. 'And so once again we must remain in Islam (that is: in absolute submission to the will of God)', Goethe writes to Johann Heinrich Meyer in a letter of 29 July 1816,[47] describing his mood of the moment; and on 20 September 1820, worrying about his daughter-in-law's health, he writes, 'There is nothing else I can say except that here too I am trying to remain in Islam.'[48]

This diction of Goethe's is entirely in keeping with the Islamic source texts he was studying. Although those Muslims who cite Goethe's statements as evidence of his conversion do not seem to be aware of it, in many passages the Quran and the Prophet Muhammad use the word 'Islam' and the related participle 'Muslim' literally – that is, in the sense of that general, natural spiritual attitude, or 'world-piety', that Goethe saw as innate in man: 'Really something of this faith is held in us all, even without being taught', he said of Islam in a conversation with Eckermann on 11 April 1827, and continued:

> 'The ball on which my name is not written, cannot hit me,' says the soldier in the battle-field; and, without such a belief, how could he maintain such courage and cheerfulness in the most imminent perils? The Christian doctrine, 'No sparrow falls to the ground without the consent of our Father,' comes from the same source, intimating that there is a Providence, which keeps in its eye the smallest things, and without whose will and permission nothing can happen.

Near the end of the conversation, Goethe concludes, 'You see that nothing is wanting in this doctrine; that with all our systems, we have got no further; and that, generally speaking, no one can get further.' But at this very point, in the highest praise of Islam Goethe has yet expressed, it is clear that he never seriously considered converting. Since he felt the fundamental doctrines to be universal, he found them in other religions as well, including his own, the Christian religion: 'The philosophical system of the Mahometans is a good standard, which we can apply to ourselves and others, to ascertain the degree of mental progress which we have attained.'[49]

Goethe praised Islam, but did he understand it correctly? On many points his interpretation stands in contradiction to the orthodoxy – that is, to the major Sunni educational institutions such as Al-Azhar University in Cairo or Ez-Zitouna in Tunis, which place their emphasis on dogma, norms of behaviour and rules of ritual. And fundamentalists who declare all heterodox believers, without exception, to be unbelievers would have to protest vehemently against Goethe's praise. On the other hand, however, Goethe's interpretation corresponds with the mystical tradition in Islam, down to details of which he could not have been aware. Although, in the history of Islam, the authors to whom he felt drawn have at times been branded heretics, they saw themselves as devout Muslims, and are revered as such to the present day. In fact, the mystics invoke the Islamic source texts no less systematically than the fundamentalists – we may recall, for example, as Goethe did, that Hafiz was not a proper name but an honorific for particularly devout Muslims who knew the entire Quran by heart, 'so that on any occasion one might quote the appropriate passages, to promote edification or to settle a dispute.'[50] Unlike the fundamentalists, however, the mystics emphasize the spirit and the universal message of the letters. It is not because Goethe had had a few lessons in Arabic, but because he was a poet, like Hafiz himself, that he showed a similar sensitivity to the poetic structure of the quranic language, which manifestly defies literal interpretation.

The sensitivity with which Goethe comprehended core tenets of Islam, adopting them sometimes literally in his own writing, sometimes expatiating on them in his thought, sometimes weaving them into his own poetic imagery, can be seen especially in the 'Talismans':

Gottes ist der Orient!
Gottes ist der Okzident!
Nord- und südliches Gelände
Ruht im Frieden seiner Hände.

God's is the Orient!
God's is the Occident!
Northern and southern lands
Rest in the peace of His hands.

The first two lines, an almost verbatim quotation from Hammer-Purgstall's Quran translation, are not only geographically completed in the second couplet but linked to two more essential motifs of the Quran, earthly peace and divine hands.

Er, der einzige Gerechte
Will für jedermann das Rechte.
Sey, von seinen hundert Namen,
Dieser hochgelobet! Amen.

He Who alone is just
Wills what's right for every man.
Of His hundred names be
This one highly praised! Amen.

The stanza introduces in a general way the names of God, which is the theme of a widely ramifying scholarly literature in Islam and, at the same time, apparently makes a conscious choice in favour of the rationalist schools of the Mutazilites and the Shiites, which place justice above all the other attributes of God, proclaiming it as a fifth obligatory article of faith for all Muslims.

Mich verwirren will das Irren;
Doch du weißt mich zu entwirren.
Wenn ich handle, wenn ich dichte,
Gib du meinem Weg die Richte.

Errancy would bewilder me;
But Thou canst untangle me.
In my actions, in my poems,
Make Thou my way straight.

The stanza relates the last two lines of the *Fatiha*, the first surah of the Quran, to Goethe's own poetry, attaining the exact quranic sense of the expression for 'error' (*Irren* in Goethe's German), the Arabic word *dalāl*, an aimless wandering. The straightness (*Richte*) corresponds to the quranic use of the word *sharia* as the way of divine guidance.

Ob ich Ird'sches denk' und sinne
Das gereicht zu höherem Gewinne.
Mit dem Staube nicht der Geist zerstoben
Dringet, in sich selbst gedrängt, nach oben.

Though I put my mind to earthly things,
Yet that brings higher profit.
The spirit, unsullied by dust,
Rushes, pressed into itself, upward.

This quatrain refers first of all to the double meaning of all mystic poetry, which definitely has a terrestrial sense while at the same time speaking in parables of transcendent themes. The spirit that rushes upwards, pressed or condensed (*dringet, in sich selbst gedrängt*), combines the quranic theme of the soul's reawakening after the death of the body with Goethe's concept of human souls as monads that aspire to join the universal soul. Finally, the last and longest of the 'Talismans':

Im Atemholen sind zweierlei Gnaden:
Die Luft einziehn, sich ihrer entladen.
Jenes bedrängt, dieses erfrischt;
So wunderbar ist das Leben gemischt.
Du Danke Gott, wenn er dich preßt,
Und dank' ihm, wenn er dich wieder entläßt.

In drawing breath are graces twain:
Inhaling air, discharging it again:
The former crushing, the latter relieving;
Such a wondrous mixture is living.
Thank thou God when He presses thee,
And thank Him when He releases thee.

I know of no other poem, Western or Eastern, that seizes the essence of Islam as easily and at the same time with such rich ambiguity as Goethe's succinct, poetically elegant 'Talismans'. This last stanza alone contains a whole library of Muslim scholarship. Yet Goethe had encountered, in the sources that were available to him, only hints at most that his own observation of the human mind's systole and diastole is one of the central topoi of Sufi theological philosophy. The Arabic technical term for it is the expression *qabḍ wa-basṭ*, which can be translated as 'contraction and expansion', but just as fittingly as Goethe's 'contracting, expanding; gathering, releasing; binding, loosing; *rétrécir* and *développer*, etc.' Inspired by verse 2:245 – 'God draws together and spreads out' – the Sufis have given the alternation of contraction and expansion a permanent place in the succession of states that a mystic goes through in the course of his forty-day, or forty-year, contemplation. What fear and hope are to the disciple are contraction and expansion to the master – not the apprehension of something that has yet to occur but the experience of God, which takes place in the present, and over which the mystic has no more influence than the breather has over his breath. The heart contracts when the I expands and expands when the I contracts, said the great mystic Bayazid Bestami, who was so filled with God that at the last degree of enlightenment he cried, 'Praise be to me!' Bayazid attained the state that comes after contraction and expansion: annihilation and being – an end of constriction in the complete emptiness of the I, an end of expansion in complete fulfilment in God.

The difference between contraction and expansion is often illustrated with an anecdote about John the Baptist and Jesus: John never laughed, while Jesus never wept; John's breast was always compressed, but Jesus' heart expanded. When they met, John asked, 'O Jesus, are you sure you will never be cut off from God?' Jesus answered, 'O John, do you doubt God's mercy? Your weeping will not change the eternal judgement; nor will my laughter influence providence.' Apparently contradictory declarations of the Prophet Muhammad are explained by saying that he was sometimes in the state of expansion and sometimes in the state of contraction; sometimes enthusiastic, sometimes doubting himself. In keeping with the sense of Goethe's last 'Talisman', of course, the two states are both graces, since each anticipates the other, and expansion would not be possible without the preceding and the subsequent constriction. Sometimes Sufis even favour the contraction, because in it they feel need more strongly, and, with need, the longing for God. In any case, the expected response, the only appropriate reaction, is to thank God both for pressing and for releasing us. The unbelievers, in the language of the Quran, are the *kuffār*, which literally means the ungrateful. Non-belief is understood essentially as an act of ingratitude. The words that Goethe puts in the Prophet's mouth in his dramatic fragment *Mahomet* precisely express the Islamic world view:

> At every silent spring, under every flowering tree, He meets me in the warmth of His love. How I thank Him – He has opened my breast and taken away the hard husk of my heart so that I may feel His name.[51]

The central importance attached to thanking or praising God in Islam follows from the quranic concept of the world, in which creation not only *was* good originally but still *is* good, at all times and in all places.

In other words, the Quran raises the biblical statement 'And God saw that it was good' (Genesis 1) to a reality that is verifiable at any time, understandable to any reasonable person – indeed, visible, audible, smellable and, not least, tangible in the body with every breath we take:

> Thou seest not in the creation
> of the All-merciful any imperfection;
> Return thy gaze; seest thou any fissure?
> Then return thy gaze again, and again,
> and thy gaze comes back to thee
> dazzled, aweary.[52]

The claim that creation itself, on careful, repeated and persistent examination, shows not the slightest flaw is a tremendous one. In view of the suffering in the world, it undeniably raises the question of theodicy, which was the starting impetus of all theological reflection in Islam. At the same time, it corresponds perfectly with Goethe's view of the world: in the *Theory of Colours* he presents his view that every earthly phenomenon without exception 'must either indicate an original division which is capable of union, or an original unity which admits of division' – that is, a harmony that is not only pre-established but present at all times in all places. This is not merely Goethe's personal conviction: he goes so far as to assert that all 'true observers of nature' must arrive at that same insight – return thy gaze again, and again: 'this is the eternal systole and diastole, the eternal collapsion and expansion, the inspiration and expiration of the world in which we live and move.'[53]

The Sufi parallel to Goethe's notion of systole and diastole as the eternal formula of life is rooted in that moment in the quranic story of the Creation, adapted from Genesis 2:7, in which God breathes His breath into man. In surah 15, verse 28:

> And when thy Lord said to the angels,
> 'See, I am creating a mortal of a clay
> of mud moulded. When I have shaped him,
> and breathed My spirit in him,
> fall you down, bowing before him![54]

The Arabic *rūḥ*, which is usually translated as 'spirit' or sometimes as 'soul', brings the lexical sense of breath with it, since the radical r-ū-ḥ with its many derivatives covers a semantic field that includes 'fresh air', 'breath of wind', 'cooling' and also 'respiration'. 'Let him who would know the divine breath look at the world', wrote the *shaykh al-akbar*, the great master of Islamic mysticism, the Andalusian Muhyiddin Ibn Arabi, who died in 1240 in Damascus:

> The world manifests itself in the exhalation of the All-merciful, with which God expanded the potential contained in the divine names, freeing it from the constricting condition of non-manifestation.[55]

When he wrote of God breathing the spirit or breath into man as the origin of tenderness, Ibn Arabi may have been thinking of the ancient notion, which was current in Islamic culture, of kissing as an exchange of souls: God as the All-loving awakens Man as his beloved by kissing him. In this theory of creation, the question posed at the outset – Who is doing the breathing? – almost answers itself: God is present in man with every breath, breathing through us; He fills us, withdraws, and fills us again. Moreover, the whole universe is the breath of the All-merciful:

> Through the All-merciful Breath God relieves every distress in His creatures. The constriction which overtakes or is found by the cosmos stems from the fact that the creatures' root lies in contraction (*qubḍa*). Everything contracted is constrained (*maḥṣūr*), and everything constrained is confined (*maḥjūr*). But since man comes into existence upon the Divine Form, he finds confinement intolerable. So God relieves that in him through this All-merciful Breath, inasmuch as His breathing is a property of the Love by which He described Himself in the saying, 'I loved to be known.' God makes man manifest through the All-merciful Breath. Hence this Divine Breathing is identical with the existence of the cosmos, and the cosmos comes to know Him as He desired. So the cosmos is identical with mercy, nothing else.[56]

Ibn Arabi not only sees an act of love in divine creation: conversely, he also sees human physical love as an act of creation that stands in a mimetic relation to God's creation of Man. And he relates the moans that a man and a woman emit during their union to the systole and diastole of the human spirit. He does so in the most concrete way conceivable, offering a phonetic analysis of the two consonants produced in moaning: the *hamza*, which represents the glottal stop before a vowel in the Arabic alphabet, and the *hāʾ*, which is always pronounced audibly in Arabic, as an aspiration or an exhalation.

Let us too imagine a lovers' bed: the lovers draw rapid breaths deep into their chests or abdomens, where they hold them for a fraction of a second, or for whole seconds longer than they would in ordinary circumstances, and their muscles contract so vigorously that they produce a glottal stop. The contraction in the ribcage or, at the height of ecstasy, behind the abdominal wall erupts in a loud, voiced exhalation. When we moan in this way, our breath does not simply flow back out through the windpipe and the mouth – it is pumped out as if by an external force. In such a moment of ecstasy, even a person of the purely immanent frame of mind could be seized with what Freud called an oceanic feeling – the sense of being united not only with one's lover but with the surroundings, maybe even with the universe:

> When two lovers kiss ardently, each of them breathes the other's saliva and is penetrated by it. Each one's breath propagates in kissing or embracing in the other, and what they exhale goes through each of the two lovers.[57]

Ibn Arabi is not the only one to say it is the breath of God that we feel in love, and specifically in that moment that in French is called *la petite mort*, although it is the moment that allows us to experience life in its greatest intensity – that is, in Goethean terms, a dying-and-living. Has the connection between Creation and sexuality, cooling breath and divine light, ever been more beautifully and succinctly expressed in verse than in Goethe's 'Blissful Longing', whose outward, literal meaning most Germans have prudishly overlooked?

> *In der Liebesnächte Kühlung,*
> *Die dich zeugte, wo du zeugtest,*
> *Überfällt dich fremde Fühlung*
> *Wenn die stille Kerze leuchtet.*

> In the cooling of nights of love
> Which begat you, where you begat,
> Strange feeling overcomes you
> When the silent candle shines.[58]

Goethe's 'cooling which begat you, where you begat' (*Kühlung, / Die dich zeugte, wo du zeugtest*) is an inspired equivalent for the sense of the Arabic *rūḥ*, the breath God breathes into man. What Goethe evidently did not know, could not have known, since otherwise he would have mentioned it at least in the 'Notes and Essays', is the epithet accorded to Jesus in Islam: *rūḥu llāh* – Spirit or, of course, Breath of God. Jesus is the only prophet to bear this honorific because his breath was able to raise the dead. The connection is the idea that the soul, which even the ancients thought was contained in the breath, rose to the lips at death. It can be reinserted into the body, however, by the life-giving breath of the lover, who awakens the beloved from near death with a kiss. In Islamic mysticism, Jesus became the prototype of the person whose incomparable love makes him a creator and hence, of all people, the most similar to God.

As I said, Goethe cannot have had more than an inkling of the specific position accorded to the Christian prophet in Islamic mysticism. Perhaps the knowledge that Jesus to the Sufis is the Spirit or the Breath of God, *rūḥu llāh*, would have led him to a new personal understanding of the Trinity and fully reconciled him with Christianity. Be that as it may, Goethe understood very well the radical nature of the surrender that Jesus exemplifies to all lovers in the Sufi teaching:

Sagt es niemand, nur den Weisen,
Weil die Menge gleich verhöhnet,
Das Lebend'ge will ich preisen
Das nach Flammentod sich sehnet.

Tell it no one, only the wise,
For the crowd simply jeer,
That vitality will I praise
That yearns to burn to death.[59]

Imagine *we* were dying. If I may generalize from the little I have heard of death and seen of it with my own eyes, our soul does not depart in a final sigh, as the poetic image has it. The breath we draw no longer returns; it remains in the breast – that is death, as far as I can testify: inhaling air, but not discharging it again. Perhaps it was that which anguished Goethe, the observer of nature, the naturalist, the student of medicine, in the sight of people dying: that man's life seems to end in constriction, not in expansion. In Ibn Arabi I found an explanation that Goethe would have liked and that might have given him some metaphysical tranquillity. It is based on verse 39:68, in which God blows the trumpet on Judgement Day – or, more precisely, He does not blow, but breathes, *nafakha* – 'and whosoever is in the heavens and whosoever is in the earth shall swoon.' Ibn Arabi, who knows the Prophet's saying that every death is like a Judgement Day, points out that *nafakha* in this passage does not necessarily mean exhaling but equally denotes inhaling: in the moment of death, God inhales the person's spirit, *rūḥ*; that is why the person seems to hold his or her last breath, and so to die under pressure. In fact, that breath is discharged – but in God; invisibly to the living, the bystanders, the relatives; and the release then is eternal. For when God breathes out – 'then it shall be blown [literally: breathed, *nafakha*] again' – and all creatures shall stand and wait. If we follow Ibn Arabi, it is God who presses Himself at our death, to release Himself only when he wakes us again; and so systole and diastole are more than just the eternal formula of life: they are the formula of eternal life.

'I would like to pray as Moses does in the Quran', wrote the 21-year-old Goethe in his first known remark on Islam: 'Lord, make room in my tight breast!'[60]

— 6 —

FILTH OF MY SOUL

*Kleist and Love**

What is love? The question sounds odd for the beginning of a literary acceptance speech, although – no, not although: *because* it is one of those few questions, perhaps the only one besides the question of death, that has preoccupied every person at least once, or indeed preoccupies everyone constantly, regardless of our origins and beliefs, qualities and propensities. What is love? That is a question that necessarily touches the private sphere, inasmuch as everyone who tries earnestly to answer it is moved by his or her individual, and hence idiosyncratic, experiences. That is something different from the question of death, whose answers are as a rule absolutely free of experience, or in any case are considered to be so in the monotheistic traditions. Love is empirical in the highest degree. Only the strange thing is: the more we – no; generalizations are out of place here, even this early on – the more I experience, the less I know. The longer, deeper, more happily or more painfully I feel it, reflect on it, observe it around me, the harder it is for me to answer the question 'What is love?'

The poets' answers, for all the enthusiasm with which I read them as a young man, satisfied me less as the years went by, and, worse, they misled me, as far as I, the misled, can judge. The poets – and this is a generalization after all, and, to make matters worse, one that literary historians must find grotesque, although it inevitably followed from the distress of the young reader, the beginning reader – the poets, I say, sang of love as a promise.

True, they spoke of suffering, described the biting of their desire, the burning of their jealousy, the beating of their disappointment. And yet

* Acceptance speech on receiving the Heinrich von Kleist Award, Berliner Ensemble, 18 November 2012.

love seemed, above the abyss of despair, of abandonment, of unquenchable yearning, to be the most magnificent, the highest of all human feelings. Human happiness – another word that we think we grasp immediately, and that slips through our fingers for that very reason – happiness seemed to depend inseparably on love – more exactly, seemed to correlate with love, whose fulfilment raises the lover up as elation, levitation, weightlessness, and so brings him closer to Heaven in a physically perceptible way, while love's affliction makes his legs literally so heavy that he can barely drag himself through the day, if he can get up at all from the bed where he lies weighted down against the earth.

In retrospect I have the impression that many poets were speaking not of love but of infatuation, the state of being in love, whose symptoms are so much easier to name – they are documented as early as five thousand years ago as the same empty feeling in the stomach, rapid pulse, rapid mood swings; and in the future, too, it will still be the same follies that lovers commit, the same vows, always sworn for eternity, often kept only a few weeks. Perhaps that is why the poets spoke to me when I too had only known infatuation, the state of being in love. Whether Werther or Hyperion – to name just the two most celebrated lovers in German literature – both of them are portrayed in the initial, and most subjectively dramatic, stage of love.

Of course that is not what is written of the Romantic heroes in so many words; of course to them it's all or nothing, a case of life and, of course, death. But if we consider which expressions and phases of our ordinary lives come closest to the situations that Goethe and Hölderlin describe, it would have to be the first, usually youthful state of being in love. And I believe that the perplexity, derision or even embarrassment that Werther's and Hyperion's endless prostrations, fiery letters and frantic cries of rapture provoke in us certainly have something to do with the perplexity, the derision and the embarrassment with which we recall the prostrations, fiery letters and frantic cries of rapture of our own youthful infatuation. The surrounding society that makes fun of the lovers' liaison may consist of a school class; the thrilling secret trysts may take place in a corner of the schoolyard – to say nothing of the bashful touch, the interminable kiss, the first time, the worshipped body naked before our eyes. Werther's yearning and Hyperion's frenzy are the yearning and frenzy of every person who believes they have found undying love.

Without denying the other dimensions of these novels, including their metaphysical import, I would insist that they are realistic, they are true for our time as well as their own, for every heart that audibly beats with affection, desire and ardour; but the poets refer to a very small segment of what love can be. It is not by chance that pre-bourgeois societies distinguished so sharply between love and the institution of marriage. What they called love was a utopia, a consistently vain wish for a life partnership that would last for years, for decades. When Goethe tells the story of unfulfilled, and unfulfillable, love in *Werther*, he takes his place in this tradition, the tradition of *Romeo and Juliet*, of the Orient's *Leyla and Majnun*. It is also the essential theme of Goethe's *Elective Affinities*, which is a drama not of marriage but of adultery; the conflict it deals with is that between passionate feeling and permanent union. Yet Hölderlin goes one step further in letting his Hyperion's enthusiasm strangely cool once he finally possesses Diotima. To notice this somewhat inconspicuous turn at the end, however, you have to be a more practised reader than I was at my first, still youthful reading of *Hyperion*. Literature, and, in the German-speaking countries, Goethe and Hölderlin in particular, have done much to develop the idea of everlasting enchantment in the close relations of two people in the contemporary nuclear family, which almost inexorably overtaxes and of course deludes them. Most marriages – this is another observation that leaves me confused – seem to fail not because of a lack of love but, because of an excess of expectations.

What divides a husband and wife when they have lived together for many years is the subject of the literature of the bourgeois marriage, which begins in the German-speaking countries perhaps with Jean Paul's *Siebenkäs*, or at the latest with Stifter's *Brigitta*. Love, in the picture that Jean Paul and Stifter paint, looks a great deal more ordinary, duller, often more dreary. The reason is not, or not entirely, that realism had come to German literature in the nineteenth century. It is also because Jean Paul's and Stifter's novels are devoted to an aspect of love that becomes relevant only once marriage for love has become the socially established ideal: namely, the aspect of a togetherness that becomes routine, that naturally becomes more ordinary, duller, often more dreary than the sensations of being in love. The marriage novel, too, upholds the ideal of love when it describes the troubles of husband and wife as a numbing of their feelings, and hence explains their crisis as a lack of affection, of devotion. That love itself can be an abyss, and that an excess of it is destructive – I didn't find that anywhere in literature. But Heinrich von Kleist was not among the poets I read as a young man; or, if I read him, I was not yet able to relate him to my own experience. Today I believe that no one has described the nature of love in German more deeply, broadly, and clear-sightedly than the poet who created the most famous expression of the lover's total bewilderment, Alcmene's 'Ach!' in *Amphitryon*.

That sigh is not simply an expression of pain, lust or longing, like the hundreds and thousands of 'Ach!'s of other poets, which could as well be replaced by words, by a 'You don't say!' or a 'Pity!' Alcmene's 'Ach!' expresses the impossibility of finding any words at all, as László F. Földényi has remarked[1] – the limitation of the language itself, and hence of communication, of understanding. Alcmene, having united with a god (and in Kleist that means, quite concretely, having slept with a god – in other words, having had ineffably good sex), can communicate her experience to no one on earth. How could she? How could ordinary mortals comprehend her celestial experience? It is anything but sentimental, Alcmene's 'Ach!'; it is more like a moan during the act of love, which becomes all the more powerful the less the lovers are able to put their experience into words. Yet Alcmene's 'Ach!' is not a joyous one, as in the ecstatic union of two bodies; it is frightful beyond measure, estranged from herself, discordant with the world. Because she experienced divine love, she is destroyed. 'Save me, ye gods!', Alcmene manages to cry before she expels her wits, her whole existence up to then – I can't help thinking: her life – in that 'Ach!'

I said that, in love, experience and knowledge are diametrically opposed. To be more precise, I should have said *opinion*, not knowledge: as a young man, if my memory does not deceive me, I had much more definite opinions than knowledge about what love is – it was what I felt so irrepressibly when I conceived a literally burning passion for a girl; that, exactly that was love, and nothing else – and woe betide any adult who dared to qualify my joy and my sorrow with sardonically raised eyebrows. The poet Kleist knows too the blaze of youthful, or in any case juvenile, infatuation, of which he tells with such stirring coolness in *The Earthquake in Chile*. Desire seems so much more ambivalent, and more dubious, more narcissistic, when it gradually shifts towards the physical – Jeronimo and Josepha in that story no more suspect it than most people who fall in love for the first time. But Kleist sees it; moreover, he ingeniously describes the depths and, more importantly, the shoals of purely erotic desire in *Amphytrion*, whose hero 'wants to be reflected in a soul / or be reflected in a joyful tear.'[2] Kleist knows the supremacy of sexual passion over reason, the vain ambition of the mere wish to conquer and the murderous hatred of one betrayed; he condenses all of this in 'The Foundling': the lust of Nicolo, who cannot break off a liaison with a significantly older courtesan in spite of his marriage; his ambition to sleep with his own adoptive mother, whom he observes night after night in a bizarre masturbation ritual, naked with a whip in front of the portrait of an earlier lover; the rape of his adoptive mother; and, finally, the hatred of his betrayed adoptive father, who kills Nicolo and, against all urging, refuses absolution before his own execution in order to continue his revenge in the 'deepest pit of Hell'.[3]

Oh yes, love can make a person rise above his own limitations, like the lawyer Friedrich von Trota who defends his client to the point of physical sacrifice in Kleist's story 'The Duel'. Love implies, first and last, 'Motherly Love', of which Kleist created an outrageous image in the anecdote with that title: 'with limbs steeled with wrath and vengeance',[4] a mother grapples with a rabid dog that has attacked her children, lets it maul her, lets it infect her with rabies, until the animal is strangled. But love can also mean the healthy pragmatism of the Marquise of O., or the suspicion of Gustave von der Ried, who shoots his lover because of a false suspicion in 'Betrothal in Santo Domingo', then shoots himself out of shame. Love can engender the raging jealousy of Thusnelda, who baits a full-grown bear to attack her lover in the *Battle of Hermann*. Love can also be the unconditional devotion and even obedience of Kate of Heilbronn, who bears the villainies and the humiliations of Count Friedrich Wetter vom Strahl with an uncomplaining patience that amounts to more than a suggestion of masochistic pleasure. And, then love can be exactly the opposite: the unconditional will to dominate the lover, to rob him of his will, as in *Penthesilea*, and Kleist knows too that the two go hand in hand, that surrender and conquest are mutually dependent. 'Those who love Kate', he wrote in a letter, 'cannot be completely without understanding for Penthesilea; they belong together, like the + and – in algebra, and are one and the same nature, only conceived from opposing points of reference.'[5]

Kleist's *Penthesilea* is the most brutal love drama in the history of German theatre. What begins as an instantaneous love between enemy war heroes ends in madness, death and cannibalism. Penthesilea throws herself on Achilles, after having shot him through the neck – after she has killed him, that is; in the middle of a pack of dogs, she rips the armour from his body and tears open his ribcage with her teeth. Blood drips from her mouth and hands as she finally lets up, leaving her lover so disfigured 'that life and putrefaction won't dispute / Possession of him'.[6] What follows, the only thing that can follow, is the stage direction 'Horrified pause'.

Kleist does not console us that love here has turned into hate. Penthesilea destroys Achilles *because* she loves him. She wants to possess him more than just body and soul, she wants to consume him entirely, and in Kleist that means, quite concretely, she wants to eat his heart. And she does eat it, Kleist leaves no doubt about it: 'She really ate him up, Achilles, for love', he wrote in a letter to his confidante Marie von Kleist.[7] When Penthesilea finally awakens from her frenzy,[8] – no fewer than twenty-six times in the play, Kleist characterizes one or the other of the two lovers as 'frenzied' ['*rasend*'] – when she recognizes Achilles dead before her, she is unable to attribute the deed to herself. As the audience we have no trouble understanding that. What is odder is that she takes it for granted that there were *two* attackers. One, she believes, murdered her lover; another devoured him. She is willing to forgive the murderer; let him escape, she says. She only wants to know who has eaten her Achilles. The murder may have been committed for base motives; that does not trouble her. But whoever 'murdered him when he was dead' must have loved him to have 'courted him with such unholy zeal': Penthesilea can explain cannibalism, the most drastic form of inhumanity, only by love, the highest expression of humanity. 'And every breast that feels is an enigma.'[9] The High Priestess implores Penthesilea to accept the terrible truth that she herself with all her hounds threw herself upon Achilles and – 'Oh my lip trembles to pronounce the word / For what you did.' Penthesilea wants to hear it from her companion Prothoë, but she is likewise unable to put what she saw into words. And exactly that, the unspeakable nature of the deed, tips the scales, so that Penthesilea, stuttering, grasps the truth:

> What! I? You mean I – him?
> Beneath my dogs – ?
> You mean that, with these hands, these little hands – ?
> And with this mouth, these lips that swell with love – ?
> Oh made for such a different service than – !

Penthesilea too is unable to finish the sentence; she cannot bring herself to utter even Alcmene's 'Ach!' 'You lie!' she says once more, and then, as if it were the only possible explanation: 'Did I kiss him to death?' Finally Penthesilea realizes that none other than she herself did the unspeakable. Yet she stammers as if to proffer excuses,

> – So it was a mistake. A kiss, a bite,
> The two should rhyme, for one who truly loves
> With all her heart can easily mistake them.

But then, when she kneels down before the body, she does not beg dead Achilles to forgive her; as a lover she knows what her lover would do: 'You forgive me!' And before she drives the dagger into her breast (the text does not say she does it out of shame, but to 'follow him, this youth' – that is, to be united with him in death) she rejects her own excuse of having acted in madness. She who could not stand the sight of a slain animal, she who 'would not crush or kick the mottled worm /

that chanced to play beneath her hovering heel',[10] she, 'this wondrous woman', as Achilles called her, 'half grace, half fury'[11] – Penthesilea confesses that she devoured her lover while fully conscious.

> How many a maid will say, her arms wrapped round
> Her lover's neck: I love you, oh so much
> That if I could, I'd eat you up right here;
> And later, taken by her word, the fool!
> She's had enough and now she's sick of him.
> You see, my love, that never was my way.
> Look: When my arms were wrapped around your neck,
> I did what I had spoken, word for word;
> I was not quite so mad as it might seem.[12]

Does the scene that Kleist shows – no, he doesn't show it; even he thought it impossible that he would ever see the play performed and, by his own testimony, did not write it for the stage – does the scene in *Penthesilea* that Kleist unfolds only before our inner eye correspond to anything in ordinary life, as the marriage novel evidently did, and as I claimed earlier that the classical love stories also did? Under the heading 'Miscellany', certainly, the newspapers occasionally mention cases of cannibalism; I remember one in particular in which the accused described his act as a labour of love. But that's not what I mean. Literature as I understand it can treat of extremely violent or especially odd, seemingly absurd, arcane, foolish, obsessive or simply unbelievable occurrences – Heinrich von Kleist himself was an attentive reader of the 'Miscellaneous' columns in the newspapers. But literature, for which Kleist is a touchstone, is not concerned with the preposterous. It uses such occurrences to shed light on the extreme, the violent, the absurd, the foolish, the inscrutable, the obsessive and the unbelievable in our own souls, in every soul. 'Don't be frightened, it is readable', Kleist continues in his letter about *Penthesilea*; 'Perhaps you would have done the same under similar circumstances.'

No one who is in his or her right mind will ever be in danger of eating his or her lover. But most people have certainly been driven out of their minds at least once by love. And they should remember that there were other undertones then besides noble, bright, selfless feelings. Perhaps they would not admit it in a public address, but at least they would admit to themselves that in love they also pursued possession, power and vanity, just as Penthesilea could have possessed, but did not want to possess, her Achilles while she was still his prisoner – she wanted first to vanquish him, dominate him, bind him to her forever, and so she unleashed the tragedy by an excess of desire.

Is it my fault that on the battlefield
I have to court his feeling with a sword?
When I assault him, what is it I want?
Is it to throw him headlong into Orcus?
All that I want, eternal gods in heaven,
Is but to draw him down upon this breast![13]

And just as Penthesilea devours her lover in her ecstasy, absorbs him bodily, ordinary people too may have the overwhelming impression, in the ecstasy that physical love bestows on them, of being united bodily with their partner, of disintegrating into *her* or absorbing *him*. It is a borderline area or, more accurately, a border-crossing area of human experience which Kleist describes so precisely and so universally – but it is an area of *experience*. 'It is true, my innermost essence is in it', Kleist wrote of *Penthesilea* in another letter to Marie – 'all the filth and splendour of my soul'.[14]

It is characteristic of Kleist's reception that his first editor, Ludwig Tieck, replaced the word '*Schmutz*', filth, with '*Schmerz*', pain: all my soul's pain. Literature must not be filthy, or, as Goethe politely wrote to keep Kleist away: 'I cannot yet warm to Penthesilea. She is of such a wonderful race, and moves in such a strange region, that I must take time to reconcile myself to both.'[15] In the nineteenth century in any case I find nothing that describes the violence of sexuality as unreservedly and as drastically as Kleist's *Penthesilea*, and, even with reference to recent decades, examples from film occur to me more readily than from literature. One would have to go farther back to find anything comparable, to classical tragedy of course, which Kleist builds on so differently, so much more persuasively than German classicism: that is where he got it, both the motif of god-eating and the gods' deadly love.

But not only there. It is certainly no coincidence that Kleist compares Achilles the lover with Christ:

Oh gods, these bloody roses!
Oh gods, this wreath of wounds around his head![16]

He also outfits the devouring near the end of the tragedy with clear allusions to the Last Supper: eating flesh, drinking blood. These have received less attention in German literary studies than his references to Greek tragedy; Kleist's understanding of love is so biblical that he would provoke a scandal in the pulpit. 'For love is strong as death', says the Song of Songs, and 'jealousy' – jealousy! – 'is cruel as the grave' – as the grave!

the coals thereof are coals of fire, which hath a most vehement flame.
Many waters cannot quench love, neither can the floods drown it.[17]

If we take these words as seriously as Kleist himself did in his life, in his loves, in his very last letters before his joint suicide with Henriette Vogel – love as strong as death, jealousy as cruel as the grave, and a fire so vehement that no water can quench it – and place the Song of Songs in the context of the passionate, sometimes violent, always sexually connoted relations that connect – we might as well say chain together – the Creator with His creatures in the Old Testament, in the Revelation of John and even in the Sermon on the Mount, nothing remains of a *loving* God, and nothing at all of a *virtuous* faith. In the Bible, after all, it is not only Solomon's Song of Songs that tells of the love between God and the people of Israel in marvellously tender, yet undisguised erotic images. It is also the book of Hosea, which is probably more representative of the whole text, in which God the jealous Lover rages so terribly that He not only chastises His beloved, the people of Israel, but strips her naked and assaults her before her lovers' eyes: 'None shall deliver her out of mine hand', roars the loving God, and, after the rape, it is certainly not with passion that the people stammer: 'Come, and let us return unto the Lord: for he hath torn, and he will heal us; he hath smitten, and he will bind us up.'[18] Love affairs such as these, which the Bible recorded two to three thousand years ago, are more real, more steeped in experience than all the romances written since – not just painful, but filthy. In a letter to his friend or lover Ernst von Pfuel, Kleist wrote:

> How we flew to each other's arms a year ago in Dresden! How the world opened up immensely, like a racetrack before our tempers trembling in the desire of competition! And now we lie, fallen upon one another, our gaze completing the course to the finish, that never seemed as glorious as now, shrouded in the dust of our fall![19]

The God of the Bible is not nice; He is choleric, wrathful, vengeful and murderous; He is magnanimous, merciful, tender and protective; frenzied is the God of the Bible – no less than Penthesilea and Achilles, He is frenzied with love. And the people of the Bible, too, do not love as people do in the soaps; they love immoderately; they are devoted to their Lord literally with body and soul; they are submissive, but also rebellious; they court the Lord when He withdraws and revile Him when He mistreats them; they find endless new words to sue for their Lover's affection. That makes the Bible great – great to unbelievers too: it tells not of the supernatural but of the full spectrum of earthly experience, and so goes beyond what is familiar, comfortable, pleasant. The Bible is divine inasmuch as it is human in the extreme. That is what also makes Kleist's poetry great, what makes it, here and there, divine. It is what German literature lacks most sorely today.

I will return once more to Alcmene's famous sigh, which I compared, not at all arbitrarily, with moaning in the act of love. In the Arabic language, sighing and moaning can be denoted by the same word: *tanaffus*. I mention this because the Islamic mystics, and in particular the Arabs among them, were great experts on sighs and can contribute to a closer hearing of Alcmene's 'Ach!' Ibn Arabi, the most famous Sufi in the history of Arabic philosophy, was the author of a veritable theology of sighing. 'When the passion of love is fulfilled in the act, the lovers breathe pleasantly into each other', Ibn Arabi wrote in the early thirteenth century in his *Meccan Revelations*, 'and deep sighs can be heard; their breath flows out in such a way that it forms the image of the beloved in the lover.'[20] Now this sigh that is at the same time a moan is written in Arabic in two letters: *hamza*, which denotes a glottal stop between two vowels (as in 'uh-oh'), and *hāʾ*, which always denotes an aspirated /h/, almost a /kh/: *oaaakh*. On the sequence of sounds that make up moaning, Ibn Arabi remarks that *hamza* and *hāʾ* are the two consonants whose place of articulation is deepest. At the physical level, these two consonants express a movement of the heart, because they are glottal sounds or, more accurately – Ibn Arabi corrects the phoneticians – pectoral sounds, which people produce when they breathe in their natural state – that is, before they learn language or when they have lost the ability to speak. 'The deep sigh that this produces is directly connected with the heart, which is the place where the sound is produced and, at the same time, the place where it is propagated.'[21] On the origin of this breath become sound, Ibn Arabi writes:

> When the lover, as the situation demands, takes on a form, he likes to moan, for the path of the pleasure desired follows this outward-flowing breath. This deep breath escaped from the source of divine love and passes through the creatures, for by it the true God would make Himself known to them so that they may recognize Him.[22]

In the sigh of sexual ecstasy – we can, we must understand Ibn Arabi in this sense – in the sigh that is at the same time a moan, God is breathing through the lovers. He is physically present in humans – the only comparable occasion in Christianity is the Eucharist. The association is still stronger in the original, since Arabic derives the words for 'soul' (*nafs*), 'breath' (*nafas*) and this 'deep sigh or moan' (*tanaffus*) from a single root, *nafusa*, so that they are inseparably linked in the minds of the speaker and the hearer. Even in the literal sense, then, moaning, as the strongest, the audible form of exhalation, escapes, flows out, from the soul. And that, exactly that, is how I imagine Alcmene's sigh: not as a sentimental 'Ach!', as in 'Ah me!' or 'Oh, heavens!', but as a low moan erupting from deep in the chest, coming from the soul, escaping, flowing: *oaaakh.*

All I have to do is imagine that Alcmene really dies with this 'Ach!' – no one dies with a cute little high-pitched startled cry. At least, the saints whose deaths are reported, whose deaths the novel *Dein Name* is concerned with, exhale the air to form a last sigh without inhaling it again. In the end, breath has no return. So if you, if ever again in a German theatre, perhaps on this very stage, you hear an Alcmene cry out a short, sassy 'Ach!', then please remember that that is not what is meant, cannot be meant, in that situation, and, for your inner ear, imitate a moan such as you would hear in a bed that could also be a deathbed.

What is love? In his *Meccan Revelations* Ibn Arabi writes that love can be a burning desire and erotic arousal. Love can be rapture, pain, howling, gloom, a wound, consumption, craving, fidelity – its forms, he writes, are innumerable. Love can take the form of withering, wilting, extreme bewilderment, longing, ecstasy, deep sighing – and Ibn Arabi devotes a separate chapter to each individual aspect. Then, however, a few pages further on, he narrates the following anecdote, naturally declaring it to be true:

> A man in love went one day to a religious leader, a sheikh, who talked to him about love. The visitor began to melt, to turn to liquid and drip down like water. His body dissolved completely, diminished to a thin wet film, and dwindled away before the sheikh. At that moment, a friend of the sheikh's came in and found no one with him. The friend asked, 'Where is so-and-so?' – 'There he is', answered the sheikh, and, pointing at the puddle, he explained to his friend the condition of that lover.[23]

I think Heinrich von Kleist would have liked this anecdote. And just like Ibn Arabi, I think, he naturally would have considered it true and reported it under the heading 'Miscellany' in his newspaper, the *Berliner Abendblätter*. Love, in the myriad forms it takes in Kleist's poetry, has nothing to do with happiness – that other word whose meaning slips through our fingers – unless in hindsight, or in the future. With the exception of the enchanted Alcmene, who awakens in greater despair from her sexual rapture, only two people in Heinrich von Kleist's complete works are happy. They are Michael Kolhaas, when he is being led to his execution, and the Prince of Homburg, when he agrees to his execution. 'Enter happiness?' reads a passage that Kleist struck out of *The Ghonorez Family*:

> Enter happiness? You can't, old man, it's bolted from inside. Come along. There's a devil behind you, he'll be cracking his whip soon, we're almost there.[24]

— 7 —

THE TRUTH OF THEATRE

The Shiite Passion Play and Alienation

When Peter Brook undertook his voyages of theatre exploration all across Africa and Asia in the 1970s, he encountered the Shiite passion play in Iran. Called *taziyeh-shabih*, or simply *taziyeh*, which means more or less 'condolence', it commemorates the martyrdom of Imam Hussein, a grandson of the Prophet. 'I saw in a remote Iranian village one of the strongest things I have ever seen in theatre', Brook later said in an interview:

> A group of four hundred villagers, the entire population of the place, sitting under a tree and passing from roars of laughter to outright sobbing – although they knew perfectly well the end of the story – as they saw Hussein in danger of being killed, and then fooling his enemies, and then being martyred. And when he was martyred the theatre form became a truth – there was no difference between past and present. An event that was told as a remembered happening in history, six hundred years ago, actually became a reality at that moment. Nobody could draw the line between the different orders of reality. It was an incarnation: at that particular moment he was being martyred again in front of those villagers.[1]

Peter Brook is not the only Western director to have come into contact with the Shiite passion play. Jerzy Grotowski and Tadeusz Kantor were also astounded to find in Iran a form of drama that quite naturally ignored the norms and conventions of bourgeois theatre and seemed to anticipate some ideas of the avant-garde. The American researcher Peter Chelkowski has written about the founder of 'poor theatre':

> Grotowski seems to be striving for what have always been the fundamental principles of Ta'ziyeh. The important difference is that Grotowski regarded the theatre as his laboratory and controls intimacy by limitation of space, number and distribution of spectators; his is a chamber theatre.

> Ta'ziyeh, on the other hand, achieves the same goal in enormous spaces and with masses of spectators.[2]

During their heyday in the nineteenth century, the passion plays did indeed draw impressive audiences. In those days, the whole country was dotted with *tekiyehs*, houses specially built for *taziyeh* performances, often splendidly furnished, with capacities of up to twenty thousand. But *tekiyehs* were also set up on village squares, in courtyards and in caravansaries. *Taziyeh* was a social event of the first order that attracted people from all walks of society and captivated them for days on end. The theatres were financed by wealthy merchants and aristocrats who displayed their piety by personally serving and giving refreshments to even the poorest spectators.

To understand the impact of *taziyeh*, we must consider the historical event that it re-creates: the passion of Imam Hussein. On 2 October 680, the first day of the Arab month Muharram, thousands of soldiers of the Umayyad caliph Yazid surround the imam, his family and a small throng of followers near Karbala, now in Iraq, and block their passage to the nearby Euphrates. Hussein has been called away from his reclusive, bookish life in Medina to help the inhabitants of the rebellious city of Kufa, who refuse to pay homage to Yazid. To the followers of Hussein, Yazid's rule is tyranny and a betrayal of the Prophet's message. Hussein waited in vain, however, for the support promised from Kufa. Thus betrayed, he negotiates with the Umayyad general Omar ibn Saad, who presses him to recognize Yazid – but Hussein remains defiant. When fighting becomes inevitable, Hussein – certain of the results of the impending battle, and already weak with thirst – releases his comrades from their oath of loyalty and urges them to flee the impending massacre. Hussein's followers refuse to abandon him, however, and so, on the morning of the tenth of Muharram 680, the imam and seventy-two comrades march to a battle that none of them survives. The women and children are carried off; the Umayyad generals send Hussein's head to the capital, Damascus, as a trophy, where Yazid exhibits it at the eastern gate of the Umayyad mosque. Hussein's body is trampled by the horses' hooves and later buried by the Bedouins of the region.

There is no historical event that moves Shiites more strongly even today than the Battle of Karbala. According to Shiite tradition, all twelve imams of Shia Islam – that is, the religious leaders who are the direct successors of the Prophet – were murdered except the last, the 'Hidden Imam', but only Hussein's fate has become a parable of the world process. He epitomizes pure goodness, justice and innocence, and his resistance stands for all rebellion against oppression and tyranny. Hussein's pain is an expression of the suffering of the human race; his death has become synonymous with humanity's betrayed hope for a better future. No event in Shiite history – least of all the Iranian revolution of 1979 – can be understood without considering the background of the Battle of Karbala.

The symbolism of those events still pervades day-to-day life. If you travel through Iranian cities in summer, you will see big tubs cooled with ice everywhere and locals offering you water. The reason for the almost religious reverence of water is the thirst Hussein suffered at Karbala. The emblem of the Shiites, worn as an amulet or held high as a standard, is the Hand of Abolfazl, Hussein's half-brother, who had his hand struck off during the battle as he was carrying water from the Euphrates to his comrades. When you write a letter in Persian to a friend or a relative, you do not close with 'affectionate regards' or 'love' but sign yourself 'your victim'. The passion of Hussein has become a founding myth in the Shiites' cultural memory. To the Shiites, the betrayal of everything the Prophet stood for, his egalitarian message and his direct successors, and, what is more, his own congregation's failure to come to the aid of the imam at Karbala make up the initial event which determines their interpretation of the subsequent, failed history of the Islamic world under Sunni usurpers – a historic Fall.

As early as four years after the massacre, penitents made a pilgrimage to the battlefield to commemorate the murder of Hussein and to lament their own omission. Over the centuries, rituals developed among the Shiites until 1502, when the first Shiite dynasty, the Safavids, took power in Iran. Now penitence and mourning, which had been practised in private or even in secret under Sunni rule, took on a public, dramatic character, and the rituals grew into spectacular processions with self-flagellation and lamentations by semi-professional singers. The Safavids promoted the ceremonies of mourning for Hussein not least for reasons of power politics: they wanted to bind the Iranians to Shia and foment resentment against the Sunnis, who still made up the majority of the population. To secure the legitimacy of an Iranian–Shiite dynasty, they needed to identify Sunni Islam with the Arabs. The cult of suffering surrounding Hussein was an effective means of doing so, since the passion and martyrdom of heroes form the pre-eminent theme of the Iranian national tradition. According to ancient Iranian beliefs, the first man, Keyumars, also died a redeeming death: all of humanity was said to be born of his sacrificed body. Hussein's martyrdom has a similar redeeming function in popular Shiite religion. Ancient Iranian legends and Zoroastrian ceremonies and laments were combined with the cult of the Third Imam. There had already been a cult of mourning, with processions and songs led by magicians, focusing on the pre-Islamic hero Siyavash. The mixture of Shiite religious themes with Persian national themes in Ashura may have been the reason for the rapid establishment of Shia Islam as the dominant religion in Iran. After all, Hussein is not only the grandson of the Arab Prophet but is also supposed to have been the husband of a Persian princess, a point repeatedly emphasized under the Safavid dynasty: in the Safavid ideology, his fate became Iran's fate – and *taziyeh* later became the national drama. But that would not be for over two hundred years yet; the earliest document of a mature Shiite passion play dates from the year 1811.

Researchers have often voiced the suspicion that street battles which took place during the processions in commemoration of the historic Battle of Karbala were used as an opportunity to present other themes of the event. Such explanations seem somewhat strained, however, when we consider the fact, for which there is still no satisfactory explanation today, that the passion play is not documented until nearly two hundred years after the development of its themes and the formation of the cult of Hussein, but then – once it had come into existence – it reached full development and became a mass spectacle throughout the entire country within just one or two decades. *Taziyeh* cannot be said to be the product of a continuous development, and the 'leap' in the history of Iranian theatre shows startling parallels with the rise of the Christian passion play in the Middle Ages, which scholars have tried in vain to present as part of the continuous development of Western theatre.

Since the late 1960s, Western researchers have studied the Shiite passion play not only with regard to its historical and religious implications but increasingly in connection with the aesthetics of drama. Again and again they have emphasized its cathartic effect: the fact that *taziyeh* puts the religious spectators in a state of utmost emotional sympathy and suspense and then sends them home released and relaxed. The overwhelming appeal of the passion plays is described in numerous travel accounts of the nineteenth and early twentieth centuries and moved Count Joseph Arthur de Gobineau to compare the Shiite passion play with Greek tragedy.[3] More recently, William O. Beeman wrote about the 'powerful catharsis of emotion' produced by *taziyeh*.[4] And Elias Canetti remarked, in what is probably the most broadly influential description of the Shiite rituals of mourning, 'The frenzy which seizes the mourning crowds during this festival is almost inconceivable.'[5]

Without denying its emotional effect on the spectators, Western and Iranian researchers alike also relate *taziyeh* to the concept of alienation.[6]

In doing so, however, they entirely neglect, as far as I can see, the fact that alienation and catharsis are two aesthetic categories which, while they are not mutually contradictory, are not commonly juxtaposed in theatre theory, except perhaps as alternatives. The expectation that theatre should effect a catharsis in the spectator is generally attributed to Aristotle, while alienation is a key device in Brecht's 'epic theatre', which uses its anti-illusionistic effect (Brecht's *V-Effekt* or alienation effect) to prevent the spectator from taking an attitude of unreflected sympathy. Brecht rejected, more vehemently than anyone else perhaps, any element of catharsis as Aristotle describes it; that was one reason why he explicitly called his dramaturgy non-Aristotelian. The scholarship on *taziyeh*, however, does not refer to alienating devices in general but sometimes refers specifically to the alienation effect as described by Brecht.[7] Ambiguous or vague terminology can impede our understanding of the theatrical aesthetics of *taziyeh*: if we represent it as a model of the Brechtian epic theatre, problems arise as soon as we consider the effects of the performances, which are opposite to the rational, didactic effect that Brecht intended. The catharsis observed seems to contrast with the style of representation and with an essential stylistic device of *taziyeh*, alienation. How can this paradox be explained?

The classical definition of alienation is Brecht's own: '*Verfremdung* estranges an incident or character simply by taking from the incident or character what is self-evident, familiar, obvious in order to produce wonder and curiosity.'[8] An abrupt, conspicuous deceleration or acceleration of an action can suffice to produce such an alienation: a hand reaching into a pocket goes unnoticed; but if done in slow motion, it attracts attention and produces expectation. One of the most important devices that seem to produce an alienation of natural and familiar elements in *taziyeh* is the conscious, ostentatious maintenance of the distance between actor and role. The actor does not try to empathize with the role in the psychological sense but, instead, intentionally limits himself to simply representing the character. Possibly the most distinct sign of this strategy is that the actor often holds a script in his hand – even illiterate *taziyeh* actors do this. This prevents from the outset the illusion by which the audience treats the action on the stage as real events. Brecht's statement, in the *Short Organon*, that the appraisal 'He didn't act Lear; he was Lear' would be a crushing blow to the actor of epic theatre[9] is no less true of *taziyeh* actors. Brecht's dictum that the actor of epic theatre only quotes a character without ever identifying with the character[10] is an exact description of the style of acting used in *taziyeh*. Just as Brecht felt it was possible for the actor to develop different feelings from those of the character he or she portrays – that the actor can and must be able to express the idea that what the character believes is not true and what the character does is reprehensible – in *taziyeh* it happens that, while playing Yazid killing his victim, the actor at the same time comments on Yazid's actions, condemning and lamenting them.

Anti-naturalism and anti-illusionism characterize not just the acting but the whole production. As in the epic theatre, no attempt is made to hide the technical and dramaturgical aids, such as costume racks, prop boxes, the orchestra and the lighting. Brecht's argument for this rejection of illusion could also be applied to *taziyeh*: 'No one would expect the lighting to be hidden at a sporting event, a boxing match for instance.'[11] Furthermore, there is no backstage in *taziyeh*. The actors never leave the performing area; when they appear in a scene, they simply step forward. Naturally that recalls modes of performance that were considered new and experimental in Western theatre especially in the 1960s. The sets and the props are multifunctional and limited to the bare minimum, in keeping with Brecht's principle that everything that is on stage must perform and that whatever does not perform does not need to be on stage. A table can function as a throne in one scene of the passion, as a hiding place in the next, and as a bier shortly thereafter. Realism is not sought after either in the set design or in the costumes. In the time of British hegemony, the villains were often dressed in British officers' jackets; in later decades they wore sunglasses. The envoys of the Byzantine Empire wear European clothes and hats. The River Euphrates is represented by a bucket of water; a heap of straw denotes the desert sand; and, when the angel Gabriel holds an umbrella in his hand, everyone knows he has just arrived from Heaven.

The role of the director in *taziyeh* strongly recalls that of the *Spielleiter* in the epic theatre, the 'auctorial narrator', as Brecht called him in the *Caucasian Chalk Circle*. In both forms of theatre, the director has control over the plot sequence and can rearrange it, comment on it, suspend the temporal continuity and so interrupt the plot, or weave another narrative thread into the action on the stage simply by announcing it. 'He intervenes quite openly in everything that happens on stage and makes no attempt to keep his directing invisible to the audience', a German missionary reported in the 1930s after attending a *taziyeh*.[12] Always on stage, script in hand, the director gives the individual actors their cues, prompts them, corrects their declamation if necessary, and lends them a hand: he may draw the hero's sword for him, for example, if the hero has no hand free, or wrap him in his shroud when the situation is hopeless. At times the director interrupts the performance, speaks to the people, comments on the scene in progress, encourages the spectators to sympathize, praises scenes that are particularly well done, apologizes for mishaps, recites prayers, or supplements the action on the stage with related stories.

One anecdote that reveals something about *taziyeh* theatrics tells of a police constable who played a lion. When he discovered his superior officer on stage in another costume, he immediately raised his lion's paw in a salute, all the while crouching on all fours. This story is only amusing to Western observers: to *taziyeh* spectators, in the context of the *taziyeh* conventions, the constable's behaviour is completely normal and legitimate: just as Brecht stipulated for the actor of epic theatre, a *taziyeh* actor cannot slip out of character because he is not identified with the character in the first place. His performance is not affected by people changing sets on stage at the same time, for example, or drinking tea, which is not unusual, or by the director handing him a prop during a scene. Such occurrences correspond exactly with the alienation effects Brecht mentions in his description of a Chinese theatre performance he attended in Moscow in 1935. In some respects, *taziyeh* applies alienation even more earnestly than Brecht, as for example when an actor goes to the edge of the stage during a scene, takes a drink of something, and returns – not because it is part of the action, but because the actor is thirsty. In this regard, *taziyeh* is more logical, for, while Brecht might have incorporated such an act to underscore the fictionality of the scene, it would have been a consciously applied device; in *taziyeh*, on the other hand, it takes place naturally, without intention, without reflection: when an actor is thirsty, he drinks.

Alienation effects can be observed not only in the production and performance itself but also in the texts, starting with the prologue and epilogue, which are practically obligatory in *taziyeh* as well as in Brecht. A characteristic text element is the prayer for the producer which the actor who plays Hussein in the play *The Martyrdom of Imam Hussein* speaks before he is beheaded: 'Pardon the organizer of this assembly, O God of All Worlds, for the love of the King of the Thirsty.'[13] In another play, a stage direction requires the Umayyad commander Omar ibn Saad, who in the story jumps his horse over a ditch, to 'dismount and run with the horse'. That is to say, the obstacle is indicated neither by a realistic ditch nor by any piece of scenery, but by the horseman suddenly stopping and beating on the horse as if he wanted to make it jump. The horse, by the way, may be just a stick – but it could just as well be a live animal if one is available.

Time and space are varied arbitrarily in the plays; the action shifts from one setting to another without a change of sets and often within a continuous scene. In a drama about Muslim ibn Aqil, a cousin of Imam

Hussein who is sent ahead to Kufa, the following verses are set in three different locations, but spoken without any division in the text or interruption in the action:

Hussein says to Muslim (in Medina):
Go; may God keep and help you,
And the blood of victory accompany you on your way.
Muslim says to the messenger (in Kufa):
I address my words to you, O well-meaning messenger.
Bring the Kufans news of my arrival,
Tell all the beloved, the light of my Lord's eye is come,
Hussein's representative, helper and cousin is come.
Thereupon the messenger says to the Kufans (at another place in Kufa):
Be notified, O Kufans, full of lamentation,
To Kufa is come the representative of Imam Hussein.[14]

Another practice reminiscent of Brecht's dramatic techniques is the *taʾliq* – that is, the interruption of the action in those plays that do not show the passion of Hussein: scenes that have a parallel with the events in Karbala are interrupted by the entrance of Gabriel, who recalls those events and calls for compassion with Hussein's family. Then, with no transition, the plot resumes.

Many other alienating practices in *taziyeh* can be mentioned: the heroes recite verse while the villains speak prose; female characters are played by men (or vice versa in women's *taziyeh*); little boys are preferred for the parts of the victims; actors wear masks; there is no fourth wall. All of these are in keeping with Brecht's instructions and conceptions. And yet *taziyeh* is not a model of epic theatre, much less a form of theatre that Brecht intended but never attained, as some researchers have called it. This can be shown with reference to the concept of catharsis.

Many Western observers of *taziyeh* have described the tremendous magnitude of the event. Like the dramatic performances of classical antiquity, *taziyeh* performances, at least in the nineteenth century, went on for several days. With the sunrise as entrance music, the passion play proper was preceded by at least two hours of dances, prayers, sermons, songs and storytelling. People smoked water-pipes; cakes soaked with musk or lozenges in the form of a seal from the soil of Karbala were served. To ease the flow of tears, the spectators chewed mastic or ate millet, for, according to Shiite folk belief, every person must have wept at least one tear for Hussein. And many tears flowed – it is not for nothing that the director and manager in *taziyeh* is titled *mo'in-e bokāʾ*, 'the weeper's aide'. Furthermore, it was not unusual for spectators to tear their clothes or beat themselves bloody with grief. One of the responsibilities of the director was to incite the audience to lamentation by gestures of mourning. To heighten their compassion, he sometimes cast children in the roles of the victims and had the scenes accompanied by instrumental music or by chanting choirs of boys or women. *Taziyeh* is a form of theatre that relies on an extreme degree of impact, and the success of a performance is directly proportional to the degree of emotional arousal. 'If the success of a drama is to be measured by the effects which it produces upon the people for whom it is composed, or upon the audiences before whom it is represented', the British officer Sir Lewis Pelly remarked in the late nineteenth century, 'no play has ever surpassed the tragedy known in the Mussulman world as that of Hasan and Husain.'[15]

The spectators' feelings reach a first high point before the actual performance when the flagellants enter. Gobineau's account shows clearly how far removed *taziyeh* is from Brecht's political, didactic theatre:

> They enter the *tekiyeh* in a procession, intoning, quite slowly at first, a litany consisting of just these two names: Hassan! Hussein! Hassan! Hussein! The tambourines accompanying them beat faster and faster. Those who carry the cymbals beat them together in time, and all of them begin to dance. The audience spurs them on, beating their breasts . . . After a short time the flagellants begin to beat themselves with their chains, first gently and with visible caution, then more vigorously and harder; those who carry needles begin to pierce their arms and cheeks; the blood flows; the crowd is enraptured and sobs; the excitement mounts, yet, when it grows too great, the leader of the troupe – who is moving through the rows, encouraging the faint and restraining the arms of those whose frenzy is too violent – suddenly stops the music, and everything ceases. It is difficult not to be moved by such a scene; one feels everything at once: pity, compassion, horror. When the dance stops, one sometimes sees penitents raise their arms wrapped in chains towards Heaven and cry with a voice so deep, and with such a commanding and trusting gaze, *Yā Allah!*, that one is struck with amazement and admiration by the transfiguration of their whole being.[16]

These outbreaks of grief are by no means always spontaneous, if by that we mean they strike the participants unpredictably. In the interaction between spectators and actors, the weeping, the extravagant moaning, wailing, lamentation and compassion are essential for the dramatic act; they are part of the ritual play. The French archaeologist Jane Dieulafoy, who travelled in Western Iran in 1881 and 1882, observed in Qazvin how the outpourings of grief at *taziyeh* are provoked according to plan and delivered at the right times by the spectators, who in this regard are an integral part of the performance.

> During the most emotional moments, the sobs of the actors join those of the crowd, and even the traitor, whose face is covered by a hood, weeps and wails on account of his villainy and the injustice he has committed. The women let out cries of pain and words of sympathy for the victims; they beat their chests and shoulders, and once they have sufficiently drawn out these expressions of emotion and sympathy, they suddenly calm down and resume the cheerful conversations they had interrupted only moments earlier. The orchestra, made up of a drum and a trumpet, stands at the corner of the carpet and intensifies the pious howling of the audience with dissonant accents. Not far off, a large man sitting on a wooden throne displays the satisfaction of an impresario presenting the audience with a first-class troupe.[17]

The exhibition and the relativity of the feelings ('they suddenly calm down and resume the cheerful conversations') have no bearing on the 'authenticity' of the experience. Or, to put it another way, the experience, the grief, the penitence are genuine – not in the everyday sense, but in the sense of theatre, of theatrical reality. The participants in a *taziyeh* – actors and spectators alike – know that they will weep when Hussein is killed, but that does not lessen the intensity of the emotion. A comparison with actors (in the conventional European, non-Brechtian sense) may illustrate what I mean: although an actor is, ideally, utterly filled and overwhelmed with the feeling of love at the moment he is displaying affection, he knows the whole time on a second level of consciousness that he is on stage and must say and do certain things so that the performance can proceed as planned and rehearsed. That these two levels of consciousness coincide does not prevent a talented actor from having a pure, spontaneous experience, nor does a sudden shift to a new situation (at the beginning of the next act, for example) inhibit his complete empathy with the character. Because this simultaneous unity and difference between the play and reality is a common occurrence in theatre – indeed, the very essence of acting – and yet a tremendously difficult one to realize, it is no wonder that a great director such as Peter Brook emphasized precisely this aspect of *taziyeh* ('. . . sitting under a tree and passing from roars of laughter to outright sobbing – although they knew perfectly well the end of the story . . . an incarnation'). In his book *The Empty Space*, Brook describes another formative experience which fits uncannily with his recollection of *taziyeh*. In the ruins of Hamburg at the end of the Second World War, he saw a performance of Dostoevsky's *Crime and Punishment*:

> By sheer necessity, all problems of theatre style vanished: here was the real main stream, the essence of an art that stems from the story-teller looking round his audience and beginning to speak. All the theatres in

> the town had been destroyed, but here, in this attic, when an actor in a chair touching our knees began quietly to say, 'It was in the year of 18— that a young student, Roman Rodianovitch Raskolnikov . . .' we were gripped by living theatre.
>
> Gripped. What does that mean? I cannot tell. I only know that these words and a soft serious tone of voice conjured something up, somewhere, for us all. We were listeners, children hearing a bedside story yet at the same time adults, fully aware of all that was going on. A moment later, a few inches away, an attic door creaked open and an actor impersonating Raskolnikov appeared, and already we were deep in the drama. The door at one instant seemed a total evocation of a street lamp; an instant later it became the door of the money-lender's apartment, and still a second later the passage to her inner room. Yet, as these were only fragmentary impressions that only came into being at the instant they were required, and at once vanished again, we never lost sight of being crammed together in a crowded room, following a story. The narrator could add details, he could explain and philosophize, the characters themselves could slip from naturalistic acting into monologue, one actor could, by hunching his back, slip from one characterization to another, and point for point, dot for dot, stroke for stroke, the whole complex world of Dostoevsky's novel was recreated.[18]

The grief that the spectators cry out points to the existential heart of *taziyeh* as a society's confrontation with death, to the collective attitude towards the ubiquity of the negative, the negating, in the vale of tears that is human life. 'The living vent on the dead their despair that they no longer give thought to themselves', Horkheimer and Adorno remarked on the Western attitude towards death in their notes on the *Dialectic of Enlightenment*. To them, the 'disturbed relationship to the dead – who are forgotten and embalmed' – was one of the symptoms of 'the sickness of experience today'. Grief, they wrote, is becoming 'the stigma of civilization, an asocial sentimentality which reveals that human beings have not yet been made to swear absolute allegiance to the realm of purposes.' Remembering the worst curse of the old Jews – 'to thee shall no thoughts be turned' – they state:

> Only when the horror of annihilation is raised fully into consciousness are we placed in the proper relationship to the dead: that of unity with them, since we, like them, are victims of the same conditions and of the same disappointed hope.[19]

By suffering with Hussein, the spectators reject the whole mediocrity of life; they wholeheartedly express their feelings, their disappointment, the pain they repress in their day-to-day lives, drawing it forth from the deepest recesses of their soul, and then go away cleansed and liberated.

Just as in Aristotle's conception, the cathartic effect of the passion play requires a specific act of empathy – empathy not with the individual actor but with the overall action on stage. That makes the boundaries between stage and auditorium permeable; the performers talk to the audience; the audience intervenes in the plot. When Hussein is about to be murdered, for example, the spectators jump up and volunteer to die in his place. They suffer guilt feelings and physical torment at having to look on helplessly as the imam is slaughtered. They tear their shirts, beat their breasts and cry out with horror. Sometimes the action arouses them so strongly that they try to lynch the actor portraying Yazid, heedless of his protest that he isn't really Yazid. This, of course, is a violation of the *taziyeh* conventions, as it means the second level of consciousness, the knowledge that the actors are only playing the historic characters, has been suspended, and it is sanctioned accordingly – as in classical antiquity, when tragic poets could be fined if they incited the people to excessive states of frenzy and grief. A certain ecstasy is required for catharsis; this was obvious to the ancient Greeks, only it was not allowed – nor is it in *taziyeh* – to override the symbolic character of the event and give rise to *real* acts.

Before Aristotle, Plato mentions catharsis in the *Phaedrus* as the second of four kinds of *thea mania*, and the medical connotation that the word has in that context (referring to the act of purging, eliminating an irritant) resonates later in Aristotle. *Taziyeh*-goers too feel both exhausted and liberated after the performances, as my older relatives reported, nostalgically recalling the great *taziyeh* extravaganzas they had attended in Isfahan. After having given up rational self-control for a certain time and given free rein to subconscious feelings, experiencing grief, anger and shame, they go home in an easy, relaxed mood – quite like that of the tragedian, if what Peter Brook observed in his many decades of theatre work is true:

> Any actor in his dressing-room after playing a tremendous, horrifying role is relaxed and glowing. It is as though the passage of strong feelings through someone engaged in strong physical activity is very healthy. I believe it is good for a man to be an orchestral conductor, good for him to be a tragedian: as a race, they seem consistently to reach a ripe old age.[20]

This experience, which is in part physical, is one of the reasons why people love *taziyeh* and why it was able to grow so rapidly in the nineteenth century, becoming a mass spectacle within just a few years. Most theologians must feel that many spectators seek not religious edification but the sensual discharge of urges and feelings – the same cathartic ecstasy that the ancient Greeks analysed. And that is no doubt one reason why some of the Shiite clergy reject this facet of popular piety. For, after all, the emotions of which Aristotle wrote and that *taziyeh* unleashes – *phobos* and *eleos* – are not the mild philanthropic virtues of 'fear and pity' that Lessing made of them in his *Hamburg Dramaturgy*; in the translation of the classical philologist Wolfgang Schadewaldt,[21] they are elemental emotions: *Entsetzen*, horror, and *gewaltige Rührung*, powerful emotion, 'the affect of grief and compassion that spontaneously seizes a person at the sight of another's suffering – with the accompanying fear that the same could happen to oneself – makes the heart soft and brings tears to the eyes.'[22] *Taziyeh* propels us, not towards the catharsis concept of bourgeois theatre, but towards Antonin Artaud. The visionary French dramatist, who died in 1948, never mentions catharsis explicitly as far as I can see, but without a doubt he accords theatre a cathartic function in writing about 'drastic purification' and about theatre as 'therapy for the soul'.[23]

Artaud's view of the world, which is fundamentally expressed in his concept of *cruauté*, corresponds with the notions and attitudes of Shiite popular piety inasmuch as Shiites define world history as 'a kind of strictness, the fundamental cruelty':[24] Shiite history begins with a martyrdom, and its continuation consists essentially of successive martyrdoms. 'For the people of God, this world is a world of suffering and sorrow; it is indeed the House of Sorrows', writes Mahmoud Ayoub in his brilliant study on Shiite piety.[25] Artaud's words could be used as a defence of the passion play against the proponents of the True, the Good and the Beautiful in religious life and in Iranian culture:

> Thus all great Myths are dark and one cannot imagine all the great Fables aside from a mood of slaughter, torture and bloodshed, telling the masses about the original division of the sexes and the slaughter of essences that came with creation. Theatre, like the plague, is made in the image of this slaughter, this essential division. It unravels conflicts, liberates powers, releases potential and if these and the powers are dark, this is not the fault of the plague or theatre, but life. We do not see that life as it stands and as it has been made offers us much cause for exaltation. It seems as though a colossal abscess, ethical as much as social, is drained by the plague. And like the plague, theatre is collectively made to drain abscesses. . . . It urges the mind on to delirium which intensifies its energy. And finally from a human viewpoint we can see that the effect of the theatre is as beneficial as the plague, impelling us to see ourselves as we are, making the masks fall and divulging our world's lies, aimlessness, meanness and even two-facedness. It shakes off stifling material dullness which even overcomes the senses' clearest testimony, and collectively reveals their dark powers and hidden strength to men, urging them to take a nobler,

more heroic stand in the face of destiny than they would have assumed without it.[26]

When the spectator offers himself for martyrdom ('Kill me! Kill me and spare the innocents!'),[27] he seeks to atone for his inaction and the failure of his co-religionists; he wants to undo the Shiite community's founding experience of having failed to come to the defence of their imam. The spectator becomes – symbolically – a martyr and yet is conscious of his own real helplessness: in this way *taziyeh*, to use a phrase of Artaud's, is an 'appeal through illustration' that can 'return the mind to the origins of its inner struggles'.[28] By touching the spectator's sense of good and evil, our heroism and fear, our love and hate, the stage play 'releases our repressed subconscious' and 'drives us to a kind of potential rebellion'.[29] Their shared experience, remembrance, suffering and symbolic resistance make the participants into a collective of the kind Artaud describes:

> Everything that acts is cruelty. Theatre must rebuild itself on a concept of this drastic action pushed to the limit. Infused with the idea that the masses think with their senses first and foremost and that it is ridiculous to appeal primarily to our understanding as we do in everyday psychological theatre, the Theatre of Cruelty proposes to resort to mass theatre, thereby rediscovering a little of the poetry in the ferment of great, agitated crowds hurled against one another, sensations only too rare nowadays, when masses of holiday crowds throng the streets.[30]

The spectacular outpourings of emotion in *taziyeh*, repulsive to Elias Canetti, who called them a collective psychosis, can be understood in Artaud's terms as symptoms of a theatre plague. Artaud compares theatre with the plague in that it brings with it an eruption of the latent, deep layer of cruelty through which all possible perversions of the spirit can be localized in one individual or one people. The eruption of cruelty in *taziyeh* is not without danger, as the actors who portray the Sunni villains regularly find. They are not only loudly vilified and taunted but also spat on and sometimes physically assaulted. The spectators especially enjoy *Omar-koshān*, the burning of an effigy of the Umayyad commander Omar ibn Saad: this is the high point of a grotesque, brutal scene which lampoons and vilifies Hussein's opponents. The people project all their feelings of hate and disgust onto the imam's murderer and let them out – a kind of utopia that turns the world upside down: 'the past is represented from the viewpoint of the victims in such a way that today's oppressors look pitiful and today's vanquished seem to be the true conquerors of yesteryear', writes Jan Assmann, describing this mechanism of a typical 'counter-history', the consequence of 'contrapresent or counterfactual memory'.[31] The oppressors of the past can be identified with real wielders of power, with dictators, colonialists or simply the major local landowner. Especially in the twentieth century, when it was prohibited, obstructed or at least marginalized by the state, *taziyeh* often took on a distinctly political, oppositional character, and during the Iranian Revolution, which was conceived as an uprising against the Yazid of its time, the month of Muharram (early December 1978) was one of the most intense and important phases.

We should not allow the links between Artaud's theatre of cruelty and the Shiite passion play to obscure the fundamental differences. For example, penitence is critically important in the Shiite religious tradition: the pious believer not only laments the fate of worlds but also ritually atones for the congregation's failure, hoping for redemption. There is nothing in Artaud's world view that corresponds to this attitude. Life is cruel, and human beings must accept it, that is all. They should be 'like those tortured at the stake, signalling through the flames';[32] Artaud does not mention penitence, and least of all redemption. Furthermore, there are unmistakable differences not only in Artaud's ideology or world view, but also in his theatrical concepts. To name just one, Artaud opposes the principle of representation. Theatre should not imitate or represent life but should, in essence, be life: 'there will be no distinct divisions, no gap between life and theatre',[33] and 'Theatre is not an art.'[34] Artaud's theory differs in this respect from Aristotelian drama, which is rooted in mimesis, the most elementary form of representation, and tends towards ritual. It also differs from *taziyeh*, which parades its representative character from beginning to end. Where Artaud sees the audience reaching a frenzy because the virus is transmitted from the actor to the spectator, allowing him to take part in the actor's manic self-experience and 'affective athleticism'[35] (Artaud compares 'actors in pursuit of their sensibility' with plague victims who run screaming after figments of their imagination),[36] the corresponding state in the *taziyeh* audience is brought about by a different process entirely: not by an extreme of sensory impressions but by the conscious use of signs in the semiotic sense. The Polish theatre theoretician Andrzej Wirth has called the passion plays a 'Persian carpet of codes', an allusion to an apt phrase of Roland Barthes;[37] the communication between performer and audience takes place by means of signals governed by a fixed protocol. For example, grief over the death of a beloved person is indicated by beating the forehead, the breast or the thighs; on receiving mournful news, the performer scatters hay on his head; hitting one hand with the other denotes a mistake. When a commander stands on his toes, spreads his arms and shouts loudly, the audience imagines a whole army listening to his speech. When a performer moves very slowly and cautiously, as if he were blind, the brightly lit stage becomes a field in the dark of night. The performer creates bright sunlight by shading his eyes with one hand. The battle scenes are likewise suggested rather than enacted, yet with no loss of dramatic momentum.

All the participants in a *taziyeh* performance share a knowledge that can be described in Jan Assmann's terms as 'mythic': Hussein's murder is not only a concrete historic event; it is also, for the cultural memory of the Shiite community, a founding myth, a source of identification. The *taziyeh* spectators know the plot and all the characters in advance; dramatic suspense in the ordinary sense is irrelevant. The goal is the complete participation of everyone present in the action and, in consequence, the evocation of the founding figures of memory, the confirmation of the collective identity. The performer's task is to awaken the shared memory by quoting characters with their attributes and actions, words or developments; when the actor touches his tongue to his lips, for example, that is enough to call to mind the whole agony of Hussein's situation, the torment of being cut off from the river for days on end in searing heat and dying of thirst. Another example: the passion play reaches its climax not when Hussein dies but as soon as he – aware of his impending martyrdom – puts on the white shroud. The climax is not the action itself; it is the sign that the action will take place. But the martyrdom is also narrated in sophisticated dramaturgical signs. For example, ten warriors of the enemy army come forward, surround Hussein and draw the circle tighter and tighter. When the imam is completely hidden from the spectators, the murderer Shemr steps into the circle to cut off his head. The horrible deed is hidden from the audience. As a signal that the execution has been carried out, some white doves that the warriors have been carrying under their coats fly up into the air – for, according to legend, doves carried the news of Hussein's death to Medina.

It tends to be the spectators – in contrast to Artaud's conception of theatre – who are seized with frenzy: instead of being 'plague-stricken' and 'infecting' the audience, the actors and the action on stage merely cause the outbreak of the 'epidemic'. That the performers and spectators commemorate a historic event by means of a conventional system of symbols, a semiotic code, and share the experience of suffering is the special power of *taziyeh*. Therein lies the difference from Artaud and, at the same time, the impossibility of producing an analogous event in contemporary European theatre. The secular society has no comparable memories and archetypal images consolidated into myths and shared by all people. Perhaps the Holocaust plays a similarly foundational, mythic role in the consciousness of Israeli society, but, in Europe and North America, neither Auschwitz nor Shakespeare is so deeply present to an audience that signs would suffice to produce a shared experience among both actors and spectators. 'The only lay equivalent one could find would be if today, for a big American group, one could dramatize with sufficient intensity the assassination of Kennedy', thought Peter Brook, and corrected himself in the same breath:

> One could touch off in shorthand the kind of very intense feelings that that event aroused; but in a sense, that is not far enough away in history to be comparable, and the relation with a higher level would not be there either.

The miracle of the past becoming present, Brook says, comes about only when the actors can count on and work with the spectators' immediate recognition and understanding of the signs, allusions and references.

> For instance, in Iran the *Ta'zieh* was brought to the Shiraz Festival – which was the most horrifying, because one actually saw how a culture can be destroyed in one night. Taking it and putting it in front of a Western festival audience that was eighty percent uninterested, untraditional, and totally alien to any religious context, you suddenly saw a basic theatre truth: that because one half was there without the other, nothing could happen at all. The deep event disappeared and in its place there was only fancy dress. The audience couldn't receive the shorthand references that trigger a total response like that in the village, where they were living all through the year in a certain structure from dawn to dusk – a structure in which they were still fragmented, but which permitted them, when the shorthand references were there in front of them, to come totally back into an ideal village for two hours: they were there reunited around what was central in their faith.[38]

Of course the cathartic moment is only one of many that constitute *taziyeh* as a form of theatre – especially since the range of themes expanded significantly in the course of the nineteenth century. In addition to the events at Karbala, the increasingly professionalized theatre troupes performed other religious stories, including many Bible stories. They also dramatized legends of the Persian heroic epic and played – sometimes immediately before the most poignant passion plays – folk comedy. Furthermore, the groups no longer limited their performances to Muharram, the month of mourning, but travelled around the country all year round. A secular form of Iranian theatre became established alongside the passion plays, a kind of commedia dell'arte called *ruhozi*, because the performances often took place in courtyards (*rū*) on wooden coverings laid over basins (*hoz*). Older relatives from Isfahan tell me that the appeal of the city's theatre culture, which was still intact up to seventy or eighty years ago, lay in the alternation of *ruhozi* and *taziyeh*, which brought the whole spectrum of human emotion into play – joy and sorrow, grief and merriment, anarchy and piety.

It was primarily the triumph of European theatre that put a rather abrupt end to this development towards an original Iranian, secular theatre. On a trip to Europe in 1873, the monarch Nasser ad-Din Shah became an enthusiastic theatregoer, and in 1886 he had the first proscenium stage opened in Tehran. The first performance was given by an ensemble of European lay actors parroting Persian texts, but soon Iranian actors were performing written Iranian comedies, such as those of Mirza Agha Tabrizi, in the Western fashion. To the new bourgeoisie, with its aspirations to a Western lifestyle, the Muharram processions with their flagellants and passion plays stood for backwardness and superstition. About the middle of the twentieth century, because the ceremonies of mourning were already opposed by the theologians and now lost the support of the political and economic authorities as well, *taziyeh* increasingly became a spectacle for the lower class and the rural population.

Not until the 1970s did many Iranian intellectuals recognize the rich theatrical aesthetics of *taziyeh* after encountering stylistic elements of the domestic theatre tradition in Western avant-garde theatre, or after their attention was drawn to *taziyeh* by travellers such as Peter Brook. Researchers, people working in theatre and cultural officials swarmed out to the villages and wrote essays and books, shot television footage, and founded a *taziyeh* institute in Tehran. They were equally fascinated by the alienation on which the theatrics of the passion play were based and by the catharsis that it can elicit in the spectators. But, to return to our earlier question, how do those go together?

In fact the intended effect of *taziyeh* can be called cathartic in the strict Aristotelian sense. Alienation, however, in the strict sense as a concept of theatre aesthetics, is not found in *taziyeh*. Those who claim otherwise evidently fail to consider the distinction between generally *alienating devices* in theatre – that is, means of breaking the illusion in representation, on the one hand, and the theoretical *concept* of alienation, established notably by Brecht, on the other. Brecht himself distinguished between alienation effects (in classical Greek or in medieval theatre, for example) and the concept of alienation as dialectical insight, in which something familiar, appearing in a new, questionable light, is perceived anew and understood as changeable. Alienation as Brecht used the term serves a certain purpose of social critique; it has 'a combative character'.[39] This specific form of alienation has its theoretical roots in Hegel's description of Socratic irony in his *Lectures on the History of Philosophy*; Brecht developed it into the concept generally used in theatre theory today with reference to dialectical materialism as its thematic basis. Yet alienation effects are also possible when their motives and purposes 'strike us as odd and suspicious', as Brecht put it in reference to Chinese theatre.[40]

Clearly, alienation effects in *taziyeh* need not serve the purposes of social criticism that Brecht put forward. The rulers, at least in the nineteenth and early twentieth centuries, found *taziyeh* a convenient means of directing people's emotions in directions that were innocuous to them. And neither the actors nor the spectators of a *taziyeh* exhibit anything like the distanced, reflective attitude that Brecht wanted to produce in the spectator. The alleged analogies between Brecht's epic theatre and the Shiite passion play do exist, but only on a purely formal level: while *taziyeh* contains remarkable alienation effects as stylistic devices, the concept of alienation in Brecht's theatrical aesthetics has fundamentally different motives, foundations and objectives. The paradox by which *taziyeh* appears to reconcile Brecht with Aristotle dissolves, since the Shiite passion plays do not exhibit alienation in the specific Brechtian sense, which is essentially defined by the purpose of social criticism. But, in addition to its different goals, *taziyeh* differs from Brecht's epic theatre in a more fundamental way. We can demonstrate this by examining the concept of empathy.

I have pointed to the actor's intentional avoidance of empathy with his role as the most important similarity between Brecht's epic theatre and the Shiite passion plays. Now empathy in theatre can take place on two levels: that of the actor and that of the spectator. Empathy on the level of the actor – that is, the actor's identification with the role – is a relatively new ideal in theatre which was systematized by Stanislavski and his school. Neither the passion play nor the epic theatre aspires to this kind of empathy. Yet Brecht also uses the concept of empathy in reference to the spectator, to designate the emotional relation between the spectator and the action on stage in Aristotelian drama, for example. Although the term cannot be derived from Aristotle's *Poetics*, it can be attributed to the object of Brecht's critique, the 'illusionist theatre' of the late nineteenth and early twentieth centuries, and Brecht himself on several occasions distinguishes the concept of empathy in classical theatre from empathy in late bourgeois theatre (although some other passages in his work suggest a direct derivation of empathy-based 'illusionist theatre' from Aristotle). Nonetheless, he suspects that the catharsis he rejects has 'as its basis some kind of empathy', according to his rather cautious phrase in a critique of the *Poetics*.[41] Brecht's reception of Aristotle has often been criticized but is undisputed at least in this one point, which is an essential one: that catharsis in Aristotle takes place 'on the basis of a singular psychological act, the spectator's *empathy* with the persons performing the action that the actors imitate'.[42] For Brecht, this 'cleansing' empathy is the identifying characteristic of Aristotelian drama. At the same time, it marks the difference between the theatrical aesthetics of Brecht's epic theatre and that of the Shiite passion play. Alienation in Brecht's sense cannot go hand in hand with empathy, which evidently occurs – in the spectator – in *taziyeh*.

If we do not limit alienation to the Brechtian definition, we may certainly say there is alienation in *taziyeh*. But, then such a broadly defined term could be applied to just about any form of theatre, except for illusionism, which, in spite of its far-reaching importance for modern Western theatre, is a marginal phenomenon from a global perspective. In the aesthetics of theatre, such a broad concept of alienation has no relevance, since it is almost identical with the artistic character of art, inasmuch as art is always a departure from everyday, pragmatic forms of representation. What is more, as far as I can see, all the theoretical reflections on alienation in this all-encompassing sense (from Aristotle's *onoma xenikon* to the *ostranenie* of Russian formalism) mention, as Brecht does, arousing the spectator's attention as a primary motive. Alienation in *taziyeh*, on the other hand, has a completely different purpose. The defeat at Karbala is held to be such a significant, extraordinary, sacred event that a realistic representation of it is not only unthinkable but impossible. We must remember that the characters in *taziyeh* are not ordinary people, as in Brecht's drama, but prophets, imams, holy men and angels, on the one hand, with superhuman qualities, and, on the other hand, villains whose turpitude, brutality and hideousness are almost those of Satan incarnate. The difference between characters like these and ordinary people is irremediable. In such a situation, a realistic representation would be absurd, impossible even for the most talented performers, and not desirable. It would not be conceivable to Shiites that an ordinary person could or should identify with Hussein, since Hussein is no ordinary person;[43] the most we can do is commemorate him. Peter Brook recognized that the prohibition of illusion in *taziyeh* is more than just a religious convention, it is a fundamental truth of theatre:

> From a certain point of view, perfectionism can be seen to be *homage* and devotion – man's attempt to worship an ideal that is linked to his pushing his craftsmanship and artistry to its limit. From another point

> of view, this can be seen as the fall of Icarus, who tried to fly above his station and reach the gods. In the Ta'zieh there is no attempt, theatrically speaking, to do anything too well: the acting does not demand characterisations that are too complete, detailed or realistic. If there is no attempt to embellish, there is in its place another criterion: the need to find the true inner echo.[44]

Taziyeh can teach us, as theatregoers influenced by cinema and television, that empathy and catharsis do not have to go hand in hand with so-called realistic representation, and indeed that the most extreme alienation effect can produce the greatest possible emotional involvement on the part of the spectator. The following anecdote may serve to illustrate this point. A *taziyeh* director from Darband who was unable to recruit a Persian actor for the role of the evil Shemr hired a Russian worker, who took on the job to earn a little money. The director outlined the part and explained to him what he had to do. The part was simplified so that the Russian, who knew only a few words of Persian, merely had to guard the bucket of water that symbolized the Euphrates. The performance began, and the Russian, in the costume of an Umayyad warrior, stood in front of the bucket holding a whip. One after the other, Hussein's children and comrades tried to get to the water, but the Russian mercilessly kept them away from it. Unfortunately, the role of Hussein was played that day by a very old man. When he approached the bucket in his turn, the Russian made no attempt to stop him. The director shouted at him to stop the old man from drinking, but the Russian answered, 'Let him drink; he's an old man!' Far from causing surprise or laughter, the incident heightened the audience's emotions. The spectators cried, 'See! How mean and evil Shemr was! He showed mercy neither to the children nor to Imam Hussein, who was the grandson of the Prophet. He killed them, but when the Russian fellow, who is outside the faith, saw the old actor with a white beard he showed him mercy and permitted him to quench his thirst.'[45] The alienation effect was by no means an obstacle to empathy; on the contrary, it heightened the spectators' compassion with the fate of the person portrayed.

The cliché is still repeated today – one that Brecht inadvertently helped to establish – that breaking down illusion by alienation is part of a politically enlightening theatre that appeals more to the intellect, while emotion, compassion and identification arise from a naturalistic performance that purports to present real feelings. In fact, a theatre that radically breaks with the illusion of reality can easily move people to tears. Children demonstrate that in their play every day. 'For secular Iranian theatre there is a great opportunity to utilize the conventions of the Ta'ziyeh performing style', wrote Andrzej Wirth:

> Having such a defined tradition of presentational acting is an advantage over the Western theatre. The naturalistic acting style, with its simplistic concept of performer–character–spectator empathy, promoted all over the world through film and television, and still strong in the bourgeois theatre, can be countered in Iran in alliance with its own performing tradition. This could mean not only the secularization of the convention, but paradoxically, also a protection of the religious theatre in its own realm from the invasion of a bastardized naturalism.[46]

Wirth expressed that hope in the 1970s. And, in fact, some performances that I saw at the Fadjr theatre festival in Tehran in the late 1990s, including both the work of an older, long-banned director such as Bahrain Beizai and the experiments of young artists who grew up after the revolution, hinted at a very distinctive language of theatre which incorporated motifs, symbols and modes of acting from the passion play. Less conspicuously, but with worldwide success, the new Iranian cinema since the revolution has developed a form of epic narrative which appears advanced to the Western audience – and no less to a Western-oriented Iranian audience – but at the same time is based on very old modes of performance. The films of the great Abbas Kiarostami reflect the conditions of their production and continually shift between the different levels of reality – for example, when amateur actors play their own true or purportedly true stories; when the director, actual or acted, intervenes in the scene being shot on the open set like the old 'aide to the weepers'; or when an actor speaks directly to the camera, breaking the spectator's keyhole perspective. Like so many other Iranian artists, however, Kiarostami in recent years has been able to work only outside the country. May Iran's aesthetic tradition once again attain more prestige in the country as well.

— 8 —

LIBERATE BAYREUTH!

Wagner and Empathy

To convey my impressions of the Wagner festival, I must begin my story before my visits to Bayreuth. For the present chapter is nothing less than a call to liberate Bayreuth from the chains with which Richard Wagner himself fettered his work, and apart from love, which is present at the birth of any heresy, there are only two possible excuses – the most intimate knowledge of a connoisseur or the most extreme naïveté – for the presumption of challenging dogmas that have been held sacred for over a hundred years of production practice, all the revolutionary directors of the intervening eras notwithstanding.

Although I often attend classical concerts, I had always given opera a wide berth, and Wagner the widest. The few images I had seen of Richard Wagner's operas, like the scraps I had heard of their music, repelled me with their pompous affectation. The bon mot attributed to Roger Waters – that if Wagner were alive today he would work with Pink Floyd – made perfect sense to me. But I was no longer interested in Pink Floyd either since Waters's attempt to create a *Gesamtkunstwerk* using the comparatively limited means of rock music. And Wagner's Germanic splendour, Wagner's anti-Semitism and Wagner's reception history, all that Teutonic flimflam that I associated with Bayreuth, confirmed me in my ignorance.

Then in 2012 I received tickets for two performances at the Bayreuth festival. I can't remember exactly what my expectations were when I left home. Curiosity was certainly involved, and something akin to a feeling of duty to visit such a landmark of German culture. I felt no ecstatic anticipation, or if I did, it was only at the prospect of a side trip to the house where the great German writer Jean Paul had lived in Bayreuth. But from the very first act, as I sat in one of the infamous wooden seats in the festival hall, a remarkable thing happened: I flipped out. If the rows of seats had not been so close together, I probably would have been head-banging as if I were at a rock concert: that's how viscerally the music of *Tannhäuser* penetrated me; that's how enraptured I was especially by the final passages when the orchestra, soloists and chorus rose to a hurricane of orgiastic force, while miraculously balancing even the most delicate note. That, to return to the apocryphal quotation, was how Pink Floyd would sound if Roger Waters had been as great a genius as Richard Wagner.

But it wasn't just the feeling of being overpowered by the auditory impression – overpowered in all the word's ambivalent senses, irritated too, sometimes even repelled by the perfection of the musical figures, by the music's seductive power, which was clear to me from the start. At the same time I was dumbfounded by the inanity that was before my eyes. As a passionate theatregoer, I have no objection to directors' forceful, extremely personal or even presumptuous interpretations, and I find the concept of 'fidelity to the work' highly dubious. So it was not the 'modernity' of the performance that was disconcerting. On the contrary, it was the utter disproportion, or rather the lack of any relation at all, between the opera's highly philosophical conceit, which would have been worthy of a refutation at least, and what was actually happening on stage; it was the incongruity of sight and sound. There was a staging that was intentionally up to the minute, with a chemical factory as the set, the obligatory video projections, all the tricks that stage technicians can muster and an ideological superstructure straight out of a deconstructivist seminar; yet at the same time the soloists and the chorus were playing a cheap theatre of empathy with which no provincial stage would hope to succeed in spoken drama today: whenever a statement was particularly laden with feeling, the right hand moved, as if driven by a spring mechanism, to the left breast, and a performer who wanted to signal resolve invariably began by making a fist. In case of infatuation, of course, the lover instantly dropped to his or her knees; and I lost count of how many times the protagonists' meaningful gazes traced the horizon – which in reality consisted of the upper circles. Most painful of all, however, were the supernumeraries, whom the director had apparently told to act like animals, with the result that ten or perhaps twenty fully grown people in ape costumes constantly crawled and squirmed, with hunched shoulders, bent arms and clawing fingers, around the leading performer, who had to pretend he was close to succumbing to a Dionysian temptation.

I wondered the whole time what could explain the outrageous discrepancy between what I heard and what I saw: on the one hand, the breathtaking complexity of the composition, the metaphysical depth and existential significance of the themes, and the stupendous brilliance of both the instrumental and the vocal performances; on the other, the artsy-craftsy obtrusiveness of the costumes, the triteness and predictability of the directorial choices, and the hoary acting. The irritation was all the greater since the director, Sebastian Baumgarten, from all I had heard and seen of his earlier work, not only remained far below Wagner's potential but also fell grotesquely short of his own. Nothing was contemporary except the set and the programme booklet; everything else, and most of all the essential part of theatre, the representation of human beings, came off as conventionally psychologizing, as if the actors were trying to parody production photos from the 1950s. I didn't know then that they might just as well have been aping photos of the previous year's production – that Wagner, evidently, is always performed like a school play.

On the second day I saw Stefan Herheim's celebrated *Parsifal*, a conceptually less ambitious but entertaining production that can only be described as successful on its own terms. Yet Herheim had not solved the crucial problem of the previous evening – the stale theatre of empathy that the actors had performed. At best, he had defused it by cleverly arranging the singers' positions to counterbalance their psychologizing acting. And his idea of setting the redemption myth in the Bundestag building in Bonn, and seating the chorus on parliamentary benches, was without a doubt original, and its execution altogether appealing; but Herheim had also dodged the religious theme itself by cleverly narrowing down the many thousands of years of metaphysical history that run through *Parsifal* to a story of modern German mentality. That is, of course, a story worth telling. But it is so much less than Wagner has to tell us. No other cycle of works in the German-speaking countries offers such an inexhaustible and ever-changing document of a society's historic experience and longing for redemption as Wagner's great operas, comparable only with Shakespeare, the classical tragedies and, to a certain extent, Oberammergau. I left Bayreuth with the ambivalent feeling that I been enriched with and at the same time robbed of something essential in my life.

As I set out for Bayreuth the second time, I was much more than merely curious or keen on culture. I wanted Bayreuth to honour its promise; I wanted for once to be more than just musically enraptured; I wanted to be taken seriously as an aesthetically and intellectually contemporary theatre spectator, an experience I certainly find in theatres – more often, in fact, than is said to be possible in the vilifications of today's theatre that are now fashionable. Perhaps, I thought, it was only by chance that, for all their differences in artistry, both of the productions I had seen affirmed the actor's empathy with his role and thematically sidestepped the admittedly unsettling, but nevertheless essential religiousness of Wagner's operas. Then, on the way there, I heard a report about the festival's opening night and was turned off by the description of the first scene: the Flying Dutchman with a trolley case and a take-away coffee. My drama teacher at school would never, I swear, have allowed an image so devoid of imagination.

I consider Christoph Marthaler, whose *Tristan und Isolde* I saw on the first evening of that year's festival, to be one of the great directors of contemporary German theatre. His flair for musical development in particular is undisputed. I thought I understood the impulse that had moved him to do away with all the splendour and pathos: Anna Viebrock's set, designed as the stuffy lounge of some bureaucratic regime; the costumes of various colours, all of them seemingly mouse-grey; his actors' movements reduced to a drawing-room play, the chorus completely banished to the wings; the lighting all from fluorescent tubes. Love, which the music heralds as absolute – such love doesn't exist in life, that much is made clear. Refraining from grand gestures, Tristan and Isolde mainly face each other as if frozen to the spot. Perhaps Marthaler intended the singers not to act at all, only to sing. The result, however, is that their acting is merely diminished: where Tristan and Isolde in the play think they are about to die, the figures in Bayreuth might have just received their tax notices. Instead of opening their eyes wide in horror, they clasp their foreheads, and instead of falling to the ground, they sit down on chairs. Instead of gazing at the horizon, they stare through each other's knees. Because Marthaler tries only to avoid the worst clichés of operatic acting but doesn't question the mode of acting itself – in other words, because he lets the singers go on pretending they really are, every second, Tristan, Isolde, Brangäne, and so on – his production offers just a different set of clichés, namely those of television acting. Instead of orgiastically melting into each other, in keeping with the musical structure of the big love scene, they hold hands, as they would in an early-evening broadcast slot.

Psychological realism is not everyone's cup of tea in spoken theatre either, least of all Marthaler's, yet it can be brought off, as directors such as Luc Bondy and Katie Mitchell strikingly demonstrate time and again, precisely in working with classic texts. But on the operatic stage, and most of all when accompanied by Wagner's enthralling and absolutely passionate music, any attempt at credible simulation of all the grand emotions of a Wagner opera is turned into farce by its outward form alone. The problem is not the emotions themselves, which of course can be grand even in the most ordinary life – just think of birth and death, of a first love or a base betrayal. The problem is that the emotions are asserted as authentic, as real, as actually being experienced now: it is simply impossible to seem at all natural while at the same time opening your mouth wide and filling the hall with song; it is not convincing to profess great love while looking at the conductor instead of your beloved. And those who do not happen to be singing at the moment do not have an easier time of it: in contrast to spoken theatre, where a dialogue is at least modelled on a real conversation, the more schematic form that an opera libretto requires, and even the length of the individual vocal parts, obliges all the other actors to freeze their facial expressions for minutes at a time in order to stay in the situation. In Hans Neuenfels's interpretation of *Lohengrin*, for example – to segue into my fourth evening in Bayreuth – poor Friedrich von Telramund is forced to spend a large part of the evening trembling with rage while waiting his turn to sing. In film, the camera would simply crop him out of the frame; in theatre, any reasonably adequate dramatic text would vary his emotion; but, in Bayreuth, Telramund must stand on the apron of the stage with chin outthrust and lips spread wide for minutes and hours on end, until the spectator grows more concerned about his facial muscles than about Lohengrin and Elsa.

Some will object that opera singers are not actors. True! The singers were cast in their roles primarily because of their vocal artistry. But, because at the same time they try to act, à la Laurence Olivier or à la Marlon Brando, as the case may be, the discrepancy I mentioned at the outset between the auditory and the visual experience arises. It is not just that their limited role-playing abilities contrast starkly with the richness of their musical expression; it is the impossibility of playing these roles at all. Wagner himself drops a hint at this, alluding again and again in his operas to the second commandment. That Elsa must not ask Lohengrin's name and Senta must not ask the name of the Flying Dutchman is grounded in one of the most important ideas of all monotheism: thou shalt not take the name of the Lord thy God in vain. Because the Absolute transcends everything human, It must not be named, hence identified, and hence translated into a human category. It can be designated only in the negative: as That Which is other than everything. Closely linked with the prohibition against speaking God's name is the prohibition against images, which is not dissolved in Christianity but only interpreted more subtly as the Middle Ages progress. Just as in Islam, it was not meant as a prohibition of pictorial representation per se. The prohibition of images is directed against the danger of mistaking human imitations for what is real, hence living, hence made by God. It is a prohibition against illusion. That is why the actors in the Christian passion play are always careful not to be identified with their roles, just as in the Shiite passion play even today the actors hold a sheet of paper in their hands although they know their lines by heart. When Peter Brook saw *taziyeh* in an Iranian village in 1970, the musicians sat under a tree, and the spectators and actors together formed a circle. One stepped forward, an inhabitant of the village, wearing rubber boots and a green neckerchief as his costume:

> He began to sing a long melodic phrase made up of a very few notes in a pattern that repeated and repeated, with words that we could not follow but whose meaning became instantly clear through a sound that came from deep inside the singer. His emotion was in no way his own. It was as though we heard his father's voice, and his father's father's, and so on back. He stood there, legs apart, powerfully, totally convinced of his function, and he was the incarnation of that figure who for our theatre is always the most elusive one of all, the hero. I had long doubted that heroes could be depicted: in our terms, the heroes, like all good characters, easily become pallid and sentimental, or wooden and ridiculous, and it is only as we go toward villainy that something interesting begins to appear. Even as I was saying this to myself, another character, this time with a red twist of cloth about him, entered the circle. The tension was immediate: the bad one had arrived. He did not sing, he had no right to melody, he just declaimed in a strong rasping tone, and then the drama was under way.

Not only is the orchestra seated in full view under a tree; not only are the costumes limited to rubber boots and pieces of green or red cloth, the green ones worn smooth, the red twisted – more importantly, no pretence is made that the actor and the character he portrays are identical. The characterization is achieved almost exclusively, and all the more grippingly, by musical means: the hero's long, melodic phrase; the singer's hard, buzzing declamation.

> The circle was operating according to certain very fundamental laws and a true phenomenon was occurring, that of 'theatrical representation'. An event from the distant past was in the process of being 're-presented', of becoming present; the past was happening here and now, the hero's decision was for now, his anguish was for now and the audience's tears were for this very moment. The past was not being described nor illustrated, time had been abolished. The village was participating directly and totally, here and now, in the real death of a real figure who had died some thousand years before. The story had been read to them many times, and described in words, but only the theatre could work this feat of making it part of a living experience.[1]

In the twentieth century, Bertolt Brecht laid ideological claim to alienation,[2] basing it on a didactic purpose of arousing not the sensations, but the intellectual understanding of the spectator. But in fact, what Brecht called alienation effects form the basic principle of all performing arts traditions all over the world. Brecht himself quite rightly called alienation the true realistic principle because it is unrealistic to ignore the theatre situation: 'But it's also a reality that we are sitting in a theatre and not with our eye pressed to a keyhole', he writes in *Buying Brass*. 'How can it be realistic to try and gloss over that fact?'[3] Nowhere, and least of all in classical theatre with its masks, have performers pretended the action on the stage was 'real', that they were really feeling love or hate when they represented that feeling. Empathy in Aristotle never means the actor's identification with the role: it refers to the audience, who are supposed to be not merely instructed, but captivated with all their senses. In contrast to the lesson Brecht inculcated in generations of directors and performers, alienation in representation is not incompatible with empathy on the part of the audience – in fact, even Aristotle's dramatic theory takes it for granted.

In painting, the discovery of perspective in the late Renaissance permitted a kind of realism that had not been possible before; with a certain delay, the onset of secularization in Western European societies also dissolved the requirement in the performing arts of maintaining a distance between the performer and the character being portrayed. Of course, that had little to do with empathy in the contemporary sense; even the open stage of Elizabethan theatre was an obstacle to any illusionistic ambition. And when the first proscenium stages were built, as the bourgeois theatre became established, it would not have occurred to any spectator to see the action as a replica of reality. To remind ourselves that empathy certainly was not meant as a kind of psychologism, we need only read Lessing's *Hamburg Dramaturgy*, or simply to imagine the technical and spatial conditions of those times: as late as the early twentieth century, before the introduction of electronically controlled lights, when the stage was illuminated only by dim gaslights or candles, it was much too dark for spectators to see a natural gesture or a natural facial expression from the distance of the stalls, much less the galleries. Accordingly, the actors had to magnify every emotion, every movement, making them overdistinct and hence emblematic. And because the stalls and the circles were also illuminated by candles or gaslights during the performance, the spectators never had the feeling of invisibility, of observing the drama as ghosts. In the theatre of the nineteenth century it was not unusual to read along in the text during the performance or to converse with one's neighbour – and if the spectators were too loud and the actors' lines were no longer audible, the actors called for quiet without interrupting the play. They could not 'break character' because they were not one with their characters in the first place. Only modern stage equipment – to say nothing of the wide, curved screens, Dolby Surround Sound and 3D glasses of today's multiplex cinemas – creates the illusion of disappearing into the picture, like the legendary Chinese painter.

In the history of theatre, Richard Wagner's misfortune is that his distinctly anti-naturalistic operatic work happened to extend into the era of naturalism. He was a contemporary not of Sophocles or Racine, with whom he probably felt a greater affinity, but of Ibsen and Strindberg. As the pictures and accounts of the first performances in Bayreuth document, Wagner did not have a realistic representation in mind; his singers' body language, for example, would more likely be associated today with ballet than with acting, so formalized, overdimensioned and yet precisely coordinated with the rhythm of the music are their crossings and gestures. Wagner was not interested in the performer's psychological empathy with his role; he wanted to induce empathy in the Aristotelian sense, the spectator's empathy with the drama itself, the captivation of all the senses.

> But only what is sensual and obeys the conditions of sensuality is true and alive. . . . The actual Art-work, i.e. *its immediate physical portrayal, in the moment of its liveliest embodiment*, is therefore the only true redemption of the artist . . . the confident determination of what was hitherto a mere imagining; the enfranchisement of thought in sense.[4]

Of course even Wagner himself used illusionistic means to draw the spectator into the action on the stage: in the first act of *Tannhäuser*, for example, the spectator was meant to believe he was actually sitting in the grotto of Venus or gazing on Wartburg Castle. To reinforce the impression of great depth, the adult pilgrims in the background were played by children. The relegation of the musicians to the invisible orchestra pit had both practical and symbolic importance for Wagner's aesthetic of total experience, which did not tolerate any distracting element that might alienate the drama. But we must not forget that the situation on the stage as a whole in the nineteenth century was still static and strictly two-dimensional, in spite of certain effects, and, by today's standards, the representation was totally unrealistic. The revolutionary innovation that Wagner introduced to concentrate the spectator's attention on the aesthetic event got caught up in the modern development of early illusionistic theatre, especially as lighting technology progressively made it possible to reduce gestures and facial expressions to ordinary dimensions. While recitative in Wagnerian opera still attests to the formalized mode of performance, which feels artificial to the novice today but was considered natural in the nineteenth century, delivery in spoken theatre increasingly resembled day-to-day communication. Yet even the most psychologically forceful acting on stage is still stylized – think of the loudness with which actors must carry on even the most intimate dialogues and monologues to make themselves heard in the back of the auditorium; and think of the audience's presence, unmistakably visible even in the dark, and unmistakably audible even when – especially when – the house is so quiet you could hear the proverbial pin drop. If we take the productions invited to the Berlin Theatertreffen festival as a measure, we observe that spoken theatre has made its event character more distinct in recent years: rather than representing reality, it emphasizes its own stage reality, reconnecting with pre-modern modes of performance. Illusionism was more persuasively pursued in film, but it could only make nonsense of the highly artificial form of opera.

I left Bayreuth the second time with the confident feeling that it was not this or that director but the contemporary conventions of theatre practice that prevent Bayreuth from redeeming the promise of Wagner's music. Adjusting one directorial screw or another from year to year won't help as long as the ideology of empathy underlying all the Bayreuth productions is not laid to rest. There is no other stage in Germany that invests so much equipment, architecture, artistic direction, lighting and stage design in creating the illusion of a unified work of art that can be reeled off like a film. But if even spoken theatre loses its soul when it behaves like cinema – what then of a Wagner opera, in which everything, from the language to the mythic characters, is unnatural, nothing is believable in the ordinary psychological sense, and everything is staged and charged with an aura of holiness? Where Bayreuth thinks its extravaganzas can compete even with today's science fiction, it only embarrasses itself, as in Hans Neuenfels's terribly expert production of *Lohengrin*, in which a hundred, or maybe it was two hundred, grown-up actors in rat costumes shrugged their shoulders, bent their arms, wiggled their fingers and still just looked like mascots in a football stadium.

What, then, is to be done? Well, first of all the orchestra would have to be brought back up onto the stage, to break with Bayreuth's holiest dogma. I know, at this point, if not before, the Wagnerians among my readers will pronounce me insane, but as long as the music is treated as background, as in cinema, the entrenched illusionism of the current Bayreuth aesthetic will prevail against all innovations. Sebastian Baumgarten's production of *Tannhäuser*, which made the most conspicuous use of alienation effects, shows most plainly that annotated text projections or spectator seats on the edge of the stage are merely cosmetic as long as the unified form of the performance is not radically broken up. Making the sound production visible would be more than a mere alienation effect: because the hidden orchestra pit was invented by Wagner himself, and is therefore considered inviolable, abandoning it would be a signal of the necessary magnitude to change the public's expectations and open them to experiments that would rethink not just the stage design yet again, but opera itself. Wagner built up the fourth wall so that nothing extraneous would disturb the sensory impression. He could not have anticipated the fact that film and television have since built the fourth wall in the spectator's minds as well.

That's right, the orchestra pit is something extraneous. The objective, essentially, is to contest the identification of the actors with their roles, a tradition which was established in the twentieth century, but which is no longer considered sacrosanct, film and television aside, except in opera, and especially in Wagner. Even in a concert performance, singers respond emotionally to the music; they let themselves be captivated by it, merge with it to the extent that they actually forget themselves in certain moments. But what theatrical devil possesses them to pretend they feel themselves one with their roles, even when they have nothing to do and can only indicate their involvement by facial acrobatics? Bayreuth should look not to Hollywood, but to Stratford, remembering Shakespeare as the model of a theatre that unites radical alienation and captivating empathy – 'a model of the theatre that contains Brecht and Beckett, but goes beyond both', in Peter Brook's words. Of course one cannot simply copy Shakespeare's theatre, but we can realize where it got its power, which is also the power of the theatrical act itself. The absence of scenery in the Elizabethan theatre was one of the things that gave it its great freedom, since the neutrality of the open stage 'enabled the dramatist effortlessly to whip the spectator through an unlimited succession of illusions, covering, if he chose, the entire physical world.'

> Compared with the cinema's mobility, the theatre once seemed ponderous and creaky, but the closer we move towards the true nakedness of theatre, the closer we approach a stage that has a lightness and range far beyond film or television. The power of Shakespeare's plays is that they present man simultaneously in all his aspects: touch for touch, we can identify and withdraw. A primitive situation disturbs us in our subconscious; our intelligence watches, comments, philosophizes. Brecht and Beckett are both contained in Shakespeare unreconciled. We identify emotionally, subjectively – and yet at one and the same time we evaluate politically, objectively in relation to society. Because the profound reaches past the everyday, a heightened language and a ritualistic use of rhythm brings us to those very aspects of life which the surface hides:

> and yet because the poet and the visionary do not seem like ordinary people, because the epic state is not one on which we normally dwell, it is equally possible for Shakespeare with a break in his rhythm, a twist into prose, a shift into slangy conversation or else a direct word from the audience to remind us – in plain common-sense – of where we are and to return us to the familiar rough world of spades as spades.[5]

Peter Brook wrote those sentences in 1968, when most European stages were still modelled on the illusionistic diorama and almost the only alternative concept was Brecht's didactic theatre, which stifled all emotion. Since then, European spoken theatre has long since found the way forward, which leads back to Shakespeare. In opera, on the other hand, and nowhere as extremely as in Bayreuth, time seems to be standing still – again, not in Wagner's day but in the mid-twentieth century, to be exact. Because the mode of representation itself seems to be frozen, the public and the critics direct their attention to the musical performance and, apart from that, almost exclusively to the ever more elaborate, ever more contemporary decors. Yet not even the Shakespearean model would be necessary to liberate Bayreuth. It would be enough just to look around Bayreuth itself, even on the sacred hilltop. Before the evening performance, the festival has for the past few years presented a children's opera. Beginning with a paintbrush rapidly sketching on a white sheet of paper the city of Nuremberg and the hero of the opera, who then enters; continuing with the feather-light tools of improvisational theatre, with actors changing roles in the middle of the stage and with enthralling musicians, the performance of the *Meistersinger* is as imaginative, earnest and enchanting as the evening shows, with their orgiastic decors and costumes, aspire to be. The work is abridged but not trivialized; there is nothing childish or pop about it; the singers – who are only the best – give it their full voice. And because everything is taken seriously, the lover's desperation and the hero's pathos turn out not inadvertently amusing, but as comical as in real life: as in Shakespeare, as in the passion play, horror goes hand in hand with laughter in Bayreuth too, at last. Both the children and the adults in the audience, whom no alienation can stop from surrendering to the music and gasping with trepidation for the hero, are delighted – and even the *Frankfurter Allgemeine Zeitung* praised the Bayreuth children's opera two years in succession as the real theatre event of the season, as a veritable tornado: 'The roof flies off. We fly off with it.'[6]

As simply as that? No, of course not. The age of the audience, the brevity of the performance, the chamber-sized orchestra all necessarily impose restrictions on the aesthetic, thematic and musical complexity of a Wagner opera. But the example made it plain to me, and evidently not only to me, what myriad modes of performance and what freedom opens up to the imagination as soon as the compulsion to call appearances real is cast off – even more so in the visible interaction with the orchestra, which is not required for all time to perform the score en bloc, as in a concert hall. Musicians too might be more comfortable sitting under a tree than in the pit.

As I sat, a few hours after the children's opera, in the proper festival performance, I felt reminded of the *taziyeh* that Peter Brook saw at the Shiraz International Theatre Festival a year after his visit to a village *taziyeh*:

> outfitted in tailor-made costumes, drilled by a professional theatre director and led by a musical conductor, the villagers stood for the first time in their lives on a frontal podium and were so blinded by the spotlights that, like the singers in Bayreuth after the introduction of electric lighting, they could make out at most the outlines of the spectators. The rubber boots worn by the village shopkeeper, in which he had looked very smart, had been replaced by leather ones, the temporary props had been replaced with well-made ones, but no one had stopped to ask what 'stuff' they were expected to do. And why? And for whom? These questions were never put, because no one was interested in the answers. So the long trumpets hooted, the drums played, and it meant absolutely nothing.[7]

Of course, *taziyeh* builds on the cultural memory and the religious conviction that are shared between the actors and the spectators. That is why its success cannot be simply translated into secularized Western society – and is no longer certain even in Iran, forty years after Brook's visit. But, at the same time, its very religiousness reminds one of a crucial aspect of Wagner's operas: their accession to the holy, which today's productions don't even try or, worse still, only pretend to find. In any case, simply breaking a cross, as in *Lohengrin*, and then putting its highly symbolic pieces back together again is a farce if the rest of the performance conveys nothing of the religious overtones of the plot and the composition. In view of current performance practice, one might object that an engagement with Wagner's syncretic religious notions is only possible when the biblical furore of an individual such as Christoph Schlingensief saves it from gravitas. And even then, one might further argue, the question remains whether there is an addressee for such a treatment in a cultural establishment that is largely indifferent to, and nowadays ignorant of, religious matters, and whether that addressee is to be found on the festival hill of all places. But if Bayreuth were to take seriously the prohibition of graven images that governed all performing arts traditions all over the world, the individual, the audience, would not have to be religious in order to give serious attention to religious themes. It is not only the singer-actors who rob the productions of their plausibility by pretending to empathize with Parsifal, Lohengrin, Tannhäuser and the rest. The assertion of empathy is also the foundation of a directorial concept of identifying with what is being represented – negatively if necessary – by making it present, and usually diminishing it in the process. But an opera that lets conflicting realities coexist instead of interpreting could afford us an experience of Wagner's themes, and of the distance that lies between him and us.

— 9 —

SWIMMING IN THE AFTERNOON

Kafka and Germany

A writer whose parents are not originally from Germany is asked no other question more often than the question of what country he calls home. The answer that my home is the German language would be as correct as it is banal. Regardless of where a German-speaking writer was born, or where he has fled to, what nationality his parents or his children have – his literature is still German literature. But what are the distinguishing features of that literature? Or, to phrase the question slightly differently: What is German about German literature? I would like to look for an answer by discussing the exemplary German writer. And, for me, that is not Goethe or Schiller, not Thomas Mann or Bertolt Brecht, but the Prague Jew Franz Kafka.

Kafka? Everyone knows the photo of the young Franz Kafka that shows him, his head turned slightly towards the camera, with a smile that is perhaps unsure or perhaps facetious, looking at a point just above the photographer's lens. It is a detail of the photo taken in 1917 on the occasion of his engagement to Felice Bauer, and it is the most famous picture of the author, the picture we all think of, practically an icon. I remember exactly what was going through my mind when I took my first steps in Kafka's world (I must have been fourteen or fifteen years old) and looked at that face every day on the book covers: he doesn't look German. The dark skin colour, the heavy eyebrows over the black eyes, the short black hair hanging so low on his forehead that not even a hint of temples can be seen, the Middle Eastern features – it is certainly no longer politically correct today to say it, but, back then, it was my immediate impression: he doesn't look German, not like the Germans I know at school, on television or on the national football team. In those days I didn't give any further thought as to what Kafka really was. I devoured his books without thinking about what cultural, social or religious experiences had gone into them. But when I asked myself which writer embodies for me what is specifically German in German literature, I knew immediately that I had to start with Kafka, with a German writer who wasn't German.

Kafka's diaries reveal how little he felt connected with Germany: they hardly even mention the land of his native language. On 2 August 1914, for example, when the First World War began, he wrote just two sentences: 'Germany has declared war on Russia', the first sentence says; and the next: 'Swimming in the afternoon'.[1] Four days later, he devoted another brief entry to political events, mentioning a patriotic parade by German-speaking citizens of Prague: 'I stand there with my malignant look.'[2] And after that: practically nothing. Kafka, who certainly does think about many other social issues, and even briefly considers going to war on the side of Austria, is not interested in the political developments in Germany. In any case, he almost never mentions Germany, neither in his letters nor in his diaries, not before, not during, and not after the First World War.

Even in September 1923, when Kafka moves to Berlin, he remains a stranger in the land of his mother tongue. His last partner, Dora Diamant, with whom he shares a flat, at first calls him a 'half-breed Indian' because of his dark skin.[3] Kafka lives in the secluded world of Steglitz, on the south side of Berlin, and steers clear of social and political events. 'You must also consider', he writes to Max Brod, 'that I am living a half-rural life here, neither under the cruel nor under the pedagogical pressure of real Berlin.' Once settled in Germany, he continues his 'Prague life'.[4] With Dora Diamant he studies Hebrew, fantasizes about going to Palestine, and lives – as an experiment – by Jewish law. He is more likely to be found in the Jewish schools than in theatres or opera houses, not only because of his interests but also for economic reasons: he can hardly afford tickets to the theatre or cinema. Kafka lives in Germany without living in Germany. He lives in a parallel society. He bears his rare trips to Berlin's city centre as a personal 'Calvary',[5] not because he abhors Berlin, but because it does not concern him. The most important author in German twentieth-century literature was indifferent to Germany: 'Germany has declared war on Russia. Swimming in the afternoon.'

Kafka had what immigrant children are supposed to be spared in Germany today: a pronounced multiple identity. By citizenship, he belonged to the Habsburg Empire and, later, the Republic of Czechoslovakia. To the Czechs, Kafka was – along with the whole German-speaking minority in Prague – simply German. Among the Prague Germans, meanwhile, someone like Kafka was considered primarily a Jew. Not even Kafka himself could say clearly to which collective he belonged. In a letter to Max Brod dated 10 April 1920, he reported on his reception in the sanatorium at Meran:

> After the first few words it came out that I am from Prague; both of them – the General, who sat opposite me, and the Colonel – were acquainted with Prague. Was I Czech? No. So now explain to those true German military eyes what you really are. Someone else suggested 'German-Bohemian', someone else 'Little Quarter'. Then the subject was dropped and people went on eating, but the General, with his sharp ears linguistically schooled in the Austrian army, was not satisfied. After we had eaten he once more began to wonder about the sound of my German, perhaps more bothered by what he saw than by what he heard. At this point I tried to explain that by my being Jewish. At this his scientific curiosity, to be sure, was satisfied, but not his human feelings.[6]

To Kafka himself, being Jewish as a cultural and political point of reference grew more and more important as he grew older, even though he did not find fulfilment in a Jewish identity. As the son of a determinedly assimilated merchant, Kafka learned little in his youth about the religion of his ancestors. He gained deeper knowledge of Jewish tradition only as an adult. Judaism for Kafka was something he yearned for rather than something he felt at home in: 'If I'd been given the choice to be what I wanted, then I'd have chosen to be a small Eastern Jewish boy', he wrote to his friend Milena Jesenská, '. . . without a trace of worry.'[7]

Reality is something else again, full of worry: 'What have I in common with Jews?', he wrote in his diary on 8 January 1914; 'I have hardly anything in common with myself and should stand very quietly in a corner, content that I can breathe.'[8] He was always aware that there was something artificial and constructed about his relation to Jewish tradition, which may have been one of the reasons for the aloofness he maintained, unlike his closest friends, towards Zionism. In the real yeshivas, the Talmud schools, there was an unbearable stench; as Kafka disconcertedly remarks on 7 January 1912: 'the students, who had no real beds, lay down to sleep without undressing, in their sweaty clothes, wherever they happened to be sitting last.'[9] Kafka's relationship with Judaism was not naïve. But unlike his connection to the Habsburg monarchy or to the German Empire, it was at least a relationship. After a meeting of the 'Jewish Society' at the Café Savoy, Kafka wrote on 5 October 1911, in his initial euphoria:

> Some songs, the expression 'yiddishe kinderlach', some of this woman's acting (who, on the stage, because she is a Jew, draws us listeners

> to her because we are Jews, without any longing for or curiosity about Christians) made my cheeks tremble.[10]

Kafka's entries about Germany and things German, rare as they are to begin with, never show such emotion – with one exception: when he mentions Goethe, Kleist or Stifter, he does so not only knowledgeably but with an enthusiasm that is rarely found anywhere else in his works. When Kafka reflects in his diaries or his notebooks about specific idioms and problems in the German language, he does so with a precision that today's guardians of the language could learn from. The motifs and narrative strategies from Jewish tradition that contemporary interpreters are so determined to identify in Kafka's work are not nearly as important as his acknowledged models in German literature. Judaism is not present at the beginning of Kafka's literary biography but is a later addition, a system of reference which he acquires and consciously applies in his mature age. Kafka's spiritual home is German literature.

It is not only Kafka who defies national attribution, co-optation, identification. The history of German literature as a whole is remarkably often disobliging towards such terms as nation, realm, fatherland. Schiller dealt with the German Empire in a single distich:

> Germany? Where does it lie? I cannot find the country.
> Where the learned land begins, the political one ends.[11]

The Germany of scholarship is not the same as the political entity. For German literature, that goes without saying, if for no other reason than that many of its protagonists were not Germans, or were not born Germans. We need not go back as far as Louis Charles Adélaïde de Chamisso de Boncourt, in whose Germanized name, Adelbert von Chamisso, a prize is awarded annually to a German writer who is not only German. Think, for example, of the 2009 Nobel Prize winner Herta Müller, the late Oskar Pastior, or Austrian and Swiss writers. Robert Walser and Heimito von Doderer are German, but not in the political sense – not German citizens, but authors belonging to German literature, which is not identical with the German nation. And, after all, the modern period in German literature had its first capital cities outside Germany: Vienna and Prague. The saying that a people finds itself in its literature has a special truth for the Germans. It was literature that helped to provide a common, specifically German self-awareness to the small and dwarf states of the late eighteenth century. The Germans famously compensated in poetry for their political fragmentation and lack of participation. As a consequence of the political supremacy of Louis XIV, the nobility spoke French into the eighteenth century, while the scholars continued to write in Latin. By beginning in the mid-eighteenth century to write in German and distance themselves from French culture, the German poets and philosophers laid the foundation for political emancipation as well. Speakers at award ceremonies and commemorative occasions are therefore fond of recalling literature's contribution to the birth of the nation. Most of those speakers overlook the fact, however, that Germany's littérateurs were thinking far beyond Germany when Germany finally crystallized as an intellectual construct and later as a political entity. The great German poets and philosophers of the late eighteenth and nineteenth centuries – a Goethe, a Kant – had their eyes not on German but on European unity. From its very beginning, the Enlightenment in Germany was not a national agenda but a European one. In literature, too, rather than clinging to any German models, writers followed literature from outside Germany, from Homer to Shakespeare to Byron. *German* was what German literature did not want to be – and what it became by its very assimilation of non-German motifs and patterns. 'Outline of the European Conditions of German Literature' was the title of August Wilhelm Schlegel's 1825 essay on the particularities of German intellectual life: 'We are, I dare say, the cosmopolitans of European culture.'[12] Or, in Goethe's words:

> But really, we Germans are very likely to fall too easily into this pedantic conceit, when we do not look beyond the narrow circle which surrounds us. I therefore like to look about me in foreign nations, and advise every one to do the same. National literature is now rather an unmeaning term; the epoch of World literature is at hand, and every one must strive to hasten its approach.[13]

Europe as a literary and political project was not supposed to level out regional and national particularities, but it was intended to dissolve the political boundaries between the nations. In this vision, writers were opposed to the nationalistic German zeitgeist which is fond of co-opting them retrospectively. At another point, Goethe says: 'At the moment when people everywhere are busy creating new fatherlands, the impartial thinker, he who can rise above his time, has his fatherland nowhere and everywhere.'[14] Opposition to the national idea grew more acute in the twentieth century, especially after the experience of the First World War: writers such as Hofmannsthal, Hesse, the Manns, Tucholsky, Zweig, Roth and Döblin upheld the dream of a democratic league of European states in the face of nationalism in Germany and Austria.

Not all, certainly, but a remarkable number of those authors who are trivialized by television today as adherents of Greater Germany were in their own time misfits and dissidents. They were persecuted, driven into exile or, in the best case, had broken relationships with their fatherland. When today's chauvinistic best-sellers cite even the author of *The Winter's Tale* as one of the reasons for their national pride, that is absurd. True, Heinrich Heine loved Germany – but he was more vociferously ashamed of Germany. And we may continue down the row of the German princes of poetry: Lessing with his tolerance play *Nathan the Wise*, which could not be performed during his lifetime, and the conclusion of his *Hamburg Dramaturgy*; Schiller with the tirades of Karl Moor in *The Robbers*; Heine and Hölderlin, Büchner and Börne. Many who are claimed as Greater Germans in the present were in their day anti-Germans, or in any case their understanding of patriotism prohibited all Germanic mythomania and all presumptions of leadership or superiority; in the twentieth century the shrewdest and most authentic representatives of German literature aimed criticism at Germany that bordered on fantasies of destruction. When Albert Einstein (one of the '100 Greatest Germans', according to a prime-time show on the German public television network ZDF) voiced the opinion after the end of the Second World War that Germany must be not only deindustrialized but reduced in population as punishment for mass murder, his German fellow exile Thomas Mann (who alone accounts for four titles among the 'Germans' Best Books') wrote, 'I can't think of much to be said against it.'[15]

On closer acquaintance, not even Germany's national poet Johann Wolfgang von Goethe is suitable for national edification. He does speak at one point, in Book 17 of his autobiography, of the 'quiet position of the German Fatherland' in which a 'highly varied gradation of ranks . . . instead of holding the several classes apart, seemed to bind them the more closely together . . . from the highest to the lowest – from the Emperor to the Jew.'[16] But, as the aforementioned Thomas Mann reminds us, at the end of a lecture he gave in May 1945 on 'Germany and the Germans' at the Library of Congress, none other than Goethe 'went so far as to wish for a German Diaspora'.[17] The remark of Goethe's that Thomas Mann cites in evidence was made in a conversation with Chancellor von Müller on 14 December 1808: 'The Germans will have to be transplanted, scattered all over the world like the Jews, before the abundance of good that is in them can be developed fully, to the benefit of all nations.'[18] A person who quotes this particular sentence at the close of the war in the capital of the nation that has conquered Germany is just as ill-suited as the writer he quotes to serve as the guarantor of a light-hearted patriotism. Goethe's relationship with the Germans was so strained that the American Secretary of the

Treasury Henry Morgenthau cited him in 1945 as a witness in favour of his plan to destroy Germany's industry: '"I have often felt a bitter pang", wrote Goethe, "at the thought of the German people, so estimable as individuals and so wretched in the whole."'[19] In the passage Morgenthau quoted, Goethe continues:

> A comparison of the German people with other peoples arouses distressing feelings in us which I try to overcome in every way; and in science and in art I have found oscillations by which one can lift oneself over them: for science and art belong to the world, and the barriers of nationality disappear before them; but the consolation they afford is only a miserable consolation and no substitute for the proud awareness of belonging to a great, strong, respected and feared people.[20]

Criticism and even rejection of Germany is a recurring theme in the history of German literature. Probably no other literature includes a national self-criticism of such severity and pervasiveness. It is by no means simply a product of the post-war period but was characteristic of German literature long before National Socialism; Thomas Mann remarked in his lecture that 'nothing could have been more faithful to German tradition' than criticism of Germany. Nearly twenty years earlier, in his *Reflections of a Nonpolitical Man*, he had already shown (more impersonally then), taking the most famous German writers as his examples,

> that it is almost part of higher German culture to present oneself as un-German and even anti-German; that a tendency toward a cosmopolitanism that undermines the sense of nationalism is, according to authoritative judgment, inseparable from the essence of German nationality; that one must possibly lose one's German character to find it; that perhaps, without some foreign admixture, no higher German character is possible; that precisely the exemplary Germans were Europeans who would have regarded every limitation to the nothing-but-German as barbaric.[21]

No matter how often the demand is made to come at last to a 'normal', relaxed attitude, the distinguishing feature of Germany's poets remains their strained relationship with Germany. They are great Germans even though, or precisely because, they struggle with Germany. In other words, Germany can be proud of those who were not proud of Germany.

Sebastian Haffner gives us perhaps the most accurate description of this paradox in his memoir *Defying Hitler*, which he wrote in exile in England in 1939: 'The nationalism of the sports clubs . . . the bombastic national self-praise in the style of the "Meistersingers", the hysteria about "German" thought, "German" feeling, "German" constancy' had been 'abhorrent and repugnant' to him even before the Nazis took power: 'It was no sacrifice to forgo it.' Nonetheless, Haffner continues, he always saw himself as a 'fairly good German' – 'if only for the shame I felt at the excesses of German nationalism.' The sentence is worth paraphrasing because it underscores the great distance that can lie between patriotism and affirmation: it was in his *shame for Germany* that Haffner saw himself as a *good* German.

When the Nazis came to power, the German patriot Haffner had no choice – he had to break free from Germany. *His* Germany had been 'destroyed and trampled underfoot' by nationalism. The conflict that confronted Haffner after 1933, he wrote, was not whether one must part ways with one's country to remain true to oneself *as an individual*. The conflict reached much deeper. It was 'between nationalism and keeping faith with one's country'. Haffner movingly describes the consequences of his decision to oppose Germany out of loyalty to Germany:

> I do not 'love' Germany, just as I do not 'love' myself. If there is a country that I do love, it is France, but I could love any country more easily than my own – even without the Nazis. However, one's own country plays a different and far more indispensable role than that of a mistress; it is just one's own country. If one loses it, one almost loses the right to love any other country. One loses the prerequisites for the delightful game of international hospitality – for exchange, mutual invitations, getting to know one another, showing off to each other. One becomes, well, 'stateless', a man without a shadow, without a background, at best tolerated somewhere – or if, voluntarily or involuntarily, one fails to follow inner emigration with the real thing, utterly homeless, an exile in one's own country. To undergo this operation, the internal detachment of oneself from one's country of one's own free will, is an act of biblical savagery: 'If your eye offend you, tear it out!'

The Germany to which Haffner remained faithful by leaving Germany was not a splotch on the map. It was an intellectual construct with specific traits:

> humanity, openness on all sides, philosophical depth of thought, dissatisfaction with the world and oneself, the courage always to try something fresh and to abandon it if need be, self-criticism, truthfulness, objectivity, severity, rigor, variety, a certain ponderousness but also delight in the freest improvisation, caution and earnestness but also a playful richness of invention, engendering ever new ideas that it quickly rejects as invalid, respect for originality, good nature, generosity, sentimentality, musicality, and above all freedom, something roving, unfettered, soaring, weightless, Promethean. Secretly we were proud that in the realm of the spirit our country was the land of unlimited possibilities.[22]

Of course the Federal Republic of Germany is not identical with the Germany Haffner carried with him in his heart when he left Germany. But it speaks well of the Federal Republic that it prefers to identify, in its collective memory, with Haffner's Germany rather than with the 'German Reich'. The battle-hungry intellectuals of the First World War are almost completely forgotten, and those of the great German intellectuals who were involved in its patriotic hysteria spoke out all the more vehemently against the national self-aggrandisement of the 1920s and 1930s. Gottfried Benn and Martin Heidegger may still be read, and here and there revered; but street names and commemorative awards tend much more strongly to honour those Germans who resisted nationalism and Nazism, often risking their lives to do so.

It was not like that from the beginning of the Federal Republic's history. Even in the 1960s, politicians and intellectuals who had returned to Germany out of exile were tainted, among conservative circles, with the odour of treason. No one today would publicly dare to reproach Willy Brandt or Sebastian Haffner for their flight from Germany. On the contrary: the Office of the Chancellor now stands at No. 1 Willy-Brandt-Allee. Regardless of how we judge Brandt's political achievements, isn't that literally wonderful – isn't it a wonder! – that the street where Germany is governed is named after a German emigrant? And the building of new synagogues in central locations is more than a sign of Jewish self-assertion. It shows that the Germany that was destroyed and trampled underfoot, the homeland of intellectuals like Haffner, has been erected again here and there: every new synagogue on German soil is a triumph not only for Judaism but for Germany – for a Germany worth living in.

We should be careful, however, not simply to assign all the music, the philosophy, the literature to Haffner's Germany and the ignorance and the lack of education and culture to the 'German Reich'. There is not one Germany of culture and another Germany of barbarism. At the Library of Congress, Thomas Mann also said:

> For that reason it is quite impossible for one born there simply to renounce the wicked, guilty Germany and to declare: 'I am the good, the noble, the just Germany in the white robe; I leave it to you to exterminate the wicked one.' Not a word of all that I have just told you about Germany or tried to indicate to you, came out of alien, cool, objective knowledge, it is all within me, I have been through it all.[23]

The barbaric Germany, too, and every German nationalism before and after it, invoked culture, appealed to Goethe and Schiller, Mozart and Beethoven. The Nazis' state – as Wolf Lepenies has pointed out

– wanted to be a cultured state; it was deadly serious about culture. Hitler, Goebbels and the other Nazi leaders prided themselves on their sophistication. Their followers admired them for their interest in art, music and architecture. Hitler spoke contemptuously of the English, saying they murdered Shakespeare's plays; he rebuked the French for their weak opera performances. After he had concluded a non-aggression pact with Stalin, Hitler promptly praised the Russian theatre scene. When the pact was broken, he denied the Soviet Union had any cultural achievement at all. But what inflamed Hitler most was the alleged barbarism of the Americans, who, he said, had closed their only opera house:

> Our standard of living is lower, I admit. But the German Reich has 270 opera theatres: a well-rounded cultural life such as they have never seen . . . After all, the Americans live like pigs in a fully tiled sty.[24]

Two hundred and seventy opera houses cannot prevent a single concentration camp. Resistance to Nazi Germany was not found in German culture generally; it was found in those specific values that the Nazis despised and that Haffner praised in Germany: humanity, openness, a brooding thoroughness in thinking, self-criticism, respect for the unconventional and idiosyncratic, good nature, generosity, freedom. As a result, the Nazis' monopolization of German literature ran up against its limits wherever the motifs of self-criticism, openness, European unity and humanism began. Goethe's cosmopolitanism, for example, fundamentally contradicted the Nazi ideology. 'And, then, what is meant by love of one's country? what is meant by patriotic deeds?', Goethe asked.

> If the poet has employed a life in battling with pernicious prejudices, in setting aside narrow views, in enlightening the minds, purifying the tastes, ennobling the feelings and thoughts of his countrymen, what better could he have done? how could he have acted more patriotically?[25]

But it was none other than Friedrich Nietzsche who reviled Germany worst: he saw it as his 'duty', he wrote, 'to tell the Germans *just what* they have on their conscience. *They have all the great cultural crimes of the past four hundred years on their conscience!*'[26] No one has been able to pack more invective against his country into one paragraph, into little more than twenty lines, than the Nazis' own favourite philosopher. Look: 'It is even my ambition to be considered the despiser of the Germans *par excellence*.' – 'I find Germans impossible. When I imagine the type of person who runs counter to all my instincts, it is always a German.' – 'But the Germans are *canaille*.' – 'You abase yourself by having anything to do with Germans.' – 'I cannot stand this race.' And so on, all in just a third of a page of his *Ecce Homo*.[27]

Neither Goethe's nor Nietzsche's cosmopolitanism and contempt for German conditions and characters saved them from being harnessed to the service of Nazism. They were not around to defend themselves. But the German language defended itself against the seduction of the Nazis. Not only has there been no Nazi literature of any distinction: even the few important poets who sympathized at first with the National Socialists lost their literary potency. The best-known example is Gottfried Benn, whose 'supple and excitingly cynical prose' changed almost overnight after 1933, as Wolf Lepenies notes:

> The sentences he publishes or speaks on the radio have all but lost their extravagance. His vocabulary remains aggressive, but is now adapted to the dominant discourse; the phrases obediently form ranks, mottos and battle cries predominate, impoverishing the once visionary vocabulary; the empty phrases clatter and the syntax obediently clacks its heels. Benn remains in the Fatherland, but the mother tongue renounces him.[28]

The German language was protected in turn by the emigrants, and hence by the Jews in particular. Because doubts had always been cast on their belonging to German culture, Jewish authors even in the nineteenth century were remarkably careful about the correctness and integrity of their language. In the twentieth century, at the same time as an almost universally anti-Semitic chauvinism was gaining strength, it was mainly Jews who not only wrote in the German language to perfection but also saw themselves as its guardians. With an exactitude we can hardly comprehend today, authors such as Karl Kraus, Walter Benjamin, Franz Kafka and Victor Klemperer combed German usage for errors, ambiguities and awkwardness. But securing their inclusion in German culture was not the Jews' only incentive to become the most fastidious custodians of the German language. Jews in Prague, such as Karl Kraus and Franz Kafka, were particularly sensitized to German usage by their bilingual situation. The environment was Czech, and especially the so-called simple people there spoke Czech. One reason for the linguistic purism of these writers was that correct German could no longer be taken for granted among the German minority. The German spoken in Prague was often dry and wooden, an institutionally fostered language for formal occasions. This alienation made it possible to consider certain words and idioms from a distance, so to speak, which would not be possible in day-to-day use.[29] Kafka himself describes life with and between two languages in a letter to Milena Jesenská, who answered his German letters in Czech:

> I have never lived among German people, German is my mother tongue and therefore natural to me, but Czech feels to me far more intimate, which is why your letter dispels many an uncertainty.[30]

Kafka, however, owed his distanced ear for his own language, undulled by the naturalness of speech, not only to his Czech surroundings but also to his background – on his father's side – in a Jewish family that had only been assimilated only for one generation. On 24 October 1911, he noted in his diary:

> Yesterday it occurred to me that I did not always love my mother as she deserved and as I could, only because the German language prevented it. The Jewish mother is no 'Mutter', to call her 'Mutter' makes her a little comic (not to herself, because we are in Germany), we give a Jewish woman the name of a German mother, but forget the contradiction that sinks into the emotions so much the more heavily, 'Mutter' is peculiarly German for the Jew, it unconsciously contains, together with the Christian splendor, Christian coldness also, the Jewish woman who is called 'Mutter' therefore becomes not only comic but strange. Mama would be a better name if only one didn't imagine 'Mutter' behind it. I believe that it is only the memories of the ghetto that still preserve the Jewish family, for the word 'Vater' too is far from meaning the Jewish father.[31]

The foreignness towards the German language that Kafka expresses here has enriched that language – and more: it has helped to perfect it, in his work and in the works of so many other writers who did not belong to Germany, or not only to Germany: 'Only a sly poacher can be such a strict gamekeeper', Kafka once said about Kraus; he might as well have been describing himself.[32] Jewish authors in particular bestowed on German literature a cultural, religious and biographical archive that has been a vital contribution to its worldwide importance. Heinz Schlaffer has pointed out that, although the Jewish proportion of the population in Germany and Austria was no more than 1 per cent, about half of the most widely recognized German writers of the twentieth century were Jews. 'If by "German" we mean not an ethnic species, but a cultural orientation, the emancipated Jews can be considered the more serious Germans', he writes in his 'brief history of German literature'. 'Hence by their expulsion and annihilation, German literature logically forfeited its position and lost its character.'[33] We will see, not today, not tomorrow, but in twenty or fifty years, how the foreignness that is now entering German literature once again as a result of immigration influences its orientation and its qualities – whether the descendants of Eastern European or Middle Eastern immigrants can restore to German literature something of the worldliness, the outward awareness or the metaphysical foundations that were characteristic of it until the Second World War. The poet's fatherland, says Goethe,

> is the good, noble, and beautiful, which is confined to no particular province or country, and which he seizes upon and forms wherever he finds it. Therein is he like the eagle, who hovers with free gaze over whole countries, and to whom it is of no consequence whether the hare on which he pounces is running in Prussia or in Saxony.[34]

Germany as a culture is not the same thing as the German nation. And so the often quoted truth that the Germans were united by their literature or their language is only half true. Often enough, what distinguished German culture was diametrically opposed to what constituted Germany as a state and a society, as a people and a nation. A reading of Ludwig Börne's memoirs of the Jewish ghetto of Frankfurt suffices to remind us that discrimination, exclusion and social contempt have been defining experiences, and not just since Hitler, for an important part of German literature. 'I've spent all afternoon in the streets, wallowing in the Jew-baiting', Kafka wrote in mid-November 1920.[35] After the First World War, when he was toying with the idea of emigrating to Palestine – that is, joining a Jewish collective – it had nothing to do with conversion or a return to his roots. It was rampant anti-Semitism that drove Kafka into Judaism. It was through the resentment against Jews that Kafka discovered himself as Jewish.

> Isn't it the natural thing to leave the place where one is hated so much? (For this, Zionism or national feeling is not needed.) The heroism which consists in staying on in spite of it all is that of cockroaches which also can't be exterminated from the bathroom.[36]

Later Kafka insists that the idea of emigrating was only a 'phantasy' – 'the kind of phantasy someone has who is convinced he will never again leave his bed. If I'm never going to leave my bed again, why shouldn't I travel as far as Palestine?'[37]

Kafka died early – early enough, I am tempted to say: for, if I am not mistaken, not a single one of his close friends survived in Germany. Those who did not make it to safety in time – mostly in what was then Palestine – suffered the hardships of political refugees, ended up stranded in cheap hotels, struggled along as illegal immigrants in foreign cities doing odd jobs, queued for visas in front of embassies, or died, like Kafka's non-Jewish love Milena Jesenská, in German concentration camps. Yes, the Germans are united by their literature, but they are not united as Germans. And so German culture is always closest to me where it stands farthest from Germany, whether out of indifference, as with Kafka, or out of opposition, as with Haffner.

Am I a German? In the football World Cup, I support Iran; I did back then when I discovered Kafka, and still I do today as I continue to read him. At the same time, there is no greater obligation for me than to belong to the same literature as the Jew Franz Kafka of Prague. His Germany is also my homeland. Another one of Schiller's *xenia*, which complements the one I quoted at the beginning, is about the 'German national character':

> To take shape as a nation, Germans, you wish it in vain;
> But take your shape the more freely, for you can, as human beings.

— 10 —

THE DUTY OF LITERATURE

Hedayat and Kafka

Sometimes literature wins in the end. Sometimes it prevails even though reason and experience teach us that it should have been stifled, banned, burnt or forgotten. Sometimes it stands up to the storms that strike from time to time, simply stands its ground, and in the end outlasts all the moralizing monitions, asserts itself against all dogmatic objections, and gathers its followers to it in the fourth and fifth generation, until finally hardly anyone dares raise their voice against it; only isolated cries of protest die away here and there; even the censors turn a blind eye because the poet has been declared a monument by the vox populi. The Iranian writer Sadeq Hedayat, who was born in 1903 in Tehran and departed this life in 1951 in Paris, is such a case.

Hedayat was long branded a decadent drug addict, dismissed as an intractable pessimist, and stamped a politically suspect nihilist by communists, monarchists and Islamists alike. His opponents have blamed him for countless suicides, sought to suppress his influence on youth, and banned his books again and again, but, if we study the past six decades of Hedayat criticism, we discover a surprising fact: the quality of his prose has practically never been contested. In Iran, a country which is prouder than any other of its poetic tradition and one whose literature is in fact a kind of sacred and yet constantly regenerating canon, that amounts almost to a certificate of immunity. And, indeed, there is no other explanation for the fact that Hedayat is always among the first to benefit from each temporary easing of the strict censorship rules, while many books that remain banned read like edifying tracts in comparison.

Hedayat's attraction is phenomenal. His texts are not easily accessible, nor are they shallowly entertaining. Their language is masterly; they are often bold in their formal structure. They do not invite identification, they offer no sympathetic heroes, they are unsettling in the relentlessness with which they distil the world's horror. The picture they paint of the country is forbidding, dark, provocative in its one-sidedness and its representation of traditional authorities. Hedayat's most acrimonious attacks were aimed at Islam, whose logic was 'the sharp sword and the begging bowl', as he wrote in his 1930 satire *The Islamic Mission to the European Countries*: 'Is Islam anything else but robbery and murder?'[1] Its Arabic is 'invented', its 'whole philosophy based on rubbish', he wrote eighteen years later in the short story *The Pearl Cannon:*

> Islam is a nauseating mixture of undigested and contradictory opinions and persuasions that were stolen and cobbled together in panic haste from other confessions, religions and old superstitions.

After all, he wrote, the origins of Islam go back to a 'conspiracy' that Jewish agents 'hatched to bring down the Persian and Byzantine empires'; the Arabs, 'those locust-eating, foul-breathed beggar kings', were much too insignificant to have perpetrated such a crime. 'But like Moses' staff that turned into a dragon, frightening even Moses himself, this seventy-headed dragon [i.e., Islam] is swallowing the world.'[2] These lines were written by the man regularly chosen in reader surveys in the Islamic Republic as the most popular writer in modern Iranian literature.

During his lifetime, Hedayat was already provoking scandals. That he criticized Islam and the Shia was the least of his offences: in the 1930s and 1940s, before the religion had been declared a revolutionary force by intellectuals such as Jalal Al-e-Ahmad, Mehdi Bazargan and Ali Shariati, it was almost considered *bon ton* to stay aloof from religious tradition. More scandalous was Hedayat's refusal to go along with the two dominant currents of Iran's early modernism. He quickly saw through the nationalism and the modernizing zeal of the dictator Reza Shah, which initially at least had captured the enthusiasm of many intellectuals; Hedayat found it superficial and totalitarian. After some initial sympathy, he later distanced himself, too, from the Tudeh Party, whose dogmatic communism continued to influence the intellectual climate of Iran into the 1950s. The break became definitive when Hedayat spoke up vehemently for Kafka, whom the communist intellectuals rejected as pessimistic and naïve. The communists' reaction was fierce, and not so different in kind from the religious outrage which intimidates critical minds in the Islamic world today. Hedayat was not to be deterred: 'Those who would brand Kafka a heretic are the numberless bridesmaids rubbing ceruse and rouge on the soulless face of the great idol that is the twentieth century.' It was a different time. It was the time of chauvinistic or left-wing ideologues, of national self-assertion and pressure from the colonial powers, of awakening and of illusions. It was not Hedayat's time. He preferred the company of Chekhov, Guy de Maupassant and Omar Khayyam to the heated debates among twentieth-century intellectuals. He took refuge in the idealized image of a pre-Islamic past or dreamt of a future Iran that would be part of a transnational world culture. He would not identify with his country as he found it. In an allusion to the martyrdom of the Shiite Imam Hussein at Karbala in the eighth century, he wrote in the mid-1930s:

> We have a fatherland like a toilet;
> Our arse is stuck in it like Hussein in Karbala.[3]

At a time when official propaganda was hailing the great nation of the Aryans, that satiric verse could easily have landed him in prison for several years. Iran, Hedayat had remarked ten years before, was a 'terrifying and painful nightmare'.[4]

Hedayat remained a marginal figure his whole life, respected by few, ill at ease with himself and the world. Anonymity, he felt, was man's fate; he resigned himself to it and worried little when his literary work was met with disdain. He never attained a presentable profession or a secure income. He spoke seldom of his family of origin, and there is no evidence that he ever saw an opportunity to found a family of his own. Far from home, Hedayat found his existence reflected in the work of Franz Kafka, to which he devoted a long essay:

> The descendant of Adam is lonely and solitary, helpless and without refuge; he carves out his nameless existence in an inhospitable country, far from his familiar surroundings. He is unable to enter into a bond with anyone, to surrender his heart to anyone, and he knows it, for his gaze and his other traits express it. He tries to hide it and tries compulsively to build a life for himself, but in his doubt he betrays himself, knowing that he is superfluous.[5]

Hedayat's life arrangements, both practical and emotional, were always tentative, as if he was always on the verge of packing up and leaving – not because he had hopes of opportunities elsewhere, but because there was nothing to hold him. Consequently, his biography is a book of restlessness. His first sojourn abroad is an example: in 1926 he travels to Europe with a coveted state scholarship to study engineering; it is the beginning of a forced march. Soon after arriving in Brussels, he leaves for Ghent, where – instead of concentrating on his studies – he writes an essay on death. But the summer of the following year finds him in Paris, where he stays until December 1928. He then moves to Reims, which he soon leaves again for Besançon. Then he tries Paris again. During all these years, Hedayat is uncertain not only about where to study but also about his subject. He starts dentistry, then changes to architecture before returning to an engineering course, while at the same time toying with the idea of becoming an art historian or a painter (as some pen and ink drawings from this period attest). In June of 1930 he returns prematurely to Tehran, against the advice of his sponsors and his family, with no degree and no prospects.

Hedayat suffered not only under the existential and political problems of the time. Even the ignominies of day-to-day life overwhelmed him. 'The whole situation is terrible and meaningless', he writes in one of his letters to Persia – letters that are worth quoting for their inimitable sarcasm:

> It's a quarter to ten here in the dormitory. Two or three reading lamps are on; everyone else is asleep. The worst of all tortures is this monstrous Turk who says his prayers five times a day – may his back be whipped for it – and fasts during Ramadan – the devil take him. God help me, he goes to bed at nine o'clock and doesn't wake until morning, and snores the whole time as if someone had shit between his lips and then turned on a mixer in his dirty mouth.[6]

If we are to believe his own testimony, Hedayat was driven to attempt suicide even by a wall clock in a Paris boarding-house whose chiming jarred him awake every hour. Unable to swim, he jumps from a secluded bridge into the Marne, unaware that a couple of lovers are enjoying themselves in a boat right under him. The young man rescues Hedayat within a few seconds. Ordinarily you tell a person whose condition is hopeless, 'Give it up, lie down and die!', Hedayat writes not much later in the story 'Buried Alive', 'But what happens when Death doesn't want you, when he turns his back on you, when he simply won't come, refuses to come to you?'[7] Perhaps such a tragicomical situation is characteristic of this Iranian poet's life: it was a continuous failure, but – and this is one thing that may distinguish it from the Romantic image of the misunderstood artistic genius driven to ruin by the world – there was absolutely nothing heroic about it. No one could have said so more soberly than Hedayat himself:

> There is nothing in the whole story of my life that would be worth calling attention to. Nothing happened that would bear consideration. I have neither an important position nor impressive qualifications. I was never an outstanding student. On the contrary: my lot has always been failure. No matter what I did, I remained unknown and insignificant.[8]

Back in Iran, Hedayat's odyssey continued – only now he changed jobs rather than cities. He began working at the National Bank, but tendered his resignation in 1932: 'Every time I leave this toilet [the National Bank], my head is spinning.'[9] He was hired by the Chamber of Commerce, and quit in 1934. His next employer was the Foreign Ministry, until 1935, when he quit to go goose hunting. When he returned to Tehran, he obtained a job with the state building company, where he lasted only two months. He went back to the National Bank, quit there for the second time in 1938, and then worked in the State Office of Music, which was closed down in 1940. In 1936, between jobs, he took advantage of a friend's invitation to visit Bombay. While Hedayat certainly had a vague interest in Indian culture, and a more concrete interest in Middle Persian – which Bombay would have been a good place to study, since there was a large Parsi community there – the actual reason for his trip was probably a different one: as his letters from this period indicate, he was eager to get away, no matter where, just to escape 'this rotten and suffocating cemetery that brings a person bad luck'.[10]

Over the years, Hedayat found no way or occasion of separating himself from his parents; he came from a family of respected civil servants but was not willing to use his family's connections to advance his career. Instead he made do with subordinate positions, usually as a translator, to support himself at least partially. He was refused a post as a lecturer in ethnology at the University of Tehran because he had fallen out with the people responsible. 'As for my own work, the less said the better', he wrote in a letter in the summer of 1931:

> Every day, all year long, they squeeze the lifeblood from your body in this God-forsaken bank. It's a dirty, mechanical kind of life. Right now I'm making new plans again. I don't expect to improve my lot, but I couldn't possibly make it worse.[11]

By this time his life's focus was on writing, and in that activity the period from 1930 to 1936 was Hedayat's most productive phase, in which he wrote his major works, including *The Blind Owl*, a disturbing, frighteningly dark novella full of mysteries that is rightly praised as the masterpiece of modern Persian prose literature. And more: if Iran contributed only one book to world literature in the twentieth century – this is it.

First published in 1936 in Bombay as a hectographed manuscript with a print run of fifty copies, each marked 'Not for sale or publication in Iran', *The Blind Owl* is the hallucination of a desperate man, governed by no logic except that of nightmares and riddled with motifs from various spheres of thought, from Sufism to modern psychoanalysis. Hedayat describes a march through the soul, but not a march along beaten tracks: it leads through that underbrush whose existence the conventional strollers among us never suspected. Faint-hearted readers would do better to avoid it; it can only be explored by efforts of superhuman strength, scythe in hand; new terrors lurk under every rotten plant, behind every dead tree. The experiences described in the book have something of the forty-day inner journeys that Islamic mystics undertake in their retreats. Hedayat's journey, however, is a horror trip.

The Blind Owl is a book of books, the kind of book that is unique in an author's bibliography because he can never squeeze such a work from himself more than once. But this should not distort our view of Hedayat's other works, which in addition to fiction include plays, essays, travelogues, translations and ethnological studies. Hedayat suffered repeatedly, for months at a time, from writer's block, but when he began writing he worked frantically. His short stories make up a kaleidoscope of outsiders: the protagonists are mostly lonesome, eccentric, sometimes helpless or spiritually crippled figures, like Davud the hunchback, Khodadad the hermit and Pat the mangy dog, who fail miserably in their hesitant pursuit of something like friendship, or even just company. In the end no course is open to them but an irreversible retreat into themselves. Once again, Hedayat's Kafka essay opens a door: 'Even in his thoughts, actions and attitudes, he is not free', Hedayat says, describing the Kafkan personality; he could just as well be describing the people in his own stories:

> His dealings with others are characterized by self-consciousness. He constantly tries to justify himself. He broods over excuses, fleeing from one to the next, but is a prisoner of his own evasiveness, unable to set foot over the line that has been drawn around him.[12]

The Message of Kafka is not only a remarkably original document of reception history, written by an Iranian author who had translated Kafka (from the French) as early as the 1940s, long before Kafka had become a common topic of exam questions and degree theses. Published in 1948, as Hedayat's last text, the essay has become his own legacy, a self-exposure and at the same time a self-justification: in writing about Kafka, Hedayat wrote about himself; in penetrating Kafka's work, he dissected his own. More an assimilation than an introduction, the essay concentrates on the moments which engage him as a writer, and with which he identifies.

Hedayat devotes a large part of his essay to Kafka's biography and reception, which he describes in keeping with the state of the scholarship then available in French. What is of lasting interest, however, are those sections which, departing from the neutral recapitulation of secondary literature, are written with visible sympathy; they are highly personal, to be sure, and sometimes – as when Hedayat dismisses religious references – reveal more about Hedayat himself than about Kafka; but that is exactly what gives them their spellbinding power, and no doubt their truth as well. In any case, the Prague Jew has an enormous influence on the atheist from Tehran – and hence on modern Iranian literature, whose most influential author is still Sadeq Hedayat. 'People will say he was a pessimistic writer and intentionally painted life more gloomy than it is', he wrote, anticipating Kafka's reception history and his own at the same time.

> Kafka lets the thieving truth of his entrails infuse his art, or, in other words, his inner truths are so numerous that they emerge by themselves and fill his entire work. He is neither optimistic nor pessimistic. All the afflictions of mankind that are recorded in his writings, and the misfortune that he chose and continuously pursued are parts of his investigation.[13]

Hedayat shared Kafka's fate of being considered decadent by his critics on the left, subversive by those on the right, and pessimistic by both. In his own intellectual milieu, among the left-leaning Tehran poets and intellectuals of the 1930s and 1940s, many of whom were suspicious of purposeless art and took it for granted that a poet was *engagé*, Hedayat was mainly accused of not being political enough. That may be a little bit surprising today, especially as his stories definitely contain social criticism, and Hedayat never disguised his criticism of political conditions. However, his sympathy for socialism was motivated less by ideological persuasion than by love for the living creatures of this earth, its people and – at least equally – animals. He was a socialist more with his heart than with his head. He sympathized emotionally with the socialist idea because he found the possessive mentality suspect, the ruling dictatorship abhorrent and the poverty of most Iranians intolerable; yet at the same time he was averse, as an introvert and a bookish man, to all ideology and political activism. In today's Iran, in the strictly ideological state that is the Islamic Republic, where questions of correct sympathies can be asked and answered on quiz shows, Hedayat's attitude gives him a new, subversive power, which may be an important reason why younger readers in particular feel sympathy with him.

Hedayat's revulsion against the political and social conditions in his country, which gave way to democratic reforms only once for a few months after the abdication of Reza Shah in the early 1940s, was directed ultimately at the political reality and was not in contradiction to his strong patriotism, which found its expression in studies of Persian folklore and popular culture and of the Middle Persian language. In his appreciation of folk customs and popular traditions, in his repeated invocations of Persia's pre-Islamic legacy, Hedayat set himself apart from the politically oppressive present, from the political dictatorship, from the cultural hegemony of Europe, and most of all from Islam, the hated 'Arab' religion. When the repressive practices of the Pahlavi monarchy became more and more manifest in the course of the 1920s, most intellectuals turned away in disgust from the swaggering patriotism of the state to become committed Marxists or to withdraw into a romantic variant of nationalism, such as Hedayat had espoused early on. It was a nationalism of the oppressed, in opposition both to the shah and to European imperialism. Although there were sympathies with Nazi Germany and the influence of European racial theories in some authors is undeniable, very few Iranian intellectuals of the 1930s were racists and fascists, least of all Hedayat. In 1937 he wrote in a letter, once again anticipating the later realization of many Iranian writers, that Goebbels and Hitler deserved to be 'spat at in the face'.[14] Without diminishing his love of country, or abandoning his interest in ancient Persian and folk culture topics, his remarks on Iran grew more sarcastic as time went on. 'That's another stupid idea: saving the reputation of the fatherland', he wrote in a letter in the late 1940s. 'What reputation, what fatherland? Maybe it would be better not to save it. Then we would be known for what we are.'[15]

Hedayat was a political writer to the extent that his lifelong theme was reality as it immediately appeared to him – inwardly and outwardly; he was critical in that he recorded the terror of that reality without fear and without deference. But he did not see it as the duty of literature to call for change, much less to advocate a certain political model. Even in his more socially critical stories, he did not fit the type of the *engagé* writer but limited himself to describing injustice. By abstaining from all commentary, moralizing undertones and glorification of the disenfranchised, he introduced a new form, often imitated since, of narrating the lives of ordinary people in Iran. Literature to Hedayat was not a manifesto, and only in his weaker stories, such as the 'Fire Worshipper', was it a vehicle for transporting a message. Hedayat was more persuasive in describing conditions than in drawing conclusions; his lasting texts are those which exemplify what he wrote about Kafka:

> He has a clear vision and a horrendous pain, and in such a way that the vision and the pain become one, and with knifelike perception he looks

> deep into the wound; but he does not believe that man can separate the noble from the evil. He wants to perform his own examination to be completely certain.[16]

In his strongest, darkest moments, Hedayat operates at the median that is equidistant from political and autonomous literature, from *littérature engagée* and *l'art pour l'art.* Theodor W. Adorno circumscribed this region in his essay on 'Commitment', taking Kafka and Beckett as his examples and contrasting them with Sartre and Brecht:

> Kafka's prose and Beckett's plays and his genuinely colossal novel *The Unnamable* have an effect in comparison to which official works of committed art look like children's games – they arouse the anxiety that existentialism only talks about. In dismantling illusion they explode art from the inside, whereas proclaimed commitment only subjugates art from the outside, hence only illusorily. Their implacability compels the change in attitude that committed works only demand. Anyone over whom Kafka's wheels have passed has lost both his sense of being at peace with the world and the possibility of being satisfied with the judgment that the course of the world is bad: the moment of confirmation inherent in resigned acknowledgement of the superior power of evil has been eaten away.[17]

Hedayat has frequently been called the 'Iranian Kafka'; the truth in the cliché is that the plot in their texts is like the blade of a guillotine; the protagonist is the condemned man. It is also true that their biographies are remarkably similar: their bureaucratic jobs, their early deaths, their publication histories, and even their physiognomies. But it is false to suggest too great a similarity between their stories. Hedayat's heroes are not nameless; their biography is self-evident, their environment is concrete and identifiable, their language is inimitably individual. Hedayat's great vocabulary, which he owes in part to his background and in part to his outstanding talent for observation and his curiosity about folk customs, wisdom and idioms, never induces him to flaunt his verbal power. On the contrary, the characteristic style with which Hedayat gave altogether new ways of expression to Iranian prose is completely free of flourishes. Not all of Hedayat's stories, of course, come up to Adorno's definition of radical art, but texts like *The Blind Owl* and *Three Drops of Blood* do more than just lament suffering; they give it a voice. That is why Hedayat's strongest stories enjoy 'the only fame worthy of the name', in Adorno's conception: 'everyone shrinks from them in horror, and yet none can deny that these eccentric novels and plays are about things everyone knows and no one wants to talk about.'[18] Their world, in the words Hedayat himself used to describe that of Kafka's stories, is 'the world of sleep which seizes people by the throat with the terror and the precision of their nightmares.'[19] Adorno pointed out the paradox that literature could help man 'only if it did not act as though it were doing so'.[20] In his *Aesthetic Theory*, he notes:

> To survive reality at its most extreme and grim, artworks that do not want to sell themselves as consolation must equate themselves with that reality. Radical art today is synonymous with dark art; its primary colour is black.[21]

Hedayat no doubt saw both the need for literature to make itself like the darkest reality ('No colour is denser than black', he wrote in a letter shortly before his death)[22] and the paradox that literature faces. It is tangible in his work; it is explicit in his essay on Kafka:

> Kafka's stories are among the darkest in literature; their movement is directed towards ultimate defeat, and it is terrible how they torture hope – not because hope is condemned in them but, on the contrary, because they cannot condemn hope.[23]

But like Adorno, who speaks of the 'minimal promise of happiness . . . which refuses to be traded for any consolation',[24] Hedayat does not abandon the utopia of art altogether: 'as perfect as the catastrophe is, yet a little opening remains; it is not clear whether the opening contains a last trace of hope, or whether hope has gone from it forever.' He maintains – in accord with Adorno – that a different reality could exist, without giving any consolation that it does exist, and without saying in what it might consist. At the same time, Hedayat knows that there is no art without the hope of a different reality.

> Although Kafka's message is as hopeless as the signpost of a dead-end street, and although he lets every desperate search and every effort end in disappointment, although annihilation looms on every side, no refuge exists, every meeting is only an encounter with futility and no territory ever appears where one could escape the breathlessness – still Kafka did not accept this world.

And Hedayat, who up to then justified the autonomy of literature, and with it his own detachment, from the standpoint of political practice, wrote in the closing paragraph of his essay on Kafka:

> This world is no place to live. It is suffocating, and that is why Kafka embarks on a quest for 'an earth, an air and a law' in which he might live in dignity. Kafka is convinced that *this world of lies, betrayal and farce must be destroyed and a better world built on its ruins.*[25]

The words set here in italics are printed in boldface in the edition I have. I do not know whether Hedayat wanted them emphasized or whether his editor is responsible. Nonetheless, the emphasis seems plausible, since the dialectic of the essay, which maintains the poet's autonomy throughout, is revealed only by this unannounced, surprising reversal. It is in fact the same dialectic that Adorno had in mind: 'All commitment to the world must be abrogated if the idea of the committed work of art is to be realized.'[26] Like Hedayat's essay on Kafka, Adorno's rejection of socialist literature and committed literature in general also ends with an affirmation of the political content of art that seems almost abrupt: he writes, in his essay on 'Commitment', that even the most sublime works conceal an 'it shall be different':

> As pure artifacts or products, works of art, even literary ones, are instructions for the praxis they refrain from: the production of right life.[27]

Wrong life was the death of Hedayat. His creative phases became progressively rarer once the political hopes that had filled him after the abdication of Reza Shah had been dispelled. Along with his use of drugs (alcohol and opium; later cocaine too), his lethargy and his loneliness grew more intense. At that time Hedayat was employed as a translator at the college of fine arts. 'Every day he comes by here for half an hour', his friend Hasan Shahid-Nura'i reported:

> First he takes off his hat and lays it in a corner. Then he sits down on a chair and rings for a glass of tea with Pahlavi sugar. Then he begins to stare at the walls for a while, and, if a newspaper happens to be lying on the desk, he looks at the front page (but without reading it). After he has drunk his tea, he puts his hat on his head and, without having said a word to anyone, goes away in the same way as he arrived. That is Hedayat's daily programme. Not a single word of my description is untrue or exaggerated.[28]

Late in 1950, Hedayat flies to Paris once more. His life in Tehran having reached its low point ('I am occupied with massacring my days'), his artistic production lamed ('try as I may, I have nothing that would be worth writing down'),[29] and his spirits further depressed by the political developments after the failed assassination of the young shah and the subsequent wave of persecution, he tries once more to escape the judgement. But the friend in France who persuaded him to come is deathly ill, Hedayat runs out of money, and he does not receive the support he hoped for from his Iranian acquaintances. After a few futile efforts to obtain a visa to travel to Geneva or London, with no money, faced with the choice of returning to his job in Tehran or being sacked (he had obtained four months' leave), he enters his humble apartment on 8 or 9 April 1951 (the precise date is unknown), goes into the little kitchen, seals up the door, opens the valves of the gas cooker, lies down on the floor and dies. 'He was the victim of his clear vision', Sadeq Hedayat wrote of Kafka.[30] It could have been his own epitaph.

— 11 —

TOWARDS EUROPE

*Zweig and the Borders**

I have a route planner on my laptop – you know, one of those computer programs that calculates the best route for you to drive. This route planner is all I need to assess what has happened to Europe in the last fifty years. First I type in North Cape, the northernmost point in Norway, and then I type in Tarifa, the southernmost city in Spain. Then I click on *Go*. The yellow battery indicator flickers – it's never done that before. The laptop clatters with exertion, it groans with indignation – but it does its duty. As soon as the program has calculated a part of the route, a chequered flag appears on the screen, like the flag they wave at the finish line of a Formula 1 race. After fifteen or twenty seconds, the laptop waves its flag to announce the result: from North Cape I drive 700 metres on a local road, bearing left at two junctions, and then, after 280 metres, I take route E69. After another 5930.2 kilometres, I turn left off the Spanish N5 onto CN340, which in 400 metres turns into the Avenida Mirador de los Rios; 600 metres farther on, I'm in Tarifa. My laptop estimates the driving time at seven days, three hours and fifty-seven minutes. It does not list any border checkpoints. I go over the route carefully: it crosses five land borders, but without a single checkpoint to queue for. That means I could drive 5931 kilometres across Europe without taking my ID along. I would pass Stockholm, Copenhagen, Hamburg, Brussels, Paris, Madrid – whatever declarations, conventions or summit meetings you might think of, nothing sums up Europe's unbelievable success better than this: Stockholm, Copenhagen, Hamburg, Brussels, Paris, Madrid, and no passport. When the Burgtheater reopened fifty years ago, hardly

* Speech on the fiftieth anniversary of the reopening of the Burgtheater, Vienna, 14 October 2005.

any of the people present would have thought possible what all of us take for granted today: a Europe without borders.

Heinrich Mann once said the Europeans' feeling of community was an invention of the poets. He may have been exaggerating, and yet it is remarkable how resolutely the poets in particular have spoken up for Europe during the past two hundred years. They were decades ahead of the politicians, if not a whole century. In 1851, when Victor Hugo, speaking in the French National Assembly, advocated a union of the democratically constituted countries, there was not a single representative present who took him seriously. Hugo's speech was drowned out by the jeers and protests of his colleagues. Arnold Rüge fared no better with the vision of a united Europe that he presented to the German National Assembly on 22 July 1848 in St Paul's Church in Frankfurt.

And fifty years ago, when the Burgtheater reopened, Europe was still far from disarming the European nationalisms, as the stir over the opening programme hints: public pressure forced the directors of the Burgtheater at that time to open the Austrian national theatre with an Austrian play. For the fiftieth anniversary of the reopening, the present directors of the Burgtheater have now invited me – a citizen of Iran perhaps, or a resident of Cologne, but certainly not an Austrian – to speak about Europe. I don't even have to mention Austria, they told me – not to say advised me. I confess: I can understand the idea behind their choice. And I like it. It speaks well of a country that it does not need to eulogize itself and, at the same time, is not so obsessed with itself that it spends all its time in self-reproach. And so I would like to talk to you about Europe, and about literature. But I am afraid I cannot oblige you by not mentioning Austria. For I think first of all, in connection with my topic, of the writers who, if they had survived, certainly would have sat here in the stalls fifty years ago. They were some of the most important and most resolute Europeans Austria has produced. I think, for example, of the Jew Stefan Zweig.

As late as 1932, Zweig wrote in an essay that Europe had finally attained once more 'one of the high points of European humanism'. With a speed that contrasted astonishingly with the laboriousness and the slowness of the post coaches and the sailing ships, the intellectual people of all nations exchanged their findings and their poetic works,

> and the problem that they belong to different nations, one a Dutchman, another a German, a third an Italian, a fourth a Frenchman and a fifth a Portuguese Jew, is of no consideration at all compared with the exhilarating feeling that they are all members of the invisible parliament of Europe, that they jointly have a heritage to govern, that all new discoveries, all new achievements of the mind belong to them in common.[1]

Note that Zweig wrote these sentences in 1932. He by no means overlooked the power of the nationalist opposition, 'the power of the little, short-sighted interests that oppose the great, necessary ideas, the force of egoism against the fraternal spirit', he wrote. Never had 'the segregation from state to state in Europe' been 'greater, more vehement, more deliberate, more organized than today'. And yet Zweig felt that Europe, after a long era of brutality and alienation, finally felt itself working again for the first time 'on a common project', a truly European literature, an awareness of a shared identity in which the diversity of language, cultures and religious traditions is appreciated as an enrichment.

> I believe that today we feel, all of us and everywhere, the electric crackling that arises from the friction of opposites, in our very nerves; we all feel that one of the two tendencies must finally gain the upper hand for the years to come. Which one will win? Will Europe continue its self-destruction, or will it become one?

Zweig had no illusions about how the balance of power stood in 1932 between the separate national interests and the supranational European idea, between resentment and the vision of linguistic and cultural diversity within a common political structure:

> Forgive me if I do not say, as many may wish: reason will triumph and soon hold the upper hand, tomorrow or the next day we will see a united Europe in which there is no more war, no isolationism and no destructive national hatred.

The 'madness of war and the post-war absurdity' had destroyed all the childlike hopefulness of his tried and disillusioned generation. For a quarter of a century Zweig had seen only political events that were directed *against* reason. His belief in Europe grew not out of an analysis of contemporary politics, but out of despair over it. His plea for Europe in 1932 was not realistic but messianic. Zweig believed in Europe, he wrote, 'as in a Gospel'. He expected a united Europe would take years and decades to be realized – so long that his generation would probably not live to see it. But the true believer does not need the confirmation of reality to know his conviction is right and true.

> And so no one today can be forbidden to write, as a European, a letter home, to call himself a citizen of the at present non-existent state of Europe, and, in spite of the borders that exist today, to feel intrinsically the fraternal unity of our diverse world.[2]

Stefan Zweig had to flee Austria in 1934. On 23 February 1942, he killed himself in Petrópolis, Brazil, near Rio de Janeiro. Today Europe is a reality. Utopian though he seemed even to himself, Zweig was right; he has triumphed over those who drove him to his death, and he has outlived those who came to this theatre fifty years ago to celebrate the rebirth of Austria instead of the end of the nationalist delusion. Stefan Zweig won and, with him, Heine, Nietzsche, Benjamin, the Mann brothers, Hesse, Hofmannsthal, Tucholsky, Döblin – to name just a few of the German-speaking writers who were at best laughed at, more often exiled, and at worst murdered by their contemporaries for their commitment to Europe.

The freedom of thought and freedom of movement that we have today cannot be taken for granted, either in the context of European history or in view of the present-day world. It makes me angry to hear Europe reduced to agricultural subsidies, free-trade zones and excessive bureaucracy. I am afraid when, increasingly often, I hear the European project talked about in disparaging or tedious tones, while more and more parties in the political centre campaign on Euroscepticism. I cannot comprehend how the European constitution was frivolously gambled away in France and the Netherlands. We travel without passports between countries that shed each other's blood a few decades ago. For sixty years there has been peace, at least in Central and Western Europe. I realize how fragile that peace is in some places. In 2005 the calendar shows not only the fiftieth anniversary of the reopening of the Burgtheater but also the tenth anniversary of the massacre in Srebrenica. Five hundred kilometres southeast of this theatre, 8000 Muslims were massacred in just a few days. The soldiers of the European Union stood idly by. It was the United States that came to the aid of the Muslims in the Balkans. I don't trust this Europe. But, after Srebrenica, it is all the more important to work on Europe.

I mention Srebrenica to make it clear that I do not want to romanticize Europe. I could also point to the growth of poverty, to the resentments that are still rampant, to Europe's inability to address the urgent problems of the world, or even to recognize them in an appropriate form. I could mention so many things about Europe that make me bitter. And yet I know of no country and no continent that looks better to me today than Europe – more just, more tolerant, more safe. We live in states in which we can vote – in my case, for Schröder or for Merkel; God knows, neither of them is the epitome of European Enlightenment, but it is a choice. When I became agitated recently talking on the telephone about my future chancellor, my cousin in Iran said to me, 'Listen, we'll take your Merkel, send her on over, and Schröder along with her. And we'll send you our bunch.' Or take just one single concept: the rule of law. I can go to a court, file a suit and hope for a fair trial, no matter whether I'm the chancellor's son or an unemployed labourer. You'll tell me the unemployed labourer can't afford a good lawyer, and other objections of that sort. But tell an unemployed labourer in Ghana, Bolivia, Syria or China to apply for free legal aid. He won't understand, no matter how good your interpreter is. He won't even comprehend something we take for granted. Not even in the United States could I say today that I would be safe from situations in which I lose all my rights. Hundreds if not thousands of young Iranians and Arabs were arrested after 11 September 2001 and taken to unknown places, without charges, without access to lawyers or their families, for months or even years. Even with all its new security laws, Europe is still far removed from that kind of legal routine.

Some time ago I received a letter from the German domestic intelligence service, the *Verfassungsschutz*. In this letter, the agency notified me that I had been investigated as part of a computer-aided search aimed at detecting Islamic terrorists. The investigation was finished and the file had been deleted. My friends said that investigating me just because of my background and my age was racist. But I thought: a secret service that respectfully informs a citizen that it has investigated him – how many are there like that? I should probably be upset about the Freedom Party of Austria's anti-Muslim campaign posters that I saw all over Vienna today – but no one is publicly upset that the Burgtheater has invited a Muslim to speak at its jubilee. No national institution in Tehran today would invite a member of the Christian or the Jewish minority as an official speaker. Nor would Stefan Zweig have been invited as an official speaker in the Burgtheater in 1932, when he wrote his essay on Europe.

As for so many Jewish intellectuals of his time, Europe for Zweig was more than just a project or a grand idea. It was an existential necessity. As a Jew, there was no place for him in Europe's nationalisms. He could flourish only in a transnational humanity united by values, by a process of secularization, not by an ethnicity, a language or a religion. Today, too, the greatest enthusiasm *for* Europe is found where a life *in* Europe is not taken for granted: in Eastern Europe, in the Balkans or in Turkey, among Jews or Muslims. If you want to know what this over-bureaucratized, apathetic, smug, unresponsive, indecisive entity called the European Union is worth, you have to go where it ends.

I did that to write this speech about Europe. I went to the people who have given up everything just to get to Europe: to the refugees at the gates of the European Union. I got back from Morocco this morning. I would like to tell you about that trip, and also about the books I took along. In addition to Stefan Zweig I had with me another author from Austria who did not live to see the reopening of the Burgtheater: Joseph

Roth. There is an early book by Roth which contains a description, still valid today, of Europe between the two world wars, a world so out of joint that its inhabitants are always suddenly finding themselves in new places, fleeing again and again, always finding themselves in new assemblages. I am referring to his 1929 novel *Hotel Savoy*. The palatial façade of the hotel that gave the novel its name still bears witness to the pre-war era; its interior shelters a motley troop of dissipated existences in makeshift accommodations: millionaires, bankrupts, currency smugglers and dancers. 'I arrive at the Hotel Savoy at ten o'clock in the morning', the first-person narrator Gabriel Dan begins his account:

> I am determined to rest for a couple of days or a week. My relations live in this town – my parents were Russian Jews. I mean to raise enough money to continue my journey westwards.
>
> I am on my way back from three years as a prisoner of war, having lived in a Siberian camp and having wandered through Russian towns and villages as a workman, causal labourer, night watchman, porter and baker's assistant. I am wearing a Russian blouse which someone gave me, breeches which I inherited from a dead comrade, and a pair of still wearable boots the origins of which I cannot myself remember. After five years I stand again at the gates of Europe.[3]

The Hotel Savoy is not a relic of some bygone era. It stands today in Tangier, 30 kilometres south of Tarifa. Its name is not Hotel Savoy but Pension de la Paix, Pension Andalus, Pension Fuentes, Pension Sevilla, Pension Hope. The dozens of Hotel Savoys that can be seen in the old medina no longer have beautiful façades. It used to be different, back when Paul Bowles lived in Tangier. The façade of the Hotel Mauritania, for example, where Bowles visited his friend Mohamed Choukri, has flaked off down to the concrete in spots – but the vestigial stucco must once have been fresh and whole. The stairs have not been refurbished for decades, but you can still imagine how the threadbare carpet that still spans the wooden floor must have glowed red when Paul Bowles walked across it daily. At the reception desk, the hotel management still asks its guests, in the same silver signs in impeccable French, to give notice the day before their departure. How happy today's guests would be to leave the Hotel Mauritania! 'But it is only possible – I mean for people like us – to live in hotels', says one of the guests in *Hotel Savoy*.[4]

Bowles wrote in his novels about Westerners grown tired of their civilization who escape from their empty lives to Africa. Today the Hotel Mauritania, like all the other boarding houses in the medina of Tangier, is inhabited by people who would rejoice at an empty Western life – as long as it was a life. They hang around in the tea houses, in their rooms, at the port – and wait. In front of the Hotel Sevilla I fell into conversation with six guests, the youngest barely twenty years old, the oldest perhaps forty. They came from all parts of Morocco, from villages, small towns, the metropolis Casablanca. Three or four of them had been to university or learned a trade; one was an engineer, another a car mechanic. The others had no qualification but their keenness. That doesn't make any difference, though. They won't find any work in Morocco anyway. I asked the group, What do they want in Europe? Work, of course, a normal life, nothing more. A little bit of assurance that you won't have to start the struggle for survival all over again every day; a chance to start a family, or at least to take your girlfriend out once in a while. A car and a holiday are not part of the normal life they dream of; it's more important to them to earn enough money to send some back to their family from time to time. Democracy? They snigger. Democracy? Oh yes, that would be grand. But, to begin with, they would be content to have health insurance.

How do they want to get across? I ask. By inflatable boat, they answer; that's the only chance at the moment. One of them fishes a piece of paper from the back pocket of his trousers: a French employment certificate. He paid 700 euros for it, 700 euros, but, when he presented it at the French consulate, the officials spotted the forgery within a few minutes. Now he's scraping the money together for a seat in the inflatable boat. No more shady tricks, he says.

I ask whether any of them has tried before to get across to Europe by boat. I've been over there twice before, says one, and looks around at the others. Three times, says the next one – once – four times – and so on. They set out at night from somewhere, get caught by the Spanish police at sea or on the beach, and are taken back to Morocco.

Many of you will remember the pictures of the derelict refugee ships, the 911 passengers who landed on the beach at Boulouris in southern France on 17 February 2001, or the death ship that the Italian authorities towed to land at Lampedusa in October 2003, whose passengers had all died of thirst. Perhaps we still have in mind the Benetton poster, or the hopelessly overloaded ship off Bari, the young Albanians jumping overboard to reach the shore. What few people know is that over 80 per cent of refugees now get across to Europe aboard small inflatable boats. When their bodies are washed ashore on European coasts, the news appears at most in the local papers of the seaside towns. If we assume that only one out of three bodies is found and registered, then 13,000 to 15,000 refugees have died in the past fifteen years, just in the area around the Straits of Gibraltar. Yes, you heard correctly: 13,000 to 15,000 dead off Gibraltar alone. That means the straits are the biggest unmarked grave in Europe.

Because the patrols in the straits are always being tightened, the boats fall back on routes that are still more dangerous, especially if they run to the West, on the open Atlantic. The 12 kilometres that separate Spain and Morocco at the narrowest point often become an odyssey of several hundred kilometres. The boats have long since begun crossing other narrows between Africa and Europe – although for an inflatable craft they are anything but narrow – between Morocco and the Canary Islands, or between Libya and Lampedusa. Fifty thousand boat people are picked up every year in the Mediterranean, either at sea or immediately after landing in Europe.

The Moroccans know the dangers of the crossing very well; they have sat in those boats. They know how slim the chances are of escaping the Spanish authorities even if they do make it to Europe. Those who take their holidays in southern Spain may have seen the men, women and children who come ashore from the inflatable boats on one beach or another and sprint past the sunbathing tourists into the bushes, trying to avoid the police. Because it is obvious where they come from, they would be deported back to Morocco immediately. The sub-Saharan refugees among them, on the other hand, can lie down in relief alongside the tourists and wait for the police to pick them up. They have destroyed their identification papers and, as long as the authorities can't find out what country they come from, they generally can't be deported. After all, what country would take them? The police take them to a camp, and from there most of them struggle on to one of Europe's major cities, where friends can help them or a member of a refugee-smuggling organization is waiting for them. For the Moroccan refugees, however, who have no chance of remaining in Europe legally, the task is not as simple as just reaching the Spanish shore. They have to do so without being noticed. The guests of the Hotel Sevilla are well informed about the Guardia Civil patrols and their radar and night vision equipment. Nonetheless, they are just waiting for an opportunity to sprint inland from the Spanish coast, for fair weather and a seat in an acquaintance's boat. And if they die?

'Then that's just how it is', one says.

'We're not suicidal', the second adds. 'There are people who cross in the autumn or winter. That's suicide. We try to be realistic. We know the risks. When we get into the boat, our chance of getting through has to be good enough in relation to the hazards.'

'But you're taking a calculated risk of dying?' I ask.

'Well, we take a risk of dying, but it's not worse than living here.'

The other men nod. None of us says anything for a while. Through the open window to the lobby I can hear someone has scored a goal –

Champions League, Real Madrid versus Olympiacos Piraeus. All the men look in through the window or the door to see the slow-motion replay. When they turn back around to me, one of them says with a grin, 'What we do is *amaliyyāt istishhādiyya*, suicide missions. The Europeans think all Arabs are suicide bombers. Well, they're right: all of us here are on a suicide mission. The paradise we're dying to get to is called Schengen.'

A few years ago, a representative survey in Moroccan secondary schools found that 80 per cent of the pupils would like to emigrate to Europe. People are always asking, Why do they hate us? I think anyone who has ever visited an Arab country can only laugh at that question: 80 per cent of Moroccan youth want to come to Europe. For a culture that is supposed to be at war with the West, 80 per cent is rather high. If they do hate Europe, it is not because of its achievements, not because of democracy and the rule of law, but because this Europe simply doesn't want them. It prefers to let these young people drown in the Mediterranean Sea every night, all summer long, rather than allowing them to enter the paradise called Schengen.

In 1929, Joseph Roth predicted his own future in *Hotel Savoy*, but he didn't end up like his first-person narrator Gabriel Dan. The man who drew on the biblical stories of flight and exile over and over again in his books had to emigrate himself in 1933. In Paris he lived in hotel rooms, worked for a few exile periodicals, became an alcoholic. On 27 May 1939, he died of the consequences of alcoholism in the Necker charity hospital in Paris. Some of the guests at the Hotel Sevilla have also fallen into addiction. Their drug is usually hashish. One of the men says himself that Tangier is rotting his mind, that he can't keep up his motivation, doesn't learn anything, sits in the tea house all day watching television, and smokes hashish in the evening. Their lives run through their fingers, just like the money they have saved and borrowed for the escape to Europe. Many of them will end up in the gutter. Many are already in the gutter. Some children have never been anywhere else. All around the vicinity of the port, you can see them in the squares that overlook the sea. They beg or play football; they watch the ships or hold bags of glue under their noses. Every night they try again to sneak into the port, to climb over the fence, to dig a hole under it, or to swim the long way around to a pier. Once they have made it into the port, they usually hide under a truck and hope that it will drive them onto one of the ferries in the morning. The ferry takes just 35 minutes to get to Europe.

Every night, from my hotel overlooking the port, I heard the dogs of the Moroccan border patrol waiting to catch the children. And yet once in a while a child makes it on board one of the ships, people say; sometimes they just try to hold onto the hull of a ship, in the water. I have no idea how that is supposed to work, but I wouldn't put it past these children to try it. Soon the European Union will be providing Morocco with sensors that detect a heartbeat or body heat. Then the children will have to stop breathing to get to Europe. They would probably try that too.

Europe keeps trying, with more soldiers, new equipment and more money, to stop the refugees in North Africa, or in the Mediterranean at the latest. But Europe has a problem. It has a formal obligation to protect human rights. All the states of the European Union have signed the Geneva Convention on Refugees. To cover up the present flagrant violation of international law, Europe would summarily declare the dictatorships of North Africa and Eastern Europe 'safe third countries' where refugees can be deported without further consideration. These dictatorships are rewarded by Europe for their cooperation. They receive not only economic aid and political support; Europe also supplies the camps to pack the refugees in, under conditions characteristic of camps in dictatorships: two hundred people to a room – men, women and children. Human rights organizations report maltreatment, rape, hunger; the worst reports are from the Libyan camps. Europe sends mattresses for these camps, wool blankets, night-vision goggles, underwater cameras, and buses for transporting inmates. Last year the Libyan government even received a thousand body bags from Italy. Europe's interior ministers are interested today only in how to close up the last mouseholes in Europe's gates. What happens outside the gates of Europe doesn't interest them. Does it interest us? Any government that understood the metaphor 'the boat is full' as referring to the hopelessly overloaded refugee ships in the Mediterranean Sea instead of to its own affluent society would soon be voted out.

On clear days, I could make out Europe from my hotel window. I couldn't understand. How many of its smartest minds Europe lost because they stood before closed borders, because they couldn't show valid ID, visas, currency! How many Europeans survived only because they were allowed to cross, sixty years ago, from Tarifa to Tangier! Every day at Europe's borders, and on the opposite coasts, the same dramatic scenes are taking place as sixty years ago: rickety boats putting out to sea from remote locations, loaded with young men, families, pregnant women, children. Boats capsizing, refugees adrift at sea until they die of thirst or cold. Every day people are killing themselves at Europe's gates when their helpers abandon them, they are captured without papers, or their forged visas are exposed. We know all that. European literature contains many descriptions of such scenes. Almost every motif of Joseph Roth's *Hotel Savoy* is found today in the guest houses of Tangier: the search for odd jobs, the waiting for transport, the hope of obtaining papers, the shame of impoverishment, the pawning of last belongings, the temptation to sell one's soul, or body, the death in the hotel bed when medicines cost more than a person can pay. Through literature, art, film, we have participated in the fates of countless European refugees. Why, when we encounter them again today from the opposite perspective, is our first impulse to insult them? Illegals, criminals, human traffickers, economic asylum, smuggler mafias, the boat is full?

I know, people will say you can't compare the two situations. But I'm not comparing the causes. I'm comparing the effects. A refugee who drowns is a refugee who drowns. A person doesn't have to be a victim of persecution on grounds of race or political persuasion to have reason enough to risk his or her life just to get to Europe. A person who is hungry and wants a piece of bread is not a parasite, much less a criminal. He or she is demanding the human right to life. He or she is yielding to the simplest, most immediate urge of all people. Every day we prevent people from surviving. We do not yield to the simplest human urge to hold out our hand to a person struggling for his or her life; instead we think we have to protect ourselves – protect ourselves from those who seek protection among us. We have made sure that the right to asylum is life-threatening. We make people travel 200 kilometres back and forth across the Mediterranean Sea in inflatable boats before they can speak the word 'asylum'. We spend billions every year to ward off those who seek refuge with us. Every child in Tangier and every organization that defends the rights of refugees in Morocco knows that the steadfastness which the European Union demands of the Maghreb states in the fight against illegal immigration is expressed in the form of beating, robbing and raping refugees. The European interior ministers know it too.

The German minister of the interior Otto Schily said Africa's problem must be solved in Africa. That sounds sensible. But we would gain a great deal if Europe would at least start solving those of Africa's problems whose causes lie in Europe. These begin with the European Union's subsidies that destroy the African cotton and sugar industries; they include the tariffs by which we exclude African products from the market; they do not end with special support for North African dictatorships. I will give you an example of what it means today when – to solve Africa's problems in Africa – Europe addresses the causes of emigration: since 2003, in Niger and adjacent states – some of which can barely be called states by now – experts and representatives of international organizations have been swarming out on so-called fact-finding missions. Their explicit objective is to investigate the causes of flight and migration and to propose ways to curb 'irregular migration'. The European experts cannot have overlooked the growing hunger, which must be the primary cause of 'irregular migration'. But their analysis doesn't say a word about it. The Western media too had few headlines to spare for the famine. But imagine how much attention the media and governments would devote to Niger if someone from Niger were to take an example from the Arab extremists and blow himself up at Vienna's central railway station. Something is fundamentally wrong if the West becomes aware of societies in distress only after they have begun producing terrorists. Without 11 September 2001, the Afghans would still be living under the yoke of the Taliban, which the Pakistani, Saudi and American intelligence services had bestowed on them in a joint venture of the dirtiest kind.

Our perception, the perception of our media, our politicians, our culture, has become as much out of joint as the world Joseph Roth wrote about. Three billion poor – that is about half of humanity – together have less income than the four hundred wealthiest families on earth; 6000 children under the age of five die every day in shacks and slums, in the villages and cities of the third world; 6000 children every day leave despairing mothers and fathers behind; 25,000 adults die every day of hunger, thirst, deprivation and exhaustion. Where are the political talk shows that discuss the Marshall Plans that could prevent their mass deaths? How many dead in sub-Saharan Africa does it take for a television network to produce a special broadcast? According to the United Nations' forecasts, two-thirds of Africa's farmland will disappear by 2025 if deserts keep growing at the current rate. There will be 135 million people looking for new livelihoods throughout the world for that reason alone. In view of this prospect, it is both cynical and unrealistic to fall back on the position that Africa's problems need to be solved in Africa. At an increasing rate, Africa's problems are going to be Europe's problems. Europe is not going to be able to keep them out, no matter how well it secures its borders.

European refugee policy today is limited largely to preventing refugees from reaching Europe. It has become an unquestioned part of security policy, shaped by the stereotypes of organized crime and terrorism. The instruments used against refugees are the same as those used against criminals and terrorists: submarines, intelligence services, night-vision devices, underwater cameras, military bases, camps, interrogation, solitary confinement, barriers, barbed wire, tear gas, rubber bullets, bending laws out of all recognition, undermining the rule of law, outsourcing torture. A year ago the Italian air force bought five American Predator drones for 48 million dollars to use – according to the official explanation – against terrorism *and* against irregular migration. These unmanned aircraft can fire rockets. Predator drones have become well known because the United States uses them to hunt al-Qaeda. Refugee protection in Europe no longer means the protection *of* refugees, but protection *against* refugees.

This summer, at the Salzburg Festival, I had the pleasure of meeting the South African author J. M. Coetzee. We both took part in a symposium at which we reflected on the title of this year's festival season: 'We the Barbarians'. In a brief, concise speech, Mr Coetzee pointed out the intentional paradox in that title. *We* can't be barbarians. By definition, if we take the word literally, only other people can be barbarians, because 'barbarian' of course means someone whose language we don't understand. To the Greeks, barbarians were everyone who didn't speak Greek. To the Arabs, the original inhabitants of Morocco were barbarians, which is why they named them that: Berbers. In the public mind, the barbarian is always the other. I think the task of literature, of art in general, is to reverse exactly this definition of the other and always to discover anew the barbaric in us – to understand what is foreign in us: 'We the Barbarians'. I call that to mind now because the artistic and literary representation of the other as a barbarian – especially when the other takes the form of the Muslim – has never, since the days of colonialism, been as common as in the European literature of recent years. We are afraid of black or Arab people invading Europe over fences and in boats. The images on television show them as anonymous masses. The political language makes them out to be a plague. Our task is to recognize them as human beings.

It is no coincidence that a white author from South Africa has called this task to our attention, not just in his speech in Salzburg but many years ago. I am referring to Coetzee's early novel *Waiting for the Barbarians*. In it, he tells about a magistrate who conducts the business of a tiny garrison town on the marches of an unspecified empire. He is not distracted by the alleged threat of the 'barbarians', a neighbouring nomadic tribe. But then a special unit of the state police arrives from the capital and constructs evidence of an allegedly imminent barbarian attack. And so the empire defends itself by going to war, by a pre-emptive strike, as it would be called today. Many nomads are killed; others are captured and mistreated in camps. The magistrate picks up a severely mistreated nomad girl. 'Come, tell me why you are here', he says to her. The girl answers, 'Because there is nowhere else to go.'[5] The magistrate takes the girl in, lives with her, and gradually begins, after many misunderstandings, to understand her. She ceases to be a barbarian. 'More ordinary than I like to think, she may have ways of finding me ordinary too.'[6] Finally, the magistrate takes the girl back to her people. When he comes back from the 'barbarian' camp, he is arrested as a collaborator and a traitor, tortured and publicly humiliated, made into a 'barbarian'.

No one likes to be brutal. No country boasts of its brutality. Brutality is always 'necessary'. The prerequisite for behaving inhumanely is to perceive the other as not human. The only way to legitimize flagrant injustice – a way that is constantly being reinvented – consists in appealing to the right of self-defence. I would like to see an aggressor who does not claim to be defending himself. 'Tell me, sir, in confidence . . . what are the barbarians dissatisfied about? What do they want from us?', the commander asks the magistrate at one point.[7] Why do they hate us?

I had Coetzee's novel in my pocket when I visited the Spanish enclave Ceuta on the Moroccan coast, 'this farthest outpost of the Empire of light', as Coetzee's narrator calls the town in the border region.[8] In the previous night, hundreds of sub-Saharan Africans had tried to get over the border fences with handmade ladders. A few refugees had made it; five had died, including an infant; dozens of refugees had fallen, severely injured, on one side of the border or the other. The Africans claimed, unanimously, that one of the dead had been shot intentionally by a Spanish border guard. In *Waiting for the Barbarians*, Coetzee writes:

> Since the news has arrived from the capital that whatever might be necessary to safeguard the Empire would be done, regardless of cost, we have returned to an age of raids and armed vigilance. There is nothing to do but keep our swords bright, watch and wait.[9]

A short way before Ceuta I see Moroccan soldiers by the roadside, between them a group of some twenty black Africans sitting on the ground, crowded close together. They are cold. The fog is thick, and most of them are wearing no more than shorts and T-shirts. The commander of the soldiers is friendly, but he says he is not allowed to give me any information, nor may I talk to any of those who have been arrested. At least he permits me to give them cigarettes. As I do that, I manage to talk with them briefly after all. But what they have to say is little more than 'Thanks'. What I can say is little more than a promise to write about their situation. What is there for us to say? Everyone present knows what is going to happen. The black people will be imprisoned for a few days and then set free near the Algerian border, in the middle of the desert, 30 kilometres from the nearest village. They'll come again. The black people know it, the soldiers know it, even the taxi driver who talks to me about the 'poor bastards' as we drive on knows it. They'll come again. Europe, too, ought to know it: they'll come again. Even if the barbed wire is twice as high: they'll come again. Even if Europe opens fire on them: they'll come again.

The border fortifications around Ceuta already look like the old German–German border: two barbed-wire fences, 3 and 6 metres high, with Guardia Civil jeeps patrolling along a road between them, watch-towers of course, video cameras, infrared cameras. The most recent improvements to the fences cost 150 million euros. The black refugees are perfectly aware that they won't get over the border unnoticed. They try to storm the fences in such numbers that the border police are over-whelmed. If five hundred people with handmade ladders rush the fence, fifty will get through – that is the formula. A few die each time, in each of these raids; the rest are deported into the desert between Morocco and Algeria, where they turn around and come back to knock again at Europe's gates – or, more precisely, to try to storm the gates.

Until two weeks ago – when the pictures of the refugees' drama found their way into our news, thanks to the dead – very few Europeans even knew of the existence of the two Spanish enclaves Ceuta and Melilla. In countries such as Niger, Nigeria and the Ivory Coast, every child probably knows about Ceuta and Melilla. I don't know. I only know that Coetzee's novel *Waiting for the Barbarians* describes Europe's border stations appallingly well: the empty, clean streets, the order, the boredom. Those who have seen the blood on the barbed-wire fences will wonder for the rest of their lives whether the barbarians are really the others.

In Tangier I talked with many black people. You don't meet them in the hotels any more, and rarely in the streets. Since the European Union has intensified its cooperation with Morocco, the police there are cracking down on illegal immigrants. If they get caught without papers, the authorities deport them into the desert. Fortunately, they are not yet particularly systematic. The police often look the other way when they see a black person. The refugees at Europe's gates have become a card the Moroccans play in their negotiations with the European Union. That is understandable from the Moroccans' point of view, since black Africans in the country want to get to Europe but, for a long time now, have been inhabiting many villages and cities in Morocco, where officially 20 per cent of the population now live below what is known in the language of the United Nations as the 'absolute poverty limit'. Imagine the black refugees in German or Austrian villages if there were comparable poverty there. For fighting Europe's battle against illegal immigration, the Moroccan state demands something in return. So the black migrants are sometimes tolerated and sometimes bullied, depending on the state of the negotiations.

At least Europe has been able to ensure that the guest houses in Tangier admit practically no black people. They now live mainly in camps outside the city and around the Spanish enclaves, in the woods, with no access to supplies, no sanitary facilities, in tents made of plastic sheeting or in the open. Out of fear of white people, they often don't even let the Doctors Without Borders into the camps. Many other black people live underground in the suburbs of Tangier or in private houses in the medina, crowding four, eight, twenty in a room, with no electricity as far as I have seen, with holes in the floor for toilets. They try to go out in the street as little as possible, especially in the daytime, to avoid encounters with the police. I was in one room that was no more than 2 by 4 metres, with no electricity and no windows. Three people lived there. They paid 60 dirhams a day, equivalent to about 160 euros a month. That is about 20 euros per month per square metre.

I sat with Osman, Stephen, Osahan and Caesar from the room above; friends of theirs were also visiting. Osman lit a candle and showed me the notebook in which he had written down the stations of his odyssey, especially the weeks in the desert after the Moroccans had deported him. Each of them had been deported to the desert at least once. I can't imagine how a person could be marooned there, even though my hosts talked about it at length. It sounded almost as if it was just one of their occupational hazards to be loaded on a truck from time to time, driven out to the desert and herded off the truck bed. Most of them had been living in Morocco for two or three years. It was more bearable when they lived in the guest houses, they said. Now they lie on their blankets waiting, day in and day out, listening to African music from a cassette recorder, if they have batteries, and staring into the dark. Once in a while they light a candle. None of the European tourists who pass, singly or in groups, by the house where Osman, Stephen, Osahan and Caesar live could know that, on the first floor, behind the clay wall, Beckett is being performed, but with no intermission, no end and no light: *Waiting for Godot*. No one could have imagined that: Godot is us.

Occasionally there are productions in which *Waiting for Godot* is set in a realistic place. Such performances, those I have seen, have never satisfied me. To me Beckett's play always belongs to an intermediate sphere, a realm between Heaven and Earth. In Tangier I discovered that *Waiting for Godot* can also be set in Hell. Only then we can't see it. The stage has no lights.

We call Osman, Stephen, Osahan and Caesar 'economic refugees', as if they were interested in profit, not survival. No one who has enough money takes a seat in an inflatable boat or hides in a refrigerated truck. Those who have money and come to increase it buy a forged passport or a visa, or pay a smuggling organization to slip them out of the airport between flights in Frankfurt or Paris. The number of 'economic refugees' who are able to buy such admission to Europe on the black market is negligible. The number of those who knock on Europe's gates at night, barefoot, drenched, hypothermic, starved and half dead of thirst is vast. It is against them that Europe is waging war in what it calls the 'Euro-Mediterranean Process'. 'Euro-Mediterranean Process' sounds like an EU programme for saving outdoor cafés or exchanging recipes. In fact, it means nothing but intensifying cooperation with dictators to protect Europe against refugees and terrorists, as you can read in the strategy papers of the EU think tanks: refugees and terrorists, in the same European breath. In the 'Barcelona Declaration' of 1995, the European Union announces it will establish an 'area of freedom and stability' in the Mediterranean region and require the 'respect of democratic principles and human rights'. But in fact, Europe continuously supports the despots south of the Mediterranean Sea, from Morocco to Algeria, Tunisia, Egypt and now even Libya. 'Strengthening the protection of refugees outside Europe as well', in the language of the European interior ministers, means declaring as many transit countries as possible to be suitable 'first countries of asylum'.[10] I did not have Orwell's novel *1984* along with me, but I found it cited often enough in the material I studied in preparation for my trip. 'Migration filter' is another fine term from the humanity department of the European Union. And 'welcome centres': the German interior minister says 'welcome centres' when he means European Union detention camps on African soil.[11] And in autumn of 1997, when large ships each carrying several hundred Kurdish asylum-seekers ran aground on the Calabrian coast, the former German interior minister Manfred Kanther found nothing better to do than to coin the term 'criminally organized illegal migration', which was to be stopped at the 'lesion of origin'.[12] A person who talks about people as an epidemic betrays Europe while pretending to defend it. A person who intones that the boat is full, and means, not the refugee ships in the Mediterranean Sea, but our affluent European societies, has abandoned the tradition on which the West is based: the tradition of the Bible.

I did not have Dostoevsky along on my trip. I hadn't imagined I would need it. But Dostoevsky is always indispensable. Immigrants roll south daily between Libya and Niger. The reason is the Gaddafi regime's agreement with Italy on preventing illegal immigration across the Mediterranean. The trip takes twelve days and nights, during which the people on the bed of the truck are dependent on a 20-litre canister of water. The asphalt road ends at Al Gatrun in southern Libya. From there it is another 1490 kilometres to Agadez, where a fleet of buses and semi-trailer trucks take the deportees to their countries of origin: 1490 kilometres of heat and fear, thirst and backache, hunger and resignation, dirt and shame. These trucks roll every day, their cargo beds full of refugees, paid for with European money. Just about a year ago, fifty refugees died at once, crushed by an overloaded truck. In the first few months after the Libyan–Italian agreement of 25 August 2004, 106 deaths were counted. No one knows how many bodies lie buried in the sand along the route: refugees who died of exhaustion or in accidents, or were robbed and left in the dunes by the smugglers who contracted with the Libyan authorities to take them home. In January of this year, a girl from Ghana was torn apart by a pack of wild dogs before the eyes of her fellow passengers. Perhaps you remember the passage in Dostoevsky's *Brothers Karamazov* in which a general has his dogs chase down a child and maul it to death, and the child's devout mother later forgives him. Ivan Karamazov rejects that forgiveness: 'I don't want harmony, for love of mankind I don't want it', he says. 'It is not worth one tear of even that one tormented child who beat her chest with her little fist and prayed to "dear God" in a stinking outhouse with her unredeemed tears!'[13]

A Dutch social-democratic justice minister, Aad Kosto, said pastors who granted refugees church sanctuary 'loved their neighbour too much'.[14] I know it is not customary to quote the Bible in theatres. Nonetheless, I would like to tell you one last story, a story of one who loved his neighbour too much – a real extremist: Jesus of Nazareth. We have forgotten that expulsion and flight are among the defining motifs of Judaism, Christianity and Islam. The Islamic calendar begins with Muhammad's flight from Mecca. According to sharia, the religious law of early Islam, asylum is an unshakable institution. In the eighth or ninth century, the Islamic legal scholars established the minimum standard by which every person who arrives in a city destitute must be received. The Bible, too, tells of refugees from the beginning. Adam and Eve fled from Paradise. Cain fled revenge; Abraham and Sarah fled to Egypt to escape hunger. Abraham's second wife, Hagar, fled into the desert as a victim of discrimination. Jacob fled because he feared Esau, Joseph because he feared his brothers. Moses is a political refugee; so is David. And Elijah flees. Joseph and Mary flee with the baby Jesus to save him from death. Imagine if they had to tell a European border guard today that they had been warned in a dream of an impending bloodbath. Europe's interior ministers can rest easy. No border guard would dare be suspected of a 'loving his neighbour too much'. He would immediately be out of a job.

But the story I wanted to recall is a different one. It's about the woman of Canaan who begged Jesus to help her child.[15] Jesus refuses because his mission is only to members of the house of Israel. He doesn't deny that the woman will be left helpless, but he can't change that. He cannot help her child, he says. The woman doesn't stop begging Jesus for help, but he always answers by 'putting his own people first'. Finally the woman prevails by saying she is asking only for crumbs, not the whole loaf. Jesus is greatly impressed by her faith: 'Be it unto thee even as thou wilt.' And lo, there was a second serving, and this time not for Israel, but for all peoples.

Europe is a wonderful country for Europeans. As urgent as its social and political problems may be – never in history has life on this continent been more peaceful and tolerant. That is no small thing, and we forget it too often. But it is not enough. Only when Europe is humane to those who do not belong to Europe will it become the 'supranational realm of humanism'[16] that Stefan Zweig believed in as a Gospel. Universalism is an essential component of the European idea in the strong sense, the idea of a secular, transnational, multi-religious and multi-ethnic intentional community that grew out of the Enlightenment and the French Revolution. It cannot be relativized; it has no fixed geographical boundaries. It cannot simply end in Tarifa or Ceuta, or at the borders of Poland or Bulgaria. Goethe is extremely clear on the necessity of feeling all nations' fates as his own. Not by chance is Immanuel Kant content with nothing less than the 'perpetual peace' of a *world* federation of constitutional republics. That is a utopia, of course, and no one knew that better than Kant, the soberest of European philosophers. But the moment Europe takes its eyes off that utopia, stops moving towards that utopia, the idea ceases to exist. A Europe that isolates itself is no longer Europe, at least not the Europe of utopians such as Goethe and Kant, Zweig and Roth, whose early hope for the United Nations or for a Europe without borders has proved to be more realistic than the pragmatic narrowness of their contemporaries. But defending the universalism of the European idea means more than just ensuring mobility and human dignity. Standing up for the universalism of the European idea also means working to spread it.

We smile smugly today when we read about the farce over the reopening of the Burgtheater fifty years ago: the indignant citizens' insistence on a purely Austrian theatre. When the Burgtheater celebrates the centennial of its reopening, people will smile smugly about the farce in which Austria is indulging over the European Union's membership negotiations with Turkey, over the indignant government representatives' insistence on a purely Christian Europe. I have to believe that's how it will be, for, if it turns out otherwise, if your government prevails, then there will be no room in Europe for me, for people like me. Europe is a utopia to me too, especially in view of this year's developments: the failed constitution, the rise of nationalist attitudes and governments in many European countries. And yet I am sure we will win, just as Stefan Zweig and the other writers I spoke of won.

> The two ideas, nationalism and supranationalism, now stand chest to chest in a crucial wrestling match, pitted one against the other; there can be no more shrinking from the problem, and the next moments must reveal whether the countries of Europe will cleave to their present economic and political enmity or finally solve this debilitating conflict by a complete unification, a supranational organization.[17]

Now I have to tell you what my route planner says when I type in Tarifa and Tangier. I hadn't thought it would accept the trip at all. But it does. In two seconds it displayed the results. I quote my laptop verbatim: Depart Tarifa on Avenida de las Fuerzas Armadas. In 0.7 km: turn right (south) on Calle Alcalde Juan. In 1.0 km: keep right (southwest) on local road. In 31.3 km: arrive in Tangier. The route planner makes it out to be the easiest thing in the world to get from Europe to Africa. It is deterred neither by Schengen nor by the sea: in Tarifa, keep right on local road; straight on; in 31.3 km, arrive in Tangier. Maybe we should follow the route planner.

— 12 —

IN DEFENCE OF THE GLASS BEAD GAME

*Hesse and Decadence**

In the early or perhaps the mid-twentieth century – it is still not quite certain today whether it was before, between or after the two great wars – the glass bead game was invented at a music conservatory in Cologne. In the beginning it was actually played with glass beads, which the first players used to signify letters, numbers, musical notes or other graphic symbols. The glass beads were soon discarded except in the name; the game itself, however, grew ever broader, more sophisticated, and more elaborate over the decades and centuries. By the time it reached its current form, probably in the twenty-second or twenty-third century, the glass bead game had encompassed the potential to set all the works and discoveries of Western culture – the world's literatures, the different sciences, the fine arts and especially music – in relation to one another and, as if in a fugue, to recombine and vary them endlessly in accordance with unchanging mathematical laws. The players of the glass bead game presented not only the works but also the possibilities of the human mind by responding to one another with abstract, sublime formulas. People travelled far to attend the annual festivals held over several days in the province of Castalia, a specialized, fairly remote and quasi-autonomous republic of scholars and artists in the European realm. Apart from the festival, travel between Castalia and the rest of the world was limited largely to teachers sent from Castalia throughout the realm and the most talented students in the realm sent to Castalia's boarding schools. The players of the glass bead game, the greatest scholars in every field and artists in the various genres, led a quiet, almost monastic life, free of economic necessity, with no personal income – that is, completely subsidized by the larger community,

* For Michael Krüger.

devoted entirely to the perfection of their work, to independent research – never subjugated to ulterior purposes – and to the education of young people.

That is the utopia that Hermann Hesse imagined in the face of Nazism, the mass murder of the Jews and the Second World War. One might say – and people did say, with a sneer, immediately after the novel's publication in post-war Germany – it was an overly modest, asensual utopia amounting to a realm of purposeless activity, of mere aesthetic ostentation, and, to top it off, an all-male utopia – a 'science fiction of introspection', as *The Glass Bead Game* was derisively called[1] because it only hints at social and political conditions and completely excludes technical development. Of all Hesse's books, the one that was met with the greatest bewilderment was his longest, his most ambitious and, in the event, his last novel. In spite of the vehemence with which it was defended by a few readers, such as Thomas Mann, Stefan Zweig – who had read drafts before his suicide in 1942 – and the future president of West Germany Theodor Heuss, and in spite of the fact that Hesse was awarded the Nobel Prize two years after its publication, *The Glass Bead Game* remained largely unappreciated, even in Hesse's later reception, including the Hesse renaissance of the 1960s and 1970s. And yet, if we hold Hesse's Castalia up to the reality of its time, and to our own, the novel contains one of the most accurate and at the same time prophetic social diagnoses in modern literature. What passes for a utopia is in fact a farewell to the political, social and intellectual world to which Hesse belonged:

> In the year 33 I had no more pleasant illusions to be destroyed, and the most infernal crimes in Hitler's Reich could not obscure my sight. Only I had faintly hoped, I admit, as everyone did, that maybe the one war would have been enough.[2]

Other intellectuals who withstood the nationalist furore had similar thoughts, of course. What is remarkable is *when* Hesse wrote so realistically about 'the year 33' – namely, on 22 March 1933. We can go down the list of the great, politically aware and courageous writers of that time, including even the most critical philosophers: two months after Adolf Hitler's appointment as chancellor, hardly anyone grasped the dimensions of the disaster to which 'the sinister tragedy of the mind, and in particular the German mind' would lead. Hesse's letter is more than just a diagnosis: it is an unusually early and accurate prognosis. Likewise, *The Glass Bead Game*, which he began writing in those same months, is anything but a naïve novel of awakening; it is, rather, a despairing novel of decline, and what declines is not just Germany,

Hesse's particular anguish over the state of that country notwithstanding. The rise of the Third Reich, to Hesse, was nothing less than the fall of Western civilization.

Some may object that we haven't perished after all. Our culture, although perhaps we no longer ingenuously call it occidental, is alive, it produces a multitude of well-known and indeed important artists, it is discussed in countless forums, it has a numerically greater audience, and it is publicly subsidized with more money than ever. On a single Saturday, a metropolis such as Berlin offers more cultural events – more theatre, film, literature, music and education – than most of the world's major cities in a whole week, than Hamburg itself in a whole month before the Second World War, or than a whole year in Lessing's day. Especially in Germany, the network of arts colleges is incomparably dense, famous throughout the world and, moreover, completely financed by the public sector, including schools for music, film, and all the fine arts and performing arts imaginable. Furthermore, the museums report new record numbers of visitors year after year. And, last but not least, culture earns more bread than it ever has before, and I am not referring only to stars whose tax returns run into seven figures. Outside Europe, or even on its southern and eastern marches, the literature business is much too small to feed more than three or four authors. In Germany alone, meanwhile, there are hundreds, probably thousands, who make their living from literature – if not from their books alone, then from readings, radio features, stipends and prizes. Culturally, in spite of all the cutbacks and economic constraints in low-income areas, Germany today is still prosperous, even blessed – and the old West is still bursting with life.

The same can be said, of course, of the future that Hermann Hesse imagines: the society whose highest art is the glass bead game is as cultured as it is peaceful. For many decades, probably centuries, it has known no wars; it has overcome the scourge of nationalism; it has opened its borders; its constitution is that of a republic. Although of course it is far from being an earthly paradise – the affairs of state are steeped in the usual intrigues and short-sighted interests, the public are often preoccupied with trivialities, the economy is anything but egalitarian – Hesse's Europe has nonetheless developed, after all its disasters, into a comfortable, liveable, constitutional and, politically, more than merely acceptable place. Most of all, however, the society values culture; it promotes the sciences, gives education the highest priority, and spends a great deal of money on festivals. In short, the province of Castalia, where scholars, artists and players of the glass bead game live, combines the characteristics of Bayreuth, Oxford and

Salem – it is Bayreuth, Oxford and Salem in one. Not in its concrete political form, certainly, or in its aesthetic notions, and least of all in its stage of technological development, but in the attitude towards life, the way peace is taken for granted and day-to-day militarism unknown, in the overall prosperity that predominates, the wealth of cultural institutions, the absence of any conflict worse than diplomatic squabbles with the neighbouring countries, which are no longer mortal enemies – in all these manifestations Hesse predicted, during Nazi rule and the Second World War, more accurately than other writers, the fall of civilization. The fall? Yes: in *The Glass Bead Game*, the decline of Western civilization is long past.

For, on a closer look, Castalia produces no new art works or new knowledge. The players of the glass bead game, and with them all the artists and scholars, are not engaged in creative competition with the generations that brought forth modern European culture, and German culture in particular, between the end of the Middle Ages and the great global wars. As imitative as they are reverent, they devote their efforts to preserving the memory of that culture whose heirs they are, researching it ever more deeply, plumbing its depths artistically as well, understanding it more purely and precisely. In the introduction to the history of the glass bead game that Hesse places at the beginning of his novel, he writes:

> We no longer have any of the exuberant fecundity of those days. For us it is almost incomprehensible that musical style in the fifteenth and sixteenth centuries could be preserved for so long a time in unalloyed purity. How could it be, we ask, that among the vast quantities of music written at that time we fail to find a trace of anything bad? How could the eighteenth century, the time of incipient degeneration, still send hurtling into the skies a fireworks display of styles, fashions, and schools, blazing briefly but with such self-assurance? Nevertheless, we believe that we have uncovered the secret of what we now call classical music, that we have understood the spirit, the virtue, and the piety of those generations, and have taken all that as our model.[3]

Is culture, at least European culture, or perhaps only German culture – in the broader sense of the term as the culture of the German-speaking region – is culture supposed to have ceased to be aesthetically productive, no longer producing original works of art but only rearranging those that already exist, setting prior achievements in relation to one another in an endless succession of new constellations? Are there supposed to be no more artists in the true, creative sense of the word, but only interpreters, great and even ingenious though they may be? That sounds absurd, absolutely grotesque. A glance at today's book market, in the record shops, down the aisles of the art fairs would seem to prove Hesse's scenario wrong. All the writers, composers, film-makers, painters and now video artists – if no new works were being created, what would their occupation consist of, day in and day out? What would my occupation consist of?

Like Thomas Mann, who felt his *Doctor Faustus* was deeply related to its contemporary *The Glass Bead Game*, Hermann Hesse in his novel presents music, and with it mathematics, as the great, enduring achievement of modern culture – not poetry and, with it, philosophy. That is hardly congruent with the position of Hesse himself, who more often listened to the composers of the dawning nineteenth century than to Bach, and whose personal cultural history would certainly not neglect Jean Paul, Hölderlin, Büchner or Kleist. The reason for the particular mention of the late baroque in the introduction of the glass bead game is its exemplary quality as a strictly formal system, organized by sequential patterns, following higher laws than subjective perceptions or intuitions. Although Hesse was an outspoken advocate of the verbal arts, in his novel he goes so far as deliberately to devalue them – whether coyly or otherwise – for example, when his narrator calls Bach's cantatas, passions and preludes the most sublime expression of Christianity but has at best a low opinion of eighteenth-century theology and church culture or of Enlightenment philosophy – that is, of discursive engagement with Christian doctrine.

I am not competent to judge the representations of music history in *The Glass Bead Game*. However, I would like to examine Hesse's diagnosis of the end of European culture as a creative culture producing new works, genres and styles in relation to Hesse's own vocation, which is one I know more about: literature. And I would like to recall a similarly famous dictum that has been no less ridiculed and declared absurd: namely, Theodor W. Adorno's 1949 pronouncement that poetry could no longer be written after Auschwitz. I find nothing ridiculous about this statement at all, except perhaps those who impertinently rubbed one poem or another under Adorno's nose to rebut him. For Adorno's meaning had nothing to do with imposing a prohibition on speech or on poetry. He followed cultural affairs in post-war Germany with curiosity, and often with enthusiasm. As far as poetry is concerned, he was so committed to the modern arts that he judged Gottfried Benn with remarkable leniency, in spite of his involvement with the Third Reich, and saw those who rejected avant-garde poetry as his real enemies. No, the adage that no more poetry could be written after Auschwitz – or, in Adorno's own paraphrase, that to write poems after Auschwitz is barbaric – makes a different point, and one that cannot be invalidated:

What is a civilization waiting for, after gassing millions of innocent people and bringing war and destruction to half the world, to acknowledge its own demise? That is the question Adorno had asked repeatedly even before the end of the war. His sentence about the end of poetry is a judgement that Auschwitz is more than just a caesura for the cultural region which, during the modern period and the Enlightenment, had begun to call itself the West in contradistinction to the Eastern Mediterranean region, to the cradle of the biblical religions, of Islam and of Orthodox Christianity: in the cultural history of the West, the gas chambers are a final full stop.

Both cultures, Orient and Occident, claim descent from Israel and from Athens; both are founded on faith in the Word: God simply said, Be it, and it was; God taught Adam the names of all things; the Gospel of St John begins, most strikingly, 'In the beginning was the Word, and the Word was with God, and the Word was God.' In its high esteem for the Word, modern European culture is still quite biblical in its construction. Moreover, it bears specifically Christian traits in its secular elaboration of John's subsequent verse, which says the Word was made flesh and dwelt among us. In contrast to the Eastern traditions, in which the second commandment remained an effective prohibition against pronouncing God's name in spite of all challenges by medieval Arabic philosophy, the Enlightenment held that truth was discursive. The belief that everything on earth must be sayable, or will become sayable in those cases for which no linguistic expression has yet been discovered, was the driving force that propelled Europe into modern civilization.

This faith in language was already faltering in Hölderlin's late poems and was shattered in the literature of the early twentieth century, as demonstrated by the necessarily failed attempts to say everything in Proust, Joyce and Musil, for example, and as theoretically established in Wittgenstein's early philosophy of language and Benjamin's philosophy of history; as visible, too, in Freud's *Civilization and its Discontents*. Thomas Mann's and Hermann Hesse's choice, in their great, definitive novels of the world war, of placing music rather than the Word at the centre, is caused by the same perception that the Word had become in modern times not merely empty but the foundation of barbarism, of the counter-Enlightenment. George Steiner has expressed this concisely with regard to Kafka:

> From the literal nightmare of *The Metamorphosis* came the knowledge that *Ungeziefer* ('vermin') was to be the designation of millions of men. The bureaucratic parlance of *The Trial* and *The Castle* have become

commonplace in our herded lives. The instrument of torture in 'In the Penal Colony' is also a printing press. In short, Kafka heard the name Buchenwald in the word birchwood. He understood, as if the bush had burned for him again, that a great inhumanity was lying in wait for European man, and that parts of language would serve it and be made base in the process.[4]

Although the actual horror exceeded anything imaginable up to then – the dehumanization of whole societies that had thought themselves civilized; the instrumentalization of the highest cultural assets to further bald, inhumane racism; the new dimensions of warfare up to and including the dropping of two atomic bombs and industrialized genocide, for which Auschwitz is iconic – nonetheless, literature, music, painting had already felt the degeneracy of their own culture between and even before the two world wars. In literature at any rate, all of the great, indeed the constitutive works of the early twentieth century are closures, surveys of a civilization, of language in general, of modern consciousness, of every nook and cranny of the managed society. And, the exclamation mark, so to speak, after this collective impression of belonging to a bygone world, is Oswald Spengler's *Decline of the West.*

The immense fascination exerted by this politically very dubious work has to do in part with the fact that it was written before the First World War, the outbreak and outcome of which seemed to confirm Spengler sooner than anyone would have thought possible. And yet the actual relevance of Spengler was revealed only later, in the 1930s, when he had long since been forgotten again and most Germans were intoxicated with their supposed resurgence: as if clairvoyant, Spengler had foreseen the reversal of democracy into a totalitarian state and the expansion of war into annihilation. And, with the war of annihilation, he had also foreseen the failure of the great political concepts of the modern era – hence the end of ideologies, and more – of all abstract ideals.

Men finally give up, not this or that theory, but the belief in theory of any kind and with it the sentimental optimism of an eighteenth century that imagined that unsatisfactory actualities could be improved by the application of concepts.[5]

Even decades later, Spengler's core idea was revived, and trivialized, as the 'end of history'. He was an extreme right-wing theoretician whose critique of liberalism, as Adorno bitterly remarked in retrospect, turned out in many ways to be superior to Marxist criticism. Where it was untrue, for example, was not in detecting disaster but in attributing necessity to that disaster.

Even now, if we compare his historic depth, his universalism and his verbal force with today's prophets of doom, we feel the whole force of the zeitgeist that Spengler both expressed and keenly encouraged. If their lamentations over the degeneration of values in society, of education in the schools, of acting in the theatre, of political culture in the talk shows, of spelling by its reform – if the lamentations of today are so much more boring and sound so blinkered and curmudgeonly, it is not because the individual diagnoses are false. On the contrary, they have been true for too long to justify the posture of breaking taboos that accompanies their pronouncement. Because they are far too late, such diatribes are directed not against the decline but against its legacy in German and European post-war culture. But no one in their right mind could wish for a restoration of the 1950s and early 1960s, and, much as one would like to complain about the schools of today for example, much as I complain as a father every day – not for a second would I wish the discipline and order of yesterday on my children. On the whole, Germany and the states of the European Union have developed in the last sixty years into the relatively comfortable, liveable, politically more than merely acceptable place that Hermann Hesse describes in *The Glass Bead Game*. Although the pre-war years may have been culturally more exciting, we can be glad we didn't live through them, if only because we would still have the war and the racial insanity ahead of us. We are living long after the decline – but that there is a life after it, quite a good, civil life in fact, that the culture has outlasted the naturally finite and also painful time of its full creative power: that is the utopian turn that Hesse appends to the apocalyptic scenarios of his era. 'Memory takes the place of full presence', Adorno wrote, perceiving the Castalian quality of present-day culture and pointing to the museum-like styling of European city centres as an example.[6]

Politically it is immediately understandable that the end of the Second World War brought with it an interruption in the continuity of historic consciousness: the focus shifted from the old European continent to America and Russia, whose relation to the traditional concept of Western culture had been an extraterritorial one. The rapid restoration of the post-war years made the intellectual break less visible, although it goes deeper. But it is to this break that Adorno refers in his dictum that poetry can no longer be written after Auschwitz: it is a rejection of the belief, inherited from Christianity and secularized by the Enlightenment, in the Word. 'All intellectual endeavours in particular have had the ground pulled out from under them', Adorno wrote as late as 1955, long after he had established himself as the most determined philosophical proponent of contemporary positions and productions, in literature as well as in music:[7] 'What can oppose the decline of the west is not a resurrected culture but the utopia that is silently contained in the image of its decline.'[8]

Indeed great, enduring works of art continued to be created after the wars, after the Holocaust, in Germany and in Europe. Adorno observed them, reviewed them, defended them: Beckett, Picasso, New Music – including Stockhausen, Cage and Kagel. However, they owed their worth and their power to the fact that they referred, as an epilogue, to the experiences of the preceding decades, as in the regression, sketched by Beckett, to the state of aphasia, for example; or in Celan's 'Death Fugue'; or in the sprawling novels of Heimito von Doderer, too big for a single reader to grasp, which pay the last respects to a visibly extinct era – and still more radically in Doderer's short and micro-novels, which consisted of just a few lines or a single sentence, mischievously subverting the modern novel's pretensions of totality. Among the Germans, the last Western poet in the strict sense was probably Heiner Müller, who was in thrall to the past even when he wrote about the present. And after him?

I do not think everything written today is worthless. If I did, I would not be a writer; I would not devote my life to literature, except perhaps as a philologist. And yet I wonder why none of us contemporary writers bears comparison with Hölderlin or Kafka, Proust or Beckett, to use these four as shorthand for the greatness of modern European literature. Occasionally I see in the newspapers, when a reviewer bears real malice towards an author whose quality is indisputable, they often resort to the ultimate argument, a real literary knockout argument: comparing the author with Hölderlin or Kafka, Proust or Beckett. Well, obviously, I think, none of us stands a chance against that. Or the other way round, the sense of immoderation, of disproportion, of really exaggerated praise when a critic gets carried away by enthusiasm to the point of ranking a contemporary author on a par with Hölderlin or Kafka, Proust or Beckett, again letting these four stand for so many others. If the author is still more or less in his or her right mind, he or she will be the first to protest and repudiate the impertinent comparison. Our novels, our poems, our plays may be good – but they can no longer redefine the novel, poetry, drama. I don't know whether this diagnosis can be extended to contemporary European music or the fine arts, taking perhaps Stockhausen's generation, or thatose of Ligeti, Picasso or Beuys, as the final cadence of an aesthetically profuse, although at the same time very warlike era. Would it not be an injustice to any living composer to compare them with Bach, Beethoven or Mahler? Or a painter with Michelangelo, Goya or Picasso?

I am sure that human creativity will produce epoch-making works in the future, but we who are living now, we who live in old Europe, will probably not be exactly the first to notice them, because they are taking shape in other places, probably in other arts than symphonic music, the modern novel and painting in perspective, which led to a rediscovery of abstraction only after it had been taken to its extreme. The theatre of empathy has long been leading an afterlife as cinema, which retains its American character even though it has long since returned to Europe and been spread to all corners of the earth. The creative phases of the arts have little connection with political stability, and the belief has likewise become untenable that development necessarily means progress. And, outside Marxism, no philosophy of history has claimed that it did. Even to Hegel, the progressing *Weltgeist* in his *Phenomenology of the Spirit* is more a parable, a literary figure, than a real discovery; and, many centuries before Spengler, the Arab Ibn Khaldun analysed the course of the world as cyclical. The tendency towards teleology, handled rather playfully by Hegel before the political ideologies – and not only Marxism – made it a serious matter, is another secular adaptation of Christian substance that became obsolete in the course of the twentieth century. Other religions besides Christianity conceive history, if not as a clear process of decay, at least as a neutral continuum in which revelation and recession alternately give way to one another.

Civilizations flourish, civilizations fade away – we may still retain this much of Spengler's seasonal metaphor today. Strictly speaking, it is banal; it goes without saying that every living thing rises and falls. The creative phase of Islamic culture began earlier and, accordingly, is long past. It is impossible in Iran and the Arab world today for anything to be created of an originality comparable with Rumi's poetry, the tales of the *Thousand and One Nights*, the philosophy of Averroes or the Taj Mahal, to use these four outstanding expressions of the human spirit as shorthand for the erstwhile greatness of Islamic culture. The breadth of thought and the philological acuity of classical Quran exegesis is worlds apart from any – and I mean any – treatise by a contemporary Islamic scholar, be it ever so modern and politically courageous. Today a universal mind like that of the mystic Ibn Arabi, whose room-filling oeuvre I consider the real pinnacle of Islamic literature, only twinkles like a star above the Muslims of today, now so far away, so faint, unknown to most, and ultimately so unimportant. The problem is not that this or that particular poet, mystic, philosopher or architect happens to be lacking at this moment. The political, intellectual, aesthetic conditions that brought forth Rumi, the *Thousand and One Nights*, Averroes and the Taj Mahal are past and beyond recall. That in itself would not be a calamity. The catastrophe of the Islamic world is that it has lost its living relation to its own past. Without Western Orientalists, who for a long time pursued their discipline archaeologically, many great works of Islamic civilization would not even have been preserved, either in literature or in architecture. But the most obvious symptom is fundamentalism, which claims to be a return to the religion's origins and yet is demonstrably a disastrous adaptation of the Protestant Reformation, cut off from its own history: there is nothing intellectually more antagonistic to the Islamic tradition than to hypostatize a bare, literally interpretable scripture.

The utopia imagined in *The Glass Bead Game* is not one of eternal duration or increasing greatness, much less earthly bliss. From a political perspective, Hesse hoped during the Nazi period for a future that would have learned from such a present. Extended to the scale of civilization, that hope is the utopian idea of preserving and continually bringing into the present what earlier generations have left us. That is exactly what religions aim to do when, in their respective central rites, they continually reiterate the initial act of revelation; and it is in that continual renewal that the culture would be secularized in the Enlightenment project. Although it is hardly religious in the usual sense of the word, Castalia is not opposed to religion; on the contrary, the province of artists and scholars strives for good, almost fraternal relations with the Holy See. Furthermore, as the glass bead game draws on all the world's arts and sciences, it also draws on the Christian and other metaphysical traditions, and the players' improvisation can take a central tenet of faith, the words of a Bible verse, a sentence from the Church Fathers or from the Latin missal as its point of departure. Yet the glass bead game itself is not theological. Hesse insists on this important point in distinguishing between art and religion. If the game is founded on a religious attitude, it is only in the strictly intrinsic sense of fidelity, of sacrifice, of faith in a higher purpose than any personal or indeed earthly interest.

What do we do, then, we who call ourselves writers, or composers or artists, or who devote ourselves to disseminating art? What makes up our legitimation, our motivation, our task, which seems to us important enough that we are willing to be fed by the public – not only by public funding but by our audience? If I were a musician or a conductor, the answer would be obvious, and yet it would be the wrong answer. For an orchestra that performs a symphony by Mozart does not simply read off the score; it interprets it, brings it into our present moment, assimilates it; and the greatest of all the presumptions that go hand in hand with any interpretation is perhaps that of minimizing the subjective element by professing fidelity to the work. Similarly, the glass bead game is explicitly not limited to recapitulating prior achievements; rather, every action sets them in a different constellation and reinterprets them, and in fact this new reading amounts to a rewriting; it is an actualization, and is naturally specific to the person performing it and to the place and the historic moment at which it is performed. Consequently, every successful glass bead game is unique – not a repetition and not repeatable. If it is not creative, then that is only in the sense that it does not use any additional elements, that it does not add any new sentences, cadences, signs and symbols. And, yes, I believe that not only a symphony orchestra or a theatre ensemble – I believe that we who work as individuals at our desks also continually extend the interpretation of the works of those who have gone before, adapting or reinventing them in ever new, surprising and also necessarily personal constellations, specific to ourselves, the given place and the given time.

We cannot transform the disintegration of a coherent concept of the world into more powerful words than Hölderlin in his late poems; we, cannot find any more apt metaphors for the lostness of modern man than Kafka, cannot describe the structure of interpersonal relations more precisely than Proust, cannot make the vacuity of language plainer than Beckett. The literature that presented itself as post-modern applied all the more profusely, whether intentionally or unintentionally, narrative techniques that originated in the past, and yet that literature never surpassed Jean Paul, much less Cervantes, whose *Don Quixote* challenged the modern novel in the very act of founding it. Nonetheless, later literature – including ours, we may hope – is justified and necessary because it does not merely mechanically imitate the traditions on which it builds but extends them and their system of signification to new themes, conditions and social situations. The famous poem of the 'Stages' – 'In all beginnings dwells a magic force' – that is contained in the epilogue of *The Glass Bead Game*, and whose moralizing, preaching tone Hesse himself sardonically unmasks in the novel, is in truth an observation on the nature of music, 'its serenity and resolution, its quality of being constantly present, its mobility and unceasing urge to hasten on, to leave the space it has only just entered.'[9] The glass beads of our culture are finite; that which seeks expression is not. But if we were to lapse into silence, we would not only forget the alphabet of European culture, and in particular German culture, which developed between the end of the Middle Ages and the great global wars: we would be betraying the future, which our testimony must help to make a better one.

Josef Knecht, the great master of the glass bead game whose biography Hermann Hesse sets down, gives up his office at the height of his art and his renown, gives up the glass bead game itself and, flouting all rules and customs, turns his back on Castalia. 'Most of us brothers of the Order take Castalia, our Order, our system of scholarship and schooling as much for granted as most men take the air they breathe and the ground they stand on', writes Josef Knecht in his letter of resignation to the educational council.

> Hardly anyone ever thinks that this air and this ground could sometime not be there, that we might some day lack air or find the ground vanishing from under us. We have the good fortune of living well protected in a small, neat, and cheerful world, and the great majority of us, strange as it may seem, hold to the fiction that this world has always existed and that we were born into it.[10]

Josef Knecht perceives that the foundations that allow a society to maintain such an elite intellectual world as Castalia are threatening to collapse. The knowledge of the artistic and scholarly traditions and the habit, the passion and the pleasure of engaging with them and keeping them alive are in decline everywhere. As schools place less and less value on the artistic, literary and historical subjects, more and more young people are cut off at the start from the sources of their culture and never even acquire the ability to contemplate the complex intellectual and aesthetic works of earlier generations, to enjoy them, to cultivate their influence in their own lives and their own world. The scholars and artists still eat their bread, Knecht writes, use their libraries, trust in their state subsidies, even expand their schools and archives – 'but if the nation no longer wants to authorize this, or if it should be struck by impoverishment, war and so on, then our life and studying would be over in a minute.' Even now, he points out, some members of the parliament raise the question quite distinctly why, faced with so many other political and especially social needs, the state spends so much money on culture. Urgently, but in vain, Josef Knecht warns the scholars and artists that 'Some day our country might decide that its Castalia and our culture are a luxury it can no longer afford. Instead of being genially proud of us, it may come round to regarding us as noxious parasites, tricksters and enemies.'[11]

It doesn't take a prophetic gift to anticipate that we who call ourselves artists, musicians and scholars will suffer the fate that Josef Knecht fears for Castalia. The deterioration of cultural education has long since passed the stage of negligible cracks. As a father and as a writer, I am meeting in schools the first generation of German teachers who are no longer readers – I mean, readers in the strong sense, people for whom reading and engaging with books is a natural part of everyday life, not one that requires any sort of inducement. The curriculum has ceased to expect the students or, perhaps more alarmingly, the teachers to read complete works; it is now possible to earn a German upper secondary leaving certificate without having read at least a Goethe or a Schiller from cover to cover and without even having heard the names of Kleist, Stifter or Döblin. Even in the universities, students are introduced to longer, more complex works at best in abridged form. And the instructors are right, in a certain sense, because their students have never learned the cultural techniques to comprehend nested sentence structures, rhythmic language, unfamiliar metaphors, intentional ambiguity, biblical, even mystically pietistic motifs, positively unpsychological descriptions of inner experiences and dramaturgical sequences that do not follow the simple model of popular movies. A drama such as *Faust* and even a novel such as Jean Paul's *Flegeljahre* is accessible to the vast majority of German university students – students of German! – only in the form of plot summaries in Wikipedia. And what's left of reading in the schools and the undergraduate courses is not aimed at awakening enthusiasm, giving free rein to associations, revealing the abundance of meaning for the students' own here and now – that is, at teaching reading itself. Instead it is aimed at training testable 'competences' precisely defined in the curriculum: terms, characteristics of periods, and the like. But it systematically kills the love of literature in the process. Knowledge is reduced to information – that is, to the utility it may have in this or that context, in this module, for that exam. What Hesse writes about the decadent era in his introduction to the history of the glass bead game is the present-day reality of European education reforms:

> People heard lectures on writers whose works they had never read and never meant to, sometimes accompanied by pictures projected on a screen. At these lectures, as in the feature articles in the newspapers, they struggled through a deluge of isolated cultural facts and fragments of knowledge robbed of all meaning.[12]

Knowledge, in the sense of information, will continue to be necessary and to be taught in schools and universities. The content of education is not decreasing – quite the contrary. But what is being taught is increasingly tied to a specific purpose: What do I need to know about Brecht for the exam? What do I need to know about literature for my job? In Castalia, too, all the primary disciplines will be maintained and will continue to be funded when nothing is left of knowledge but information: 'Mathematics is needed, after all, to devise new firearms', Josef Knecht writes. What Knecht sees as endangered is culture as a sufficient purpose unto itself; it is art as an activity that is not subject to the logic of production; what the glass bead game embodies as the most extreme, the least economical and, hence, the most endangered part of the province of learning: ‘no one will believe – least of all the military – that closing the Vicus Lusorum and abolishing our Game will cause the country and people the slightest loss.’[13]

In our country, too, the value of cultural education is questioned more and more openly. In commercial television, which public television emulates more closely year after year, an asocial aura no longer characterizes the prole but, rather, the educated middle-class figure, and a person who voluntarily appears in the upper grades of a German secondary school with a work of older literature that is not on the best-seller lists, and goes so far as to open it at lunch break or during a free period, must live with the stigma of a misfit, an oddball or, in the current slang pejorative that suggests a bizarre reversal of Christian values, a ‘victim’. Intellectual snobbery has ceded the field to its opposite – pride in one’s ignorance. The title of a recent German film comedy sums it up: *Fack ju Göhte!* With the simple message that no viewer should be ashamed of his or her lack of education and culture, it was not only the most popular film in German cinemas in recent years but was also awarded state-sponsored prizes and celebrated in the newspapers for its ‘absolute topicality’.[14]

I don’t know whether the devaluation of literature – and it’s not just ebbing interest that I experience at schools and even universities (not always and not everywhere, but alarmingly often, and from teachers as well as students): it is an aversion, it is an ostentatious disparagement, at least of difficult literature, works that require effort, discipline and knowledge – I don’t know whether it is matched by an analogous devaluation of music, specifically classical music. But it would seem so from the figures and findings presented by the German School Music Association, for example: a third of the planned music lessons at grammar schools don’t take place; at the lower secondary schools, more than half are cancelled – and music has been slashed from curricula to begin with. Not even one-fifth of all primary school children in Germany have regular music lessons.[15] We are committing an offence against future generations, barring them from the intellectual archives of our culture, by failing to teach them in the schools and universities the ability to contemplate the complex intellectual and aesthetic works of earlier generations, to enjoy them, to cultivate their influence in their own lives and their own world. We cannot force our children to use the archives. But we should make sure they get the library card – it costs so little. ‘On the heels of civilization is an earth full of slag heaps and rubbish tips', Hesse noted shortly before beginning work on *The Glass Bead Game*,

> the useful inventions result not only in fine World Expositions and elegant automobile salons; they are also followed by armies of miners with pale faces and miserable wages; they are followed by diseases and desolation; and if mankind possesses steam engines and turbines, it pays for them with infinite devastation on the face of the earth and in the image of man . . . while at the same time there is no price at all to pay for the fact that man has invented the violin, and that someone has written the arias in *Figaro*. Mozart and Mörike did not cost the world much; they were as cheap as sunshine; any employee in an engineering firm costs more.[16]

Josef Knecht leaves Castalia to become a teacher at an ordinary school. He explains his decision by a parable:

> A man sits in an attic room engaged in a subtle work of scholarship. Suddenly he becomes aware that fire has broken out in the house below. He will not consider whether it is his function to see to it, or whether he had not better finish his tabulations. He will run downstairs and attempt to save the house. Here am I sitting in the top story of our Castalian edifice, occupied with the Glass Bead Game, working with delicate, sensitive instruments, and instinct tells me, my nose tells me, that down below something is burning, our whole structure is imperiled, and that my business now is not to analyze music or define rules of the Game, but to rush to where the smoke is.[17]

If we apply Knecht's parable to our own situation, very few of us are drawing the same conclusions. We think we can get some relief from the rising heat by opening the windows towards the market, towards popularization, simplification and compression into mass-marketable formats. But the air that blows in from that direction only fans the flames. To put out the fire that is spreading through the lower floors, it would be more helpful to do the obvious thing and run downstairs – that is, go to the kindergartens, offer our services to the schools and, while we're at it, storm the ministry of education, whose curriculum treats the artistic subjects as substandard goods. Because childhood is the only time when it is possible to develop the interest, and also the pleasure, in playing with glass beads – in reading just as in listening, in writing just as in making music. Josef Knecht, the supreme and most renowned player of the glass bead game, finds the education of a single gifted child important enough to devote the rest of his life to it. But he has barely taken up his first teaching post when he dies upon jumping into an ice-cold alpine lake. He wanted to follow his pupil, a gifted but difficult boy who mistrusted all authorities but was a passionate athlete; Knecht did not want to look a coward and a slacker in front of the boy but wanted to win his respect and comradeship: an ordinary accidental death, yet at the same time Knecht became what enthusiastic readers are called in German schoolyards: a victim.

Our Castalia, too, so diversely and marvellously developed in the form of our cultural institutions, will continue to exist a while yet with little damage. The literature business, for example, will most likely survive long enough for writers of my generation to grow old in it. And, afterwards, literature will not simply close its doors but will shrink to normal proportions, to those that can already be observed outside Europe, or even on its southern and eastern marches. There will still be readers even then, when literature has become a marginal pursuit like philately, far from public perception. General contempt actually boosts the enthusiasm of some individuals, a counter-development that is already observable in schools and universities and among younger authors, scholars and readers. They will probably be the 'individuals and small groups' who once, before, between or after the great wars, 'had resolved to remain faithful to true culture and to devote all their energies to preserving for the future a core of good tradition, discipline, method, and intellectual rigor', as Hesse puts it in the introduction to *The Glass Bead Game*.[18] And even if no one but archaeologists studies Western literature – like the classical literature of the Orient today – then other formats, genres and styles, perhaps electronic ones, can still develop to pervade the world aesthetically. Our yearning for the past ceases the moment we picture any specific past, including the past of our schools. If I, a man of books, see only decadence, it is because I lack the sensory apparatus to perceive the new growth that every decay must bring with it.

As you can see, I am trying – in vain, I fear – to close on a less blinkered and curmudgeonly note than the diatribes I decried at the outset. And what I feel is really not so much anger or indignation. In fact, the marvellous and rich development of European and, in particular, German cultural life in the past sixty years, the great support, devotion and attention that our society has given to music, literature and the arts, seems to me miraculous and, seen from the perspective of 1945, no less utopian than the glass bead game. I am grateful for that; I owe my livelihood as a writer to that public support, devotion and attention. It is sadness, rather; sentimentality too, I admit; and most of all shame that it is ultimately our fault, as the heirs of Hölderlin and Kafka, Proust and Beckett, to use these four once more as shorthand for modern European literature, if these great, exhilarating traditions should lose their currency in our generation – for that would mean our own books did not have enough to say. 'Above all we forget that we ourselves are a part of history, that we are the product of growth and are condemned to perish if we lose the capacity for further growth and change', Josef Knecht writes in his farewell letter: 'We are ourselves history and share the responsibility for world history and our position in it.'[19] The awareness of that responsibility is gravely lacking in our Castalia too.

13

THE VIOLENCE OF COMPASSION

*Arendt and Revolution**

There are many prizes awarded in Germany, and no doubt most of them bear the name of a deceased writer, scholar, politician or patron of the arts. The prize awarded in Hannah Arendt's name has a remarkable suffix: it is a prize 'for political thought'. I must admit that I was spontaneously pleased with that expression: political thought. At the same time I wondered just what it meant. The question 'What is political?' is much easier to answer thanks to Hannah Arendt, who thought about it again and again in the last decades of her life, and even wrote a book about exactly that. We can also give definitions of political judgement, political philosophy and political action based on her words. But what does it mean to think politically? How is political thought different from non-political thought? And, since I happen to be the one receiving this prize, what might be political about my thinking?

An obvious strategy would be to define political thought by analogy, since it is related to politics and hence to the political space – that is, in Hannah Arendt's definition, to the world that lies between people. Perhaps she would have accepted such an explanation, derived as it is from her concept of the political. And yet, if we try to apply that definition to her own work, the relatively neutral attribute of relating to the public space falls short. For Hannah Arendt accords to the nature of politics a valuation that is itself political and not justifiable by political science: politics is 'the cause of freedom against tyranny'.[1] Arendt characterizes political thought much more profoundly – perhaps not as she would define it, but as her books exemplify it for me – by three phrases in which she refers to the work of others, not her own. It is an

* Acceptance speech on receiving the Hannah Arendt Prize for Political Thought, Bremen City Hall, 2 December 2012.

expression of her noblesse, incidentally, that she explains what she strives for by citing the achievements of other authors.

The first phrase I would like to mention is from a dedication to her teacher Karl Jaspers, from whom she learned 'to find my way around in reality without selling my soul to it the way people in earlier times sold their souls to the devil'.[2] This phrase expresses a triad of essential motifs in Hannah Arendt's work: the will to understand reality – to find one's way around in it – and, at the same time, the will to change that reality if necessary – not to acquiesce in it – and, finally, the belief that reality can be changed, hence in free will and in the mission of reason – instead of the submissive assumption that it is as inexorable as the devil. Thought, by itself, is a process of clarifying and condensing concepts. Political thought, on the other hand, as Arendt exemplifies it, deciphers what is as what has been made, and is hence by nature rebellious. In attempting to understand circumstances, it never accepts them as necessary. Necessity, Arendt writes a few lines further on, is only 'a will-o'-the-wisp that tries to lure us into playing a role instead of attempting to be a human being.' Attempting to be a human being – that is an extraordinarily vague and altogether pathetic expression such as one rarely finds in Arendt. And yet it is both well placed and expressive, since political thought, although it proceeds analytically, is nonetheless based on a preconceptual act of empathy, of human sympathy or solidarity, whether in the form of compassion or of anger.

In connection with Gotthold Ephraim Lessing – to come to her second characterization of political thought – Hannah Arendt points out that the Greek theory of emotions counted not only compassion but also anger among the pleasant feelings, while hope was reckoned along with fear as unpleasant. This appreciation of anger has to do not with the degree of agitation associated with the emotion but with the degree of 'awareness of reality', as Arendt states: 'In hope the soul overleaps reality, as in fear it shrinks back from it. But anger . . . reveals and exposes the world.'[3] Anger and compassion are not words that spontaneously come to mind when we read Hannah Arendt. As elegant as her prose is, it is also cool, pointedly rational, almost detached, and free of rhetorical effects. Her clarity is most distinct in comparison with her philosophical teachers, with the solemnity of Karl Jaspers and the murmuring of Martin Heidegger. Nonetheless, I believe her repulsion of all sentimentality reflects the excess of sentiment that burns in an excess of adversity. And the adversity that Arendt faces is more than existential, for its source is more than the possibility of her individual extinction. Her adversity is at the same time collective, since the extinction of her entire people is also imminent, and with it her past, her memory, her very name. Murder is one thing, but the inconceivable intent of the Nazis was to leave no one alive to mourn those they murdered and so make the worst curse of the Jews come true: 'May you perish from remembrance.'

This brings me to the third phrase that Hannah Arendt used to characterize another author but which just as aptly could describe herself: in regard to Stefan Zweig, she refers to 'the pitiless accuracy which springs from the calm of absolute despair'.[4] I can think of no more apt description of her great works of history, and first among them *The Origins of Totalitarianism*. One aspect among many others that make this book seem so incredible today – the span of her arguments, her analytical penetration of historic experience, the originality of her interpretative synthesis, her clear awareness of the times – is the date of its publication, immediately after the Second World War, before the dead had even been counted, before the survivors had had a chance to collect their wits, when the images of the death camps were being shown – not in history classes but in the newsreels. Even though the book is practically contemporary with the catastrophe, which affected Arendt personally, it has the appraising perspective of history. Hardly a phrase can be found in it that is on its surface accusatory; nothing in it plays on feelings, nothing indulges, nothing stirs the reader by verbal effects. Arendt wrote the almost one thousand pages without a single exclamation mark, without superlatives, without rhetorical questions appealing to empathy, without calls to indignation and outrage. Compassion and anger are transformed in Arendt's political thought into a different, invisible state.

She rarely permits herself the ceremonious tone of a statement of principles, and then only when introducing an ideal in order to demonstrate its inadequacy. For example, the declarations of the Rights of Man by the American and the French revolutionaries mark for Arendt the political beginning of the modern age:

> The declaration of the Rights of Man at the end of the eighteenth century was a turning point in history. It meant nothing more nor less than that from then on Man, and not God's command or the customs of history, should be the source of Law. Independent of the privileges which history had bestowed upon certain strata of society or certain nations, the declaration indicated man's emancipation from all tutelage and announced that he had now come of age.[5]

These are well-turned and well-chosen words, at once lofty and uplifting, and would make a fine adornment to any commemorative speech on the Enlightenment, on Europe, on Western civilization. Yet, in

Hannah Arendt, words such as these are not part of an edifying treatise on human progress; they introduce the closing section of a chapter that ought to disturb even the reader of today as few other historical analyses of the twentieth century have done: the chapter on 'The Decline of the Nation-State and the End of the Rights of Man'. The unctuous tone rarely seen in Arendt's writing graces her praise of the Rights of Man just as she sets out to explain its aporia. And Arendt herself leaves no doubt that one problem lies in the solemnity of the language itself, which has come down to us from the nineteenth century. Just a page further on, she remarks:

> Even worse was that all societies formed for the protection of the Rights of Man, all attempts to arrive at a new bill of human rights were sponsored by marginal figures – by a few international jurists without political experience or professional philanthropists supported by the uncertain sentiments of professional idealists. The groups they formed, the declarations they issued, showed an uncanny similarity in language and composition to that of societies for the prevention of cruelty to animals.

The exposition that ensues of the dilemmas facing the modern nation-state is compellingly logical, historically grounded, and nightmarish in its hopelessness: for the nation-state does not simply fail to defend human rights – much worse, it is structurally incapable of universally defending those human rights that were proclaimed at the time of its creation. The French Revolution, which conceived humanity as a family of nations, saw humanity's rights as accruing to the members of a nation. That meant, however, that the rights of man were linked to the rights of the citizen.

> The full implications of this identification of the rights of man with the rights of peoples in the European nation-state system came to light only when a growing number of people and peoples suddenly appeared whose elementary rights were no more safeguarded by the ordinary functioning of nation-states in the middle of Europe than they would have been in the heart of Africa.

When the last multi-ethnic empires were dissolved at the end of the First World War, and all over the continent arose nations – some of them arbitrarily constructed – whose peoples were by no means congruent with their inhabitants, everywhere minorities were left over who were not provided for in the old trinity, imaginary as it was to begin with, of people, territory and state. While the recognized minorities had, if not equality, then at least legal rights as citizens, the many millions of refugees and stateless persons who had no papers at all at the end of the war found themselves in a much more dramatic situation. Because they did not enjoy the protection of any government, they could rely only on their minimal, allegedly innate human rights. Only there was no one, no national or international authority, that could guarantee those stateless persons their rights:

> The Rights of Man, supposedly inalienable, proved to be unenforceable – even in countries whose constitutions were based upon them – whenever people appeared who were no longer citizens of any sovereign state. To this fact, disturbing enough in itself, one must add the confusion created by the many recent attempts to frame a new bill of human rights, which have demonstrated that no one seems able to define with any assurance what these general human rights, as distinguished from the rights of citizens, really are.

The minorities, refugees and expelled persons in the aftermath of the First World War at least seem to have felt they had effectively no human rights, for, whenever they organized, they always invoked their rights as Poles, as Jews or as Germans. It did not occur to any of them to appeal to human rights. 'Their plight is not that they are not equal before the law, but that no law exists for them.'

Some of Arendt's readers have suggested applying her arguments to the refugees of our time – those who have no passports or residence permits, people living without a legal status. Whether or not that is helpful, I believe Arendt's thesis of the end of the Rights of Man is relevant today in another, much more comprehensive sense: it concerns the very essence of the nation-state. It is interesting to note that Hannah Arendt spoke of the end of the Rights of Man at a time when the General Assembly of the United Nations had just unanimously adopted the Universal Declaration of Human Rights. There is no doubt that she approved of the progress made in international law after the Second World War, including the Geneva Convention Relating to the Status of Refugees, the United Nations High Commissioner for Refugees and the International Court of Justice in The Hague. The purpose of these institutions is precisely to ensure the rights of those who have no rights under any nation-state. And yet, even though we owe democracy itself to the origin of the nation-state, in essence the problem of the nation-state remains. When the sovereignty of the people supplanted the absolute rule of princes, it brought with it the necessity, which persists today, of defining who makes up the people and who does not belong to the people. The principle of popular sovereignty compels the nation-state to make this distinction, this identification: 'Where persons of other ethnic origins are found within the nation, national feeling calls for them to be either assimilated or expelled.'[6]

Since the Second World War, Europe has certainly reduced the potential for conflict that lies in this distinction between citizens and non-citizens, and the situation cannot be compared with the one Hannah Arendt witnessed, in which non-citizens were first marked, like lepers, and later slaughtered like animals. And yet the discussions about the rights of others that were carried on long before Nazism, and are being carried on again today, about the rights of minorities, of persons of other faiths, of immigrants and even of tourists, who, depending on their country of origin, in order to obtain a visa must present file folders full of guarantees, bank statements, title deeds, insurance policies, and education and employment certificates – these discussions are not understandable without considering the foundations, and also the pitfalls, of the modern nation-state as it has developed in consequence of the French Revolution. Both the discussions and the actual passport checks have their roots in the question: Who is 'we'? True, this 'we' has become more permeable. The son or daughter of an immigrant can accede to high state office or to academic honours. But even the word 'integration', which has acquired a normative status, suggests that the discussion is still founded on the idea of a somehow unified people to which an outsider must bring qualifications, make contributions. The very word 'integration' denotes a one-sided process: an individual or a group integrates into an existing whole. In Germany there may be reasons to continue to conceive the people as something uniform, as a collective which has proved to be ethnically and religiously extendable but which remains linguistically and culturally more or less homogeneous. We should be aware, however, as Hannah Arendt was, of the genesis of this pretension and not mistake it for a law of nature. Popular sovereignty, for example, had entirely different meanings in the American and French revolutions, and accordingly the problems posed by immigration today take quite different forms in the United States and in Europe.

In the French Revolution, the emphasis shifted early on from the republic to the people: the permanence and identity of the state would be guaranteed not by the institutions of the state but by a putative will of the people, which was conceived, after Rousseau, as a unity, but which in the actual course of the revolution became a coerced unanimity. The Fathers of the American Revolution, on the other hand, never understood the word 'people' to denote something singular; immigration from so many different countries made it natural to see the society as a plurality to be culturally unified, democratically organized. Consequently, the most important and most significant of all revolutionary acts was felt to be the adoption of a constitution, whereas in other revolutions, and not only in Europe, the new constitutional state was always in danger of being swept aside by an appeal to public opinion, or to the *volonté générale*, as if the people really shared just a single opinion, a single will. For Hannah Arendt, Robespierre's betrayal in dissolving the political clubs with the argument that there was only one great *société populaire*, the French people, is more than just a seizure of power by a single faction. It stands as an example, she points out in the German version of *On Revolution*, of the fundamental deception of nationalism, 'which sets a delusion in the place of a living reality'.[7]

It would be much more convenient not only for the Germans, but also for the nations that were victorious in the Second World War, to be able to dismiss Nazism as an aberration in Western civilization, isolated from the other Western democracies – as barbarism and, hence, as that word implies, as something foreign, obscure; something with no causal connection to European history. At this point, Hannah Arendt, much closer to the *Dialectic of Enlightenment* than to the apologetics of her own teachers, shows how nationalism was inherent in the origins of the French Revolution itself and was by no means limited to Germany, but only took its most radical form there as National Socialism. The fact that Europe did not overcome that tyranny in the people's name on its own – that it took the help of the United States to do so – was not, Arendt finds, the result of geostrategic or military circumstances: it followed logically from the history of revolutions. Hence it is not surprising that she was very much in favour of the project of European unity after the Second World War but very sceptical about its chances of succeeding. As late as 1958 she feared that Europe would no more find a way out of its organization in nation-states than the Europe of late antiquity had escaped from its organization in city-states.[8]

Nazism is defeated, we may well say in late 2011 – in spite of the shock of the serial murders exposed by the recent suicide of two right-wing assassins. Nazism is defeated, but the nationalism from which it sprang is not. So, although it is only by random coincidence that they all occurred in 2011, the attacks of the NSU are not entirely unconnected with those in Oslo and Utøya a short time before, and not only confront Germany and Norway with a new quality of xenophobic terror but also drastically illustrate the decline of the European project. That decline did not just begin with the financial crisis, of course. The financial crisis is an expression and a consequence of a political crisis that began years ago, in the transition from the generation with first-hand memories of the horrors of war to our generation, to those born later who cannot appreciate the miraculous character of European unity from our own experience – who, in the West at least, have not experienced directly what bondage means.

To ascertain that the European project is in decline, we do not need to look disparagingly at neighbouring countries where right-wing populist, xenophobic, staunchly anti-European parties are on the rise and, in some cases, participating in coalition governments. When a leading spokesman of the party of Konrad Adenauer and Helmut Kohl, the chairman of their parliamentary group in the Bundestag, triumphantly declares that Europe finally speaks German again,[9] and does so the day before a visit by the British prime minister, that is more than just diplomatic imbecility. It is historical amnesia to a degree that must frighten any reader of Hannah Arendt. (Before anyone on the other side of the political spectrum nods too smugly, I would like to recall that a prominent left-wing politician recently reintroduced the connection between race and intelligence, namely – and significantly for our topic – by the no less imbecilic and even more amnesiac reference to a higher intelligence of the Jewish people.)

But to return for a moment to the chairman of the Christian Democrat parliamentary group in the Bundestag: this triumphant German is the same one who announces up and down the country that, since the Germans are Christians, they ought to devote themselves particularly to the defence of Christendom, which suffers persecution as no other religious community throughout the world. I will not examine this assertion here, much less weigh the numbers of Christian victims against those of other religious or ethnic minorities in the world who are also victims of persecution. Instead I will stick with Hannah Arendt and recommend her book *On Revolution* to the chairman of the CDU parliamentary group in the Bundestag for a different reason. Although written by a Jew, it contains, in a brilliant double interpretation of Dostoevsky's 'Grand Inquisitor' and Melville's *Billy Budd*, one of the most precise and most forceful descriptions of the benevolence that Jesus of Nazareth brought into the world, or at least into the history of religion: 'his ability to have compassion with all men in their singularity, that is, without lumping them together into some such entity as one suffering mankind.'[10] Every person, every ordinary person, acts, thinks, judges, loves as a member of a community, guided by his or her *sensus communis*, as Hannah Arendt explains elsewhere with reference to Kant. At the same time, every person, by the simple fact of being a person, is a member of a world community. A person who acts politically, Arendt emphasizes, should be conscious of being, if not in reality, then at least ideally, a citizen of the world and should be guided by his or her world citizenship.[11] This is the dilemma in all politics: to act on the sense of one's own community yet without overlooking the valid interests of other communities. That is the dilemma that the prophets of the Old Testament faced and, later, the Islamic Prophet too: to preach to their own people a message that was actually addressed to all humanity. Jesus' compassion, as Hannah Arendt interprets it, goes much further: it not only oversteps but demolishes the boundaries of the communal. The notion that Jesus of Nazareth would subscribe to an appeal to aid only, or especially, the Christians in the world is irreconcilable with the sense of the Gospel. His compassion does not collectivize; it is radically directed towards the individual – all individuals; it is the first truly universal love in the recorded history of humanity.

When Hannah Arendt, a German Jewish emigrant, illustrates the highest degree of compassion by way of the person of Jesus Christ, the founder of a different community, and one that has mostly been hostile to the Jews for almost two thousand years, it tells us something about her personality. When she sees the greatness of the story that Dostoevsky and, indirectly, Melville tell about Jesus in the fact 'that we are made to feel how false the idealistic, high-flown phrases of the most exquisite pity sound the moment they are confronted with compassion',[12] that tells us something about the feeling produced by reading her texts.

It is characteristic of the political thinking that Hannah Arendt exemplifies that she not only describes compassion in its highest degree but, at the same time, perceives its social ambivalence and immediately subdues the passion again. Like love, compassion 'abolishes the distance, the in-between which always exists in human intercourse'. However, by that very quality – because it abolishes 'the worldly space between men where political matters, the whole realm of human affairs are located', compassion is politically irrelevant. It is 'with compassion, and not for lack of arguments' that Jesus listens in silence to the Grand Inquisitor's speech; from the beginning he is 'struck, as it were, by the suffering which lay behind the easy flow of his opponent's great monologue.'[13] And when the Grand Inquisitor has finished, Jesus is still not capable of answering him in words. His only response is a kiss. And Billy Budd, at the foot of the gallows, is similarly reconciled, in a last, stammering cry, with his judge, who is suffering pangs of conscience.

> Jesus' silence in 'The Grand Inquisitor' and Billy Budd's stammer indicate the same [thing], namely their incapacity (or unwillingness) for all kinds of predicative or argumentative speech, in which someone talks *to* somebody *about* something that is of interest to them both because it *inter-est*, it is between them. Such talkative and argumentative interest

> in the world is entirely alien to compassion, which is directed solely, and with passionate intensity, towards suffering man himself.

Someone who has a saint's deep compassion for the poor – to illustrate Hannah Arendt's thought with an example – joins them, to help them or to share their poverty. But such a person rarely sets out to change the conditions that cause poverty. If such saintly people are moved, by whatever circumstance, perhaps the distress of the masses or the pleas of the needy, to act in the political sphere, their excessive compassion becomes a hazard, pushing them to 'shun the drawn-out wearisome processes of persuasion, negotiation, and compromise, which are the processes of law and politics.' Excessively empathic people will tend by nature to lend a voice 'to the suffering itself, which must claim for swift and direct action, that is, for action with the means of violence.'[14] Violence, however, in Arendt's view, can never do more than defend the boundaries of the political field. Where violence penetrates into politics itself, politics is finished.

Much has been written about Hannah Arendt's attitude towards the Jewish question during the Second World War and towards the founding of the state of Israel. Her accusations against the Jewish councils and her sympathy with the Jewish resistance fighters, her plea for a Jewish army and her criticism of the transfer agreement – positions that have actually been held by revisionists – cannot be understood except with reference to her attitude on compassion. Arendt did not tolerate charitable talk about victims or appeals to sympathy for them, for, if freedom was a mercy, it would cease to be a human right. In 1962 she wrote a letter to James Baldwin criticizing him for supporting blacks by attributing so many good qualities to them: their beauty, their capacity for joy, their warmth, their humanity; these, Arendt wrote, are the characteristics of all oppressed peoples:

> They grow out of suffering and they are the proudest possession of all pariahs. Unfortunately, they have never survived the hour of liberation by even five minutes.[15]

These lines display a similar realism, and a similar severity, to those with which Hannah Arendt saw her own people during the catastrophe. Perhaps her attitude can be summed up in this way: for the sake of compassion, compassion must be banned from politics. Justice must be done to the oppressed not because they are good people, but because they are people. Arendt makes a strict distinction – some have said, especially in the controversy over her essay on the race riots in Little Rock, *too* strict – between morality and legality. Social discrimination against blacks is morally reprehensible, she wrote, but legitimate. Only the state must treat all people equally. Private citizens, on the other hand, are free to prefer the company of their own community and to exclude another community. A sign of a good state, she writes elsewhere, again citing Immanuel Kant, is that a bad man can be a good citizen.[16] On the basis of this political philosophy, and not out of sympathy for the Arabs, to whom she had devoted little attention, Arendt vehemently condemned the Zionist movement's and, later, the Israeli state's policy of displacement. Her position that the founding act of one nation must not bring with it the degradation of another nation was not a plea arising from compassion but one based on principle, on a categorical imperative to be exact. Those who violate the rights of others destroy the basis of their own political existence as well.

As Hannah Arendt shows in her discussion of the influence of Rousseau, who considered compassion the principle of all true human relations, that noblest of passions changed in the political field into absolute mercilessness, and the French Revolution of 1789 ultimately led to catastrophe – and the same can be said of all the other great revolutions since: not only the Russian Revolution of 1905, as Hannah Arendt found, but also the Iranian Revolution of 1979. The misfortune of the Iranian Revolution is that it was likewise 'deflected almost from its beginning' from the course of

> the foundation of freedom and the establishment of lasting institutions . . . through the immediacy of suffering; it was determined by the exigencies of liberation not from tyranny but from necessity, and it was actuated by the limitless immensity of both the people's misery and the pity this misery inspired.

In Iran, too, the original protagonists of the revolution, the bourgeoisie with its intellectuals, students, women's rights activists, engineers and businesspeople, for whom the cause of freedom was at stake, were displaced, driven away or physically destroyed by those acting in the name of the common people, in particular the population in the slums of the cities, the 'needy' or *mostazafin*. To use Robespierre's sentence from his accusation against Louis XVI, which became almost an axiom to the French revolutionaries, Ayatollah Khomeini declared very early on that whatever served the purposes of the revolution was legal, going so far as to declare even the sacred law of Islam obsolete where its abrogation would serve the interests of the new state. In Iran, this revaluation of law as a means to an end marked the beginning of the purges and mass executions.

> Who would deny that the law knows no mercy? But we must not forget that when people abolish the law, no matter why, it is always brute violence that takes its place. Nothing teaches that more aptly than the history of revolutions.[17]

Only one revolution, in the history Hannah Arendt recounts in her book, was spared the excesses of virtue, and that was because it was the only one not cursed with poverty, so that the necessary pragmatism of politics was 'never put to the test of compassion'.[18] Because she consistently described the American Revolution as the more successful of the West's two great revolutions, Arendt was often either co-opted or dismissed as a right-wing theorist, especially in her early reception. Her Americanism, however, does not fit any right–left model. What animates it is, rather, a plea for a multicultural society, understood not as 'anything goes' but as the strictly equal treatment of different people before the law. As a historian Arendt had studied, and as a Jew she had directly experienced, how the European type of nation-state forces people into an identity, whether that of assimilation or that of the pariah. In America, however, she was able to belong without quite belonging.

The loyalty she felt as an American citizen motivated her to criticize American politics almost with the same passion that was suspect to her as a historian. In regard to the question what political thought means, her objections against McCarthy and against the Vietnam War are not the most crucial aspects of that criticism. Other American intellectuals criticized their country with similar or greater severity, and indeed one might define the intellectual as someone who reflects critically on his or her own society. Thinking politically means trying to understand the world in all its ambivalence, inconsistency and complexity. Hannah Arendt underscored the relative success of the American Revolution yet at the same time pointed out its deficiency. In her interpretation, the disappearance of the concept of the public from the original expression of the *pursuit of public happiness*, leaving in the Declaration of Independence simply the right of the *pursuit of happiness*, is an example that illustrates the spreading conception of freedom, still influential in America today, 'as the right of citizens to pursue their personal interests and thus to act according to the rules of private self-interest.'[19] Yet Arendt not only explained the evil spirit of unbridled capitalism and individualism by its descent from the spirit of the American Revolution; she also pointed to that revolution's limited, 'little more than local importance' – that is, its failure to usher in a new world order of freedom.[20]

> The reason for [its] success and failure was that the predicament of poverty was absent from the American scene but present everywhere else in the world.[21]

Moreover, the relative ease and the social balance of the American society, Jefferson's 'lovely equality', which made the non-violent course of the revolution possible in the first place, was built on slave labour. In other words, the greatest triumph of freedom in the history of the West was achieved, in Hannah Arendt's analysis, thanks to the worst possible exploitation. The American Revolution was successful because compassion played no part in it. Yet that noblest of all passions plays no part only because the revolutionaries closed their eyes completely to the plight of the black people who, in the mid-eighteenth century, made up almost a quarter of the population. It is precisely this kind of antagonism, ambivalence, aporia that characterizes political thought as Hannah Arendt exemplifies it. It is thinking without the balustrade of systems, ideologies and wishes; it is as confusing, suspenseful, unsafe and paradoxical as real human experience.

Because it strives to judge both history and current events in all their contradictory aspects, never deciding on a single point of view, such thought can be co-opted by all kinds of agendas by singling out one aspect or another. And so, in the course of her reception history, Hannah Arendt has been pronounced sometimes a leftist and sometimes a rightist thinker; sometimes a supporter and sometimes an opponent of Zionism; sometimes an apologist and sometimes a denouncer of America; sometimes a champion and sometimes a critic of the European project. She seems to have been aware that this extreme polarity in her reception is rooted in the structure of her thinking, although, again, in her elegant discretion she spoke of it only in paying tribute to others. In her speech on Lessing that I quoted at the outset, she said that, to him, criticism was

> always taking sides for the world's sake, understanding and judging everything in terms of its position in the world at any given time. Such a mentality can never give rise to a definite world view which, once adopted, is immune to further experiences in the world because it has hitched itself firmly to one possible perspective. . . . To be sure, we are still aware that thinking calls not only for intelligence and profundity but above all for courage. But we are astonished that Lessing's partisanship for the world could go so far that he could even sacrifice to it the axiom of noncontradiction, the claim to self-consistency, which we assume is mandatory to all who write and speak.[22]

What would Hannah Arendt have said about the Arab Spring? Her prophecy that in world politics 'those will probably win who understand revolution, while those who still put their faith in power politics in the traditional sense of the term and, therefore, in war as the last resort of all foreign policy may well discover in a not too distant future that they have become masters in a rather useless and obsolete trade'[23] – this sentence has gained a new currency in view of American Middle East policy after 11 September 2001 and of Western amazement at the Middle Eastern liberation movements of recent years. The will to freedom that was observed in the summer of 2009 in the streets of Tehran, and soon afterwards in Tunisia, Egypt, Libya, Bahrain, Yemen and Syria, would certainly have captured Arendt's enthusiasm, and she would certainly have argued against theories that ascribe political passivity to the culture of certain nations. And yet, Arendt would probably not look very optimistically at the Middle East in these days, for unfortunately it recalls 1789 more than 1776. If we follow her historical analysis, revolutions do not succeed in countries cursed with poverty. And, in fact, among all the Arab countries, the chances of establishing a constitutional democracy are best in Tunisia, which has a comparatively balanced social structure. In the other Arab countries, and especially in Egypt, we can already observe how the revolutionary movement is splitting into the primarily young, primarily middle-class activists, who continue to struggle for political freedom, and the inhabitants of the slums, for whom, after their initial euphoria, the question of how to earn a living is now more urgent than ever since the disturbances of the revolution have brought the economy to its knees. As it was in post-revolutionary France, the call for a firm hand that promises to end the chaos of the young and fragile democracy may soon be heard in the Arab countries too.

But who knows? The political thought that Hannah Arendt exemplifies is not limited to learning from history: it also incites us to refute history. Whatever the coming years may bring for the Arabs, the fact that they once succeeded in changing what had previously seemed ordained by God, that they were able, peacefully, largely spontaneously, without outside help, without heroic leaders, to overthrow dictators who had posed for years and decades as their fathers – and fatherhood is not an elected office – the fact of this patricide, which all observers and, more importantly, most Arabs themselves would have thought impossible or, more accurately, would have found unthinkable, will inscribe itself in their collective memory, as Arendt correctly predicted in regard to the Hungarian uprising of 1956: even failed revolutions can have a political effect by being remembered. For the first time in modern history, the Arab societies have experienced history as something that doesn't simply happen but is made. Whoever acts as their leader in the years to come, no matter what authority he may claim, his statues will no longer be thought immovable.

To walk the long road from liberation to freedom is not a task for the Arabs alone. In the sense of the world citizenship that Hannah Arendt called for as the basis for political action, it is also a task for us – and not just our human rights NGOs. What the Arab nations need most urgently now is not a declaration of their rights; it is a tangible contribution to the reduction of mass poverty, such as the removal of import tariffs, an end to subsidized agricultural exports that destroy local farming, the development of infrastructure – of electricity, water, energy, education – and of course economic aid and integration in the European single market, better in the short than the medium term. Yes, that would be expensive; it would cost much more than declarations that recall the sentimental language of societies for the prevention of cruelty to animals. But how much would Europe lose, politically, economically and strategically, if the history of its own revolution were to repeat itself south of the Mediterranean Sea? Just as America after the war did not offer the Germans a prospect for the future out of compassion, it would be in the enlightened self-interest of the European countries today to stop investing in dictatorships and start investing in freedom.

Only one neighbour of the Arab nations has more at stake on Tahrir Square than the Europeans: that is the state of Israel. The lasting peace that was always Hannah Arendt's vision as a Jewish thinker will come about in the Middle East only when tyranny is overcome. To those who think that is unrealistic in view of the election results in Egypt and Tunisia, and in view of the increasing repression in Israel itself, I would point out that political thought, as Arendt exemplifies it for me, expected nothing less than miracles – 'not because we believe in miracles, but because human beings, as long as they are able to act, are able to achieve the improbable and the incalculable, and constantly do achieve it, whether they know it or not.'[24] And so, to close as paradoxically as she experienced the world, I will hope with Hannah Arendt that the Arab revolutions do not prove Hannah Arendt right.

— 14 —

TILTING AT WINDMILLS

*Mosebach and the Novel**

Today the German Academy for Language and Literature honours a writer who seems to have little in common with the German literature of recent decades. In what group, school or current could we classify Martin Mosebach? Who would be the colleagues with whose work his corresponds? Heimito von Doderer comes to mind as an influence, the more readily as Mosebach refers to him from time to time – but Doderer, too, was a literary eccentric; admiration for him is in itself a credential of anachronism. If the year of Mosebach's birth weren't printed on the dust jackets of his books, we wouldn't even be able to assign him to a certain generation. From his debut, he came on with the stylistic sureness of an old master, and since then his language has grown younger, his motifs broader; Mosebach turns his attention to the world beyond the German bourgoisie, whose decline is one of his lifelong themes.

Long unnoticed by any kind of wider public, his books have accumulated over a quarter of a century to form a true oeuvre, a shelf of stories, travelogues, essays, plays, poems and, above all, the eight novels, weighty not only in literary merit. Martin Mosebach writes thick books – five hundred pages, six hundred pages, eight hundred pages; and, although numbers are generally uninformative, in this case they do provide a first indication of what distinguishes him from the literature of his time and where we might look for his literary relations. Martin Mosebach writes novels!

A novelist, some may say, so what? The publishers' catalogues are full of novels. Any text that is a hundred pages long – no matter how big

* Speech to the German Academy for Language and Literature on the presentation of the Georg Büchner Prize to Martin Mosebach, 27 October 2007.

the type is, as long as it's a hundred pages, or even ninety, but no short stories please, and please, please no poetry, and least of all an anthology; we want something to read right through – gets labelled a novel. Never mind the fact that most novels aren't novels at all, that they fulfil none of the criteria that characterize the classic novel except in length, that they are not set in a broad imaginary world and do not grasp the full social import of a historic experience, the complexity of motifs and characters, the diversity of modes of expression and speech registers – it makes no difference.

Certainly many novels are still being created, sometimes great ones, in Germany as elsewhere, for which the publishers and distributors quite rightly claim affiliation with the genre. But they follow – or at least they tend to follow – a specific, more recent tradition, namely the Protestant tradition of the *Bildungsroman*, which of course developed in the eighteenth century in reaction to the society novels from France and England. No longer the whole world, but the world from the point of view of a specific person, often an artistic figure or a fool, usually narrated in the first person or by a named narrator character – this alone expresses the fragmented, subjectivized relation to reality that characterizes human experience after the Reformation and the Enlightenment. No major Catholic authors enter the field until the turn of the nineteenth century, and for a hundred years they remain the exception. Only in the first half of the twentieth century did German literature temporarily lose its ties to the Protestant outlook and come to be written in large part, perhaps in its most significant part, in the Catholic or Jewish circles of the multicultural Habsburg monarchy. Post-war literature, on the other hand – regardless of the religious background of its best-known proponents – sees life once more from the worm's-eye rather than the bird's-eye view, reducing the world at the same time to its suchness; it is anti-metaphysical but takes social criticism to didactical extremes – and to that extent it is, at its core, for all its ostensible secularity, prototypically German and Protestant.

Of course, I am merely sketching tendencies in contemporary literature in a few broad strokes, and Martin Mosebach is not the only eminent German writer to whom they do not apply – but among living authors there is probably none whose work runs so vehemently counter to the general course of development. Mosebach believes in the novel – the novel in the strict sense, the French or Russian sense; the novel as the presumption of creating an image of reality, of reality in its entirety, of a society, an era, a state of affairs, condensed into a city, a neighbourhood, a milieu or a year. That is why novels require temporal or spatial distance and are remarkably often written in exile. That is why

Mosebach writes many of his books abroad. From outside it is easier to get a view of the whole, of the human comedy, with the sublime and the ridiculous, the king and the fool, the lover and the chastiser.

Consider his novels *The Bed*, *A Long Night*, *The Tremor*[1] and all the others. Think of their unvarying plot trajectories consisting of a brief gamble and a lasting failure; examine their characters, as expressively drawn as those in Chekhov's plays, down to the minor parts; remember in particular the protagonists, always slightly awkward in their blundering march through the foreign country that the world is to them; consider the rich use of stylistic devices, of sarcasm, of grotesque, of humour in many forms, the slightly mocking – no, self-mocking – tone. Why do all of these characteristics, for all their idiosyncrasy, for all their secession from contemporary literature, still seem familiar? From what lineage are they descended? We must look farther back than to Heimito von Doderer, much farther back than Marcel Proust; farther than Stendhal or Honoré de Balzac, the realistic novelists of the nineteenth century with whom Mosebach is often associated; even farther than Eichendorff or Moritz; we must go back to the very beginning of the modern novel to find the source of Mosebach's tone. We must go back to the *Ingenious Gentleman Don Quixote of La Mancha* by Miguel de Cervantes Saavedra.

Like Cervantes in his *Don Quixote*, Mosebach in his novels rejects an outdated conception of life and literature dominated by entrenched forms, values and rituals precisely by pretending to adhere to it in the extreme. Each of his sentences is well formed, his grammar always correct, the rhythm constantly buoyant, the narrative strictly chronological and, at first glance at least, of such authorial integrity as if Joyce and Adorno had never existed. Likewise the social conditions: in Mosebach's novels, people still have artistic sense and lunch at 12 noon; there are historic private banks and couples who – hold onto your seats – move in together only after the wedding. No sex before marriage! In the West German reality of the new millennium, in which Christian Democrats pronounce same-sex marriage one of the inalienable achievements of the Enlightenment, to be approved by all candidates for naturalization, even the suggestion of a virgin marriage seems as antiquated as the ideals of chivalry during Cervantes' lifetime.

But our contemporary Mosebach is much too observant to fail to notice that his protagonists are more passé than progressive. That is why he is interested in them. And he is much too reflective an author to ignore the crisis of realistic narrative in the twentieth century, which goes hand in hand with the cinema's mass reproduction of realism. As absurd as it would be to declare Cervantes the last representative of the medieval romance of chivalry, it would be equally erroneous to consider Mosebach a reactionary who is out to restore the novel of the nineteenth century and its bourgeois world along with it: he lampoons both the garb in which his works come attired and the lifestyle they seem to celebrate.

Just as Cervantes placed his *Don Quixote* in a realistic setting, Mosebach sets his novels in a social reality that is identifiable right down to the street names, petrol stations and references to real persons and current political events – of course, only in order to contrast the prosaic real world with an imaginary one in which even the minor characters are caricatures, more valiant in their anxiety, more profound in their superficiality, subtler in their stupidity than we real people. In order to be so poetically charged, the world in which Mosebach's novels are set has to be as ordinary as possible. What La Mancha is to Cervantes – the unspectacular, arid region of his childhood – post-war Frankfurt is to Mosebach, with its ten-lane traffic strips and its grim suburbs, its four-storey architectural abominations of the reconstruction period alongside the forty-storey ostentation of today, and in the middle of it the farce of a brand-new historic city centre. 'It is part of my particular relation to my native Frankfurt that I see it as one of the most disfigured and ugly cities in Germany, while in my imagination and my inner image of the city I think of it as one of the most beautiful cities I know': so begins one of the many essays in which Martin Mosebach describes the setting of his life and his literature.

Because his chosen literary genre forbids him, like Cervantes, the supernatural, he must instead – and here, not least, he is quite Catholic – make even the most ordinary situation parabolic, miraculous, whether a cow walking through the lobby of an Indian airport, an ant burning on the hearth, or a cat slinking past the hero. All those animals – it is no coincidence that they play a similarly prominent role in Mosebach's novels as in *Don Quixote*. In the adventures of the sheep, the bulls or the pigs, Cervantes, too, finds the mute beasts the ideal surface on which to project a strange, magical reality in order to demonstrate, not the existence of magic, but the prosaic nature of our existence. Only to Don Quixote is the great, thick cloud of dust on the horizon is raised 'by a mighty army of countless different peoples'. To the reader, what the comical knight meets in combat remains a flock of sheep. As amusing as his subsequent debacle is, Cervantes' novel nonetheless evokes a feeling of regret that we live in a world in which sheep are only sheep and knights are only laughing stocks.

Just as it is only in Don Quixote's eyes that the windmills are enormous giants flailing about with their arms, the marionettes live people, the brass basin a helmet, likewise the greatest scenes in Mosebach's novels describe a drama that is played out only in the mind of the protagonist. The darkness in *A Long Night* – to mention just one example – is nothing but an ordinary power outage in a vacant office building, but the way Mosebach describes the existential despair in which the protagonist Ludwig Drais skids about searching first for the exit, then for the lavatory – this is more than just slapstick: it develops from an insignificant incident into a virtually biblical parable of human ridiculousness, although of course it is amusing only to the gods or, in this case, the reader. Ludwig Drais himself doesn't even have the consolation of knowing that his suffering is heroic, as in the old books. All he knows is that he needs to get to the loo. 'Had there always been such an unbridgeable chasm between literature and life?' asks the narrator near the end of *A Long Night*. Literature, he finds, tells of fatal occurrences, of love and jealousy, crime and punishment. Ludwig's life contained all of that: the love of a married woman, betrayal, even death.

> Wasn't that material for a gripping story? How must they feel, the people to whom all that happens? The heroes of such novels – they really were heroes, because the novels described heroic struggles in which the people were defeated by the institutions, the institutions were defeated by the people, and everything was defeated all together by crime and punishment.

Here and on the pages that follow in the novel, we see distinctly how Mosebach too pronounces a literary tradition outdated by continuing it under contemporary conditions and with the conscientiousness of one who mourns its passing. Heinrich Heine called *Don Quixote* 'the greatest satire against human zeal', but it could only be written by someone who was himself a zealot, who still belonged to that world of honour, erudition and passion that he carried to its grave.

Mosebach's works are no more progressive than *Don Quixote*, which, in contrast to the trend of its time, sounds no anti-absolutist or anti-Catholic notes. Respect is due to that which vainly resists decay, and sympathy is with the loser. That may sound conservative, but it is, rather, the scepticism of those who do not equate development with progress. Mosebach's gaze is directed backwards, it is true. But whichever way he looks – whether at Germany, Egypt or India – he is always interested in the splendour of the past, to the extent that it is in fact past. His novels describe the ephemeral in order to wield it against the present, contesting its claim to permanence. In the literary world of Martin Mosebach, life in itself is decay, and that does not imply that human conditions were ever better.

I asserted at the outset that Martin Mosebach believes in the novel. That is of course a literary genre that, in its beginnings, still bears distinct traces of older narrative forms, in particular the epic and the collection of tales in a frame story. While the outer plot of such a novel is oriented after a modern dramaturgy of exposition, action and resolution, in reality it consists of a thousand individual stories inserted more or less smoothly in that plot. This is noticeable in the fact that, once you know the outline, you can start in reading almost anywhere. The whole is always present in each part. This narrative principle is older than *Don Quixote*; it is found in the *Decameron*, in the *Divine Comedy* and, of course, in the literary tradition of the Orient and al-Andalus, which Cervantes uses as explicitly as Dante and Boccaccio before him. The Persian mystic Maulana Rumi titled one of his collections *Fīhi mā fīhi*: 'In it is what is in it.'

What is modern about *Don Quixote* is not its imaginary world but that world's collapse; not the literary form per se but the use of that form in quotation, which breaks it. In presenting his novel as the translation of a story by an Arabic author, bought in the market of Toledo, and then adding a second part, purportedly written later, in which all the characters are familiar with the published first part of the story, Cervantes is playing with literary pretences, layers of reality and the reception of his own works. Mosebach, too, while adhering so strictly to form, takes the verbal posture of quotation, expressly using exactly those idioms that the dictionary brands as archaic, and at the same time the form repeatedly comes unglued. Characters such as Mr and Mrs Kn. in *A Long Night* are introduced just before the end of the story and described in full detail, only to leave again suddenly and never reappear in the rest of the book. Or look at the construction of his novels: in *The Tremor*, for example, the mistress from Frankfurt just happens to appear at the court of the rural Indian king – who of course snatches her away right under the hero's nose, only to lose her to her other lover, the Frankfurt art guru who also just happens to be on a tour of India: this is so transparent that we realize how little Mosebach cares about the structure he seems to be using – always the same group of characters, a similar plot, remarkable coincidences, the same ironic tone. What makes Mosebach different is not the stories, which seem to be arbitrary, interchangeable, but the courage to dive into an individual situation, a marginal episode of maybe ten, maybe five, maybe two minutes of real time, as if into a rushing river, to let it carry us along for ten, fifteen, thirty pages, without a thought for reaching the shore, for what may be happening outside, in the story. These passages in Mosebach's novels feel to me like the improvisations in jazz or rock music, which often develop out of banal songs and, in their best moments, leave the composition far behind them, completely forgetting it for a while.

This truly mystical surrender to the object of his narrative goes farthest, so far, in Mosebach's second-to-last novel, *The Tremor*, which starts out in Frankfurt, like a typical Mosebach story, but then transforms in its second part into a literary meditation, one big description of a situation, out of all proportion to the much shorter first part and the tiny denouement. In these two hundred and some pages, in which practically nothing and everything happens, compressed into a few scenes, Mosebach doesn't just break open the form of the novel, he explodes it. Tension, real time and dramatic development in the conventional sense are irrelevant. In it is what is in it. In *The Tremor* Mosebach reveals that his faith in the novel is as audacious, as presumptuous, as absurd and even as ridiculous as Don Quixote's belief that he is a knight. But by the collapse of that belief – this is the twist – Don Quixote becomes a knight, his windmills become giants, Martin Mosebach creates a novel.

His latest novel, *The Moon and the Girl*,[2] is quite different, much more concentrated, tighter too, strictly and evenly organized. Here again we find what makes his style so brilliant: the melodic rhythm; the elegance of his ramified syntax, revealing that sentence structure is a branch of architecture; the fine sarcasm; the delightful anticipation of the coming metaphor that every 'as if' elicits. And yet even the balanced chapter outline is unconventional. The chapters, except the last, are all the same length, as if Mosebach had counted the pages, and they all follow the same structure, alternating between narration and inserted reflections that feel like a musical refrain. The structure is frighteningly perfect – and yet that is not what thrills this eulogist, for one, about the laureate. Naturally we younger readers want the explosion, not the perfection; what interests us about the plot is most of all the digression. But, on the other hand, something emerges further in *The Moon and the Girl* that was not yet present in the early novels, with their fairly endearing characters, and that only in *West End*, in *A Long Night* at the latest, takes on the unsettling quality I find indispensable in literature: what emerges is malice. It is no accident that *The Moon and the Girl* contains the first cold-blooded murder in a Mosebach novel. Literature has to be malicious, it has to hurt; for the sake of humanity itself, it has to be merciless in its view of human beings.

— 15 —

ONE GOD, ONE WIFE, ONE CHEESE

Golshiri and Friendship

I was on holiday when I learned of Hushang Golshiri's illness. A radio station called me on Easter Monday to ask me about the banning of newspapers and the arrests in Iran. What ban, what arrests?, I asked. I let the editor quickly give me the information he had received from the news agencies, thanked him and said good-bye. I pushed the red button that is the mobile substitute for hanging up the phone and immediately dialled Hushang Golshiri's number in Tehran. In the time it took to get a scratchy ringing tone on the line, I was able to hope that the situation was not as bad as the reports made it sound. But when his wife Farzaneh Taheri answered, her 'Hello' seemed to confirm my fears. After a brief greeting ritual, I learned that I was wrong and was also right. Golshiri was not in jail, but he had collapsed and was in intensive care. The doctors suspected lung cancer. They would know more tomorrow or the next day. He was unconscious most of the time. When he opened his eyes briefly, he only looked at her sadly.

He had last visited us six months earlier, in autumn of 1999. He was waiting for a visa for England, where he wanted to talk to two or three publishers who were interested in texts of his. He had submitted his application at the consulate in Düsseldorf during his previous visit. They would contact him as soon as the visa was granted, they had told him. There was no way to find out from the consulate how the matter stood. When I called, either the line was busy or no one answered, or else a woman answered and then left me on hold. Perhaps she made bets with her colleagues on my patience. Golshiri had experience with that kind of thing. He dismissed my suggestion that we go to Düsseldorf and try our luck. During his previous trip to Germany, he had gone to the consulate personally and waited there hours to be told they would get in touch with him in due course. It was good for us that the British were being so fussy and obliging him to honour us a little longer with his presence. In Persian you say things like that when you mean: Great, we can play some more backgammon. Well, then, get the backgammon board, he growled. We went to our rooms to put on our pyjama trousers and met again in the living room. For a proper game of backgammon in Iran you have to wear pyjama trousers because they give your legs enough freedom to sit comfortably on a Persian rug (jogging pants fulfil the same purpose, but how pitifully their thick fabric bunches up, like rolls of fat, on a man's legs, compared with the generous billows of pyjama trousers). I made tea, poured pistachios in a bowl, and sat down with him on the carpet. Usually he emerged from our nocturnal tournaments the winner, and then he would shower me with scorn for days. Foreigner! Amateur! And you call yourself an Isfahani!

How he could taunt. Even I had tears in my eyes, while my wife Katajun Amirpur was doubled over with laughter. And how he could parry my taunts! Even the rare times that I won, I was still the one who got the shower. But of course I was outmatched: I with my broken Persian, and he, the great poet, whom even his political opponents and the state-approved papers in Iran acknowledged as the most artful among all contemporary prose writers (and whose sympathy they would have been glad to claim for that reason). When I talked with Golshiri, I often had a sudden feeling that something had gone over my head. I never got that feeling except with him. Then I would realize he'd made yet another joke too subtle for me to notice it. He took a mischievous pleasure every time I missed the turnoff into irony or grotesque, and he reiterated the path to his punch line, step by step. He saw it as teaching me a lesson, and that's what it was.

Golshiri had worked for a few years as a village schoolteacher near Isfahan after finishing school himself, and since becoming famous overnight in the late 1960s with his short novel *Prince Ehtejab* he had espoused the cause of young writers in Iran as no other author of his generation did, looking after them and teaching them in spite of being banned from such activities – Golshiri remained an educator every second of his old age. He couldn't help trying to save everyone from their mistakes. That was also a significant motivation for his political activity: he couldn't help being publicly indignant about censorship, the lack of freedom, the barbarism of the cultural officials in Iran, long after it had become life-threatening to do so. He always said, Don't bother me with politics, and then he was the first and sometimes the only writer in Tehran to pick up the phone and give an interview to the foreign broadcasters' Persian-language services, to fax articles to us in Germany, to invite his colleagues to a meeting and launch declarations of protest.

That was in the evil hours, of which he suffered through so many in his last years: the murders of his friends, the attacks on him, the arrests and interrogations. In his best hours, of which life also gave him a few towards the end, he was an arrogant, opinionated and madly funny teacher in every situation, a mixture of a fusty schoolmaster, Groucho Marx and the old sage in a Buddhist fable. Even when he played backgammon, he never stopped lecturing (when he played with me, in any case). A bad move by his opponent was likely to unleash a thunderstorm of remonstrations and advice. When I did the washing up, too, he knew how to do it better. Perhaps this trait had its cause in his origins, which are also mine. Isfahanis are legendary not only as misers but especially as know-it-alls and compulsive meddlers in all kinds of affairs that are none of their business. And when two Isfahanis come together, there is no saving the world, which in this case consisted of my wife and my daughter, from laughing itself silly.

I had the feeling Golshiri felt at ease in our home. He avoided his acquaintances and admirers, of which he had whole armies in Cologne, as in almost every metropolis. He rarely went out and, in contrast to his earlier visits, he had no desire to go to the theatre, the museums or a café. And our backgammon sessions no longer lasted, as they used to do, until morning. It was evident that his strength was ebbing. He didn't drink, almost never smoked, and ate little. On the other hand, he took a long nap every day. He said himself the silence did him a world of good; he was finally able to relax. I accepted his explanation and still blame myself for not taking him to a doctor who might have discovered the tumour.

Sometimes he scolded me for not helping my wife more with the housework, but I had agreed with her to spend whatever time I could spare from work with him; after all, he was our guest. Since I couldn't tell him that, Golshiri considered me an incorrigible male chauvinist. He really was concerned about our relationship and worried that, in my paternal bliss, I was forgetting my good fortune in having the love of a wonderful wife (since he didn't give me or any other man credit for good taste, he ascribed our relationship to the mercy of heavenly providence). He liked Katajun very much. When they talked, they always did so in a very particular jocular-dallying tone all their own. If anything was left over from dinner, he did his utmost to persuade her to serve it to us the next day. After meals, even bodily force couldn't stop him clearing the table and putting the plates in the dishwasher (he wasn't completely debilitated after all). Golshiri liked how I treated my daughter, and that I did everything Iranian men of his generation never did: changed her nappies, fed her, took her along, together with him, whenever I had an errand to run.

A few months earlier, in February 1999, the five of us – Golshiri, Farzaneh, Katajun, our baby daughter Ayda and I – attended the great celebrations of the twentieth anniversary of the revolution in Tehran. I wanted to write something about it for the newspaper, and then everyone wanted to accompany me. He, the infamous and often persecuted critic of the regime, never would have dreamed that he would one day take part in a commemoration of the revolution, but when I said I wanted to go, he was immediately enthusiastic. As we walked to Freedom Square among the hundreds of thousands of demonstrators, we were quite a conspicuous quintet: our clothes, the women's loose headscarves, Golshiri's intellectual goatee and my clean-shaven cheeks identified us as members of a social class that took part in the Islamic Republic's parades as often as Lutherans in Holy Communion. Golshiri collected the flyers of the various groupuscules fighting for particularly extremist positions among the partisans of the revolution. The 'Staff for the Revival of "Commanding Good and Forbidding Evil"', for example, distributed a brochure that gave 'all people of sense and values' detailed instructions on how to bring undesirable journalists and authors to trial. Another group we encountered is renowned for storming the offices of critical publications, waylaying young couples in the parks, and beating people who have any kind of divergent opinion or appearance. Again and again Golshiri stopped, caught up in a conversation at a stand or a book table. His looks and his talk struck the people as odd, but he made them smile again and again with his friendly chaffing. Some recognized him, but no one was unfriendly towards him. In any case, Golshiri was not really the cause of their amazement. Protruding from my long black coat, unusual enough in itself on the national holiday, Ayda's little face, masked in cap and scarf, was a much greater curiosity to the demonstrators. I had harnessed her to my chest with the baby carrier, and, since she was now over two months old, she was facing forwards and observing the revolutionary world with great big eyes.

Golshiri was delighted with the baby carrier because it indicated a new, and in a way very old, relationship between parents and children, but also because he was tickled to see the people, especially the women, all heavily veiled, reacting with curious looks and incredulous whispers to the baby in its father's coat. At dinner in Cologne he lectured us again and again on how good it was that many young men had a different relationship with their wives and children than in his generation. He himself, he said, had used to be a typical Middle Eastern man who never touched anything in the household except the meals set before him. Then one day, on his way home, he had seen his wife, several months pregnant, standing in a long queue to buy milk. That had been during the war; Golshiri hadn't given a thought to anything but literature, politics and the various meetings of the various groups and associations. He went to his wife and took her place, telling her to go home and rest. Ah! Has it dawned on you, Farzaneh had jeered at him, that there may be other things in our life besides literature and politics?

He had a greater respect for her than one might expect of a famous older gentleman (but Farzaneh herself is a courageous intellectual, and a well-known literary translator, whose determination would teach respect to more Middle Eastern men than him). He scrupulously avoided arousing even a spark of her dreaded jealousy, and, if she had any cause to raise her eyebrows after a reading or a reception because Golshiri's charm had got the better of him again, he could plan whole campaigns to appease her. Time after time he praised – his eyes on me, the corners of his mouth raised wickedly – the worth of fidelity and mutual support. Although the reminiscences with which he regaled us every evening revealed a past that can only be called eventful in every respect, Golshiri assured us, when he had let slip an excessively libertine anecdote, that marriage had reformed him. He was happy to expatiate, however, on who of his colleagues had consorted with whom when, and he raged against any writer who dallied instead of devoting himself to literature, the resistance and his wife, especially as the secret service dug around in everyone's private lives. And what terrible taste those colleagues had, anyway!

When he spoke of Farzaneh and their two nearly grown-up children, however, he was like a man newly in love who can't believe his good fortune. His prudent character was not native to him. I believe it came from humility: he had seen a lot, and now he wanted to hold onto the good things life had given him. Because in Iran there is almost no cheese except from sheep's milk, I put delightful cheeses from France, Italy and Spain on the table every evening to spoil him. But every day Golshiri touched nothing but the Turkish sheep's cheese, saying, One God, one wife, one cheese. He honestly said that every evening until it became a proverb in our house. When I had to explain why, in spite of all the work I had to do and my neglected household duties, I couldn't miss the live broadcast of the second-division match between 1st FC Cologne ('the Real Madrid of the West', as I tried to explain to him) and some smalltown kickers, including the pre-match programme and the managers' interviews, I said, One football club. Golshiri, who didn't know the first thing about football, sat down next to me on the sofa, and in the second minute of play began to curse my Cologne side, the poor quality of the match, the amateurish tactics, the clumsy performance, the lack of playing culture. Naturally not a single pass or dribble was good enough; naturally he could have handled the ball better, even at his age. Only when 1st FC Cologne lost – to whom else but their rivals Mönchengladbach – did he stop teasing. With no ironic overtones, he consoled me and asked Katajun to show me some affection that night, 'just for once'.

After dinner we usually went down to the bank of the Rhine, remembering nights beside the *Zāyanderūd*, the 'life-giving river' of Isfahan. We talked almost always about poetry and language. Golshiri was interested in hearing about the latest developments in German literature and the debates in the cultural pages. We also talked at length about the aesthetics of the Quran, on which we had both written, from different points of view. Although Golshiri had once stood politically on the far left, towards the end of his life he became a more and more resolute champion of the individual and the particular versus the universal and general in both his literary and his political interests – he didn't distinguish between the two. Golshiri found frightening, for example, what people said of Ayatollah Khomeini: that when he lived in Najaf, in Iraq, he never glanced right or left when he walked from his house to the mosque every day, and that he never took a walk to the river during the fourteen years he lived there. Worse still, Golshiri insisted, was that the people said such things *in praise* of Khomeini. He called Khomeini's behaviour 'prophetlike' – by which he did not mean to insult the prophets. What he meant was, you observe life – this life today – this simple, little life – the river, that duck there, the dinner we just ate, even the cheese; he meant, you sweep your room, you put a flower on the table – and here was someone, this Khomeini, who could disdain and ignore all that. When Golshiri's leftist freedom fighters went to sleep at night, they would pick the hardest patch of ground they could find. And, when he was with them in prison, he found the blows they gave each other and him in play were worse than the interrogators' tortures.

Golshiri no longer believed in all that. The normal, average person in this world, he said, doesn't need to devote his life to such utopian ideals any more. People know you can't suddenly change the way life is, that you can't set the world in order once for all time, that it's a dangerous idea. Any judgement that is made for all time is dangerous. Really modern literature, he said, is this: to get away from both poles of prophecy, the positive and the negative. Nietzsche was a great man, but from within his thought came fascism, and from within Christianity came the Middle Ages and burning people alive, and from one-sided Islam, as he called it, came all this that we have now. People could profess their faith, pray every day, have a relationship with God, and so on, he said, but when somebody brings that into the society and says, I am God's representative, he should be certified, or at least put under supervision, because he's a danger to human society.

We talked about things like that on the banks of the Rhine. I remember a great deal of it; I made notes afterwards of some of it. On the way back we thought about what kind of car I should buy, because, after years of ecologically motivated, loudly proclaimed abstinence, I had decided for Ayda's sake to throw my self-imposed dogma to the winds. Golshiri respected my green conscience but was glad of every dogma defeated. Besides, he thought a young family needs a car. He said that to Katajun, too, who thought there was no use for a car in the city. But with a car, Golshiri said, we could go to the countryside at weekends and enjoy life. And so we walked along the rows of parked cars and debated what model would suit us best. I argued tenaciously for a big old saloon car – as big and old as possible (but with a catalytic converter for the environment's sake), while he stressed the issues of economy and reliability. He endorsed my father's advice to buy a used Mercedes. I was afraid a Mercedes would be too bourgeois, but Golshiri praised German automotive engineering and dismissed my worries as twaddle. To compare the various models we often criss-crossed our neighbourhood near the Rhine. Naturally cars didn't interest him in the least – he didn't even have a driver's licence to my knowledge – but, because they interested me at that time, they interested him too.

Finally I sent a fax, in the name of the newspaper I was working for then, to the press attaché of the British embassy in Berlin. The same day I received a call from the consul in Düsseldorf, who was terribly sorry and invited Golshiri to come and pick up his visa any time he liked, regardless of the opening hours. Golshiri was thoroughly impressed with me and the newspaper. He wanted to go to Düsseldorf straight away, before the British changed their minds. I wanted to register my new car the next day – a used Mercedes – so my mother went with him to the consulate. They left our flat one morning, chattering in Isfahani Persian, and came back only towards evening – still chattering – my mother having obliged Golshiri to accompany her on an extensive stroll through the shopping arcades. Golshiri filled the rest of the evening with anecdotes about my mother, who had gone along as his guide but would have been hopelessly lost in Düsseldorf without him, of course. Apparently the two of them had had a spirited debate in front of a bus ticket vending machine, since my mother, on some principle no doubt rooted in her Isfahani background, had insisted on taking a bus from Düsseldorf main station to the consulate. Golshiri had at first been sympathetic to my mother's insistence, but when, a quarter of an hour later, she still hadn't found out which button to push, he grew restless and tried to persuade her to take a taxi. But my mother could not be moved – even Golshiri had met his match.

Two or three days later, Golshiri was off to London, intending to return to Tehran from there. Because there were no cheap flights on such short notice, I suggested he take the Eurostar. He, the world traveller, was scared to death he might get lost changing trains in Brussels, but the travel agent and I were able to persuade him, by detailed explanations using maps of the Brussels railway station, that it was easier to get from Cologne to London by train than to get from the south side of Tehran to the west side by taxi.

A few months later, in early February 2000, we met again in Tehran. Golshiri and his family were in good spirits, for the process of reform seemed to be making progress. The parliamentary elections had brought the results he had hoped for, the newspapers were more courageous than ever, and the founding of a writers' union, a lifelong project of Golshiri's, was coming along. The censors had also signalled they would allow some of his books to be printed. As I almost always did, I spent my last evening at the Golshiris' home and went from there to the nearby airport for a night flight. It had been a long time since I had had such a relaxed evening in Tehran and laughed so much.

When all the reform-oriented newspapers were banned and critical authors arrested in the spring of 2000, Golshiri was too sick to know it. The day I learned of his illness, I had to write an article. A long-smouldering conflict with Katajun flared up that evening, and I took my laptop and went to sit outside a taverna. I wrote about the repression in Iran, about friends at the newspapers who had been so hopeful during my visit two months before but were now in jail or, at best, unemployed; I wrote about the end, for the foreseeable future, of my own hopes, and I thought all the while about Hushang Golshiri in the intensive care unit. Everything melted down into a despair in which the possible end of my marriage, my own little familial bliss, seemed trivial. But it was sad that we had quarrelled just now, when Golshiri lay dying: he had entreated us so often to be attentive to each other, perhaps because he had perceived the conflict before we did.

In the weeks that followed, I talked often with Farzaneh on the telephone. Golshiri, his head shorn, his bushy goatee shaved off, dwindled to a skeleton within days and must have had a look of death in his face even while the doctors still radiated confidence. When he awoke from his unconsciousness for brief intervals, he used the few words that were still within his power to console his family with hints of a few jokes before falling asleep again, and on 5 June 2000 he awoke no more in this world.

The day before the funeral, I decided to fly to Tehran. This time it was really risky to enter the country. The conservative press had been printing inflammatory articles, and my cousin in Isfahan had been informed that I was the subject of investigations. No one but my wife and my editors knew I was going. My parents would have dragged me out of the aircraft with their own hands if they had known I was going to Tehran and not to Hamburg. Least of all did I tell anyone in Tehran I was coming. In any case, because I could stay only a short time, I had decided to get a hotel room. In contrast to my previous trips to Iran, I was really afraid I might be arrested at the airport in Tehran, but, in contrast to my previous trips, Katajun didn't try to dissuade me from going. She was worried but, because she had immediately understood that I had to go, and why, she showed me only her love and not her fear. That brought us very close together. Unlike her, however, I was nervous and agitated, which I rarely am ordinarily (except when 1st FC Cologne are playing, of course). On Wednesday I booked the flight and cancelled it again several times before finally telling Mr Kochems of the Aventuras travel agency at 1:45 p.m. that I would fly. I wasn't sure whether I was behaving like a little child, whether it was extravagant and overly sentimental to go all the way to Tehran for a funeral, especially under the circumstances. But at 3 o'clock, sitting in the train to Frankfurt, I grew calm. I was still calm in Tehran when they took away my passport and I waited to be interrogated, calmer than I would have thought possible. It was a calm that didn't come from me; it came from him. I knew I was doing something I had to do. I knew it was the right thing. I explained to the officer that I had come to Iran to bury my friend and teacher Hushang Golshiri. The officer questioned me about everything imaginable and diligently wrote down my answers. Then I had to sign what he had written. To my amazement, after expressing his condolences, he produced my passport, put it in my hand and dismissed me.

I reached my hotel about five in the morning. Three and a half hours later I got a taxi. Thousands of people had gathered in front of the Iranmehr hospital. I pushed my way into the hospital and said my name at a door where family members went in and out. For a few seconds I stood where Farzaneh could see me so that she would know I had come. She was in no condition to say anything, or even to make a sign. Her face was swollen with tears like the breast of a nursing mother. I exchanged a few words with the children, went back out the door and disappeared into the crowd of mourners.

After the funeral I went back to the hotel. I had booked my return flight not for that night, but the next, to have time to meet at least a few of my friends from the banned newspapers. But now I just wanted to go home. This trip belonged to my farewell to Golshiri. I couldn't get the Lufthansa office on the telephone, so I went there to change my flight. I spent the evening at the Golshiris' home, where his closest friends, students and relatives had gathered. Golshiri and I had initiated a project of inviting young Iranian authors to Germany and publishing an anthology of new Iranian literature. He had spoken so enthusiastically at his readings in Germany about the work of younger writers that we had obtained the support of the Goethe Institute and the House of World Cultures. I talked with Farzaneh about what I would have to do to carry on the project in Golshiri's spirit. Talking about continuing his work and his cause on the day of the funeral helped her a little bit, it seemed to me. I made some notes, and she introduced me to his closest students. I told her the event series and the anthology would have Hushang Golshiri's name in their titles.

When I boarded my plane, I was greeted by the same stewardess who had seen me off the night before. That was a short trip, she said, smiling. I just wanted to tell someone *auf Wiedersehen*, I answered.

— 16 —

SING THE QURAN SINGINGLY

*Neuwirth and Literalist Piety**

Some time ago, a group of Salafi Muslims announced they would give every German a readily understandable edition of the Quran. To invite their contemporaries to read the Quran, the Salafis wanted to stand in pedestrian zones and to go around ringing doorbells. At the same time, they planned a poster campaign with the slogan 'Read!' In the readily understandable translation that they proposed to distribute in the pedestrian zones, 'Read!' is the beginning of the 96th surah, and, in the Salafi reading, it is the very first word God addressed to the Prophet: *iqraʾ bi-smi rabbika llāḏi khalaq / khalaqa l-insāna min ᶜalaq* – 'Read! In the name of thy Lord who created / Created Man from a clot of blood.'

The announcement caused a considerable public stir – indeed, a commotion – in Germany. The Salafi Muslims were the leading story in the news broadcasts and on the front page of the national newspapers, and were discussed in the talk shows of the public television networks. The German interior minister expressed his concern, and the security agencies announced they would keep them under observation. The Salafis denied all allegations of extremist attitudes and pointed out that the Bible too is distributed free in readily understandable translations. Their campaign, they said, was not intended as proselytism – the concept doesn't exist in Islam, they said – but as *daᶜwa*, merely an invitation. And what's wrong with people reading the Quran, just as they read the Bible?

Indeed, what's wrong with it?

Like so many discussions that escalate into minor hysterias through the multiple amplifications by which public opinion is shaped today,

* Speech to the German Academy of Language and Literature in honour of Angelika Neuwirth, recipient of the academy's Sigmund Freud Prize for Scholarly Prose, 2013.

the campaign to give away the Quran faded away as rapidly as it had appeared. The Salafis didn't have enough money to print eighty million or fifty million or even just one million copies of their Quran, and there were not enough volunteers to invite people all over the country to read it. In the end it transpired that the Quran had been distributed only in those pedestrian zones which also contained television cameras. And yet the question hung in the air, in the public air: Who could object to people reading the Quran the same way they read the Bible?

There were the answers of the newspapers and talk shows, the interior minister and the security agencies. More interesting, more coherent, even more politically relevant answers might have come from philology – at least, from such a philology as that of Angelika Neuwirth. If one were to try to reduce her scholarship to a common denominator, to a single statement, a fundamental theme, it would be this: the Quran itself objects to being read like a Bible. Its objections begin with the dating of the 96th surah, which, if read carefully, can hardly be the earliest, and continue with the simple Arabic wording, which the Salafis evidently didn't understand: the imperative *iqraʾ* in the Arabic of the Quran doesn't mean 'Read!'; it means 'Recite!', 'Declaim!' or 'Repeat after me!' The Quran itself explicitly denies that the Prophet was shown a written text or anything comparable with the tablets given to Moses. The mode of revelation is mentioned again and again as words spoken aloud, chanted or even sung: *rattili l-Qurʾāna tartīla*, as another Quran passage puts it. The poet Friedrich Rückert translated the passage more beautifully, and more accurately, than all the Salafis, as '*Singe den Koran sangeweise*' – sing the Quran singingly.

All sacred texts were originally meant to be recited, including of course the Bible, which was also recited in Mecca and Medina in Muhammad's day, not read silently. And yet the Quran, with its linguistic structure, is a completely different text: it is not a Bible. As logical, even as trivial as this statement sounds, its implications have been flagrantly ignored – not only by the general public but also in Oriental studies, which grew out of Christian theology and in particular out of Old Testament scholarship. It is thanks not least to the early investigations of Angelika Neuwirth that this insight has come to prevail since the 1980s, at least among Western scholars of Islam: the Quran is neither a sermon about God nor spiritual poetry, nor is it prophetic oratory in the sense of the ancient Hebrew genre. And the Prophet did not compose his proclamation as a book that people normally read and study alone, silently. The Quran, by its own self-definition, is the liturgical recitation of God's direct speech.

That is why the Quran, unlike the Bible, has necessarily remained a text for recitation, even after the invention of the printing press. The written page is secondary: in principle, it is nothing more than a prompt. Similarly, a translation of it can be an aid but never a substitute for the word itself. In a Quran recitation, it is God who speaks; we cannot read His word, strictly speaking; we can only hear it. According to the Islamic tradition, Muhammad did not receive the text in writing; he heard his revelation told to him orally and subsequently recited it to his fellows. 'Embellish the Quran with your voices,' he exhorted them, 'for a beautiful voice magnifies the beauty of the Quran.' And the Quran attests to its own aesthetic power, as in verse 39:23:

> God has sent down the fairest discourse as
> a book, consimilar in its oft-repeated,
> whereat shiver the skins of those who fear
> their Lord; then their skins and their hearts
> soften to the remembrance of God.[1]

The passage precisely defines the effect, or at least the postulated effect, of a Quran recitation: it first causes gooseflesh (this is exactly the process indicated by the verb *taqsha^c irru*, here rendered as 'shiver'), then soothes the hearer in body and soul, making him ready to celebrate God. The passage makes plain that religious insight is received aesthetically by hearing an utterance that is called fair, and that it makes the listener shiver, gives him gooseflesh: it is an experience of beauty.

It has often been pointed out that, in the phenomenology of religion, there is a correspondence not between Jesus and Muhammad but between Jesus and the Quran. Each of them is the theological centre of the religion by virtue of being the Word of God: one is the Word of God made flesh; the other is the Word of God made oratory. That is to say, in highly oversimplified terms, the Quran is to Islam what Jesus is to Christianity: God's earthly embodiment; it is not the 'incarnation' but the 'inverbation' of God. Christ is the manifestation of God in this world, accessible to mortals, and their connection to Him; no man cometh unto the Father but by him. The analogous role in Islam is that of the book, not the Prophet. As for the gospels, they are comparable more with the hadith and the sunnah, which recount the words and deeds of the Prophet Muhammad. The ritual prayer that Muslims are supposed to perform five times daily consists mainly of repeating surahs of the Quran, and Angelika Neuwirth points out that such Quran recitation has a quasi-sacramental character: although Islam does not have the concept of sacrament, speaking God's word with one's own mouth, receiving it through one's ears, contemplating it in one's heart, is by nature a sacramental act; the believer does not merely commemorate the divinity but assimilates it physically, like the body of Christ in the Last Supper (this, incidentally, is why Quran singers must carefully rinse their mouth and clean their teeth before beginning the recitation); God appears, or, more precisely, God resounds in the moment mortals speak His words. Listening to the Quran has a value in itself; it is not, or not only, a means to mentally comprehending its thematic content. The first thing is the Quran's sensory – and that means primarily auditory – reception and its audible recitation. Ibn Hanbal, the founder of one of the four Sunni schools of law, asked God in a dream whether one should listen to the Quran 'with comprehension' or 'without comprehension'. God answered the theologian, 'With or without comprehension.'[2]

The quasi-sacramental nature of Quran recitation is also at the root of the great importance attached to memorizing the Quran in traditional Muslim societies. The principle of beginning every Muslim school curriculum with learning Quran verses by heart has remained unbroken for centuries. Still more than hearing them recited, meditatively repeating the revealed verses (*ḏikr*) and, ideally, learning them by heart in their entirety (*ḥifẓ*) represents the absorption of God's word and hence, to continue the analogy with the sacrament, the assimilation of God. If lessons in Quran schools from Kuala Lumpur to Duisburg consist primarily of memorizing the Quran, it is not for lack of modern teaching methods but the logical consequence of the Muslim conception of the scripture. Just as baptism is a step on the path of Christian life, and Christian religious instruction is centred on preparation for the sacraments of communion and confirmation, a true Muslim education necessarily involves learning a number of surahs by heart. The obligation of prayer alone has the consequence that every halfway devout Muslim always carries at least a few short surahs of the Quran within him. The reputation of being a *ḥāfiẓ* – that is, being able to recite the whole Quran by heart – brings prestige and reverence to the believer and his family.

The Quran must be recited: this is not only a theological requirement that follows from the Islamic concept of the revelation, from the Quran's claim to be the direct speech of God. More importantly, the Quran unmistakably exhibits its recitative character in its linguistic structure – for example, by the highly developed onomatopoeia of many surahs. Other characteristic elements include repetition, refrains, and the rhyming cadences at the ends of long verses, which are pointless and even irritating when pronounced in a normal speaking rhythm but contribute substantially to the poetic power of a cantilena-style recitation. Those who study the Quran in translation under a desk lamp will hardly notice its timbres and its rhythms. And more: parallel constructions, clausula verses with various functions, interspersed meditative passages, and refrains may appear superfluous, boring or naïve to the eye of the Western silent reader. But, to the Muslim listener, it is precisely these features of the text that create its aesthetic appeal. The recitative form brings with it frequent changes of grammatical person, sentence fragments, anacolutha – the whole spectrum of living speech. The Quran's narrative often takes the form of dialogue, yet without marking the places where the speaker changes or the direct speech starts and stops. 'The reciter can mark them with little effort, and the listener can understand them with less still', writes the Arabist Stefan Wild of Bonn, 'but the silent reader of today loses the thread and complains of faulty logic and the lack of a "pleasing form".' For Muslims, however, this musical quality of the Quran is the greatest – nay, the definitive – miracle of Islam.

And now Salafi Muslims appear on German television and announce they will distribute the Quran unasked in pedestrian zones and at the doors of people's homes. Anyone who has read one book, even one essay, on the Quran by the non-Muslim scholar Angelika Neuwirth will understand the arrogance of the orthodox in ignoring the text's linguistic structure and reception history – and realize what a sacrilege they are committing in their zeal.

Think of the fact that, even today, the Quran in most Muslim households is kept in the highest place, wrapped in a precious cloth. Even reciting, listening to, or touching the Quran requires, if not ritual purity, then at least, in all Islamic traditions, a reverent, humble and contemplative attitude – when the person concerned is a Muslim, and more so in the case of a person of another faith. For a Muslim experiences, in reciting the Quran or hearing it recited, nothing less than a reiteration of the act of the initial revelation – it is not a human voice that speaks to us; it is God Himself. Muslim military leaders in the olden days avoided carrying manuscripts of the Quran with them into battle so that God's oratory would not fall into unbelievers' hands, and members of other faiths were sometimes prevented from learning the Arabic language with the argument that, if they did, they might recite the Quran. These are odd examples, perhaps even extreme ones, and yet they give an idea of the scruples Muslims have always had in regard to the Quran. Meanwhile, the Salafisx want to distribute the Quran like a leaflet or a free sample – with no qualms that the Quran might then land, like all leaflets and free samples, in the nearest rubbish bin.

And what an edition, what an orthodox but dull German edition of the Quran the Salafis wanted to distribute! Altogether too readily understandable, it distorts the Quran in its very core. Even the beginning of the 96th surah, which they quote on their posters, the alleged exhortation of the Prophet to read – in the Arabic, it is a rhymed couplet: *iqraʾ bi-smi rabbika llāḏi khalaq / khalaqa l-insāna min ʿalaq*. It rhymes, as all verses of the Quran rhyme, without exception. The Quran is in structured, rhythmic and onomatopoetic language. You can't simply read it the way you would read a story or a legal text. If you open it unawares, you are at first confused; the Quran appears incoherent; you are irritated by the many repetitions, the incomplete or mysterious sentences, the allusions, the persistently enigmatic references, the reckless changes of topic, the ambiguity of the grammatical person and the polysemous images.

Reading longer passages of the Quran with comprehension is difficult in pedestrian zones. Even during our lifetimes, Western scholars influenced by Bible studies have contested the authenticity of the Quran by pointing to its chaotic, seemingly almost random structure. The Quran in its present form, they said, is the product of a later time and has many different authors whose texts were collated arbitrarily. Muslims naturally reject that, for a later date of origin and an anonymous, collective authorship would invalidate the foundations of Islam.

I would recommend to all Salafis to read Angelika Neuwirth. She won renown as a scholar with her first major work by demonstrating, through a microscopically close reading of the Meccan surahs, the poetic cohesion, the consistent imagery and the substantial textual integrity of the Quran. The very features that the casual reader, and a fortiori the reader of a readily understandable translation, finds enigmatic, incoherent, tiring – the repetitions, the anacolutha, the sudden changes of grammatical person and the seemingly surreal metaphors – constitute the quality of the Quran's language for the Arabic listener (and are the reason why James Joyce was fascinated by the text). Thus historically critical Quran scholarship, which the Salafis often say is opposed to Islam, generally confirms the traditional conception of the Islamic salvation history. The Quran is substantially the work of a single time and of a single ingenious mind of great linguistic gifts. But who is that mind?

Angelika Neuwirth's answer to this question is much more uncomfortable to Salafi Muslims. For, in her works written after the *Studies on the Composition of the Meccan Surahs*, she turns her attention to the oral nature of the Quran and documents its performative elements. That means the Quran is not only a text that must be recited, that can only be realized in performance, like sheet music. Not only that: the text itself as we know it is in part a transcript, written and edited after a public recitation, a performance. That is, the Quran consists not only of the statements of a speaker but also includes the interjections of a believing or unbelieving audience – and the spontaneous reactions to those interjections – which repeatedly lead to abrupt changes of topic.

But that means that the Prophet's first listeners, the Muslim community, make a substantial contribution to the text of the Quran, and their transition from an oral to a written culture takes place in the Quran itself. If our reading of the Quran is as exact as the example Angelika Neuwirth sets, it is clear that it is not a dictation but a conversation: pro and con, question and answer, riddle and solution, admonition and awe, promise and hope, the voice of an individual and the refrain of a chorus. That God speaks in the Quran – that is a matter of faith. But to realize that, in the Quran, man answers – all you need is philology.

The conversation that is the Quran takes place not only with the Prophet's immediate listeners on the Arabian peninsula in the seventh century. In her more recent works, building up to the many volumes of her Quran commentary, Angelika Neuwirth exposes how the Islamic revelation is embedded in the culture of late antiquity – in the same era and the same cultural sphere that also shaped Jewish and Christian theology.

I do not mean she delivers one of the customary lists of all the places Arab thought has influenced Western scholarship. That a major current of the European Enlightenment has its source in Arab culture, particularly in Judaeo–Islamic philosophy, has been known in Germany at least since the Jewish studies movement of the nineteenth century, even if the news hasn't reached the current minister of the interior. But Angelika Neuwirth is interested in something else: she makes it clear that the Quran itself, the founding document of Islam, is a European text – or, inversely, Europe belongs, by its very creation, in part to Islam. No security agency can defuse such explosive research. It will shake the foundations of our intellectual landscape for a very long time.

Angelika Neuwirth's latest work, the first volume of her Quran commentary, hints at how enriching this tremor could be. By tracing the diverse biblical, Platonic, patristic and Talmudic relations, as well as the ancient Arabic and intra-quranic references, especially by taking seriously the Quran's linguistic structure as a poetic text, as a score for singing recitation, she reveals how very deeply the Quran has breathed in the whole culture of the Eastern Mediterranean – and how very much it permeates our culture in turn as it breathes out. If any text in the history of world religions is the conversation that our academy so often invokes – the conversation that Hölderlin says we are – it is the Quran. And at the same time it is the music that he says we shall be.

Appendix

ON THE SIXTY-FIFTH ANNIVERSARY OF THE PROMULGATION OF THE GERMAN CONSTITUTION*

Messrs Presidents, Madam Chancellor, honourable members of the Bundestag, your Excellencies, dear guests,

Paradox is not one of the customary stylistic figures of legal texts, which naturally strive for the greatest possible lucidity. A paradox is necessarily enigmatic in nature; it is appropriate where an unambiguous expression would be tantamount to a lie. For that reason it is one of the most frequently used devices of poetry. And yet no less a legal text than the constitution of the Federal Republic of Germany begins with a paradox. For if human dignity were inviolable, as the first sentence states, then the state would not have to uphold it, much less defend it, as the second sentence requires. Dignity would exist independently, untouched by all power. By a simple paradox, hardly noticeable at first glance – dignity is inviolable and yet needs to be defended – the German constitution reverses the premises of previous German constitutions and declares the state to be, not the telos, but the servant of the people, of all human beings, of humanity in the strong sense. Verbally, it is – I hesitate to call it brilliant, because that would be aestheticizing an eminently normative text – it is only perfect.

And we cannot explain the impact, the incredible success of this constitution without acknowledging its literary quality. In its substantial features and statements, in any case, it is a remarkably beautiful text, and was meant to be so. It is well known that Theodor Heuss, the first president of the Federal Republic, thwarted the original version of the first article on the grounds that it was bad German. But *Die Würde des Menschen ist unantastbar* is a superb German sentence, so simple, so complex, immediately obvious – 'human dignity is inviolable' – and

* Speech to the Bundestag, Berlin, 23 May 2014.

yet all the more unfathomable the more we think about the sentence that follows it: *Sie zu schützen ist Aufgabe aller staatlichen Gewalt*; it is the duty of all state power to defend it. The sentences cannot both be true, but in combination they can come true – only in combination; and, indeed, they have come true in Germany to a degree that few or none would have thought possible on 23 May 1949. Comparable perhaps only with the Luther Bible in this respect, the German constitution has created a reality by the power of the word.

'All persons shall have the right to free development of their personality' – how odd it must have seemed to most Germans, worried about sheer survival in the rubble of their cities, how odd they must have found the prospect of developing something as intangible as their own personality – but what a compelling idea it was at the same time. 'All persons shall be equal before the law' – the Jews, the Sinti and the Roma, the homosexuals, the disabled, all those on the margins of society, the dissenters, the strangers: until then they had been unequal before the law, so they had to be made equal. 'Men and women have equal rights' – the weeks and months of resistance to this article in particular is the clearest proof that, in 1949, men and women were not thought to have equal rights; the sentence acquired its truth only in practice. 'Capital punishment is abolished' – this was not the will of the majority of Germans, who in a survey favoured retaining capital punishment by a three-quarters' majority, yet it is widely approved today. 'All Germans shall have the right to move freely throughout the federal territory' – this sentence was almost embarrassing to the members of the Parliamentary Council in view of the refugee crisis and the lack of housing, and sixty-five years later freedom of movement is guaranteed throughout not only reunified Germany but half of Europe. The Federal Republic may 'consent to such limitations upon its sovereign powers as will bring about and secure a lasting peace in Europe' – this article anticipated, in 1949, a united Europe, and more: the United States of Europe. And so on: prohibition of discrimination, freedom of religion, the freedom of art and science, freedom of opinion and assembly – when the constitution was promulgated sixty-five years ago, these were statements of principle rather than descriptions of reality in Germany. And at first it did not look as if the Germans would hear the appeal that lay in these both simple and forceful articles of faith.

Public interest in the constitution was, in retrospect, disgracefully small, and approval among the population was marginal. When asked when Germany had fared best, 45 per cent of the German respondents in a representative survey chose the German Empire, 7 per cent the Weimar Republic, 42 per cent the period of Nazi rule, and only 2 per cent the Federal Republic – 2 per cent! How glad we must be that the politicians who attended the beginning of the Federal Republic were guided in their actions not by surveys but by their convictions. And today?

I have no doubt that the members of the Parliamentary Council, should they be watching our commemoration from some celestial seats of honour, would be content and very much surprised at the roots that freedom has put down in the past sixty-five years in Germany. And they would probably notice and nod approvingly at this significant detail: that the promulgation of the constitution is being commemorated today by a child of immigrants, and one who belongs to a different religion from that of the majority. There are not many states in the world where that would be possible. Even in Germany a short time ago, let us say on the fiftieth anniversary of the constitution, it would have been difficult to imagine the commemorative speech in the Bundestag being delivered by a German who is not only German. In the other state whose passport I hold, it is still unthinkable, in spite of many protests and many victims in the name of freedom. But I would also like to say from this podium, Messrs Presidents, Madam Chancellor, Honourable Members, dear guests, and not least his Excellency the Ambassador of the Islamic Republic, who is also watching today, although not from a celestial seat: it will not be sixty-five years, or even fifteen years, before a Christian, a Jew, a Zoroastrian or a Baha'i as a matter of course delivers the commemorative speech before a freely elected parliament in Iran.

This is a good Germany, the best one we have known, the president of the Federal Republic said recently. I cannot dispute it. No matter what period of German history I consider, there is none in which people lived in greater freedom, peace and tolerance than in our time. And yet the president's statement would not flow so smoothly from my lips. Why is that? One might dismiss such unease at expressing pride in our country as typical German self-loathing and, in doing so, overlook the very reason why the Federal Republic has become liveable and even lovable. For when and how did Germany – the Germany that was viewed with suspicion because of its militarism as early as the nineteenth century and appeared to be thoroughly dishonoured after the murder of six million Jews – when and how did it regain its dignity? If I had to name one day, an isolated event, a single gesture in German post-war history which seems to merit the word dignity, it was – and I am sure a majority of the Bundestag, a majority of Germans, and also a majority of those in the celestial seats, will agree – it was Willy Brandt's genuflection in Warsaw.

That is even odder than the paradox that begins the constitution, and probably unique in the history of nations: this state attained dignity by an act of humility. Is not heroism usually associated with fortitude, with virility and hence with physical strength, and most of all with pride? But here a man showed greatness by stifling his pride and shouldering guilt – and, what is more, guilt for which he personally, as an opponent of Hitler and an exile, was least responsible – here a man proved his honour by his public shame; here a man so conceived his patriotism that he knelt before Germany's victims.

I am not given to sentiment in front of the screen, and yet I felt as so many did when, on his hundredth birthday, the films were replayed of a German chancellor who steps back from the monument at the site of the Warsaw Ghetto, hesitates a moment, and then, to everyone's surprise, drops to his knees – I cannot watch that even today without tears coming to my eyes. And the strange thing is: along with everything else, along with the emotion, the remembrance of the crimes, the unending astonishment, they are also tears of pride, of the very muted and yet definite pride in such a Federal Republic of Germany. That is the Germany I love: not the boastful, strong-man, proud-to-be-German or Europe-finally-speaks-German Germany, but a nation exasperated with its history, dissatisfied and struggling with itself to the point of self-incrimination, yet which has grown wiser through its error, has outgrown pageantry, humbly calls its constitution a 'basic law', prefers to show strangers a bit too much friendliness, too much trust, than ever to lapse into hostility and insolence again.

It is often said, and I have heard speakers say it at this podium, that the Germans should finally return to a normal, relaxed attitude towards their nation – that it's now long enough since Nazism was overcome. And I always wonder what those speakers mean: there never was a normal, relaxed attitude, even before Nazism. There was an excessive, aggressive nationalism and, as a counter-current, a German self-criticism, a plea for Europe, an appeal to world citizenship (and also to world literature for that matter) which was unique in its determination, at least in the nineteenth century. 'A good German cannot be a nationalist', Willy Brandt said confidently in his Nobel Lecture: 'A good German knows that he cannot refuse a European calling. Through Europe, Germany returns to itself and to the constructive forces of its history.'

Since the late eighteenth century, since Lessing at least, who despised patriotism and was the first German to use the word 'cosmopolitan', German culture has often stood in diametrical opposition to the nation. Goethe and Schiller, Kant and Schopenhauer, Hölderlin and Büchner, Heine and Nietzsche, Hesse and the Mann brothers – all of them struggled with Germany, saw themselves as citizens of the world and believed in European unity long before politicians discovered the project.

It is this cosmopolitan line of German thinking that Willy Brandt continued – not only in his struggle against German nationalism and for a united Europe but also in his early plea for *Weltinnenpolitik*, a 'global domestic policy', in his commitment to international development, and during his chairmanship of the Socialist International. And it puts the Germany of today in what is perhaps not a very advantageous light when, in television debates before the parliamentary elections, practically nothing is said about foreign policy, when a constitutional body trivializes the upcoming European elections, when the developmental aid of such a strong economy is below the average of the OECD states – or when Germany admits just ten thousand of the nine million Syrians who have lost their homes in the civil war.

After all, the involvement in the world that Willy Brandt exemplifies has always implied, conversely, more openness to the world. We cannot commemorate the constitution without remembering all the mutilations that have been inflicted upon it here and there. In comparison with the constitutions of other countries, its wording has been changed unusually often, and few of those modifications have done the text good. What the Parliamentary Council expressly put in general and overarching terms, the Bundestag has burdened from time to time with detailed regulations. The most severe deformation is that of Article 16, linguistically and otherwise. The very constitution in which Germany seemed to have codified its openness for all time now locks out those who are most urgently in need of our openness: the victims of political persecution. A wonderfully concise sentence – *Politisch Verfolgte genießen Asyl*, 'Persons persecuted on political grounds shall have the right of asylum' – was amended in 1993 into a monstrous provision of 275 words, stacked wildly one on top of another and closely convoluted just to hide one thing: the fact that asylum has practically ceased to be a fundamental right in Germany. Is it really necessary to recall that Willy Brandt, whose name brought approving nods from many of you throughout this chamber, was a refugee, an asylum-seeker?

Today, too, there are people, many people, who depend for their safety on the openness of other, democratic countries – and Edward Snowden, whom we have much to thank for in regard to the defence of our fundamental rights, is one of them. Others are drowning every day in the Mediterranean, several thousand every year, and very probably during this celebration. Germany does not have to receive all those that labour and are heavy laden. But it does have sufficient resources to defend victims of political persecution instead of shrugging off the responsibility onto so-called third countries. And out of properly understood self-interest it should give other people a fair chance to apply for immigration legally, so that they don't need to resort to the right of asylum. For there is still no sign, twenty years later, of the unified European refugee law that was talked of in 1993 in justifying the amendment, and the textual abuse alone that was inflicted on the constitution is painful enough. The right of asylum was robbed of its substance; Article 16 was robbed of its dignity. May the constitution be cleansed of this hideous, heartless stain by its seventieth anniversary at the latest.

This is a good Germany, the best one we have known. Instead of closing itself off, it can be proud that it has become so attractive. My parents did not flee Iran for political reasons. But, after the coup against the democratic Mossadegh government in 1953, they were glad, like many Iranians of their generation, to be able to study in a freer, more just country. After their studies they found work, they watched their children, grandchildren and even great-grandchildren grow up; they have grown old in Germany. And this whole big family, now grown to twenty-six people, counting only direct descendants and their spouses, have found happiness in this country. And not only we: many millions of people have immigrated to the Federal Republic of Germany since the Second World War – counting the expellees and the ethnic German immigrants, more people than half the current population. Even compared with other countries, that is a tremendous demographic change which Germany has had to master within a single generation. And I think, on the whole, Germany has mastered it well. There are cultural, religious and, most of all, social conflicts, especially in the metropolitan areas; there are resentments among Germans and there are resentments among those who are not only German; unfortunately, there is also violence and even terror and murder. But, on the whole, life in Germany is decidedly peaceful, still relatively just, and much more tolerant than it was as late as the 1990s. Without actually noticing it, the Federal Republic has accomplished a magnificent work of integration – and I have not yet mentioned reunification!

Perhaps there could have been a little more recognition here and there, a visible, public gesture especially towards my parents' generation, the generation of the 'guest workers', for all they have done for Germany. But, conversely, perhaps the immigrants too have not always made it sufficiently plain how much they appreciate the freedom in which they share in Germany, the social balance, the professional opportunities, the free schools and universities, an outstanding health-care system by the way, the rule of law, a sometimes painful and yet precious freedom of opinion, the freedom of worship. And so, in closing, I would like to speak in the name of – no, not in the name of all immigrants: not in the name of Djamaa Isu, who hanged himself with a belt almost exactly one year ago today in the Eisenhüttenstadt refugee camp, for fear of being deported to a so-called third country without consideration of his request for asylum; not in the name of Mehmet Kubaşık and the other victims of the National Socialist Underground, who for years were libelled as criminals by the investigating authorities and the biggest newspapers in the country; not in the name of even one of the Jewish immigrants or returnees, who can never consider the murder of almost their entire people redressed – but in the name of many, of millions of people, in the name of the 'guest workers' who have long since ceased to be guests; in the name of their children and grandchildren, who naturally grow up with two cultures and, at long last, with two passports as well; in the name of my literary colleagues, for whom the German language too is a gift; in the name of the football players who will give everything they've got for Germany this summer in Brazil, even if they don't sing the national anthem; in the name of the less successful, the needy and even the delinquent, who belong just as much to Germany as the Özils and the Podolskis; especially in the name of the Muslims, who enjoy rights in Germany that, to our shame, are denied Christians in many Islamic countries today; thus in the name of my devout parents and an immigrant family of twenty-six – I would like to say, with at least a symbolic bow: thank you, Germany.

ON RECEIVING THE PEACE PRIZE OF THE GERMAN PUBLISHERS' ASSOCIATION*

On the day I received the news of the Peace Prize of the German Publishers' Association, the same day, Jacques Mourad was abducted in Syria. Two armed men entered the monastery of Mar Elian on the outskirts of the small town of Qaryatain and demanded to see Father Jacques. They found him no doubt in his bare little office, which also served as his living room and bedroom, seized him and took him with them. On 21 May 2015, Jacques Mourad became a hostage of the so-called Islamic State.

I first met Father Jacques in the autumn of 2012, when I was travelling through an already war-torn Syria to report on the events there. He was responsible for the Catholic parish of Qaryatain and also belonged to the community of Mar Musa, which was founded in the early 1980s in a derelict early Christian monastery. It is a special, probably a unique Christian community, for it is devoted to the encounter with Islam and love for Muslims. While conscientiously following the commandments and rituals of their own Catholic church, the nuns and monks engage equally earnestly with Islam and take part in Muslim traditions, including the observance of Ramadan. It sounds mad, even ludicrous: Christians who, as they themselves put it, have fallen in love with Islam. And yet this Christian–Muslim love was a reality in Syria only recently, and still is in the hearts of many Syrians. With the work of their hands, the kindness of their hearts and the prayers of their souls, the nuns and monks of Mar Musa created a place that seemed to me a utopia, a place which – although they did not ignore the divisions of the present – anticipated nothing less than an eschatological reconciliation, took for granted that reconciliation will come. A seventh-century

* Given on 18 October 2015 in St Paul's Church, Frankfurt am Main.

stone monastery, amid the overpowering solitude of the Syrian desert mountains, which was visited by Christians from all over the world but where, day after day, still greater numbers of Arab Muslims – dozens, even hundreds – knocked at the door to meet their Christian brethren, to talk, to sing and to keep silence with them, and also to pray according to their own Islamic ritual in a corner of the church that was kept free of images.

When I visited Father Jacques in 2012, the founder of the community, the Italian Jesuit Paolo Dall'Oglio, had just been expelled from the country. Father Paolo had been too outspoken in his criticism of the Assad government, which responded to the Syrian people's demands for freedom and democracy – demands they had raised peacefully for nine months – with arrests and torture, with truncheons and assault rifles, and finally with horrific massacres and even poison gas, until the country descended into civil war. But Father Paolo had also opposed the leadership of the recognized Syrian churches, which had remained silent about the government's violence. He had tried in vain to raise support in Europe for the Syrian democratic movement and had called in vain on the United Nations to impose a no-fly zone or at least to send observers. He had warned in vain of a sectarian war if the jihadists were the only ones to receive support from abroad while the secular and moderate groups were neglected. He had tried in vain to break through the wall of our apathy. In the summer of 2013, the founder of the community of Mar Musa secretly returned to Syria to try to help some Muslim friends who were in the hands of Islamic State and was himself abducted by Islamic State. Since 28 July 2013, Father Paolo Dall'Oglio has been missing without trace.

Father Jacques, who now bore sole responsibility for the monastery of Mar Elian, is a very different kind of person: not a gifted orator, not charismatic, not a temperamental Italian but, like so many Syrians I met, a proud, deliberate and extremely polite man, quite tall, with a broad face, his short hair still black. I did not get to know him well, of course; I attended Mass, which consisted of enchantingly beautiful singing as in all Eastern churches, and observed how warmly he chatted with the faithful and with local dignitaries at the lunch that followed. When he had said good-bye to all the guests, he led me to his tiny room for half an hour, placing a chair for me next to the narrow bed upon which he sat for the interview.

It was not only his words that amazed me – how fearlessly he criticized the government and how openly he also spoke of the hardening taking place in his own Christian community. What made an even more profound impression on me was his demeanour: I experienced him as a quiet, very conscientious, introverted and ascetic servant of God who, now that God had given him the task of ministering to the beleaguered Christians in Qaryatain and leading the monastic community, was devoting all his strength to carrying out this public duty as well. He spoke quietly and slowly – usually with his eyes closed – as if he were consciously slowing down his pulse and using the interview as a brief rest between two more strenuous commitments. At the same time he chose his words very carefully and articulated his thoughts in polished sentences, and what he said was so clear, and so politically incisive, that I asked him repeatedly whether it might not be too dangerous to quote him directly. Then he opened his warm, dark eyes and nodded wearily – yes, I could print everything, otherwise he would not have said it; the world had to learn what was happening in Syria.

This weariness – this was also a strong impression, perhaps my strongest, of Father Jacques – it was the weariness of one who not only acknowledged but, indeed, affirmed that he might not find rest before the next life; it was also the weariness of a doctor or a fire-fighter who husbands his strength in the face of mounting adversity. And Father Jacques was indeed a doctor and fire-fighter too in the midst of the war, not only for the souls of those living in fear but also for the bodies of the needy, to whom he gave food, shelter, clothes, protection and, above all, loving attention in his church, regardless of their religion. To the end, the community of Mar Musa sheltered and cared for many hundreds if not thousands of refugees, the vast majority of them Muslims, at the monastery. And not only that: Father Jacques managed to keep peace, even between the different faiths, at least in Qaryatain. It is chiefly thanks to him, the quiet, serious Father Jacques, that the various groups and militias, some of them aligned with the government and some opposed to it, agreed to keep all heavy weapons out of the town. And he, the priest critical of his Church, was able to persuade almost all the Christians in his parish to stay. 'We Christians are a part of this country, whether the fundamentalists here and in Europe like it or not', Father Jacques told me. 'Arab culture is our culture!'

The demands of some Western politicians to admit Arab Christians in particular made a bitter impression on him. The same West that cared not one iota about the millions of Syrians of all confessions who had demonstrated peacefully for democracy and human rights, the same West that had devastated Iraq and supplied Assad with his poison gas, the same West that was allied with Saudi Arabia, the main sponsor of jihadism – this same West was now concerned about the Arab Christians? He could only laugh at the idea, Father Jacques said, with a perfectly straight face. And, with his eyes closed, he continued,

'With their irresponsible statements, these politicians promote the very confessionalism that threatens us Christians.'

The responsibility grew constantly, and Father Jacques bore it as patiently as ever. The community's non-Syrian members had to leave the country and took refuge in northern Iraq. Only the seven Syrian monks and nuns stayed behind, dividing themselves between the monasteries of Mar Musa and Mar Elian. The front was constantly shifting, and Qaryatain was ruled sometimes by the state and sometimes by opposition militias. The monks and nuns had to come to terms with both sides and, like all the inhabitants, to survive the air raids whenever the little town was in opposition hands. But then Islamic State advanced ever deeper into the Syrian heartland. 'The threat from IS, this sect of terrorists who present such a ghastly picture of Islam, has arrived in our region', Father Jacques wrote to a French friend a few days before his abduction. The message to her continues, 'It is difficult to decide what we should do. Should we leave our homes? We are loath to do that. It is dreadful to admit that we have been abandoned – especially by the Christian world, which has decided to keep its distance so as not to endanger itself. We mean nothing to them.'

Two phrases are striking in these few lines of a simple e-mail, no doubt written in haste – phrases which are both characteristic of Father Jacques and a standard for all intellectual integrity. In the first phrase, Father Jacques writes, 'The threat from IS, this sect of terrorists who present such a ghastly picture of Islam'; the second phrase, referring to the Christian world: 'We mean nothing to them.' Father Jacques defended the community he does not belong to and criticized his own. A few days before his abduction, when the group that pretends to represent Islam and claims to apply the law of the Quran was already an immediate physical danger to him and his parish, Father Jacques still insisted that these terrorists were distorting the true face of Islam. I would take issue with any Muslim whose only response to the phenomenon of the Islamic State was the worn-out phrase that their violence has nothing to do with Islam. But a Christian, a Christian priest who could expect to be expelled, humiliated, abducted or killed by followers of another faith, yet still insisted on defending that faith – such a man of God displays a magnanimity that I have encountered nowhere else, except in the lives of the saints.

A person like myself cannot and must not defend Islam in that way. The love of one's own – one's own culture, one's own country and also one's own person – manifests itself in self-criticism. The love of the other – of another person, another culture and even another religion – can be far more effusive; it can be unreserved. It is true that the prerequisite for love of the other is love of oneself. But one can only fall in love, as Father Paolo and Father Jacques did with Islam, with the other. Self-love must be a struggling, doubting, constantly questioning love if it is to avoid falling prey to narcissism, self-praise, self-satisfaction. How true that is of Islam today! Any Muslim who does not struggle with it, does not doubt it and does not critically question it does not love Islam.

I am thinking not only of the horrific news and the still more horrific pictures from Syria and Iraq, where the Quran is held aloft at every act of barbarism and 'Allahu akbar' is cried out at every beheading. In so many other countries too – indeed, in most countries in the Muslim world – state authorities, state-associated institutions, theological schools and rebel groups all appeal to Islam as they oppress their own people, discriminate against women, and persecute, expel or massacre those with different ideas, religious beliefs or ways of life. Islam is invoked to justify stoning women in Afghanistan, murdering whole classes of schoolchildren in Pakistan, enslaving hundreds of girls in Nigeria, beheading Christians in Libya, shooting bloggers in Bangladesh, detonating bombs on marketplaces in Somalia, murdering Sufis and musicians in Mali, crucifying dissidents in Saudi Arabia, banning the most important works of contemporary literature in Iran, oppressing Shiites in Bahrain, and inciting violence between Sunnis and Shiites in Yemen.

The vast majority of Muslims certainly reject terror, violence and oppression. This is something I have experienced directly on my travels; it is not an empty slogan. On the contrary: those who cannot take freedom for granted know its value best. All of the mass uprisings of recent years in the Islamic world have been uprisings for democracy and human rights: not only the attempted – although mostly failed – revolutions in almost all the Arab countries but also the protest movements in Turkey, Iran and Pakistan and, not least, the revolt at the ballot box in the last Indonesian presidential election. The streams of refugees likewise indicate where many Muslims hope to find better lives than in their home countries: certainly not in religious dictatorships. And the reports that reach us directly from Mosul and Raqqa attest not to enthusiasm, but to the panic and despair of the population. Every relevant theological authority in the Islamic world has rejected the claim of IS to speak for Islam and has explained in detail how its practices and ideology go against the Quran and the basic teachings of Islamic theology. And let us not forget that those who are fighting on the front lines against Islamic State are themselves Muslims – Kurds, Shiites and also Sunni tribes and the members of the Iraqi army.

All of this needs to be said to expose the illusion that is being propounded in unison by the Islamists and the critics of Islam alike, namely that Islam is waging a war against the West. More accurately, Islam is waging a war against itself – that is to say, the Islamic world is being shaken by an inner conflict whose effects on the political and ethnic map may well come close to matching the dislocations that resulted from the First World War. The multi-ethnic, multi-religious and multicultural Orient, which I studied through its superb literary achievements of the Middle Ages, and which I came to love as an endangered, never whole yet still vital reality during long stays in Cairo and Beirut, as a child during summer holidays in Isfahan and as a reporter at the monastery of Mar Musa – this Orient will have ceased to exist, like the world of yesteryear which Stefan Zweig recalled with nostalgia and sorrow in the 1920s.

What happened? Islamic State was not founded yesterday, nor did it begin with the civil wars in Iraq and Syria. Though its methods meet with abhorrence, its ideology is none other than Wahhabism, which exerts its influence in the remotest corners of the Islamic world today and, in the form of Salafism, has become attractive especially to young people in Europe. Since we know that the schoolbooks and curricula of Islamic State are 95 per cent identical with the schoolbooks and curricula in Saudi Arabia, we also know it is not just in Iraq and Syria that the world is strictly divided into what is forbidden and what is permitted – and humanity divided into believers and unbelievers. A school of thought that declares all people of other religions heretics, and berates, terrorizes, vilifies and insults them, has been promulgated for decades, sponsored with billions from oil production, in mosques, in books and on television. If you denigrate other people systematically, day after day, it is only logical – how well we know this from our own history, from German history – that you will end up declaring their lives worthless. That such a religious fascism has become conceivable at all, that IS is able to recruit so many fighters, and still more sympathizers, that it has been able to overrun entire countries and capture major cities with hardly a fight – this is not the beginning but the endpoint to date of a long decline, and I am referring not least to the decline of religious thought.

I took up Middle Eastern studies in 1988; my topics were the Quran and poetry. I think everyone who studies this subject in its classical form reaches a point where they can no longer reconcile the past with the present. And they become hopelessly, hopelessly sentimental. Naturally the past was not simply peaceful and colourfully diverse. As a philologist, however, I was dealing mostly with the writings of the mystics, philosophers, rhetoricians and theologians. And I, or rather we students, can only marvel, then and now, at the originality, the intellectual scope, the aesthetic power and the great humanity we find in the spirituality of Ibn Arabi, the poetry of Rumi, the historiography of Ibn Khaldun, the poetic theology of Abd al-Qahir al-Jurjani, the philosophy of Averroes, the travel reports of Ibn Battuta, and the tales of the *Thousand and One Nights*, which are worldly – yes, worldly and erotic, and feminist too, incidentally, and at the same time infused with the spirit and the verses of the Quran on every page. These were not newspapers, of course; the social reality of that civilization was, like any other, greyer and more violent. And yet these documents of their age tell us something about what was once conceivable, even taken for granted, within Islam. None of this can be found in the religious culture of modern Islam, nothing whatsoever that is even remotely comparable, that is as fascinating, as profound as the writings I came across as a student. To say nothing of Islamic architecture, Islamic art or Islamic musicology: they no longer exist.

Let me illustrate the loss of creativity and freedom in the context of my own field: there was a time when it was conceivable, and even taken for granted, that the Quran is a poetic text which can only be grasped using the tools and methods of literary studies, exactly the same as a poem. It was conceivable and taken for granted that a theologian was at the same time a literary scholar and an expert on poetry, and in many cases a poet himself. In our time, my own teacher Nasr Hamid Abu Zayd in Cairo was charged with heresy, driven from his university and even pronounced divorced from his wife because he conceived quranic studies as a form of literary scholarship. In other words, an approach to the Quran which was once taken for granted, and for which Nasr Abu Zayd was able to cite the most important scholars of classical Islamic theology, is no longer even acknowledged as thinkable. Anyone taking such an approach to the Quran, even though it is the traditional one, can be persecuted, punished and declared a heretic. And yet the Quran is a text that not only rhymes but speaks in disturbing, ambiguous and enigmatic images; nor is it a book at all so much as a recitation, the score of a chant that moves its Arab listeners with its rhythm, onomatopoeia and melody. Islamic theology not only examined the aesthetic peculiarities of the Quran; it declared the beauty of its language to be the authenticating miracle of Islam. All over the Islamic world today, however, we can observe what happens when one ignores the linguistic structure of a text, when one no longer adequately understands or even acknowledges it: the Quran is degraded to a reference manual in which people look up arbitrary keywords using a search engine. The powerful eloquence of the Quran becomes political dynamite.

We read so often that Islam must be cleansed by the fire of Enlightenment or that modernity must win out over tradition. But that is perhaps too simplistic when we consider that Islam's past was so much more enlightened, and its traditional writings at times more modern, than the current theological discourse. Goethe and Proust, Lessing and Joyce were not out of their minds, after all, to have been fascinated by Islamic culture. They saw something in the books and monuments that we no longer perceive so easily, brutally confronted as we often are by contemporary Islam. Perhaps the problem of Islam is less its tradition than its nearly total break with that tradition, the loss of its cultural memory, its civilizational amnesia.

All the peoples of the Orient experienced a brutal modernization imposed from above in the form of colonialism and secular dictatorships. The headscarf – to name one example – the headscarf was not abandoned gradually by Iranian women: in 1936, the shah sent his soldiers out into the streets to tear it from their heads by force. Unlike Europe, where modernity – in spite of all the setbacks and crimes – was ultimately experienced as a process of emancipation and took place gradually over many decades and centuries, the Middle East experienced it largely as violence. Modernity was associated not with freedom, but with exploitation and despotism. Imagine an Italian president driving his car into St Peter's Basilica, jumping onto the altar with his dirty boots and whipping the pope in the face: then you will have a rough idea of what it meant when, in 1928, Reza Shah marched through the holy shrine of Qom in his riding boots and responded to the imam's request to take off his shoes like any other believer by striking him in the face with his whip. And you will find comparable events and pivotal moments in many other Middle Eastern countries which, instead of slowly leaving the past behind, demolished that past and tried to erase it from memory.

One might have thought that the religious fundamentalists who gained influence throughout the Islamic world after the failure of nationalism would have valued at least their own culture. Yet the opposite was the case: by seeking to return to a supposed point of origin, they not only neglected Islamic tradition but resolutely fought it. We are surprised by Islamic State's acts of iconoclasm only because we have not noticed that there are virtually no ancient relics left in Saudi Arabia. In Mecca, the Wahhabis have destroyed the tombs and mosques of the Prophet's closest kin, including the house in which he was born. The historic mosque of the Prophet in Medina has been replaced with a colossal new building, and on the site where, until a few years ago, the house of Muhammad and his wife Khadija stood there is now a public toilet.

Apart from the Quran, my studies were focused mainly on Islamic mysticism, Sufism. Mysticism sounds like something marginal, esoteric, a kind of underground culture. In the Islamic context, nothing could be further from the truth. Well into the twentieth century, Sufism formed the basis of popular religion almost everywhere in the Islamic world; in Asian Islam, it still does. At the same time, Islamic high culture – especially poetry, the fine arts and architecture – was infused with the spirit of mysticism. As the most common form of religious life, Sufism was the ethical and aesthetic counterweight to the orthodoxy of the legal scholars. By emphasizing God's compassion above all and seeing it behind every letter of the Quran, by constantly seeking beauty in religion, acknowledging truth in other forms of faith too, and explicitly adopting the Christian commandment to love one's enemies, Sufism infused Islamic societies with values, stories and sounds that could not have resulted from literalist reading alone. As the Islam of daily life, Sufism did not invalidate the Islam of law but complemented it and made its day-to-day form softer, more ambivalent, more permeable, more tolerant; and, most of all, through music, dance and poetry, it opened Islam to sensual experience.

Hardly any of this has survived. Wherever the Islamists have gained a foothold, from the nineteenth century in what is now Saudi Arabia to recent events in Mali, they began by putting an end to public Sufi rituals, banning the mystics' writings, destroying the tombs of the saints, and cutting the long hair of the Sufi leaders or killing them outright. But not only the Islamists: the reformers and the enlightened religious philosophers of the nineteenth and early twentieth centuries also found the traditions and customs of popular Islam backward and antiquated. It was not they who took Sufi literature seriously but the Western scholars, Orientalists such as the Peace Prize winner of 1995, Annemarie Schimmel, who published scholarly editions of the manuscripts and so saved them from destruction. And, even today, only a handful of Muslim intellectuals address the treasures found in their own tradition. The destroyed, neglected, rubbish-filled old city quarters all over the Islamic world, with their ruined architectural monuments, symbolize the decline of Islamic thought every bit as vividly as the biggest shopping mall in the world, which has been built in Mecca right beside the Kaaba. You have to picture this – you can see it in photos: the holiest place in Islam, this simple and superb edifice where the Prophet himself prayed, is literally towered over by Gucci and Apple. Perhaps we should have listened less to the Islam of our grand thinkers and more to the Islam of our grandmothers.

To be sure, people have started restoring buildings and mosques in some countries, but only after Western art historians or Westernized Muslims like myself came along and recognized the value of the tradition. And, unfortunately, we came a century too late, when the buildings had already crumbled, the building techniques had been forgotten, and the books had been erased from memory. But we believed there was still time to study the remains thoroughly. Now, as a reader, I almost feel like an archaeologist in a war zone, gathering up relics hastily and often haphazardly so that future generations will at least be able to view them in museums. Certainly Muslim countries are still producing outstanding works, as we can see at biennials and film festivals, and once more at this year's book fair. But this culture has hardly anything to do with Islam. There is no Islamic culture any more – at least, none of quality. What we now have bursting all around us and raining down on our heads is the debris of a massive intellectual implosion.

Is there any hope? Until our last breath there is hope – that is what Father Paolo, the founder of the community of Mar Musa, teaches us. Hope is the central theme of his writings. The day after his disciple and deputy was abducted, the Muslims of Qaryatain flooded into the church, unasked, and prayed for their Father Jacques. That must surely give us hope that love works across the boundaries between religions, ethnicities and cultures. The news and the pictures of Islamic State have produced a powerful shock and have set opposing forces in motion. Finally, a resistance to violence in the name of religion is taking shape in the Islamic orthodoxy as well. And, for some years now – perhaps less in the Arabian heartland of Islam than on the periphery, in Asia, South Africa, Iran, Turkey and, not least, among Muslims in the West – we have witnessed the development of a new religious thought. Europe too had to reinvent itself after the two world wars. And perhaps I should mention, considering the flippancy, disdain and open contempt which our politicians – no, which we as a society – have shown towards the European project of unification, the most politically valuable project ever initiated by this continent, perhaps I should mention at this juncture how often people bring up the subject of Europe with me on my travels: as a model, almost a utopia. Anyone who has forgotten why there needs to be a Europe should look at the emaciated, exhausted, frightened faces of the refugees who have left everything behind, given up everything, risked their lives for the promise that Europe still represents.

That brings me back to the second phrase of Father Jacques's that I found remarkable, his statement about the Christian world: 'We mean nothing to them.' As a Muslim, it is not my place to cast blame on the Christians of the world for failing to aid, if not the Syrian and Iraqi peoples, then at least their own brothers and sisters in faith. And yet I too cannot help thinking it when I experience the lack of interest of our public sphere in the seemingly apocalyptic disaster in the East, which we try to repel with barbed-wire fences, warships, stereotypes and mental blinkers. Just a three-hour flight away from Frankfurt, whole ethnic groups are being exterminated or expelled, girls are being enslaved, many of humanity's most important cultural monuments are being blown up, cultures are disappearing, and with them an ancient ethnic, religious and linguistic diversity that, in contrast to Europe, had still persisted to a certain extent into the twenty-first century – but we join together and rise up only when one of the bombs of this war strikes us, as it did on 7 and 8 January in Paris, or when the people fleeing this war come knocking at our gates.

It is a good thing that our societies, responding better than they did to 11 September 2001, have opposed terror with freedom. It is uplifting to see so many people in Europe, and especially in Germany, supporting refugees. But this protest and this solidarity too often fall short of becoming political. We are not having a broad dialogue in our society about the causes of terror and refugee movements, about how our own policies may in fact be exacerbating the disaster taking place just outside our borders. We are not asking why our closest partner in the Middle East is Saudi Arabia, of all countries. We are not learning from our mistakes when we roll out the red carpet for a dictator like General el-Sisi. Or we are learning the wrong lessons if we conclude from the disastrous wars in Iraq or Libya that it is best not to get involved even when genocide begins. We have not come up with any way to prevent the murders being committed by the Syrian regime against its own people for the past four years. We have likewise resigned ourselves to the existence of a new religious fascism whose territory is roughly the size of Great Britain and extends from the Iranian border almost to the Mediterranean. Not that there are any simple answers to such questions as how a metropolis like Mosul can be liberated – but we are not even asking the question in earnest. An organization like Islamic State, with an estimated 30,000 fighters, is not invincible to the world community – we cannot allow it to be. 'Today they are in our country', said the Catholic archbishop of Mosul, Yohanna Boutros Moshe, when he asked the West and the great powers to help drive IS out of Iraq. 'Today they are in our country. Tomorrow they will be in yours.'

I hesitate to imagine what else has to happen before we agree with the archbishop of Mosul, for the logic of Islamic State's propaganda is to kindle ever higher degrees of horror with its images in order to penetrate our consciousness. Once we ceased to be outraged at the sight of individual Christian hostages saying the rosary before being beheaded,

IS started beheading whole groups of Christians. When we banished the decapitations from our screens, IS torched the ancient artworks in the National Museum in Mosul. Once we had become inured to the sight of smashed statues, IS began levelling the ancient ruins of whole cities like Nimrod and Nineveh. When we stopped worrying about the expulsions of Yazidis, the news of mass rapes briefly jolted us from our slumber. When we thought the terrors were confined to Iraq and Syria, snuff videos reached us from Libya and Egypt. When we had grown accustomed to the beheadings and the crucifixions, they beheaded their victims first and then crucified them, as they recently did in Libya. Palmyra is not being blown up all at once but, in fact, one building at a time, at intervals of several weeks, in order to produce a fresh news item each time. This will not stop. IS will go on escalating the horror until we see, hear and feel in our European day-to-day lives that this horror will not end by itself. Paris will have been only the beginning, and Lyons will not be the last beheading. And, the longer we wait, the fewer options we will have. In other words, it is already far too late.

Can the recipient of a peace prize call for war? I am not calling for war. I am merely pointing out that there is a war – and that we too, as its closest neighbours, must respond to it – possibly by military means, yes, but above all with far more determination than we have shown up to now, in our diplomacy and in civil society. For this war can no longer be ended in Syria and Iraq alone. It can only be ended by the powers behind the warring armies and militias: Iran, Turkey, the Gulf states, Russia and the West. And only when our societies cease to accept the madness will our governments take action. Whatever we do at this point, we will probably make mistakes. But our greatest mistake would be to go on doing nothing, or too little, against the mass murder being carried out by Islamic State and the Assad regime on Europe's doorstep.

'I have just returned from Aleppo', Father Jacques continued in the e-mail he wrote a few days before his abduction on 21 May:

> this city which sleeps by the river of pride, which lies at the centre of the Orient. It is now like a woman consumed by cancer. Everyone is fleeing Aleppo, especially the poor Christians. Yet these massacres strike not only the Christians, they strike the entire Syrian people. Our purpose is difficult to achieve, especially in these days since the disappearance of Father Paolo, the teacher and initiator of dialogue in the twenty-first century. In these days we are living that dialogue as a communal, shared suffering. We are sad in this unjust world which bears a share of the responsibility for the victims of the war, this world of the dollar and the euro, which cares only for its own peoples, its own prosperity, its own safety, while the rest of the world dies of hunger, disease and war. It

seems their only aim is to find regions where they can wage wars and further increase their trade in arms and aeroplanes. How do these governments justify themselves, when they could end the massacres but do nothing, nothing at all?

I do not fear for my faith, but I fear for the world. The question we ask ourselves is this: Do we have a right to live or not? The answer has already been given, for this war is a clear answer, as clear as sunlight. So the real dialogue we are living today is the dialogue of mercy.

Courage, my dear, I am with you and embrace you.

Jacques

Two months after the abduction of Father Jacques, on 28 July 2015, Islamic State took over the small town of Qaryatain. Most of the inhabitants managed to flee at the last moment, but two hundred Christians were kidnapped by IS. Another month later, on 21 August, the monastery of Mar Elian was destroyed by bulldozers. You can see in the pictures posted online by IS that not one of the 1700-year-old stones was left standing. Another two weeks later, on 3 September, photos appeared on an Islamic State website showing some of the Christian hostages from Qaryatain sitting in the front rows of a school auditorium or municipal hall, their heads shaven, some of them little more than skin and bone, their faces void of expression, all of them marked by their captivity. Father Jacques is recognizable in the photos, wearing plain clothes, likewise emaciated and with his head shorn, the shock clearly visible in his eyes. He is covering his mouth with his hand, as if unwilling to believe what he is seeing. On the stage of the hall we see a broad-shouldered, long-bearded man in combat fatigues signing a contract. It is what is known as a dhimmi contract, which subjugates Christians to Muslim rule. They are forbidden to build churches or monasteries or to carry crosses or Bibles on their person. Their priests are not allowed to wear clerical attire. Muslims must not hear the prayers of Christians, read their writings or enter their churches. The Christians are not allowed to bear arms and must obey the instructions of Islamic State unconditionally. They must bow their heads, endure all injustices in silence, and also pay a poll tax, the *jizya*, to be allowed to live. The contract is sickening to read: it divides God's creatures quite clearly into first- and second-class persons and leaves no doubt that there are also third-class persons whose lives are worth even less.

It is a calm but utterly depressed and helpless glance that Father Jacques casts at us in the photo as he covers his mouth with his hand. He had expected his own martyrdom. But to see his parish taken captive – the children he baptized, the lovers he married, the elderly to whom he promised the last rites – must be enough to drive him mad, to drive mad even a man as deliberate, inwardly strong and devoted to God as Father Jacques. After all, it was for his sake that the other captives had stayed in Qaryatain instead of fleeing Syria like so many other Christians. Father Jacques no doubt believes that he bears guilt; but God, I know this much, God will judge him otherwise.

Is there hope? Yes, there is hope, there is always hope. I had already written this speech when, five days ago, on Tuesday, I received the news that Father Jacques Mourad is free. Inhabitants of the town of Qaryatain helped him escape from his cell. They disguised him and managed to get him out of the IS-controlled area with the help of Bedouins. He has now returned to his brothers and sisters of the Mar Musa community. Apparently a number of people were involved in the rescue, all of them Muslims, every one of them risking his or her life for a Christian priest. Love worked across the boundaries between religions, ethnicities and cultures. And yet, as magnificent as this news is – indeed, as wondrous as it is in the literal sense of the word – sorrow nevertheless outweighs the joy, and, most bitterly, Father Jacques's own sorrow. Indeed, the lives of the two hundred other Christians in Qaryatain may well be in greater danger now than before his escape. And there is still no trace of his teacher, Father Paolo, the founder of the Christian community that loves Islam. Until our last breath there is hope.

The recipient of a peace prize should not call for war. But he can call to prayer. Ladies and gentlemen, I would like to make an unusual request – although, in a church, it is not really so unusual after all. I would like to ask you to refrain from applauding at the end of my speech and instead to pray for Father Paolo and the two hundred captive Christians of Qaryatain, for the children Father Jacques baptized, for the lovers he married, for the elderly to whom he promised the last rites. And if you are not religious, then let your wishes be with those who have been abducted, and with Father Jacques, who struggles with the fact that only he was freed. What are prayers after all but wishes addressed to God? I believe in wishes, and I believe that they have power in our world, with or without God. Without wishes, mankind would never have built one stone upon one another, the stones it so recklessly demolishes in war. And so I ask you, ladies and gentlemen, to pray for Jacques Mourad, pray for Paolo Dall'Oglio, pray for the Christians of Qaryatain, pray or wish for the liberation of all hostages and the freedom of Syria and Iraq. I invite you to stand up so that we can answer the snuff videos of the terrorists with a picture of our brotherhood.

Thank you.

ABOUT THE TEXT

All the texts have been reviewed and newly translated or revised for this book; some differ substantially here from the form of their original publication. Except where otherwise noted, the passages from the Quran follow the author's German translation, drawing on those of Friedrich Rückert and Max Henning. Bible passages follow the King James Version. Arabic and Persian terms, names and titles are given in simplified transliteration except in bibliographical notes.

1 Don't Follow the Poets!

The Quran and Poetry

Originally published as 'Poetry and Language', in Andrew Rippin (ed.), *The Blackwell Companion to the Qur'ān* (Malden, MA, and Oxford, 2006, pp. 107–19). This chapter and the next are based on lectures I gave at the Institute for Advanced Study, Berlin. Although they are mainly introductions to my two previously published monographs, *God Is Beautiful* and *The Terror of God*, the publisher proposed including these texts here as the books are quite large, and I have often been asked for a more concise treatment of those topics which are particularly relevant to current discussions. Those who are familiar with the books may skip over these two chapters or may read them for the new ideas that have been added.

2 Revolt against God

Attar and Suffering

Originally published in *Wespennest* 150 (March 2008).

3 World without God

Shakespeare and Man

The text is based on a speech I gave at the opening of the annual conference of the German Shakespeare Society in Bochum on 20 April 2012. First published in *Akzente* 59/4 (2012). I am grateful to Sabine Schülting and Tobias Düring for their valuable comments.

4 Heroic Weakness

Lessing and Terror

Originally published as *Vergesst Deutschland: Eine patriotische Rede* [Forget Germany: a patriotic address] (Berlin: Ullstein, 2002). For the present book, I have omitted some references to literary history and added ideas from my essay in *Toleranz: Drei Lesarten zu Lessings Märchen vom Ring im Jahre 2003* [Tolerance: three interpretations of Lessing's fable of the ring in 2003] (Göttingen: Wallstein, 2003). I am grateful to Maik Baumgärtner and Bettina Eltner for their valuable comments.

5 God Breathing

Goethe and Religion

The text is based on a speech I gave at the opening of the annual conference of the German Goethe Society in Weimar on 23 May 2013. First published in *Goethe-Jahrbuch 2013*. I am grateful to Petra Oberhauser and Jochen Golz for their valuable comments.

6 Filth of My Soul

Kleist and Love

First published by the Heinrich von Kleist Society in *Kleist-Jahrbuch 2013*. I am grateful to Günther Blamberger for his valuable comments.

7 The Truth of Theatre

The Shiite Passion Play and Alienation

A very early version of this text was published as 'Katharsis und Verfremdung im schiitischen Passionsspiel' [Catharsis and alienation in the Shiite passion play] in *Die Welt des Islams* [The world of Islam] 39 (1999), pp. 31–63.

8 Liberate Bayreuth!

Wagner and Empathy

Originally published in *Die Zeit*, 16 August 2002. I am grateful to Carl Hegemann for his valuable comments.

9 Swimming in the Afternoon

Kafka and Germany

Speech delivered at the Konrad Adenauer Foundation, Berlin, 13 December 2006, at the invitation of the president of the Bundestag. Originally published in Bernhard Vogel (ed.), *Was eint uns? Verständigung der Gesellschaft über gemeinsame Grundlagen* [What unites us? Society's agreement on shared foundations] (Freiburg im Breisgau: Herder, 2008, pp. 78–98).

10 The Duty of Literature

Hedayat and Kafka

Originally published as 'Der Auftrag des Dichters: Ṣādeq Ḥedāyat über Kafka und über sich selbst' [The poet's purpose: Ṣādeq Ḥedāyat on Kafka and on himself], in Stephan Guth, Priska Furrer and Johan Christoph Bürgel (eds), *Conscious Voices: Concepts of Writing in the Middle East: Proceedings of the Berne Symposium July 1997* (Stuttgart: F. Steiner, 1999, pp. 121–242).

11 Towards Europe

Zweig and the Borders

Originally published as *Nach Europa: Rede zum 50. Jahrestag der Wiedereröffnung des Burgtheaters* [To Europe: speech on the fiftieth anniversary of the reopening of the Burgtheater] (Zurich: Ammann, 2005).

12 In Defence of the Glass Bead Game

Hesse and Decadence

The text is based on a speech I gave at the invitation of the Körber Foundation to open the conference on 'The Art of Music Education' on 22 January 2014. First published in *Akzente* 61/2 (2014).

13 The Violence of Compassion

Arendt and Revolution

Originally published in *Frankfurter Rundschau*, 5 December 2011.

14 Tilting at Windmills

Mosebach and the Novel

First published in the German Academy for Language and Literature's *Jahrbuch 2007*.

15 One God, One Wife, One Cheese

Golshiri and Friendship

Originally published as an afterword to the novel *Prinz Ehtedschab* [Prince Ehtejab] by Hushang Golshiri, trans. Anneliese Ghahraman-Beck (Munich: Beck, 2001, pp. 129–40).

16 Sing the Quran Singingly

Neuwirth and Literalist Piety

The text is based on a speech to the German Academy of Language and Literature in honour of Angelika Neuwirth on the occasion of her receiving the 2013 Sigmund Freud Prize. Parts of the text recapitulate the ideas I discuss in *God Is Beautiful.*

On the Sixty-Fifth Anniversary of the Promulgation of the German Constitution

Originally published in *Der Spiegel*, 26 May 2014.

On Receiving the Peace Prize of the German Publishers' Association

Originally published as a commemorative volume by the German Publishers' Association with an English translation by Wieland Hoban; translation revised for the present book by Tony Crawford.

NOTES

Preface

1 Heinrich Heine, 'The Romantic School', trans. Helen Mustard, in *The Romantic School and other Essays*, ed. Jost Hermand and Robert C. Holub. New York: Continuum, 2002, pp. 1–127, at p. 92.
2 Ibid., p. 69.
3 Heinrich Heine, 'Jehuda ben Halevy', trans. Hal Draper, in Ritchie Robertson (ed.), *The German–Jewish Dialogue: An Anthology of Literary Texts, 1749–1993*. Oxford: Oxford University Press, 1999, p. 84.
4 Heinrich Heine, *Heinrich Heine's Life Told in His Own Words*, ed. Gustav Karpeles, trans. Arthur Dexter. New York: Henry Holt, 1893, p. 340.
5 M. Werner (ed.), *Begegnungen mit Heine: Berichte der Zeitgenossen*, 2 vols. Hamburg: Hoffmann & Campe, 1973, vol. 2, p. 174; quoted in Karl-Josef Kuschel, *Gottes grausamer Spaß? Heinrich Heines Leben mit der Katastrophe*. Düsseldorf: Patmos, 2002, pp. 92–3; quoted here in Alfred Werner's translation after his article 'Cedars of Lebanon: Heinrich Heine to His Eckermann', *Commentary* 20 (July 1955), pp. 71–3.
6 'The Asra', trans. Aaron Kramer, in *The Poetry and Prose of Heinrich Heine*, ed. Frederic Ewen. New York: Citadel, 1948, p. 145.
7 Almut Shulamit Bruckstein Çoruh, *House of Taswir: Doing and Undoing Things*. Paderborn: Wilhelm Fink, 2014, pp. 9–10.

Chapter 1 Don't Follow the Poets!

1 *The Koran*, trans. Arthur J. Arberry. Oxford: Oxford University Press, 1998, verse 14:4.
2 Shlomo D. Goitein, *Studies in Islamic History and Institutions*. Leiden: Brill, 1966, p. 8.
3 Ibn Kaṯīr, *As-Sīra an-nabawīya*, 4 vols, ed. Muṣṭafā᾽ Abdulwaḥīd. Beirut, 1407/1987.
4 Ibn al-Manẓūr, *Lisān al-ʿarab*, 15 vols, Beirut 1375/1961; vol. 8, p. 183.
5 Verse 26:224, trans. Arberry.

6 Octavio Paz, *The Bow and the Lyre*, trans. Ruth L. C. Simms. Austin and London: University of Texas Press, 2009.
7 Adonis [Ali Ahmad Sa'id], 'The Dead God', in *Mihyar of Damascus, His Songs*, trans. Adnan Haydar and Michael Beard. Rochester, NY: BOA, 2008, p. 70.
8 Roman Jakobson, 'What Is Poetry?' in *Language in Literature*. Cambridge, MA: Harvard University Press, 1987, pp. 368–78, at p. 369.
9 Clifford Geertz, 'Art as a Cultural System', *Modern Language Notes* 91 (1976), pp. 1473–99, at p. 1490.
10 Franz Kafka, 'The Silence of the Sirens', in *The Great Wall of China*, trans. Willa Muir and Edwin Muir. New York: Schocken, 1970, p. 143.

Chapter 2 Revolt against God

1 *Moṣibatnāmeh*, ed. Nurāni Wesāl. Tehran, 1973/1994, pp. 77–8. Hellmut Ritter retells many of the stories from Attar's *Book of Suffering* in his pioneering work on Attar, *The Ocean of the Soul: Man, the World and God in the Stories of Farīd al-Dīn ᶜAṭṭār*, trans. John O'Kane. Leiden: Brill, 2003. I will add references to these retellings where available. In this case, see Ritter, p. 56.
2 *Moṣibatnāmeh*, p. 67.
3 Ibid., p. 132.
4 Ibid., p. 57.
5 Ibid., p. 342; Ritter, *The Ocean of the Soul*, p. 177.
6 Georg Büchner, *Danton's Death*, in *Danton's Death, Leonce and Lena, Woyzeck*, trans. Victor Price. Oxford: Oxford University Press, 1988.
7 *Moṣibatnāmeh*, pp. 336–7; Ritter, *The Ocean of the Soul*, p. 64.
8 *Moṣibatnāmeh*, pp. 215–16; Ritter, *The Ocean of the Soul*, pp. 183–4.
9 *Moṣibatnāmeh*, p. 300; Ritter, *The Ocean of the Soul*, p. 177.
10 *Moṣibatnāmeh*, pp. 90f.
11 Ibid., p. 223.
12 Yvan Goll, *100 Gedichte*. Göttingen: Wallstein, 2003, p. 123.
13 *Moṣibatnāmeh*, p. 249; Ritter, *The Ocean of the Soul*, p. 183.
14 Job 31:19–20; 28.
15 Ernst Bloch, *Atheism in Christianity: The Religion of the Exodus and the Kingdom*, trans. J. T. Swann. New York and London: Verso, 2009, p. 96.
16 Georg Büchner, *Lenz*, trans. Richard Sieburth. New York: Archipelago, 2004, pp. 73–5.
17 Arthur Schopenhauer, *Manuscript Remains: Berlin Manuscripts (1818–1830)*, trans. E. F. J. Payne, ed. Arthur Hübscher, 4 vols. Oxford: Berg, 1988, vol. 3, p. 63.
18 Emmanuel Levinas, *Difficult Freedom: Essays on Judaism*, trans. Seán Hand. Baltimore: Johns Hopkins University Press, [1963] 1976, pp. 142ff.
19 *Moṣibatnāmeh*, p. 251.
20 Ibid., p. 271.
21 Ibid., p. 196.
22 Ibid., p. 133; Ritter, *The Ocean of the Soul*, p. 588.
23 *Moṣibatnāmeh*, p. 17.
24 Deuteronomy 32:39.
25 *Moṣibatnāmeh*, p. 300.

26 Ibid., pp. 299f.; Ritter, *The Ocean of the Soul*, p. 266.
27 *Moṣibatnāmeh*, pp. 125ff.; Ritter, *The Ocean of the Soul*, p. 342.
28 *Moṣibatnāmeh*, p. 18.
29 Heinrich Heine, letter to Hermann Heine, 19 November 1855. Quoted in *Säkularausgabe der Werke – Briefwechsel – Lebenszeugnisse*, ed. Fritz H. Eisner, 27 vols. Berlin and Paris, 1972, vol. 23, p. 470.
30 Heinrich Heine, *Testamente*, quoted in *Sämtliche Schriften*, ed. Klaus Briegleb, 6 vols. Munich, 1997, vol. 6/i, p. 549.
31 Quoted in Emil L. Fackenheim, *God's Presence in History: Jewish Affirmations and Philosophical Reflections*. New York: New York University Press, 1970, p. 76.
32 Quoted in Anson Laytner, *Arguing with God: A Jewish Tradition*. Northvale, NJ, and London: J. Aronson, 1990, pp. 228–9.
33 Quoted ibid., p. 229.
34 *Moṣibatnāmeh*, 101; Ritter, *The Ocean of the Soul*, p. 413.
35 Job 13:15.
36 Farīdoddin ᶜAṭṭār, *Tazkerat ol-ouliyā'*, ed. Parwin Qā'emi. Tehran, 1381/2002, p. 565.
37 Zvi Kolitz, *Yosl Rakover Talks to God*, trans. Carol Brown Janeway. New York: Vintage, 2000, p. 24.
38 Angel Wagenstein, *Isaac's Torah*, trans. Elizabeth Frank and Deliana Simeonova. New York: Other Press, 2001, p. 36.
39 Quoted in Shmuel Boteach, *Wrestling with the Divine: A Jewish Response to Suffering*. Northvale, NJ: J. Aronson, 1995, pp. 111–12.
40 Immanuel Kant, 'On the Miscarriage of All Philosophical Trials in Theodicy', trans. George di Giovanni, in *Religion and Rational Theology*, ed. Allen W. Wood. Cambridge: Cambridge University Press, 1996, pp. 24–38, at p. 33.
41 Susan Neiman, *Evil in Modern Thought: An Alternative History of Philosophy*. Princeton, NJ: Princeton University Press, 2002, p. 16.
42 Ibid., p. 14.
43 Ernst Bloch, *Avicenna und die Aristotelische Linke* [Avicenna and the Aristotelian left], Frankfurt am Main: Suhrkamp, 1963, p. 11.
44 Translator's note: The reference is to a speech by the German head of state Christian Wulff on 3 October 2010.
45 María Rosa Menocal, *The Arabic Role in Medieval Literary Theory: A Forgotten Heritage*. Philadelphia: University of Pennsylvania Press, 2003, p. 3.
46 Johann Wolfgang von Goethe, 'Prometheus', trans. David Luke, in *Selected Poetry*. London: Penguin, 2005.
47 Fyodor Dostoevsky, *The Brothers Karamazov*, trans. Richard Pevear and Larissa Volokhonsky. London: Vintage, 2004, p. 245.
48 Albert Camus, *The Plague*, trans. Robin Buss. London: Penguin, 2001, p. 169.
49 Albert Camus, *The Rebel*, trans. Anthony Bower. London: Penguin, 2000, pp. 30–31.
50 Karl-Josef Kuschel, 'Ist Gott verantwortlich für das Übel? Überlegungen zu einer Theologie der Anklage' [Is God responsible for evil? Reflections on a theology of indictment], in Gotthard Fuchs, *Angesichts des Leids an Gott glauben? Zur Theologie der Klage* [Belief in God in the face of suffering? On the theology of indictment]. Frankfurt am Main: Josef Knecht, 1996, pp. 227–261, at p. 250.

Chapter 3 World without God

1 *King Lear*, IV.vi.132.
2 Johann Wolfgang von Goethe and Friedrich Schiller, 'On Epic and Dramatic Poetry', in *Correspondence between Schiller and Goethe from 1794 to 1805*, trans. George H. Calvert. New York and London: Wiley and Putnam, 1845, vol. 1, p. 379.
3 *King Lear*, IV.vii.46–8.
4 Ibid., IV.i.25–6.
5 Ibid., IV.i.27–8.
6 Ibid., I.iv.186–7.
7 Ibid., V.iii.278.
8 Harold Bloom, *Shakespeare: The Invention of the Human*, New York: Riverhead, 1999, p. 512.
9 Ibid., p. 479.
10 *King Lear*, I.i.233–4.
11 What is remarkable is that, in the chief source of Shakespeare's tragedy, an old play by the Queen's Men titled *The True Chronicle History of King Leir*, Lear's test of his daughter's love is supported by rationally understandable arguments. That means Shakespeare purposely reinforces the impression that the king's action is perfectly arbitrary. Stephen Greenblatt, *Will in the World: How Shakespeare Became Shakespeare*. New York: W. W. Norton, 2004, pp. 327–8.
12 *King Lear*, I.i.9–10.
13 Ibid., I.i.20–23.
14 Ibid., IV.vi.76–7.
15 Ibid., III.ii.37.
16 Ibid., V.iii.20–21.
17 Ibid., IV.i.36–7.
18 Ibid., V.iii.258–9.
19 Ibid., V.iii.172–3.
20 Ibid., I.ii.116–25.
21 Georg Wilhelm Friedrich Hegel, *Hegel's Aesthetics: Lectures on Fine Art*, trans. T. M. Knox. Oxford: Oxford University Press, [1975] 1988, vol. 2, pp. 1227–8.
22 *King Lear*, IV.vi.103–4. I find Günther's translation, deviating here from earlier German versions, reduces the text to one of the possible meanings: '*die sagten, ich war doch ihr ein und alles; 's war gelogen, ich bin nicht fieberfest.*'
23 Ibid., III.ii.1–9.
24 Ibid., I.ii.1–2.
25 Theodor W. Adorno, *Aesthetic Theory*, trans. Robert Hullot-Kentor. London: Bloomsbury, 2013, p. 291.
26 *King Lear*, I.iv.115–24.
27 Ibid., I.iv.125.
28 Ibid., I.iv.129.
29 Ibid., I.iv.187–8.
30 Indira Ghose, *Shakespeare and Laughter: A Cultural History*. Manchester: Manchester University Press, 2008, pp. 189–90.
31 Leo Tolstoy, *Tolstoy on Shakespeare: A Critical Essay on Shakespeare*, trans. V. Tchertkoff and I. F. Mayo. New York and London: Funk & Wagnalls, 1906, p. 3.

32 George Orwell, 'Tolstoy and Shakespeare', in *The Collected Essays, Journalism, and Letters of George Orwell*, ed. Sonia Orwell and Ian Angus. Boston: Nonpareil, 2000, vol. 2, pp. 127–30; and 'Lear, Tolstoy und the Fool', in *Essays*. London: Penguin, 2000, pp. 401–16.
33 Tolstoy, *Tolstoy on Shakespeare*, p. 113.
34 Ibid., p. 114.
35 Ibid., p. 124.
36 Ibid., p. 123.
37 *King Lear*, V.iii.290.
38 Ibid., V.iii.323–4.
39 Ibid., I.ii.2–3.
40 Ibid., I.ii.127.
41 *Hamlet*, IV.iv.33–5.
42 Ibid., IV.iv.36–9.
43 *King Lear*, I.ii.172.
44 Ibid., I.ii.111–14.
45 Ibid., I.ii.105–8.
46 Ibid., I.iv.95.
47 Ibid., IV.vi.179–80.
48 Ibid., IV.vi.172.
49 Ibid., V.iii.307–11.

Chapter 4 Heroic Weakness

1 The police officer was killed using a Tokarev and a Radom, which were also found in the rubble.
2 *Philotas*, trans. Ernest Bell and R. Dillon Boylan, in *The Dramatic Works of G. E. Lessing*, ed. Ernest Bell. London: George Bell & Sons, 1878, vol. 1, p. 109.
3 *Philotas*, pp. 112ff.
4 I have discussed the intellectual and biographical background of the 11 September attacks in *Dynamit des Geistes: Martyrium, Islam und Nihilismus* [Spiritual dynamite: martyrdom, Islam and nihilism] (Göttingen: Wallstein, 2002).
5 'Lieb, nett und niemals böse', *Der Spiegel*, 24 September 2001.
6 *Stern*, 27 December 2001.
7 *Cicero*, 22 November 2011.
8 Lessing, *Hamburgische Dramaturgie*, in *Werke*, vol. 4, p. 318.
9 *Philotas*, p. 124.
10 In the original: *Bei allen Kebabs herrschen Angst und Schrecken. / Der Döner bleibt im Halse stecken, / denn er kommt gerne spontan zu Besuch, / am Dönerstand, denn neun sind nicht genug.*
11 German: *Döner-Morde.*
12 *Der Spiegel*, 15 April 2006.
13 *Der Spiegel*, 21 February 2011.
14 Letter to Johann Wilhelm Ludwig Gleim, 14 February 1758, quoted in Wilfried Barner, Gunter E. Grimm, Helmut Kiesel and Martin Kramer, *Lessing: Epoche – Werk – Wirkung* [Lessing: era; work; influence]. Munich: Beck, 1995, p. 255.
15 Letter to Friedrich Nicolai and Moses Mendelssohn, 29 March 1757, quoted in

Hugh Barr Nisbet, *Gotthold Ephraim Lessing: His Life, Works, and Thought*. Oxford: Oxford University Press, 2013, p. 237.

16 Nisbet, *Gotthold Ephraim Lessing*, p. 236.

17 Daniel Kehlmann, 'Toleranz und Ärger' [Tolerance and anger], in Heinz Ludwig Arnold (ed.), *Mit Lessing ins Gespräch* [To converse with Lessing]. Göttingen: Wallstein, 2004, pp. 28–31, at p. 28.

18 Quoted in Nisbet, *Gotthold Ephraim Lessing*, p. 508.

19 G. E. Lessing, *Nathan the Wise: A Dramatic Poem in Five Acts*, trans. Bayard Quincy Morgan, in *Nathan the Wise, Minna von Barnhelm, and Other Plays and Writings*, ed. Peter Demetz. New York: Continuum, [1991] 2004, p. 235.

20 17th 'Letter on Literature', quoted in Nisbet, *Gotthold Ephraim Lessing*, p. 254.

21 Lessing, *Ernst und Falk: Gespräche für Freimaurer* [Ernst and Falk: dialogues for freemasons], quoted in *Werke*, vol. 7, p. 459.

22 *Nathan the Wise*, p. 231.

23 For more detail, see my essay in Angelika Overath, Navid Kermani and Robert Schindel, *Toleranz: Drei Lesarten zu Lessings Märchen vom Ring im Jahre 2003* [Tolerance: three interpretations of Lessing's fable of the ring in the year 2003]. Göttingen: Wallstein, 2003, pp. 33–45.

24 *Der Spiegel*, 12 December 2011.

25 Thilo Sarrazin, *Deutschland schafft sich ab: Wie wir unser Land aufs Spiel setzen* [Germany's self-destruction: how we are putting our country at risk]. Munich: Deutsche Verlags-Anstalt, 2010, p. 316.

26 *Lettre International*, September 2009.

27 Achim Bühl, *Islamfeindlichkeit in Deutschland: Ursprünge, Akteure, Stereotype* [Islamophobia in Germany: origins, actors, stereotypes]. Hamburg: VSA, 2010, p. 138.

28 *Lettre International*, September 2009.

29 Sarrazin, *Deutschland schafft sich ab*, p. 386.

30 *Hier & Jetzt: Radikal rechte Zeitung*, December 2010, p. 25.

31 Ibid., p. 21.

32 Bühl, *Islamfeindlichkeit in Deutschland*, p. 140.

33 Hannah Arendt, 'On Humanity in Dark Times: Thoughts about Lessing', address on accepting the Lessing Prize of the free city of Hamburg, in *Man in Dark Times*. New York: Houghton Mifflin Harcourt, 1970, pp. 17–18.

34 Ibid., p. 18.

35 Letter to Johann Wilhelm Ludwig Gleim, 16 December 1758, quoted in Nisbet, *Gotthold Ephraim Lessing*, p. 235.

36 *Philotas*, p. 132.

Chapter 5 God Breathing

1 Johann Wolfgang von Goethe, *West-östlicher Divan* [West-eastern divan] in *Werke* [Works], ed. Erich Trunz, 14 vols. Munich, 1998 (hereafter 'Hamburg edn'), vol. 2, p. 10.

2 *Wilhelm Meister's Apprenticeship and Travels*, trans. Thomas Carlyle, ed. Nathan Haskell Dole. Boston: Niccolls, 1901, vol. 2, p. 129.

3 *The Poems of Goethe: Translated in the Original Metres by Edgar Alfred Bowring*. London: Parker, 1853, p. 264.

4 *The Auto-Biography of Goethe: Truth and Poetry: From My Own Life*, vol. 1, trans. John Oxenford. London: Henry Bohn, 1848, p. 321.
5 Ibid., pp. 18–19.
6 Ibid., p. 30.
7 Namely '*ein Scheisding*'; letter to Johann Gottfried Herder, c. 12 May 1775, in *Goethes Werke* [Goethe's works], 143 vols. Weimar, 1887–1919; repr. Munich, 1987, supplemented by vols. 144–6: addenda and index to part 4: *Briefe* [Correspondence], ed. Paul Raabe, vols. 1–3. Munich, 1990 (hereafter 'Weimar edn'), part 4, vol. 2, p. 262.
8 Letter to Johann Kaspar Lavater, 29 July 1782, in Weimar edn, part 4, vol. 6, p. 20.
9 Friedrich Heinrich Jacobi to Goethe (draft), November 1815, in *Goethes Gespräche: Eine Sammlung zeitgenössischer Berichte aus seinem Umgang auf Grund der Ausgabe und des Nachlasses von Flodoard Freiherrn von Biedermann* [Goethe's conversations: a collection of contemporary reports from his commerce based on the edition and the estate of Baron Flodoard von Biedermann], ed. Wolfgang Herwig, 5 vols. Zurich, 1965–87, vol. 2, p. 21.
10 Letter to Christian Gottlob Voigt, 27 December 1789, in Weimar edn, part 4, vol. 9, p. 171.
11 *Wilhelm Meister's Apprenticeship and Travels*, vol. 3, p. 121.
12 *Goethes Gespräche*, vol. 3, p. 604 (7 April 1830).
13 Quoted in *Goethe-Handbuch*, 5 vols, ed. Bernd Witte, Theo Bück, Hans-Dietrich Dahnke, Regine Otto and Peter Schmidt. Stuttgart and Weimar, 1996–9, vol. 4, part 1, p. 523.
14 *The Auto-Biography of Goethe*, vol. 1, p. 113.
15 *Goethes Gespräche*, vol. 3, part 1, p. 603.
16 *Conversations of Goethe with Eckermann and Soret*, trans. John Oxenford. London: Smith, Elder & Co., 1850, 2 vols, vol. 1, p. 120 (4 January 1824). [Oxenford's translation abridges the doctrine of the Trinity to 'I was required to believe other points'; cf. Johann Peter Eckermann, *Gespräche mit Goethe*, ed. Regine Otto. Berlin and Weimar, 1982, p. 470.]
17 *Goethes Gespräche*, vol. 2, p. 724; letter to Karl Ludwig von Knebel, 22 August 1817, quoted in Weimar edn, part 4, vol. 28, p. 227.
18 Ibid.
19 Goethe, *Maxims and Reflections*, trans. Elisabeth Stopp, ed. Peter Hutchinson. London: Penguin, 1998, p. 109 (no. 808).
20 Letter to Sulpiz Boisserée, 25 February 1832, quoted in Weimar edn, part 4, vol. 49, p. 250.
21 Quoted in Goethe, *West-östlicher Divan*, ed. Hendrik Birus. Frankfurt am Main: Deutscher Klassiker Verlag, 2010, p. 909.
22 Goethe, 'Einwirkung der neueren Philosophie' [Influence of modern philosophy], Hamburg edn, vol. 13, p. 27.
23 Goethe, *Geschichte der Farbenlehre*, Hamburg edn, vol. 14, p. 36.
24 Goethe, *The Metamorphosis of Plants*, trans. Douglas Miller, ed. Gordon L. Miller. Cambridge, MA: MIT Press, 2009, p. 44.
25 Goethe, *Maxims and Reflections*, p. 33 (no. 278).
26 Goethe, *Theory of Colours*, trans. Charles Lock Eastlake. London: Murray, 1840, p. 15.
27 Goethe, *Maxims and Reflections*, p. 109 (no. 809).
28 5 May 1786, quoted in Weimar edn, part 4, vol. 7, p. 214.

29 Quoted in Katharina Mommsen, *Goethe and the Poets of Arabia*, trans. Michael A. Metzger. New York: Camden House, p. 80.
30 Goethe, *Maxims and Reflections*, p. 109 (no. 810).
31 Quran 2:164, trans. Arberry.
32 *Goethes Gespräche*, vol. 3, part 1, p. 63.
33 Goethe, *West-östlicher Divan*, p. 10. Albany: State University of New York Press, 2010.
34 9 August 1782; Weimar edn, part 4, vol. 6, p. 36.
35 Trans. Arberry.
36 *Theory of Colours*, p. xxxix.
37 A. J. Arberry, *Fifty Poems of Ḥāfiẓ*. Cambridge: CUP, 1962, p. 103.
38 *Faust Part 2*, trans. Martin Greenberg. New Haven, CT: Yale University Press, 1998, Act II, p. 114.
39 Letter to Count Moritz von Brühl, 23 October 1828, quoted in Weimar edn, part 4, vol. 45, p. 32.
40 *Goethes Gespräche*, vol. 3, part 1, p. 108.
41 Letter to Adolf Oswald Blumenthal, 28 May 1819, quoted in Weimar edn, part 4, vol. 31, p. 160.
42 Letter to Johann Kaspar Lavater, 4 October 1782, Weimar edn, part 4, vol. 6, p. 66.
43 *The Auto Biography of Goethe*, vol. 2, trans. A. J. W. Morrison. London: George Bell & Sons, 1881, p. 23 (emphasis added).
44 *The Auto-Biography of Goethe*, vol. 1, p. 302. [Goethe's translator Oxenford included the German words in brackets and noted, 'If we could make use of some such verbs as "inself" and "unself," we should more accurately render this passage.']
45 Quoted in *West-östlicher Divan*, ed. Hendrik Birus, p. 549.
46 Letter to Adele Schopenhauer, 19 September 1831, Weimar edn, part 4, vol. 49, p. 87.
47 Weimar edn, part 4, vol. 27, p. 123.
48 Letter to Karl Friedrich Zelter, 20 September 1820, Weimar edn, part 4, vol. 33, p. 240.
49 *Conversations of Goethe with Eckermann and Soret*, vol. 1, pp. 391–2.
50 Goethe, 'Notes and Essays for a Better Understanding of the *West-East Divan*', trans. Martin Bidney and Peter Anton von Arnim, in *West-East Divan*, trans. Martin Bidney, p. 202.
51 Quoted in Katharina Mommsen, *'Orient und Okzident sind nicht mehr zu trennen': Goethe und die Weltkulturen* ['Orient and occident are no longer separable': Goethe and the world's cultures]. Göttingen: Wallstein, 2012, p. 95.
52 67:3–4, trans. Arberry.
53 *Theory of Colours*, pp. 293–4.
54 Trans. Arberry.
55 Muhyiddin Ibn Arabi, *Die Weisheit der Propheten (Fuṣūṣ al-ḥikam)* [The wisdom of the prophets], trans. Titus Burckhardt and Wolfgang Herrmann. Zurich: Chalice, 2005, p. 101.
56 Quoted in William C. Chittick, *The Sufi Path of Knowledge: Ibn al-Arabi's Metaphysics of Imagination*. Albany: State University of New York Press, 1989, p. 131.
57 Muhyiddin Ibn Arabi, quoted after *Abhandlung über die Liebe (aus den Futūhāt al-makkiya)* [Treatise on love: from the Futūhāt al-makkiya, the

Meccan revelations], trans. Maurice Gloton and Wolfgang Hermann. Zurich: Chalice, 2009, p. 97.
58 *West-östlicher Divan*, vol. 2, p. 18.
59 Ibid.
60 Letter to Johann Gottfried Herder, mid-July 1772, in Weimar edn, part 4, vol. 2, p. 17.

Chapter 6 Filth of My Soul

1 Lázsló F. Földényi, *Heinrich von Kleist: Im Netz der Wörter*, trans. Akos Doma. Munich: Matthes & Seitz, 1999, pp. 15ff.
2 Heinrich von Kleist, *Amphytrion*, trans. Marion Sonnenfeld. New York: Frederick Ungar, 1962, p. 52.
3 Heinrich von Kleist, 'The Foundling', trans. David Constantine, in *Selected Writings*. London: Dent, 1997, p. 365.
4 'Mutterliebe' ['Motherly love'], in Heinrich von Kleist, *Sämtliche Werke und Briefe* [Complete works and correspondence], ed. Helmut Sembdner. Munich, 1993, vol. 2, p. 77.
5 Letter to Heinrich Joseph von Collin, 8 December 1808, in *Sämtliche Werke und Briefe*, vol. 2, p. 818.
6 Heinrich von Kleist, *Penthesilea*, trans. Joel Agee. New York: HarperCollins, 1998, p. 143.
7 Letter to Marie von Kleist, late autumn 1807, in *Sämtliche Werke und Briefe*, vol. 2, p. 796.
8 Except where otherwise indicated, subsequent references are to scene 24 of *Penthesilea*, pp. 130–48.
9 *Penthesilea*, p. 59.
10 Ibid., p. 128.
11 Ibid., p. 118.
12 Ibid., pp. 145–6.
13 Ibid., p. 48–9.
14 Letter to Marie von Kleist, late autumn 1807, in *Sämtliche Werke und Briefe*, vol. 2, p. 797.
15 Letter to Heinrich von Kleist, 1 February 1808.
16 *Penthesilea*, p. 142.
17 Song of Songs, 8:6–7.
18 Hosea 2:10; 6:1.
19 Letter to Ernst von Pfuel, 7 January 1805, in *Sämtliche Werke un riefe* vol. 2, p. 749.
20 Muhyiddin Ibn Arabi, *Abhandlung über die Liebe (aus dem Futūhāt al-makkiya)* [Treatise on love: from the Futūhāt al-makkiya, the Meccan revelations], trans. Maurice Gloton and Wolfgang Hermann. Zurich: Chalice, 2009, p. 89.
21 Ibid., p. 196.
22 Ibid., pp. 81–2.
23 Ibid., p. 167.
24 Heinrich von Kleist, *Die Familie Ghonorez*, variant draft of lines 2630–1, in *Sämtliche Werke und Briefe*, vol. 1, p. 832.

CHAPTER 7 THE TRUTH OF THEATRE

1 'Leaning on the Moment: A Conversation with Peter Brook', *Parabola* 4/2 (1979), p. 52.
2 Peter J. Chelkowski, 'Ta'ziyeh: Indigenous Avant-Garde Theatre of Iran', in Chelkowski (ed.), *Ta'ziyeh: Ritual and Drama in Iran*. New York: New York University Press, 1979, pp. 10–11.
3 M. le Comte de Gobineau, 'Le Théâtre en Perse' [Theatre in Persia], in *Les Religions et les philosophies dans l'Asie centrale* [Religions and philosophies in central Asia], ch. 13. Paris: Didier, 1900, pp. 359ff.
4 William O. Beeman, 'Cultural Dimensions of Performance Conventions in Iranian Ta'ziyeh', in Chelkowski (ed.), *Ta'ziyeh*, pp. 24–31, at p. 25.
5 Elias Canetti, *Crowds and Power*, trans. Carol Stewart. New York: Continuum, 1978, p. 149.
6 Translator's note: I use the traditional English term 'alienation' for Brecht's *Verfremdung*; 'alienation' here always corresponds to *Verfremdung* and 'alienation effect' to *V-Effekt* or *Verfremdungseffekt* in the original. On the drawbacks of this choice, and of the alternatives, see the editors' remarks in their general introduction to the revised third edition of *Brecht on Theatre*, trans. John Willet et al., ed. Marc Silberman, Steve Giles and Tom Kuhn. London: Bloomsbury, 2015, pp. 4–5.
7 E.g. Parviz Mamnoun, 'Ta'ziyeh from the Viewpoint of the Western Theatre', in Chelkowski (ed.), *Ta'ziyeh*, pp. 154–66.
8 Bertolt Brecht, 'On Experimental Theatre', in *Brecht on Theatre*, p. 143.
9 Bertolt Brecht, *Short Organon for the Theatre*, ibid., pp. 229–54, at p. 243.
10 See Bertolt Brecht, 'The Street Scene', ibid., pp. 176–83.
11 Bertolt Brecht, 'Stage Design in the Epic Theatre', quoted in 'Short Description of a New Technique of Acting that Produces a *Verfremdung* Effect', ibid., pp. 184–95, at p. 189, n. 3.
12 Herbert W. Duda, 'Das persische Passionsspiel' [The Persian passion play], *Zeitschrift für Missionskunde und Religionswissenschaft* 4 (1934), pp. 97–114, at p. 102.
13 Parviz Mamnoun, *Ta'ziya: schi'itisches–persisches Passionsspiel* [Taziyeh: the Shiite–Persian passion play]. Vienna: Notring, 1967, p. 48.
14 Ibid., pp. 72–3.
15 Sir Lewis Pelly, *The Miracle Play of Hasan and Husain*. London, 1879; quoted in Chelkowski (ed.), *Ta'ziyeh*, p. xv.
16 Gobineau, 'Le Théâtre en Perse', pp. 377–8.
17 Jane Dieulafoy, *La Perse, la Chaldée et la Susiane* [Persia, Chaldea and Susiana]. Paris: Hachette, 1887, p. 109; quoted in Heinz Halm, *Shi'a Islam: From Religion to Revolution*, trans. Allison Brown. Munich: Markus Wiener, 1997, p. 73.
18 Peter Brook, *The Empty Space*. New York: Touchstone [1968] 1996, p. 80.
19 Max Horkheimer and Theodor W. Adorno, *Dialectic of Enlightenment: Philosophical Fragments*, trans. Edmund Jephcott. Stanford, CA: Stanford University Press, 2012, pp. 178–9.
20 Brook, *The Empty Space*, p. 136.
21 Wolfgang Schadewaldt, *Tübinger Vorlesungen* [Tübingen lectures]. Frankfurt am Main: Suhrkamp, 1991, p. 17.
22 Wolfgang Schadewaldt, 'Furcht und Mitleid?' [Fear and pity?], in *Hellas und*

Hesperien: Gesammelte Schriften zur Antike und zur neueren Literatur [Hellas and Hesperia: collected writings on antiquity and modern literature], 2 vols. Zurich and Stuttgart: Artemis, 1970, vol. 1, pp. 194–236, at p. 203.
23 Antonin Artaud, *The Theatre and its Double*, trans. Victor Corti. London: Oneworld, 2010, p. 21.
24 Ibid., p. 74.
25 Mahmoud Ayoub, *Redemptive Suffering in Islam: A Study of the Devotional Aspects of Āshurā in Twelver Shi'ism.* The Hague: Mouton, 1978, p. 25.
26 Artaud, *The Theatre and its Double*, p. 21.
27 Yann Richard, *Le Shi'isme en Iran: iman et révolution.* Paris: Librairie d'Amérique et d'Orient, 1980, p. 81.
28 Artaud, *The Theatre and its Double*, p. 20.
29 Ibid., p. 18.
30 Ibid., p. 60.
31 Jan Assmann, *Cultural Memory and Early Civilization: Writing, Remembrance and Political Imagination.* Cambridge: Cambridge University Press, 2011, pp. 66–7.
32 Artaud, *The Theatre and its Double*, p. 7.
33 Ibid., p. 91.
34 Ibid., p. 124.
35 Ibid., pp. 93ff.
36 Ibid., p. 16.
37 Andrzej Wirth, 'Ein Perserteppich von Codes: Versuch, das iranische Passionsspiel Ta'zieh als ein System von Zeichen zu beschreiben' [A Persian carpet of codes: an attempt to describe the Iranian passion play *ta'zieh* as a system of signs], *Theater heute* 19/10 (1978), pp. 32–7; and 'Semiological Aspects of the Ta'ziyeh', in Chelkowski (ed.), *Ta'ziyeh*, pp. 32–9, at p. 34.
38 Brook, 'Leaning on the Moment', p. 52.
39 Brecht, 'Short Organon', p. 261.
40 Brecht, '*Verfremdung* Effects in Chinese Acting', in *Brecht on Theatre*, pp. 151–8, at p. 155.
41 Brecht, *Schriften zum Theater: Über eine nicht-aristotelische Dramatik* [Writings on theatre: On non-Aristotelian drama]. Frankfurt am Main: Suhrkamp, 1964, p. 24.
42 Ibid., p. 22.
43 See Mamnoun, 'Ta'ziyeh from the Viewpoint of the Western Theatre', pp. 157–8.
44 Peter Brook, *There Are No Secrets: Thoughts on Acting and Theatre*. London: Methuen, 1995, p. 42.
45 Mejdid Rezvani, *Le Theatre et la danse in Iran.* Paris: Maisonneuve & Larose, 1962, pp. 86–9, quoted in Muhammad Ja'far Mahjub, 'The Effect of European Theatre and the Influence of its Theatrical Methods upon Ta'ziyeh', in Chelkowski (ed.), *Ta'ziyeh*, pp. 137–53, at pp. 146–7.
46 Wirth, 'Semiological Aspects of the Ta'ziyeh', p. 39.

CHAPTER 8 LIBERATE BAYREUTH!

1 Peter Brook, *There Are No Secrets: Thoughts on Acting and Theatre*. London: Methuen, 1995, pp. 39–42.

2 Translator's note: As in the previous chapter, I use the traditional English term 'alienation' for Brecht's *Verfremdung*; 'alienation' here always corresponds to *Verfremdung* and 'alienation effect' to *V-Effekt* or *Verfremdungseffekt* in the original. On the drawbacks of this choice, and of the alternatives, see the editors' remarks in their general introduction to the revised third edition of *Brecht on Theatre*, trans. John Willet et al., ed. Marc Silberman, Steve Giles and Tom Kuhn. London: Bloomsbury, 2015, pp. 4–5.
3 Bertolt Brecht, 'Messingkauf, or Buying Brass', trans. Romy Fursland and Steve Giles, in *Brecht on Performance*, ed. Tom Kuhn, Steve Giles and Marc Silberman. London: Bloomsbury, 2014, p. 64.
4 Richard Wagner, 'The Art-Work of the Future', in *Richard Wagner's Prose Works*, trans. William Ashton Ellis. London: Kegan Paul, Trench, Trübner & Co., 1895, vol. 1, p. 73.
5 Peter Brook, *The Empty Space*. New York: Touchstone, 1996, pp. 86–8.
6 See *Frankfurt Allgemeine Zeitung*, 26 July 2012 and 9 August 2013.
7 Brook, *There Are No Secrets*, p. 43.

Chapter 9 Swimming in the Afternoon

1 Franz Kafka, *Diaries, 1914–1923*, ed. Max Brod, trans. Martin Greenberg with Hannah Arendt. New York: Schocken, 1965, p. 75.
2 Ibid., p. 78.
3 Hans-Gerd Koch (ed.), *'Als Kafka mir entgegenkam . . .': Erinnerungen an Franz Kafka* ['As Kafka came towards me . . .': remembering Franz Kafka]. Berlin: Wagenbach, 1995, p. 174.
4 Letter to Max Brod, 25 October 1923, in Franz Kafka, *Letters to Friends, Family and Editors*, trans. Richard and Clara Winston. New York: Schocken, 1977, p. 387.
5 Koch, *'Als Kafka mir entgegenkam . . .'*, p. 176.
6 Letter to Max Brod and Felix Weltsch, 18 April 1920, in *Letters to Friends, Family and Editors*, p. 233.
7 Franz Kafka, *Letters to Milena*, ed. Willi Haas, trans. Tania and James Stern. New York: Schocken, 1962, p. 196.
8 Kafka, *Diaries 1914–1923*, p. 11.
9 Franz Kafka, *Diaries, 1910–1913*, ed. Max Brod, trans. Joseph Kresh. New York: Schocken, 1965, p. 220.
10 Ibid., pp. 80–1.
11 Friedrich Schiller, *Sämtliche Werke*, 5 vols, ed. Peter-Andre Alt, Albert Meier and Wolfgang Riedel. Munich: Hanser, 2004–11, vol. 1, p. 267.
12 August Wilhem Schlegel, 'Abriß von den Europäischen Verhältnissen der Deutschen Literatur' [Outline of the European conditions of German literature], in *Kritische Schriften*, Berlin, 1828; quoted in Paul Michael Lützeler, *Europa: Analysen und Visionen der Romantiker* [Europe: the Romantics' analyses and visions]. Frankfurt am Main: Insel, 1982, pp. 373–84, at p. 375.
13 *Conversations of Goethe with Eckermann and Soret*, trans. John Oxenford, 2 vols. London: Smith, Elder & Co., 1850, vol. 1, p. 351 (31 January 1827).
14 Letter to Johann Jakob Hottinger, 15 March 1799, in *Goethes Werke* [Goethe's works], 143 vols. Weimar, 1887–1919; repr. Munich, 1987, part 4, vol. 14, p. 41.

15 Thomas Mann, letter to Agnes E. Meyer, 14 December 1945, in *Briefwechsel 1937–1955*, ed. Hans Rudolf Vaget. Frankfurt am Main: Fischer, 1992, p. 650; quoted in Wolf Lepenies, *Kultur und Politik: Deutsche Geschichten* [Culture and politics: German stories]. Munich and Vienna: Hanser, 2006, p. 315.
16 *The Auto-Biography of Goethe: Truth and Poetry: From My Own Life*, vol. 2, trans. A. J. W. Morrison. London: George Bell & Sons, 1881, p. 98.
17 Thomas Mann, *Germany and the Germans*. Washington, DC: Library of Congress, 1945, p. 19.
18 Goethe, *Conversations and Encounters*, ed. and trans. David Luke and Robert Pick. Chicago: Henry Regnery, 1966, pp. 76–7.
19 Henry Morgenthau, Jr., *Germany Is Our Problem*. New York: Harper & Brothers, 1945, p. 104.
20 *Goethes Gespräche*, vol. 2, pp. 866–7.
21 Thomas Mann, *Reflections of a Nonpolitical Man*, trans. Walter D. Morris. New York: Unger, 1987, p. 48.
22 Sebastian Haffner, *Defying Hitler: A Memoir*, trans. Oliver Pretzel. New York: Farrar, Straus & Giroux, 2002, pp. 221ff.
23 Mann, *Germany and the Germans*, pp. 18–19.
24 Quoted in Lepenies, *Kultur und Politik*, 137–8.
25 *Conversations of Goethe with Eckermann and Soret*, vol. 2, p. 428 (early March 1832).
26 Friedrich Nietzsche, *Ecce Homo*, in *The Anti-Christ and Other Writings*, trans. Judith Norman. Cambridge: Cambridge University Press, 2005, p. 140.
27 Ibid., p. 142.
28 Lepenies, *Kultur und Politik*, p. 123.
29 Cf. Klaus Wagenbach, *Franz Kafka: Biografie seiner Jugend* [Franz Kafka: biography of his youth]. Berlin: Wagenbach, 2006, p. 94.
30 Kafka, *Letters to Milena*, p. 30.
31 Kafka, *Diaries, 1910–1913*, p. 111.
32 Gustav Janouch, *Gespräche mit Kafka*. Frankfurt am Main: Fischer, 1951, p. 50; quoted in Wagenbach, *Franz Kafka*, p. 89.
33 Heinz Schlaffer, *Die kurze Geschichte der deutschen Literatur* [The brief history of German literature]. Munich: Deutscher Taschenbuch, 2003, p. 140.
34 *Conversations of Goethe with Eckermann and Soret*, vol. 2, p. 427 (early March 1832).
35 Kafka, *Letters to Milena*, p. 213.
36 Ibid.
37 Ibid., p. 236.

Chapter 10 The Duty of Literature

1 Ṣādeq Hedāyat, *Al-Baᶜṯa al-islāmiya ilā l-bilād al-ifranjīya*, first published in its entirety in Maḥmud Katirāʾi (ed.), *Ketāb-e Ṣādeq Hedāyat*, Tehran, 1349/1970. Very few copies of this book are extant because it was censored and taken off the market in 1970 right after its publication; an Iranian dissident group later published a facsimile edition in Paris. Quoted here after Ṣādeq Hedāyat, *Kārewān-e Eslām; Afsāneye Āfarinesh; Ḥājji Āqā*, Stockholm, n.d., p. 41. An unsatisfactory German translation of this satire was published

in Aschaffenburg in 1999 under the title *Karawane Islam: Die islamische Mission in Europa.*

2 Ṣādeq Hedāyat, *Tup-e morvāri*; the text was published only once in Iran, to my knowledge, in 1979, under the pseudonym Hādi Ṣedāqat, an anagram of Ṣādeq Hedāyat which he had used in publishing another story critical of Islam, *Hājji Āqā*. Quoted here after the edition published in Los Angeles in 1986, pp. 28ff.

3 *Yek vatan dārim mānand-e hala / Mā dar an hamcon Hoseyn dar Karbala.*

4 Unpublished letter of 6 October 1925.

5 *Payām-e Kāfkā* [The message of Kafka], Tehran, 1342/1963, p. 12.

6 Letter to Taqi Razavi, 26 February 1929. The complete letter, with the comments about prayers and fasting and the vulgar expressions censored out, is published in Maḥmūd Bahārlu (ed.), *Nāmehā-ye Ṣādeq Hedāyat*, Tehran, 1384/2005, pp. 154–5.

7 *Zendeh be gur*, Tehran, 1342/1963. Quoted here after *Die blinde Eule: Ein Roman und neun Erzählungen* [The blind owl: a novel and nine stories], trans. Bahman Nirumand. Frankfurt am Main: Eichborn, 1990, pp. 251–2.

8 Quoted in Hasan Tāhbāz (ed.), *Yādbudnāme-ye Ṣādeq Hedāyat be-monāsebat-e hastādomin sāl-e tavallod-e u* (German title: *Gedenkschrift für Ṣādeq Hedāyat zu seinem 80. Geburtstag* [Commemorative anthology for Sadeq Hedayat on his 80th birthday]), Cologne: Bider, 1983, p. 17.

9 Letter to Taqi Raẓavi, 13 January 1931.

10 Letter to Mojtabā Minovi, 12 February 1937, quoted in Ṣādeq Hedāyat, *Majmuᶜa-i az āṯār-e*, ed. Moḥammad Bahārlu, Tehran, 1372/1993, p. 709.

11 Letter to Taqi Raẓavi, 29 August 1931.

12 *Payām-e Kāfkā*, pp. 12–13.

13 Ibid., p. 32.

14 Letter to Taqi Razavi.

15 Letter to Hasan Sahid Nurā'i.

16 *Payām-e Kāfkā*, p. 32.

17 Theodor W. Adorno, 'Commitment', in *Notes to Literature*, trans. Shierry Weber Nicholsen. New York: Columbia University Press, 1992, vol. 2, pp. 76–94, at p. 90.

18 Ibid.

19 *Payām-e Kāfkā*, p. 54.

20 Adorno, 'Commitment', p. 93.

21 Adorno, *Aesthetic Theory*, trans. Robert Hullot-Kentor. London: Bloomsbury, 2013, p. 53.

22 Letter to Abolqasem Engavi Sirazi, 14 January 1951, quoted in *Majmuᶜa-i az āṯār-e*, p. 741.

23 *Payām-e Kāfkā*, pp. 66–7.

24 Adorno, 'Commitment', p. 90.

25 *Payām-e Kāfkā*, pp. 43–4.

26 Adorno, 'Commitment', p. 191 (trans. modified).

27 Ibid., p. 93 (trans. slightly modified).

28 Letter to Seyyed Moḥammad Jamālzādeh, 19 August 1948, quoted in Ṣādeq Hedāyat, *Nāmehā*, ed. Moḥammad Bahārlu, Tehran, 1372/1993, p. 343.

29 Letter to Hasan Shaḥid-Nurā'i, 27 August 1950, quoted ibid., p. 343.

30 *Payām-e Kāfkā*, p. 32.

Chapter 11 Towards Europe

1 Stefan Zweig, 'Der europäische Gedanke in seiner historischen Entwicklung' [The historical development of the European idea], in *Die schlaflose Welt: Aufsätze und Vorträge aus den Jahren 1909–1941* [The sleepless world: essays, 1909–1941], ed. Knut Beck. Frankfurt am Main: Fischer, 1990, pp. 185–210, at p. 195.
2 All quotations up to here: ibid., pp. 206ff.
3 Joseph Roth, *Hotel Savoy*, trans. John Hoare. Woodstock, NY: Overlook Press, 1986, p. 6.
4 Ibid., p. 18.
5 J. M. Coetzee, *Waiting for the Barbarians*. New York: Vintage, 2004, p. 43.
6 Ibid., p. 61.
7 Ibid., p. 54.
8 Ibid., p. 114.
9 Ibid., p. 41.
10 Quoted in *iz3w*, no. 280 (October 2004).
11 The expression *Begrüßungszentren* was the runner-up for the distinction of 'ugliest word of the year' [*Unwort des Jahres*] in 2004.
12 Quoted in Helmut Dietrich, 'Das Mittelmeer als neuer Raum der Abschreckung: Flüchtlinge und Migrantinnen an der südlichen EU-Außengrenze' [The Mediterranean as a new region of deterrence: refugees and migrants at the southern border of the EU], 2004, www.ffm-berlin.de/mittelmeer.html.
13 Fyodor Dostoevsky, *The Brothers Karamazov*, trans. Richard Pevear and Larissa Volokhonsky. London: Vintage, 2004, p. 245.
14 '*Kerkasiel is naastenliefde-exces*', said Secretary of State Aad Kosto of the Dutch Labour Party, according to the newspaper *Reformatorisch Tagblad* of 19 May 1993. Kosto was appointed minister of justice a short time later.
15 Matthew 15:21–8.
16 Zweig, 'Der europäische Gedanke', p. 194.
17 Ibid., p. 208.

Chapter 12 In Defence of the Glass Bead Game

1 Joachim Kaiser, 'Science-Fiction der Innerlichkeit', in Volker Michels (ed.), *Materialien zu Hermann Hesses 'Das Glasperlenspiel'*, 2 vols. Frankfurt am Main: Suhrkamp, 1973–4, vol. 2, pp. 215–20.
2 Letter to Helene Welti, 22 March 1933, ibid., vol. 1, p. 63.
3 Hermann Hesse, *The Glass Bead Game*, trans. Clara Winston and Richard Winston. New York: Vintage, 2000, p. 19.
4 George Steiner, *Language and Silence: Essays on Language, Literature and the Inhuman*. New Haven, CT: Yale University Press, 1998, p. 50.
5 Oswald Spengler, *The Decline of the West: An Abridged Edition*. Oxford: Oxford University Press, 1991, p. 390.
6 Theodor W. Adorno, 'Wird Spengler recht behalten?' [Will Spengler be right in the end?], in *Gesammelte Schriften* [Collected writings], ed. Rolf Tiedemann. Frankfurt am Main: Suhrkamp, 1970–86, vol. 20, pp. 140–48, at p. 142.
7 Ibid., p. 141.

8 Adorno, 'Spengler after the Decline', in *Prisms*, trans. Samuel and Shierry Weber. Cambridge, MA: MIT Press, 1981, pp. 51–72, at p. 72.
9 Hesse, *The Glass Bead Game*, p. 421.
10 Ibid., p. 327.
11 Ibid., p. 330.
12 Ibid., p. 14.
13 Ibid., p. 341.
14 *Die Zeit*, 5 December 2013; see also Joachim Güntner's commentary in *Neue Zürcher Zeitung* of 14 January 2014. The film's title is a German phonetic rendering of the phrase 'Fuck you, Goethe'.
15 See Holger Noltze, *Die Leichtigkeitslüge: Über Musik, Medien und Komplexität* [The lie of easiness: on music, media and complexity]. Hamburg: Körber-Stiftung, 2010, p. 60.
16 Hermann Hesse, 'Feuerwerk' [Fireworks], in *Die Kunst des Müßiggangs: Kurze Prosa aus dem Nachlaß* [The art of idleness: posthumous short prose], ed. Volker Michels. Frankfurt am Main: Suhrkamp, 1973, pp. 320–21.
17 Hesse, *The Glass Bead Game*, p. 326.
18 Ibid., p. 16.
19 Ibid., p. 332.

Chapter 13 The Violence of Compassion

1 Hannah Arendt, *On Revolution*, London: Penguin, 1990, p. 11.
2 'Dedication to Karl Jaspers', trans. Robert and Rita Kimber, in Arendt, *Essays in Understanding: 1930–1954*, ed. Jerome Kohn. New York: Harcourt Brace, 1994, pp. 212–16, at pp. 213–14.
3 'On Humanity in Dark Times: Thoughts about Lessing', trans. Clara Winston and Richard Winston, in Arendt, *Men in Dark Times*. New York: Harcourt, Brace & World, 1968, pp. 3–32, at p. 6.
4 'Portrait of a Period', in Arendt, *The Jew as Pariah: Jewish Identity and Politics in the Modern Age*, ed. Ron H. Feldman. New York: Grove, 1978, pp. 112–124, at p. 113.
5 Arendt, *The Origins of Totalitarianism*. Cleveland and New York: World, 1958, p. 290. The quotations that follow are from subsequent pages.
6 'Nationalstaat und Demokratie' [Nation-state and democracy] (1963), first published in *HannahArendt.net: Journal for Political Thinking* 2/1 (September 2006).
7 *Über die Revolution*. Munich: Piper, 1974, p. 308. [Translator's note: In translating her own works between German and English, Hannah Arendt freely adapted them to the different audiences. I cite the German where the English does not contain the given reference.]
8 See '"Mir ist der Ausdruck 'europäisches Denken' verdächtig": Hannah Arendt auf dem Internationalen Kulturkritikerkongress 1958 in München' ['I find the expression "European thinking" suspect': Hannah Arendt at the International Conference on Cultural Criticism, Munich, 1958], *HannahArendt.net* 4/1 (May 2008).
9 15 November 2011, at the CDU party conference in Leipzig.
10 Arendt, *On Revolution*, p. 85.

11 See Arendt, *Lectures on Kant's Political Philosophy*, ed. Ronald Beiner. Chicago: University of Chicago Press, 1992, pp. 75–6.
12 *On Revolution*, p. 85.
13 Ibid., p. 86.
14 Ibid., p. 86–7.
15 'The Meaning of Love in Politics: A Letter by Hannah Arendt to James Baldwin' (21 November 1962), *HannahArendt.net* 2/1 (September 2006).
16 *Lectures on Kant's Political Philosophy*, p. 17.
17 *Über die Revolution*, p. 117.
18 *On Revolution*, p. 95.
19 *On Revolution*, p. 135.
20 *On Revolution*, p. 56.
21 *On Revolution*, p. 68.
22 'On Humanity in Dark Times', pp. 7–8.
23 *On Revolution*, p. 18.
24 'Einführung in die Politik II' [Introduction to Politics II], in Arendt, *Was ist Politik? Fragmente aus dem Nachlass* [What is politics? Posthumous fragments], ed. Ursula Ludz. Munich: Piper, 1993, p. 35.

Chapter 14 Tilting at Windmills

1 *Das Bett*, Hamburg: Hoffmann & Campe, 1983; *Eine lange Nacht*, Berlin: Aufbau, 2000; *Das Beben*, Munich: Hanser, 2005.
2 *Der Mond und das Mädchen*, Munich: Hanser, 2007.

Chapter 16 Sing the Quran Singingly

1 Trans. Arberry.
2 Abu Hamid Muhammad al-Ghazālī, *Iḥyā ʿulūm ad-dīn* [The revival of the religious sciences], 4 vols, Cairo, 1358/1939, vol. 1, p. 274.

INDEX